Writing Sri Lanka

What is the place of contemporary Sri Lankan literature in English within the wider postcolonial literary canon and context? How does the work of resident writers relate to that of internationally acclaimed writers who have left the country? And to what extent has Sri Lankan literary production at home and abroad been shaped by the civil war that continues to tear the island apart?

Focusing on ways in which cultural nationalism has influenced both the production and critical reception of texts, Minoli Salgado offers a detailed analysis of eight leading Sri Lankan writers – Michael Ondaatje, Romesh Gunesekera, Shyam Selvadurai, A. Sivanandan, Jean Arasanayagam, Carl Muller, James Goonewardene and Punyakante Wijenaike – and rigorously challenges the theoretical, cultural and political assumptions that pit 'insider' against 'outsider', 'resident' against 'migrant', and the 'authentic' against the 'alien'. By interrogating the discourses of territoriality and boundary marking that have come into prominence since the start of the civil war, Salgado works to define a more nuanced and sensitive critical framework that actively reclaims marginalised voices, and draws on recent studies in migration and the diaspora to reconfigure the Sri Lankan critical terrain.

Minoli Salgado teaches English at the University of Sussex. She has published widely in postcolonial studies, particularly on migration and postmodernity in the literature of South Asia and the South Asian diaspora.

Postcolonial Literatures

Edited in collaboration with the Centre for Colonial and Postcolonial Studies, University of Kent at Canterbury, this series presents a wide range of research into postcolonial literatures by specialists in the field. Volumes will concentrate on writers and writing originating in previously (or presently) colonised areas, and will include material from non-anglophone as well as anglophone colonies and literatures. The series will also include collections of important essays from older journals, and re-issues of classic texts on postcolonial subjects. Routledge is pleased to invite proposals for new books in the series. Interested authors should contact Lyn Innes or Rod Edmond at the Centre for Colonial and Postcolonial Studies, University of Kent at Canterbury, or Routledge's Commissioning Editor for Literature.

The series comprises three strands.

Routledge Research in Postcolonial Literatures is a forum for innovative new research intended for a specialist readership. Published in hardback, titles include:

1. *Magical Realism in West African Fiction: Seeing with a Third Eye* by Brenda Cooper
2. *The Postcolonial Jane Austen* edited by You-Me Park and Rajeswari Sunder Rajan
3. *Contemporary Caribbean Women's Poetry: Making Style* by Denise deCaires Narain
4. *African Literature, Animism and Politics* by Caroline Rooney
5. *Caribbean-English Passages: Intertextuality in a Postcolonial Tradition* by Tobias Döring
6. *Islands in History and Representation* edited by Rod Edmond and Vanessa Smith
7. *Civility and Empire: Literature and Culture in British India, 1822–1922* by Anindyo Roy
8. *Women Writing the West Indies, 1804–1939: 'A Hot Place, Belonging To Us'* by Evelyn O'Callaghan
9. *Postcolonial Pacific Writing: Representations of the Body* by Michelle Keown
10. *Writing Woman, Writing Place: Contemporary Australian and South African Fiction* by Sue Kossew
11. *Literary Radicalism in India: Gender, Nation and the Transition to Independence* by Priyamvada Gopal
12. *Postcolonial Conrad: Paradoxes of Empire* by Terry Collits
13. *American Pacificism: Oceania in the U.S. Imagination* by Paul Lyons
14. *Decolonizing Culture in the Pacific: Reading History and Trauma in Contemporary Fiction* by Susan Y. Najita
15. *Writing Sri Lanka: Literature, Resistance and the Politics of Place* by Minoli Salgado

Postcolonial Literatures makes available in paperback important work in the field. Hardback editions of these titles are also available, some published earlier in the Routledge Research strand of the series. Titles in paperback include:

Postcolonial Studies: A Materialist Critique by Benita Parry
Magical Realism in West African Fiction: Seeing with a Third Eye by Brenda Cooper
The Postcolonial Jane Austen edited by You-Me Park and Rajeswari Sunder Rajan
Contemporary Caribbean Women's Poetry: Making Style by Denise deCaires Narain

Readings in Postcolonial Literatures offers collections of important essays from journals or classic texts in the field. Titles include:

1. *Selected Essays of Wilson Harris* edited by Andrew Bundy

Writing Sri Lanka

Literature, resistance and the politics of place

Minoli Salgado

Routledge
Taylor & Francis Group
LONDON AND NEW YORK

First published 2007
by Routledge
4 Park Square, Milton Park, Abingdon, Oxon OX14 4RN

Simultaneously published in the USA and Canada
by Routledge
605 Third Avenue, New York, NY 10017

First issued in paperback 2012

Routledge is an imprint of the Taylor & Francis Group, an informa business

Typeset in Baskerville by
Book Now Ltd, London

British Library Cataloguing in Publication Data
A catalogue record for this book is available from the British Library

Library of Congress Cataloging in Publication Data
Salgado, Minoli.
Writing Sri Lanka: literature, resistance, and the politics of place/Minoli Salgado.
p. cm. – (Routledge research in postcolonial literatures; 15)
Includes bibliographical references and index.
1. Sri Lankan literature (English)—History and criticism. 2. Politics and literature—Sri Lanka–History–20th century. 3. Politics and literature–Sri Lanka–History–21 century. I. Title.

PR9440.S25 2007
820.9′5493–dc22 2006023103

ISBN 13: 978–0–415–65343–5 (pbk)
ISBN 13: 978–0–415–36418–8 (hbk)
ISBN 13: 978–0–203–01536–0 (ebk)

for my mother
Indira Salgado

to the memory of my father
Kenneth Salgado

and for Shaun

Contents

Contents

Acknowledgements

A list of acknowledgements cannot quite do justice to the full range of literary and critical encounters that have gone to make up this book, or to the memory of debt. Researched and written in the fractured spaces generated by four trips to Sri Lanka between December 2002 and April 2006, I was privileged to exchange views with Jean Arasanayagam, Neloufer de Mel, Nihal Fernando, D.C.R.A. Goonetilleke, Ashley Halpé, Carl Muller, Jehan Perera, Sasanka Perera, Walter Perera, Neluka Silva, Punyakante Wijenaike and Rajiva Wijesinha, whose voices came to inform and inflect much of what I wrote. Many of them gave generously of their time and resources, going out of their way to help procure material that was out of print or hard to find. Jean Arasanayagam and Punyakante Wijenaike also granted me permission to cite material from work that is privately published or unpublished, and the International Centre for Ethnic Studies permission to cite selected poems from *Apocalypse '83*.

Further invaluable assistance was provided by members of staff at the British Council, Gratiaen Trust, International Centre for Ethnic Studies in Kandy, Marga Institute, National Library, National Peace Council of Sri Lanka, Social Scientists' Association, University of Colombo library and University of Sussex library, while Harrison Perera at the University of Peradeniya library went beyond the bounds of duty.

In addition, Aparna Halpé, Dilesh Jayanntha, Sharanya Jayawickrama, Ranjini Mendis, Arun Mukherjee, Ramani Samarasinghe, Charles Sarvan and Sarah Williams freely shared information and material that have proved serendipitous.

I would also like to express my gratitude to the following people: Nirmala Salgado, who responded patiently and positively to my numerous queries on aspects of Buddhist historiography, thought and practice; Elleke Boehmer, Peter Morey, Meenakshi Mukherjee and Susheila Nasta, for their long-term support and encouragement; Liz Thompson and Polly Dodson at Routledge; and Lyn Innes, who believed in the book from the beginning.

The award of a research fellowship from the Leverhulme Trust enabled me to embark on this study, while an eight month period of research leave funded by the Arts and Humanities Research Council (AHRC) and the Department of English at Sussex allowed me to complete it. This book would have taken much longer to write without their support.

I have been fortunate, for many years, to have had the opportunity to teach at an institution that has invested in interdisciplinarity, and students on the MA courses 'The Migrant Writer: Postcolonialism and Creativity' and 'Narrating the Past: Postmodernism, History and Postcolonial Literature' have been one of the most enduring sources of encouragement. I would like to thank them for their enthusiasm and spirit of critical inquiry, which have done much to make me feel the need for this study, and for doing me the inestimable service of nudging me out of my comfort zone.

Colleagues, past and present, at the University of Sussex who have provided a context of support include Peter Boxall, Deborah Cherry, Vinita Damodaran, Denise deCaires Narain, Elena Gualtieri, Andrew Hadfield, Margaret Healy, Laura Marcus, Stephanie Newell, Sybil Oldfield, Vincent Quinn, Nicholas Royle, Daniel Rycroft, Alan Sinfield, Lindsay Smith, Sophie Thomas, Maya Unnithan, Norman Vance and Marcus Wood.

Finally I would like to thank those members of my family who shared the journey: my mother, who did so much to help keep me on track that I cannot imagine having written this book without her; Shaun, who made me realise that the courage of my convictions lay in the writing; and Roshan and Dilhan, for their patience and loving reminders of the world outside the book.

Introduction

> The tidal wave that brought in its wake death and destruction to Sri Lanka, also assisted over 300 convicts, serving their terms in the high-security Matara jail, to make a successful bid for freedom, police sources said.
>
> *The Island*, 27 December 2004

This news, written a day after the event, is preceded by the headline article 'Lanka's *Day After Tomorrow* – Tsunami kills over 3,000' and is subtitled 'Sri Lanka worst hit' 'India sends warships for relief work'. The South Asian tsunami, to which this report refers, destroyed three-quarters of Sri Lanka's coastline, killed about 35,000 people in the country and displaced a further two and a half million. It was a natural disaster of unprecedented proportions: it made the earth wobble on its axis, caused smaller islands off Sumatra slip – altering the regional map – and took the lives of an estimated quarter of a million people in all. Remote towns and villages that were almost unknown outside their national boundaries became international bywords for disaster as reporters all over the world tried to situate, fix and habilitate the news, reaching for words and images to give narrative and meaning to an event of such magnitude that its full scale – the sheer enormity of loss and destruction – would not be known for months afterwards. There were the inevitable inaccuracies – evident here in the claims that Sri Lanka was the worst affected country and in the underestimation of the number of dead – marking the factual slippages of an emergent narrative: 'history', re-written daily, was emphatically provisional. It was emergent and contingent, marked as a palimpsest through simultaneous inscription and erasure in ways that replicated the obliterating force of the waves themselves.

These conceptual paradigms linking the provisionality of history with the instability of geographical location are central to this study. Boundaries – spatio-temporal, discursive and communal – appeared to be destroyed *and* reinforced by the tsunami. The dramatic human and geographical displacements caused by the waves seemed – in the first instance – to displace old narratives of belonging, breaking down the boundaries of communally inscribed difference as Sri Lankan military personnel and Tamil Tiger cadres united to get relief to the worst affected regions of the North East, and communities from across the country linked resources in their efforts to help. As Jehan Perera, the Media Director of the National Peace Council, observed a few days later, there was a 'spontaneous outpouring of solidarity that transcend[ed] region and race'.[1] Yet within days the instabilities generated by new affiliations and an altered geography began to give way as the indelible markers of communal difference and political dissent quickly resurfaced, marking out old tensions symptomatic of the twenty-year civil war and the inevitable erosion of social ties: political squabbles over the distribution of aid, claims of biased and uneven relief, reported selective looting of destroyed and damaged homes and a fear that buried landmines in the war zone might have been dislodged by the impact of the waves creating new, unmarked no-go areas. Exactly one year later – after the election of a new president – an escalation of armed conflict in the North and East reveals that though the tsunami shifted the country it had failed to displace political boundaries.[2] Although the country had experienced a seismic shift, a morphology of erasure, geographical redefinition and destruction of communities, the boundaries of difference not only appeared to persist, but, according to one report, had been accentuated, 'deepening political fault-lines'.[3] And now, at the time of writing, the political landscape appears to be changing yet again, with the renewal of peace negotiations in 2006 interrupted by what is being termed a 'low intensity' war.

How does one effectively gain a purchase on what David Scott has described as a moment of considerable instability and uncertainty when hitherto established and authoritative conceptual paradigms and political projects seem no longer adequate to the tasks of the present, and when, at the same time, new paradigms and projects have yet to assert themselves?[4] Given the radical ruptures and instabilities of the recent Sri Lankan past and the fluctuations of its divided and divisive political present, is it possible to render with any certainty a clear historical trajectory, present a 'totalising' picture (as at least one critic asks of Sri Lankan writers) or achieve narrative settlement? How do writers attempting to convey the experience of living in Sri Lanka since the escalation of conflict in 1983 try to habilitate their work in such a shifting and provisional landscape? And how do literary critics – both inside and outside the country – successfully mediate textual products generated from a context that is not only provisional and unstable but itself subject to the contestatory dynamics of competing nationalisms? Of course all history is provisional and contingent and all contexts inherently unstable, constituted as they are through discourse. But the problem of negotiating the relationship between history (as factual event), historiography (or the discursive construction of the past) and literary writing is especially pertinent to the critic of Sri Lankan writing in English, for here we have an emergent literature whose very terms of affiliation are being subject to contestation at the very moment of evolution. After a twenty-year period following Independence in which anglophone literature was 'neglected [. . .] and even reviled'[5] as a result of the cultural nationalism generated by the 'Sinhala Only' Act, there has been a marked surge in the production of English literary texts in Sri Lanka. This has coincided both with the period of heightened political unrest in the country, culminating in the civil war,[6] and the emergence of a postcolonial disciplinary perspective that has brought increased international attention to literatures from former British colonies such as Sri Lanka. I am not suggesting that an anglophone literary tradition did not exist before the 1970s in Sri Lanka as this is self-evidently untrue,[7] but rather that the conditions that have created the disciplinary context for the study of a body of literature known as 'Sri Lankan writing in English' have emerged during a critical period when the very boundaries of the nation and the basis of national affiliation are being tested and contested in the country. It is a context charged with what Graham Huggan calls 'invidious questions of "eligibility"', so that the evaluation of a literary work may be mediated not only or always on the basis of discursive dynamics or textual considerations, but also on the basis of its perceived cultural legitimacy.

By focusing on spatial registers – territory, space, place and home – I aim to offer a grammar of critical analysis that effectively intervenes in and deconstructs the historically inflected register of both Sinhala and Tamil nationalism while addressing the political conditions in which the literature has been produced. On the understanding that we are indeed, as Scott suggests, working within the historical paradigm of a Gramscian interregnum, I aim to mediate established conceptual paradigms of territoriality and boundary marking with the aim of creating a space for new ones to emerge. Sinhala nationalism, in particular, has operated on the understanding of spatio-temporal continuity, of granting a timeless continuum to Sinhala presence and ownership of the land. By emphasising the territorial implications both within the texts and critical contexts of reception and production, I intend to rupture the assumptions underpinning this continuity – to reveal the fissures in belonging and identify some of the sites of contention and belonging.

My study of textual territoriality thus moves between these poles of analysis: the locatedness of literary criticism and the territorial markers to be found within the texts themselves. It aligns itself with some of the critical objectives of recent cultural and historical studies which work to modulate and unsettle the hegemonic prescriptives informing monogenist, totalising and exclusionary nationalist narratives,[8] but distinguishes itself from them in its literary emphasis, drawing strong connections between the differential discourses which serve to locate texts and the internal registers of alterity to be found within them. My approach is mediated by my own experience of multiple displacement. As a migrant Sri Lankan now resident in England, born in Malaysia to Sri Lankan parents whose close connection to their native land was reflected in my initially being raised apart from them with my grandparents at 'home', I am conscious both of the spatiality of my historical experience and of the historical contingency shaping a mobile identity – my experience of 'home' constructed through the interplay between dwelling and travelling. Yet I aim to activate this in the service of what Anthony Appiah has called a 'rooted cosmopolitanism' working within the cultural coordinates of a specific historical moment in Sri Lanka in order to create a context where dialogue between the local and global may be enabled.

I have chosen to analyse the work of eight, established, post-Independence Sri Lankan writers, writers who have been recognised for their contribution to

Sri Lankan writing in English in Sri Lanka or abroad. Most, if not all, of the resident writers in this study are little-known outside Sri Lanka, in contrast to the migrant writers whose work has gained international acclaim. This is inevitably leading to the creation of two distinct, asymmetrical Sri Lankan literary canons and a context of critical reception in which there is little dialogue between the two fields, despite that fact that the writers themselves work to challenge national and cultural boundaries, actively creating the context for cultural interchange and dialogue. I am of the conviction that bringing the work of resident and non-resident writers into creative and critical alignment is an essential means of creating a context of cultural accommodation that not only works in the service of a more open and sensitive evaluation of texts, but also promises to effectively dismantle some of the discursively constructed cultural boundaries to which the country has been increasingly subject.

Inevitably this study is subject to boundary marking of its own, particularly in its selection of authors and texts. It is not an encyclopaedic survey of the field or a chronicle of literary history, nor does it attempt a comprehensive analysis of each of the writers, most of whom have been highly prolific. Rather I have selected texts which, in my view, incorporate spatial tropes that elucidate how the nation is imagined in their work. I have focused – with one exception – on novelists, partly in order to create a common generic ground to my analysis and partly out of a recognition that it is in the novel that the nation most effectively gains imagining. (The exception is of course Jean Arasanayagam, who is best known as a poet. Her work, explicitly exploring and contesting boundary marking and territoriality, insists upon inclusion.) As Timothy Brennan has observed,

> It was the *novel* that historically accompanied the rise of nations by objectifying the 'one, yet many' of national life, and by mimicking the structure of the nation, a clearly bordered jumble of languages and styles. [. . .] Its manner of presentation allowed people to imagine the special community that was the nation. [. . .] In its hands, 'tradition' became what Hobsbawm calls a 'useable past', and the evocation of deep, sacred origins – instead of furthering unquestioning, ritualistic reaffirmations of a people (as in epic) – becomes a contemporary, practical means of *creating* a people. [original emphasis][9]

This choice may well be contentious – literary production in Sri Lanka is much more variously marked, covering plays, poetry and translations – but I have privileged the need for analytical consistency and rigour over the desire to be more inclusive in an effort to set a coherent and consistent framework that supports future study in the field; one which, it is hoped, will open up for discussion many of the texts that I have not been able to incorporate here.

Any discussion of literary canonisation in the Sri Lankan context also needs to acknowledge the uneven, contestatory and highly variable social and cultural formations governing the emergence of a hierarchy of aesthetic value. We need to draw a distinction between literary production in Sri Lanka – in all its rich diversity – and the institutional canonisation of texts through literary awards and dissemination through school and university curricula. Literary awards such as the Gratiaen Prize and the State Literary Award have, to date, recognised and responded to the wide range of literary production in English and English translation, whereas the assimilation of the work of Sri Lankan writers into a putative canon of 'English literature' in educational establishments (where the analysis of 'postcolonial literature' has yet to get a firm footing) is markedly more variable and contested. It is of course from within the university context that literary production gains sustained critical evaluation and from here that the terms, codes and criteria of literary analysis are formally generated. My study aims not so much to evaluate the process of canonisation *per se* – a process that requires a socially situated mediatory practice analysing the connections between the production, distribution and marketing of texts and the institutional structures that endorse criteria for the evaluation of them – but rather to engage with and contest the discursive formations *within* literary analysis that work to privilege certain forms of writing over others. The cultural nationalism to be found in Sri Lankan literary criticism is largely generated from an institutional context in which canonical English texts still hold sway, marking the precarious positioning and cultural instabilities attendant upon the formation of an emergent 'Sri Lankan' canon. My analysis of its terms is largely directed at assessing the impact and relevance of this critical discourse on and to literary production as I believe that such a focused engagement is a precondition for a broader evaluation of the process of cultural legitimation marked by literary canonisation.

The study is divided into three parts. Part 1 is made up of an extended chapter that establishes the historical, theoretical and methodological basis of my study. It considers the boundary marking evident in the arbitration of an emergent postcolonial canon, caught between the legitimating discursive strategies of post-colonial nationalism and post-national metropolitan bases. It suggests that both literature and the critical reception of texts are constitutive of territorial relations in a way that intersects with social and political discourses of the time, and it considers territoriality as a political strategy, as a critical manoeuvre in literary studies and as a defining framework for literary production in the context of war. It develops these ideas by historically positioning the development of writing in English in relation to linguistic nationalism, and concludes with a consideration of two forms of critical territoriality in Sri Lankan literary studies, exploring the epistemological connections between them.

Parts II and III focus on the analysis of the work of individual 'resident' and 'migrant' writers respectively. The aim here is to create a context that registers the radically different sites of production and reception of the two groups while also attending to the contingent historical spaces occupied by individual writers. This structure offers a basis for comparative evaluation while working to question the very distinctions between the two categories in order to generate the development of a critical discourse that might formulate alternative models of identity and belonging. By comparing 'resident' constructions of space, place and home with 'migrant' representations, I move towards a critique that intersects with the constructions of territoriality evaluated in Part I, revealing how textual production can reformulate constructions of the insider and outsider which intersect with – and can entrench or challenge – cultural formulations of national, ethnic and other bordered identities. I conclude, as I have begun, with a brief, personal reflection on the locatedness of the past and its relationship with our construction of difference, suggesting that it is in our dislocated desires for an openly constructed past that we can recreate our origins in ways that might lead toward a transformed and transformative future.

Part I

1 Literature and territoriality

Boundary marking as a critical paradigm

Etymologically unsettled, 'territory' derives from both *terra* (earth) and *terrēre* (to frighten) whence *territorium*, 'a place from which people are frightened off'.

Homi K. Bhabha, *The Location of Culture*[1]

Sri Lankan literature in English constitutes an emergent canon of writing that has yet to find settlement in the field of postcolonial studies.[2] It occupies an uncertain territory, which, in recent years, has itself been marked by the competing ethnic nationalisms of civil war and of contestatory constructions of home and belonging. The upsurge of literary production in English in the past thirty years has corresponded with the dynamic growth of postcolonial studies from the metropolitan centre, the international acclaim granted to writers such as Michael Ondaatje and Romesh Gunesekera, and, as significantly, with a period of heightened political unrest in Sri Lanka – a context of production and reception that is shaped by a politics of affiliation and competing claims to cultural authority. It is worth reminding ourselves that unlike most postcolonial nations, Sri Lanka's national consciousness developed significantly after Independence and did so along communal lines.[3] The 1950s witnessed the dramatic decline of Ceylonese or multi-ethnic Sri Lankan nationalism in favour of Sinhala linguistic nationalism along with the sharpening of Sri Lankan Tamil nationalism[4] – a combination that culminated in the communal violence of 1983 and the start of the military conflict. As a result the accelerated production of Sri Lankan literature in English is historically situated within a context of evolving and contested claims to cultural legitimacy. The precise location of Sri Lankan writers within postcolonial studies and the extent to which their work is domesticated and habilitated within a corresponding emergent Sri Lankan canon thus depends on a complex range of social, cultural and historical factors demarcating different lines of affiliation from diverse and divergent sites of production, reception and accommodation. In determining the boundaries of what constitutes 'Sri Lankan literature in English' there is therefore a need to engage with the contexts of cultural contestation in which postcolonial canonisation meets the legitimating strategies of national affirmation – a context of social and cultural instability whereby a resident writer may well be rendered an outsider, and 'Sri Lankan' writers abroad may find themselves deemed foreigners in their native land.

Chelva Kanaganayakam's nuanced consideration of some of the difficulties of evaluating the emergent canon of Sri Lankan writing raises several important issues that are pertinent here. Having attested to the crucial role played by literary critics in 'filtering' Sri Lankan literature for an international audience – a task that directly affects the pedagogic construction of the canon – he reveals the radically different evaluations of a Sri Lankan writer which puts him in the 'awkward situation of being praised for [his] Sri Lankan sensibility by one critic and condemned for not being Sri Lankan by another' so that a non-Sri Lankan reader 'would have a hard time deciding whether a writer is a traitor or patriot, an essentialist or an authentic voice'.[5] It is a critical context in which, according to Kanaganayakam, 'the line that separates aesthetic criteria and political conviction becomes extremely thin'. It is notable that he is conspicuously attentive to the role of critics in Sri Lanka, 'a small group' of people working within the context of conflict and violence in which 'the polarization that has taken place between the major ethnic groups has made a common ground increasingly difficult', so that 'what is offered as literary criticism may well be the expression of a personal bias'.[6]

Drawing together the many strands of Kanaganayakam's cautious and considered evaluation it can be seen how the ideas expressed in his essay could be taken further. It could be argued that, given the context of cultural contestation that marks Sri Lanka's recent political history, the literary criticism generated by 'personal bias' does not merely constitute an isolated expression of a subjective opinion operating within a culturally conflictual context, but rather enacts a form of discursive 'boundary marking' that engages in a politics of inclusion and exclusion that has a symbiotic relationship with the politics of cultural nationalism that informs – and is in turn shaped by – current political events. Before I continue, I would like to stress that this is in no way intended to represent Kanaganayakam's critique. Rather it constitutes a resettlement of some of his observations within the context of territoriality – a cultural and political dynamic that I aim to use as a critical paradigm on the basis that it informs the discursive register of both literary texts and critical responses. While it has been argued that writers in English are operating in fields that are remote from political realities,[7] the terms on which their work is assessed both from within and outside Sri Lanka are largely based upon discursive constructions of allegiance, affiliation and legitimacy that serve the needs of various forms of cultural reclamation. While all literary criticism is by definition discriminatory, the practice of critical territoriality enacts a practice of inclusion and exclusion that works not so much to interrogate or deconstruct difference or to draw lines of affiliation between diverse contexts of belonging and thereby create contexts of accommodation, but instead to further generate a practice of cultural boundary marking that has its political corollary in cultural nationalism.[8] I am not suggesting that all Sri Lankan literary criticism is marked by such a manoeuvre – later in this chapter I will show how this is clearly not the case – but rather that there is a discernable tendency to invest in such critical practices that need to be identified and addressed at this early stage of Sri Lankan literary emergence in postcolonial studies if the concept of a Sri Lankan literary 'canon' is to have any useful meaning at all.

This is not an appeal for critical consensus – the sheer range of critical responses to the work of Sri Lankan writers both inside and outside the country could be read as an indication of plurivocity – nor does it stake an interest in the questionable value of canon-formation itself, rather it is a call for identifying the salient critical strands engaging in specific strategies of exclusion so that the 'boundaries' of Sri Lankan writing, the sites of cultural contestation and resistance, are exposed in ways that allow for a more inclusive practice of cultural accommodation that might, in turn, feed into a politics of accommodation. The increasing polarisation in Sri Lankan literary studies, with writers subject to analysis of their work on the basis of what Graham Huggan calls 'invidious questions of "eligibility"',[9] reveals the urgent need to generate a mode of critical inquiry that works to dismantle cultural prescriptives of authenticity and allegiance and engage with a mode of discourse attentive to alternative lines of affiliation and, as significantly, sensitive to the varied and contrastive dynamics of belonging to be found in the texts themselves. Such an inquiry is particularly pertinent given that writers are increasingly scripted as cultural ambassadors – both within the country, where anglophone writers are in the privileged position of having the potential to reach an international audience,[10] and abroad, where such writers effectively do. It is necessary therefore to analyse the terms that demarcate the authenticated 'Sri Lankan writer' from his or her 'expatriate' counterpart – a subject central to this chapter. This process is enabled by a critique that draws into alignment 'resident' and 'expatriate' writers, creating a context for comparative analysis that is nevertheless attendant to their radically different sites of textual production and reception – an approach that informs this study as a whole, shaping its structural dynamics. The need for such an engagement, addressing and deconstructing critical territoriality, can be seen when the cultural contradictions underpinning accommodation into an authenticated Sri Lankan experience are exposed – evident here in a Sri Lankan critic's consideration of the emergent canon:

> the responsibility for that part of the post-colonial struggle which involves the making of the Lankan canon in English falls very squarely on bi-culturals who more obviously than most others are characterised by their symbiotic natures. These biculturals [sic] are called upon to engage with the relationship/tensions between the two aspects of their symbiotic personalities in a manner that allows what can be felt to be an authentic contemporary Lankan experience to emerge with conviction.[11]

Here the mediatory position of those who occupy a borderland identity are recoded and ruptured into the dualistic logic of 'biculturalism' – a term split in its conscription to the service of an essentialised 'authentic Lankan experience'. I will be analysing this passage in more detail later, but use it here to reveal the way in which the very terms of accommodating culturally liminal subjectivities have, as their basis, a monocultural centrism that resists rather than engages with the complex sites of affiliation that such subjectivities can occupy.

In a different vein, another Sri Lankan critic – resident outside the country and alert to the significance of Sri Lankan 'expatriate' literary production – has marked a distinction between these literary products and their counterparts from within the country in terms that could be interpreted to privilege a specific reading of culture:

> The 1980s [. . .] witnessed instances of expatriate activity that reveal a deep-reaching sensitivity to specific events at 'home', that have either had significant effects on the 'home' culture or other potential for such effects. [. . .] Opinions may vary regarding the value of these activities. I must it leave [sic] to my readers to determine whether some of them are contributory to, or destructive of, Sri Lankan national culture.[12]

This observation is attentive to the impact of 'expatriate activity' on the 'home' culture – implicitly acknowledging the close connection between these two spaces of representation and the transformative potential of literature, its destabilising effects. It forms part of a detailed and extensive analysis of the English-educated community which gives numerous examples of the socio-cultural and political roles of Sri Lankan expatriates, effectively demonstrating the gradual fragmentation of 'national culture' and its expansion into what the critic calls the 'periphery'.[13] Yet the terms of evaluation cited here have been re-sited by a resident critic to invite an evaluation of 'expatriate' literature on the basis of its impact on an authenticated 'Sri Lankan national culture' in ways that *resist* critical mediation between these sites.[14] This refocusing of the original terms of analysis effectively creates a context in which literary products from outside the country can be screened – or 'filtered' to use Kanaganayakam's felicitous phrase – on the basis of authentication by a Sri Lankan cultural 'centre'.

While there are numerous distinctions to be drawn between 'expatriate' texts and literary products from 'home', and there is certainly a need to address the impact of literary products legitimated in metropolitan centres on the marginalised national centres at 'home', what interests me here is the basis on which some of these distinctions are made. Exile and expatriation are not simply a question of geography; writers, as this study emphatically shows, can be displaced in a myriad ways at home. I will return to this point later, but now wish to raise an issue that directs much of this study: the process of 'ex-patriating' texts – excluding them from the borders of authenticated belonging in ways that might transform the 'expatriate', or even the self-exiled resident writer, into an *ex-patriot*. Both the passages cited above enact a form of critical boundary marking that operates within a discursive paradigm which repeats and revises broader claims to national affiliation that are themselves the subject of literary representation in the work of writers both in and outside Sri Lanka. The literature 'of' Sri Lanka (and what a burden of significance this small word carries) can thus be subject to conscription on the basis of contested notions of belonging in which 'home' and 'homeland' stand as symbolic markers of inclusion and exclusion. As will be seen in my analysis of the work of individual writers in succeeding chapters, texts from both inside and outside the country reflect complex negotiations of territory and identity and reformulations of the constructions of the insider and outsider which intersect with – and can entrench or challenge – cultural formulations of national identity and belonging. Thus within the contestatory dynamics of the postcolonial positioning of Sri Lankan writing in English, literature and the critical reception of texts do not simply reflect but are themselves constitutive of territorial relations in ways that intersect with the divisive discourse of competing constructions of the national space and the very real displacements and geopolitical ruptures generated by political violence. Yet while literary texts may engage with varieties of displacement, opening up for analysis the multiple mediations of belonging and affiliation and thereby revealing the contingent boundaries of 'home' and 'homeland', critical territoriality – by which I mean the overdetermined evaluation of texts in terms of an authenticated national culture – works to constrain these areas of debate, regulating the boundaries of belonging in ways that serve a specific politics of location. The interconnected dynamics between territoriality as a political strategy, as a critical manoeuvre in literary studies and as a defining framework for literary production in the context of nationalist activism thus require closer analysis. What follows is a brief consideration of these connections that works both to contextualise critical territoriality by revealing some of its social and political coordinates and to outline some of the connections between different readings of territoriality in order to show the ways in which they might collectively work to demarcate the boundaries of belonging in which Sri Lankan literature is evaluated.

The politics and practice of territoriality

> The term 'border villages' is a misnomer. [. . .] Sri Lanka is a single unitary state and has no borders within it.
>
> D.C.R.A. Goonetilleke[15]

> Territory is no doubt a geographical notion, but it is first of all a juridico-political one: the area controlled by a certain kind of power.
>
> Michel Foucault[16]

Foucault's definition clearly links spatial practice with the practice of the state and highlights the normative role played by the state in enforcing and simultaneously disguising boundary markings. Territory is here defined performatively in that it is through the self-determining act of territorialism – the control and ownership of land – that it gains definition. For others territory is defined through the spatial idiomatics of territoriality – encompassing terms such as 'territorial integrity', 'hallowed ground' and 'homeland'– which, according to Ericksen, are linked to sensitising concepts that explain how people tie themselves to the land.[17] In a different vein, political geographers such as Michael Shapiro have focused on cultural difference in claiming that territoriality can be marked ethnocentrically, in that it is ethnographically constructed reflecting how collectivities locate themselves and construct cohesive identities.[18] While these definitions of territory and territoriality help define the differing disciplinary boundaries of their interlocutors, they also serve to highlight the complex connections between territoriality, spatial idiomatics and ethnocentricity, which have all been central in shaping both political history and literary production in Sri Lanka since Independence and have come to prominence in the past twenty years, since the start of the civil war.

This war has been waged on the basis of the right to self-determination and territorial control, resulting in competing constructions of nationhood, home and belonging. The Tamil demand for an independent homeland, Eelam, has been countered by the state assertion of the need to preserve the 'unity and territorial integrity' of the island. This territorialising spatial discourse has been reinforced by material spatial transformation: the creation of new sites and boundaries, such as militarised zones, checkpoints and indeterminate areas (the 'no-man's-land') between army occupation and guerrilla control, the internal and external migration of one and a half million people[19] and the enforced population resettlement generated by war, and more recently by the South Asian tsunami, the LTTE practice of ethnic cleansing in northern areas since 1990,[20] the disfigurement of the landscape through the ravages of military conflict and natural disaster, and the breakdown of land links between the northern city of Jaffna and the South, which have collectively served to provisionally partition the country and generate an altered geography. As Chelva Kanaganayakam pointed out in an article published in 2000, 'in a country which measures approximately 250 miles between its two furthest points, more than ninety miles are not connected by roads or the railway'.[21] In the topography generated by the displacement of war, culturally hybrid borderlands have been replaced by military boundaries that reinforce ethnic difference, thereby furthering the discourse of territoriality[22] and leading one analyst to claim that 'the current boundary is ethno-national in character'.[23] Such discourse has also influenced economic and political development. The Mahaweli Project – Sri Lanka's most expensive irrigation project, made possible through massive foreign loans in the mid-1970s – was promoted on the basis of nationalist rhetoric that compared it to the ancient irrigation systems of Sinhalese kings.[24] This project was enforced through resettling nearly 130,000 families – including 100,000 Sinhalese peasantry into Tamil-dominated areas – and also resulted in the dramatic cultural and material dispossession of the indigenous forest dwellers of Sri Lanka, whose dwelling space and hunting lands were made into a national park.[25] The relocation of the capital from Colombo to Kotte also served to mark a shift away from the island's colonial past towards an identification and reintegration with the pre-colonial period of Sinhalese rule – a territorial project of nationalist reclamation replicated in a different form in the burgeoning discovery of ancient Buddhist relics that serve to reclaim the land as a sacred space.[26]

These nationalist imperatives have gained particular urgency in the twenty years of armed conflict, when the cultural construction of what constitutes 'home' and 'homeland' has been foregrounded. Home is, as Rosemary Marangoly George points out, built upon 'a pattern of select inclusions and exclusions. Home is a way of establishing difference'.[27] It is within the trope of home that physical and psychic space converge and coalesce into a potent symbol of the circumscribed and situated self. The discursive construction of an 'imagined homeland' extends this symbol into a public, national space, but it disturbs its apparent coherence by its very location within the textual imaginary. The terms overlap, but they draw upon different models of location and, as will be seen, for many it is the disjunction between the two that generates alienation, when one's home and one's homeland occupy different spaces of representation.

Soon after Independence in 1948, the spatialisation of the Sri Lankan nation inscribed a Manichean cartography based on what Sankaran Krishna has called an 'originary hierarchy of authenticity'. Quoting the island's earliest texts, which were written by Buddhist clergy, political leaders repeatedly identified the island nation as 'Dhammadipa' and 'Sihaladipa'[28] – the land of the Buddha's teaching and of the Sinhalese people – entrenching a cultural homogeneity and exclusivity that have relegated the non-Sinhalese to the status of 'permanent guests', a people who are literally 'out of place'.[29] As James Duncan has pointed out (in words that substantiate Dennis Austin's claim that Sri Lankan history is 'more made up than most'[30]):

> The written history of Lankan society is among the world's most ancient. This unbroken record has been and is the venerated text, the ethnic scripture, of this passionately political people. To follow and fulfil this textual tradition was to have political legitimacy, thus it is written history and written mythology that provided the reference for the struggle for political power.[31]

These lines reveal temporal instability – the historical record '*has been and is* the venerated text' (my emphasis) and 'provided the reference for the struggle for political power' – indicating the author's uncertainty over the political use of mythology in the present. A raft of separatist policies after Independence, most notably the 'Sinhala Only' Act of 1956 which made Sinhala the sole official language in the very year that commemorated the 2500th anniversary of the Buddha's death with its attendant calls to make Buddhism the state religion, made it clear how national myths could be used in the service of exclusionary political objectives and reveal how the nation is culturally produced within specific codes of signification.

The discursive constructions of 'nation' and 'homeland' continue to be sites of contestation. One of the earliest initiatives in the peace negotiations of 2002 identified the need to construct a new spatial term, and the demand for a 'separate homeland' – with all its exclusionary registers of secession and ownership – was replaced by the rather more fluid formulation: 'areas of historical habitation'.[32] This term, while affirming the historical claims of the Tamil people to their ancestral home, simultaneously denies stability and coherence to the terrain over which they may be granted conditional control, and works to situate the Tamils in a system described by Deleuze and Guattari as 'itinerant territoriality' – a people whose settlement may well be temporary and subject to change.[33] The new term, it could be argued, offers a precarious occupancy, with the Tamils marked as resident outsiders, bearing credence to Sankaran Krishna's claim that in Sri Lanka the multiethnic state is incomprehensible to the popular mind and the writer Jean Arasanayagam's assertion that in the country 'each new settler [is] an invader'.[34]

The discursive registers of Tamil nationalism, on the other hand, tend towards a separatist logic that embraces irredentism, with its call for political autonomy in a region considered by Tamil nationalists to constitute a former independent Tamil kingdom – one unconquered by any colonial power apart from the Portuguese.[35] Drawing largely upon a diasporic base for its financial support, Tamil nationalism in its militant form has gained demographic expression within the country in the systematic ethnic cleansing of the Jaffna Peninsula[36] and a corresponding cultural expression in the call for a pure Tamil movement purged of Sanskritic, Aryan and 'northern' influences. It is strengthened by major commemorative rituals inside and outside Sri Lanka that create and sustain a collective memory of warrior sacrifice, courage and honour, following a calendar whose printed form, in a 1998 version, marked the death of Hitler with explicit praise and admiration for the German dictator.[37]

Territoriality is thus not only a geographical inscription but also a textual one, discursively shaped and itself shaping the discourse of belonging. It directly affects the political and cultural landscape of writers and the production and reception of literary texts. In Sri Lanka – where there has been a dramatic increase in literary production since the escalation of armed conflict – the link between literature and nationalist inscriptions of belonging is strong. Key issues such as the role of the writer, who has the right to write the nation and how the nation should be written have become sites of contention, both within the literature and, equally significantly, in the critical reception of texts.[38] Sri Lankan literature since the war thus brings to crisis many of the key debates in postcolonial studies reflecting struggles over issues of legitimacy, authenticity, canonicity and the politics and representation of belonging and exclusion. The literary territoriality marked by spatial configurations of nation, landscape, home and belonging, and by linguistic markers of geopolitical discourse and ethnically differentiated discourse, needs to be considered in relation to the boundary marking generated within critical practice and the politics of belonging and affiliation encoded in it.

It could be argued that this is particularly necessary given the radically different constraints within which Sri Lankan texts written inside and outside the country operate. The position of 'expatriate' literature is dictated by factors informed by its publication and ready availability within the metropolitan centres in which postcolonial studies has its base. Given that Sri Lankan texts written from within the country are almost entirely published locally – with little or no editorial support, poor distribution and a very limited print run[39]– the constitution of 'Sri Lankan' literature outside Sri Lanka is coming to be increasingly dictated by the terms set by 'expatriate' writers, resulting in a canon of writing *set apart* from the emergent canon in Sri Lanka which looks more to local writers and the work of selected non-residents for its base. The conditions are thereby being created for a polarised dynamic of competing claims to authority from outside and inside Sri Lanka in which the cultural mediations evident in the literature itself are in danger of being displaced or silenced.

'Expatriate' writers have an advantage over their 'resident' counterparts in that while their work may be – and often is – scrutinised in relation to constructed notions of cultural authenticity, these are not the only terms on which their work is assessed. Shyam Selvadurai is also situated as a Canadian gay writer and A. Sivanandan as a Marxist internationalist, and Michael Ondaatje's work is analysed from a range of poststructuralist perspectives incorporating meta-fictionality, the visual arts and chaos theory. What is more, polarised critical positions on, say Ondaatje, outlined by Chelva Kanaganayakam, or Selvadurai in Daniel Coleman's evaluation, describe tensions between clearly defined critical positions or fields – the opposition between nativist or nationalist readings and migrant and exilic ones, or the intersecting marginalities attending postcolonial and queer studies, in ways that bring into the open the process of critical arbitration and its terms of evaluation.[40]

Resident writers, on the other hand, do not have the luxury of being positioned in such an open critical field. As Kanaganayakam has shown, their work, published and distributed locally, is not readily available to international readers, who are almost entirely dependent on local critics to define and place the work in its cultural context[41] – critics who are influenced by and are in turn influencing the nationalist discourses of the day. Even in India, where Sri Lankan writers are increasingly being published, availability remains limited due to restricted distribution, so the texts have yet to gain a critical base in literary studies there.[42] An exegetical study of textual territoriality thus requires a mediatory critical practice that moves between different poles of analysis: the locatedness of literary criticism and the territorial markers to be found in the texts themselves. These markers are, as I will now show, multiple, varied and contestatory – resistant to domestication and any easy distinctions on the basis of domicile. In the next section, therefore, I provide an outline of some of the ways in which spatial idiomatics gain literary expression in a range of Sri Lankan texts.

Writing space

Sri Lankan writing since the war has emerged out of a context shaped by a tension between an overdetermined spatial discourse – what political geographers describe as the 'territorial trap' – on the one hand[43] and cultural and spatial shifts of seismic proportions on the other. In the words of Sankaran Krishna, it is a situation in which the making of the nation 'is coeval with its violent unmaking'.[44] This disjunction between the fixity of territorial discourse and the dislocations of war has generative potential in providing the conditions of possibility for the emergence of new narratives of belonging. As anthropologists have observed, deterritorialisation – and one can add to this reterritorialisation – serves to unsettle and challenge accepted notions of nativeness.[45] Given that in Sri Lanka nationalism has long been defined in communal terms and identities are increasingly communally based, the unsettling effects of a twenty-year war provide opportunities for identifying the boundaries of specific contestational sites between competing ethnic nationalisms – both of which draw upon the premise that the nation should be ethnically homogenous – as well as other forms of cultural contestation.[46] In these terms Sri Lankan literature since the war could be seen as articulating and testing the viability of new formulations of belonging, mapping geographies that, in Cleary's re-citing of Said, chart the desire '"to reclaim, rename, and re-inhabit" the alienated landscape through the imagination'.[47]

The tendency has manifested itself in both popular and literary fiction. The 'national romance'– that is, across-the-barricades stories of relationships that challenge the ethnic divide (notably in Karen Roberts' *July* (2001)) – together with the crime novel and the political thriller (for example Jeanne Cambrai's' *Murder in the Pettah* (2001) and David Blacker's *A Cause Untrue* (2005)) are popular forms that work to critique the state-sanctioned cartography of the nation by drawing upon the discourse of justice and morality to realign established boundaries, while detective fiction has elided into the literary uncanny in Michelle de Krester's historical novel *The Hamilton Case* (2004).[48] This increasing focus on displacement has found expression in novels that focus exclusively on boundary crossing from the war zone, such as Nihal de Silva's *The Road from Elephant Pass* (2003) and C. Suryakumaran's *Kilali Crossing* (2002), and the exploration of indeterminate spaces and compromised alliances, such as Chandraratna Bandara's translated novel *Hostage City* (1993; trans. Vijitha Fernando). The political thriller, with its creation of an underworld marked by paranoia and subterfuge, is notable for sharing imaginative affinities with literary texts such as Ondaatje's *Anil's Ghost* (2000) and *Handwriting* (1998), which explore fugitive space and hidden history through metaphoric registers of excavation and burial, and Romesh Gunesekera's *Heaven's Edge* (2002), a dystopian fantasy set in a future marked by guerrilla warfare and random state violence – the latter sharing some of the apocalyptic drive of Rajiva Wijesinha's political satire *Days of Despair* (1989) and Tennyson Perera's translated novel *Thunder* (1999; trans. Tilak Balasuriya).[49] For both Ondaatje and Gunesekera the recourse to a subterranean mapping of the nation is influenced by the fact that in their reading of the nation political forces resist legibility. Other genres that have increased in popularity since the start of the war are the personal memoir – a form that can offer sanctuary in a hermetically sealed past, distanced from the political discord and violent uncertainty of the present – and the short story. The latter form, one that invites plurivocity, has developed dramatically in recent years and has found notable exponents in, amongst others, Neil Fernandopulle and Jagath Kumarasinghe, while the innovative reach of Tissa Abeysekara's work resists categorisation altogether. Another notable literary intervention is playwright Manuka Wijesinghe's recently published first novel *Monsoons and Potholes* (2006), which contrasts with Abeysekara's lyrically weighted reading of myth and, in its assured and exuberant interplay between personal, national and mythological histories, bears striking imaginative affinities with Rushdie's *Midnight's Children.* The sheer range of writing and writers – with recent Gratiaen Prize winners drawn from the fields of molecular biology and the aviation industry – reveals an increasing democratisation and pluralism in literary production in English that challenges the rather tired charge of elitism levelled at such work.

The development towards new cartographies can also be measured by a consideration of the work of the two writers who – according to one critic – kept anglophone writing going during the dry decade following the 'Sinhala Only' Act.[50] Both James Goonewardene and Punyakante Wijenaike show a shift in spatial register after the escalation in political violence in the 1970s and 1980s. Goonewardene abandoned his critique of the pastoral idyll for an engagement with ecology and the geopolitical construction of the state as an organism in *One Mad Bid For Freedom* (1990) and a focus on tribalism in his last novel. Wijenaike, who, in her strongest novels, had explored the gendered space of the *walauwe* – or traditional ancestral home – reflecting on the alienation of women within their dwelling space, transferred this dynamic of estrangement to an explicitly political context in her award-winning novel *The Enemy Within* (1998), which focused on the Central Bank bomb explosion of 1996. Drawing upon the capital's spatial history as a former fortress, Wijenaike explores the experiences of a range of residents living in a state of siege, restricted as much by their own fear as by instruments of the state. Her work more than that of any other local writer in English explores Homi Bhabha's formulation of the uncanny or 'unhomely' as the manifestation of an absent presence that serves to menace the scene of representation.

Both these writers work to deconstruct models of a unitary, homogenous nation and do so by relocating national space as exilic space through mobile structurations of home and belonging. Their different spatial configurations do more than this; they work to confound assumptions underlying any easy distinctions between 'resident' and 'expatriate' writing by exploring diverse modalities of alienation. Much of this study seeks to dismantle polarised categorisations that conscript writing to critical territoriality, but for now a brief comparison of boundary marking in the work of a 'resident' and 'expatriate' writer will further illustrate my argument on the urgent need for such a critical manoeuvre.

'Resident' and 'expatriate' cartographies

Boundaries are central tropes to a range of Sri Lankan texts. David Sibley has shown how 'moral panics heighten boundary consciousness' and has claimed that boundaries 'assume considerable significance because they are simultaneously zones of uncertainty and security'.[51] Boundaries figure prominently in both Shyam Selvadurai's *Funny Boy* (1995) and Jean Arasanayagam's work. Selvadurai, the product of an inter-ethnic marriage, and Arasanayagam, a Burgher married to a Tamil, are both caught in the interstices of contested ethnic identities, and both were displaced by the anti-Tamil violence of 1983 – Selvadurai as a political refugee in Canada and Arasanayagam as an internal refugee. Their work thus registers displacement in ways that accommodate it as not only external but also internal to the nation.

Selvadurai's novel *Funny Boy* depicts the coming-of-age of a cross-dressing Tamil boy, Arjie, who unwittingly gets embroiled in a range of inter-ethnic relationships, notably his aunt's inter-ethnic relationship with a Sinhalese man and his own affair with a Sinhalese boy, Shehan, just before the Colombo pogrom of 1983. The novel thus aligns itself with national romances such as Karen Roberts' *July*, in which ethnic identity is marked in exclusionary terms in order to explore the possibilities for communal connection. What distinguishes Selvadurai's work is that the romance between Arjie and Shehan addresses the boundary marking created by both ethnic intolerance and homophobia. Selvadurai's mediation of emergent homosexuality is played out through foregrounding the mobility of the desiring self across clearly defined ethnic and gender categories, which are, in turn, given concrete spatial coordinates in the text. 'Most people marry their own kind', Arjie is told, and he is left to consider the ways in which his own life inverts the terms on which the statement is made.

Charting a clearly segregated terrain of permitted spaces and forbidden zones, the focus of the novel rests on the negotiation, invasion and violation of politicised, gendered and socially stratified spaces, mapping the larger struggle for territorial control in the country. The emphasis on essentialised ethnicities and segregated physical space allows Selvadurai to focus on the relative fluidity of relationships and the physical mobility of his central character, providing a context of constraint that allows us to witness the process of emergence of a bordered sexual identity. As a result there has been a tendency, both within Sri Lanka and abroad, to read Selvadurai's work as a diasporic reflection on migrant sexuality. Both Daniel Coleman and Raj Rao situate it in these terms, the latter claiming that '*Funny Boy* adds to the slowly growing body of gay writing on [rather than from] the Indian subcontinent' and concludes by dissociating it from what he calls the 'Sri Lankan literary tradition'.[52] It is, we are told elsewhere, 'the story of one young boy's interior formation and integration set against *the backdrop* of his country's disintegration' (my emphasis)[53] – a backdrop that was almost effaced in Sri Lanka where the novel was primarily positioned as a gay text, and responses ranged from one writer's enraged evaluation of the novel as filth[54] to a national debate on the need to repeal the anti-sodomy law after the Sri Lankan President read it.

My concern here is not that so much attention was granted to the novel's negotiation of gay identity, but with the use of exclusionary critical registers that fail to evaluate the construction of ethnicity that frame the conditions of emergence of mobile sexuality. The novel intersects with and interconnects gay, diasporic and Sri Lankan cultural registers, and the fact that, as Raj Rao points out, political events are presented 'from a Tamil point of view, with no references to Tiger atrocities' requires a reading of the way all identities get staged.[55] Kanaganayakam's positioning of Selvadurai as a Colombo Tamil who has access to a syncretic linguistic register – in the novel Arjie is placed in the Sinhala rather than the Tamil stream – also needs to be brought into play here as it helps identify the specific politics of location that activate the text's 'queer' identity.[56] If ethnic essentialism is constructed from a syncretic cultural space – and there is plenty of evidence in the novel to support this – then the articulation of discrete Tamil and Sinhala identities is further problematised. To displace the text into a queer, diasporic space is to dramatically reduce its ideological investment in critiquing ethnically bordered discourse and its role in determining the cultural matrices of an emergent Sri Lankan canon. It is perhaps through such manoeuvres that ethnic politics and displacement come to be de-linked in the work of a political exile.

In contrast, Jean Arasanayagam's extensive oeuvre registers a different range of approaches to exile which collectively chart a development from a personal to a public voice. A writer of Burgher descent, she has acknowledged that her relationship to the land is marked by its provisionality – a sense of ancestral 'tenantship'.[57] Her work registers alterity in three key ways: the critique of territorial discourse focusing on borders and boundaries in short stories and drama; the development of a fluid and mobile subject positioning, shifting between the boundaries of marginalised ethnic identities (Burgher and Tamil) in biographical prose (such as *Peacocks and Dreams*) and poetry; and an unsettling internalisation of difference resulting in the dissolution of boundaries and a mergence between speaking subject and landscape in verse. This generic diversity and subjective flexibility does not however ally itself with the postmodern celebration of liminal identity found in Ondaatje's *Running in the Family* or the delight in a hybridised, anarchic linguistic register found in Carl Muller's Burgher trilogy. Rather, as Neloufer de Mel has succinctly pointed out, 'her writings imply that syncretism is never an *equal* mixing of diverse inheritances, that cosmopolitanism is classed and raced, and that identity is as much about political exigency dictated by the dominant hegemony'.[58] Yet while her work resists ethnically marked readings there has been a tendency to ethnically overdetermine her work by emphasising her mediation of Burgher and Tamil identity, diverting attention away from the focus of her writing, which rests – as I show in a later chapter – on the broader dynamic of a subjectivity struggling against the erasure imposed by such territorial markings. These divergent scriptings of 'ethnicity' in the work of the 'expatriate' Selvadurai and the 'resident' Arasanayagam reveal that the textual accommodation of difference can be marked in ways that disturb categories of belonging bound by geographical readings of place. An engagement with the spatial idiomatics underpinning texts can thus challenge the overdetermined reading of texts in relation to their sites of production by revealing the contestatory boundaries in which belonging itself is enunciated. It is in these sites, I argue, that the 'nation' is opened up as a provisional, contingent and negotiated space.

There is clearly a need to find a critical discourse for the fractured spaces inhabited by Arasanayagam and Selvadurai, one that is responsive to the varieties of victimisation, the hierarchies within hybridity and the contingency of contested frontiers. Dislocating the work of these writers from the polarised discourse of 'resident' and 'expatriate' readings and from interpretative strategies that write into or write over the exclusivity of ethnic identity markers remains a precondition for deterritorialising Sri Lankan writing from existing exclusionary binaries, challenging constructions of ethnicity and enabling a transactional ethics to emerge from the violence of ethnic intolerance. Concomitant with this project is one that works to identify some of the specific strategies of exclusion through which critical territoriality is enacted. To reveal, in other words, the ways in which apparently divergent modes of critical evaluation of Sri Lankan literature in fact can delineate mutually reinforcing lines of affiliation. This is the subject of my final section, but before I begin identifying and analysing these different modes, it is first necessary to explore one of the key critical boundaries applied to the studies of

English writing from Sri Lanka, one based on the exclusivity of the English language itself.

The edge of English

English is colloquially referred to as 'kaduwa' or 'sword' by Sinhala speakers, a term that reflects its status as an instrument of empire that effectively divides a subject peoples. Critics have contended that the term was coined and gained currency somewhere between the late 1960s and early 1970s,[59] a decade or so after the 'Sinhala Only' Act, and that it originated among rural or semi-urban children and youth in their response to English classes in government schools where it was worn 'not as a badge of privilege but as a mask, and a very vulnerable one at that'.[60] The term, then, does not so much discursively enact a decolonising strategy of cultural reclamation from the former colonial power, but rather it registers an internalised counter-hegemonic resistance to the power of the English-educated, who continued to hold key positions of power and influence in the country *after* the nationalist imperatives underpinning the 'Sinhala Only' Act had come into effect.[61] When situated in the political and historical context in which it evolved, the 'kaduwa' of English can be seen to be less a marker of cultural reclamation – a term wielded to minoritise the English language[62] – and more a register of the very *uncertainty* of such reclamation within the context of cultural fragmentation in the nation, as fluency in English, the language of the international community, is seen to be indispensable for access to positions of social and material privilege in the country.[63] Constitutionally recognised as a link language in 1978,[64] this discursive *kaduwa* is clearly a sword with a double edge: one that socially and culturally divides the nation in ways that create very real material inequities between peoples, and also one that effectively connects the English-speaking elite to other postcolonial elites within and outside the country and to the wider global community as well. Indeed its significance as a link language is such that it has been suggested that the very downgrading of the English language has been a contributory factor in the division between racial groups and religious communities such 'that the troubles of 1983 were largely due to the fact that this important cultural function of English and the English-educated had ceased to operate effectively'.[65]

It is this unstable positioning of English as a language whose use works to both divide and connect peoples, creating alternative lines of affiliation, which is central to my analysis of cultural and critical boundary marking. The assumption that almost all resident Sri Lankan writers in English are from a materially privileged minority is not in dispute here: it is evident in the fact that the cultural effects of constitutionally enforced linguistic nationalism have for some time compelled those who wish to learn English fluently – and are not born into a family in which it is spoken at home – to pay for their own tuition.[66] But rather it is the assumption that the use of English itself has the *singular and unilateral* effect of social and cultural exclusion, that it marks a stable boundary and a determinable cultural centre, which I wish to challenge. 'English' is of course not itself singular or homogenous; its very insertion within a radically alternative cultural context insists upon its mutation into multiple 'englishes'.[67] What is more as a recent study of 'Sri Lankan English' has shown, all speakers of English in the country use a hybridised form of the language – a fact that is not only unacknowledged but actively resisted by members of the elite, who prefer to believe they are using 'Queen's English'.[68] Yet the tendency to read the literary products of Sri Lankan writers in relation to the fixity of class difference and either their conformity to or their deviation from a putative 'standard' English not only assumes the stability of a medium that, like all linguistic mediums, is historically and culturally contingent (so that the 'standard' that is referred to is subject to change), but also results in forms of evaluation that differentiate texts on a highly selective construction of difference and belonging. It results in markedly variant – and often contradictory – scriptings of the 'place' of English in anglophone texts which can be used to arbitrate and determine cultural legitimacy. Hence it is possible for one critic to suggest that James Goonewardene's lack of deviation from formal English and his inability to communicate 'broken English' are markers of his elitism, for another to claim that the morphological borrowings from the indigenous language register another writer's alienation, and another to contend that the hybridised play of Jagath Kumarasinghe's short stories effectively ground the work in Sri Lanka.[69] These readings register the ways in which linguistic markers of difference are scripted to serve specific readings of national culture and, when taken collectively, reveal that English in Sri Lanka does not in fact have a stable cultural base, centre or constituency at all.

The assumption of the singularity of English and its unilateral connection to the imperial centre is evident in the infamous statement by the young bilingual poet Lakdasa Wikkramasinha, who contended in 1965:

> I have come to realize that I am using the language of the most despicable and loathsome people on earth; I have no wish to extend its life and range, enrich its tonality.
>
> To write in English is a form of cultural treason. I have had for the future to think of a way of circumventing this treason; I propose to do this by making my writing entirely immoralist and destructive.[70]

The denigration of literature in English through the 1960s and until the period of the first JVP (or People's Liberation Front) insurrection was in part facilitated by the failure of anglophone writers to directly address some of the dramatic social upheavals affecting the country and choose instead to focus on rural themes in keeping with the nationalist project of connection with the masses. Rajiva Wijesinha has reflected on the social and cultural contradictions underpinning such efforts:

> In the first few decades after independence we had the irony of the classes that spoke English striving desperately to describe village maidens flinging themselves into wells, while writers at home in Sinhala described the upper classes in unrealistic if not quite Dickensian terms – and in terms of their relationship with other classes, rather than their interactions amongst themselves.[71]

This desire to *bridge* difference can demarcate an arena where contested and contradictory constructions of identity clash, a space of representation that actively engages with hegemonic political prescriptives in ways that, far from being external or peripheral to the discourse of ethnonationalism, instead articulates the very difficulties of accommodation within competing hierarchies of belonging. The instabilities of discourse – as Bakhtinian analysis shows us – indicate sites of radical affiliative uncertainty in literature. Bakhtin's seminal analysis of the coexistence of linguistic forms and their contestation has specific implications for the study of English literature produced in Sri Lanka, for here the cultural conflicts of ethnic, class and gender differentiation are internally marked by the linguistic register of writers who are also almost all bilingual, familiar both with English and another tongue, familiar in other words with (at least) two distinct cultural registers and a historical and political context in which language-use has been contested on the basis of ethnicity. A consideration of linguistic hybridity in the work of Jean Arasanayagam and Carl Muller can be used to assess the level of cultural exchange, permeability and accommodation of difference in the country. As Burgher writers they belong to the one community distinguished on the basis of their hybridity, part of a mixed-race minority who are English-speaking descendants of the Dutch and Portuguese who had once ruled the island. As their first language is English the subversion of normative English discourse to be found in their work can be read as largely a conscious effort. What follows is a brief overview that attempts to open up the borders of 'English' writing, indicating some of the ways in which dialogism and discursive hybridity can mark the difficulties of cultural accommodation in the country.

Language, as Bakhtin has shown, is materially produced and culturally determined – an index of social change and conflict. Individual words and phrases, both oral and written, are sites of cultural conflict, their juxtaposition embodying a clash of competing discourses and ideologies. Language, and in particular the discourse of novelistic fiction, can thus be decentred, dialogic and hybridised; 'a mixture', as Bakhtin puts it, 'of two social languages within the limits of a single utterance, an encounter, within the arena of an utterance, between two different linguistic consciousnesses, separated from one another by an epoch, by social differentiation or by some other factor'. Bakhtin distinguishes between 'polyglossia', the interaction between two or more languages within a given culture, and 'heteroglossia', a diversity of unofficial forms of a particular national language leading to internal differentiation.[72]

Jean Arasanayagam, as already indicated, occupies a nebulous borderland: as a Burgher woman married to a high-caste Tamil, she was rejected by her Tamil in-laws and, on the basis of her inter-ethnic marriage, was victimised during the anti-Tamil riots of 1983, during which she was forced to seek shelter in a refugee camp. This experience of double exclusion has a direct bearing on the construction of ethnic and cultural difference in her work. While her own social and cultural position may be liminal, in-between fixed identities, the linguistic registers of her prose are strikingly marked by their polyglossia, the juxtapostion of discrete languages. In *Peacocks and Dreams* (written 1984; published 1996), an evocative, mythopoeic reconstruction of her husband's childhood in a Tamil village, Arasanayagam inserts Sanskrit terms into normative English, transforming the dominant English idiom by making interpretation dependent upon an understanding of Hindu myth and religion.[73] She further dialogises the work by rhetorically addressing the boy (who was her husband) directly in the opening story:

> But you tasted nectar once and you were a deity too, let us give you a name – Small god of the Grove. The trident twirled for you and Siva invited you into that dream of *Kailasa.*
>
> Why don't you return to your village, you had a home there once. Is it too late? The black *naga* rears its hood, uncoiling itself. The sky darkens with the spread of its malignant hood. Siva stirs the earth in his *tandava* dance but his thunderous step can no longer destroy the evil *asuras* that ravage the land. Your prayers to Ganesh, Skanda, Vishnu, Siva are as distant as a madman's mutter wandering through its own confusions as shells fly cracking the roofs, skullblows smashing the bone into smithereens.[74]

This disorientating passage registers cultural difference through its dependence on Hindu ideas and terminology as individual words from the subaltern discourse are isolated, italicised and set apart from standard English. These words are integral to the meaning of the piece (which focuses on the way Siva's regenerative dance of creation and destruction has been stilled by the violence of war – how the divine order has been broken) but their very differentiation registers the fault lines, fractures and disjunctures of the cultural world described. The text's plurivocity thus registers cultural dissonance by the self-conscious insertion and awkward accommodation of an alternative discourse into 'standard' English idiom. Even the promise of code-switching on a metaphoric level is not realised – the sky, we are told, is not itself analogous to a cobra's hood (a potentially striking image) but only 'darkens' with it. The linguistic register of *Peacocks and Dreams* reveals an important aspect of her work: that the accommodation of difference is impossible for Arasanayagam within the Tamil context.[75] It here reminds us that exclusion is not the preserve of one community and registers the extent to which Arasanayagam's work is attentive to multiple fault lines.

Linguistic hybridity has the potential to subvert dominant discourses. As Homi Bhabha has shown, in hybridised discourse narrative authority is articulated 'with a range of differential knowledges and positionalities that both estrange its "identity" and produce new forms of knowledge, new modes of differentiation, new sites of power'.[76] But, as this passage shows, in Arasanayagam's work dialogicality – also to be found in her poetry, which sometimes draws upon a Sinhala and Dutch lexicon – is used to register the coexistence of discrete worldviews and their incommensurability.[77] While, on the one hand, her work unsettles the heirarchy of discourses through linguistic juxtapostion, discrete languages are held in tension, words connect only to collide, and cultures clash to produce an idiom in which there is no easy accommodation of difference.

In contrast to Arasanayagam's polyglossic juxtaposition of different languages, Carl Muller's work contains a syncretic linguistic register celebrating an anarchic, hybridised Sri Lankan English, or 'Singlish' as it is commonly called.[78] His bawdy novel *The Jam Fruit Tree* (1993) is fully heteroglossic, describing the contestation of voices and dialects within a language, and, unlike Arasanayagam's work, it does not require the reader to have a working knowledge of a subaltern discourse to understand its meaning. Here, an elderly Burgher couple, Maudiegirl and Cecilprins, contemplate the prospect of one of their daughters marrying a Sinhalese:

> 'I die and go and cannot see even one married,' Maudiegirl would grumble and Cecilprins would make the old rattan chair creak and say: 'What's this silliness you're saying. If anything wrong with you can bring doctor, no?' But he knew. Deep inside. Over fifty years of married life and all it stood for was not lost on this man. 'Anna doing the dance with Sinhalese fellow. So what to do? You want Sinhalese son-in-law, I suppose.'
>
> Maudiegirl glared and let loose one of those rare shafts of wisdom that was based, even if she did not know it, on pure logic. 'So never mind. You thinking we are special or something? Good to go to top market buying *bombili* (the dried "Bombay duck" – a thin eel-like fish that is found in abundance in Indian waters) from Sinhalese man. Good to get children's bicycle made by Sinhalese man. Good to eat rice and curry and *stringhoppers* (steamed circlets of flour – a favourite breakfast dish in Sri Lanka) like Sinhalese man. When want to cut tree in the backside you call Sinhalese man, no? Firewood bringing Sinhalese man. Plucking coconuts who? Dhoby who? All over people Sinhalese, no? Father telling in church love the neighbour. See, will you, who neighbour is. Sinhalese, no?'[79]

The novel effectively parodies standard English idiom, using a mongrelised, dialogical discourse to reflect cultural negotiation rather than cultural conflict.[80] Sri Lankan words are italicised *and* immediately decoded; they are culturally differentiated and unmarked (their etymology is not provided) simultaneously marking and crossing the lexical boundaries of a culture. Thus while Arasanayagam's work registers the difficulties encountered by the hybridised subject and the awkwardness of overcoming cultural boundaries, Muller's novels revel in the indeterminacy of their cultural location. Significantly, it is the Sinhalese subject who is displaced here, requiring translation, as mongrelised 'Singlish' takes precedence.

Between them Arasanayagam and Muller unsettle the hegemonising view of English as a singular discourse with a unilateral affiliation with the former colonial power and their neocolonial successors. What is more, these brief extracts reveal the complex ways in which hierarchic constructions of difference can be challenged and transcended through unsettling linguistic registers; manoeuvres that call for pluralist readings of culture and identity. Between the clash of cultures found in Arasanayagam's reflections on childhood in Tamil Sri Lanka and the syncreticism of Muller's reconstruction of a suburban past, the gap between alienation and accommodation is not only marked but mobilised into an articulation of the margins of national belonging. It reveals how those who are displaced or occupy cultural borderlands are creative agents in the construction of the nation.[81] Yet, as will be seen, literary manoeuvres can all too often be contained by critical strategies that work to re-territorialise texts. Identifying strategies of critical exclusion thus remains a precondition for the process of creating a transactional ethics in literary studies in Sri Lanka. I will now attempt to identify some of the key modes of critical territoriality, revealing how apparently antagonistic modes of analysis can work to reinforce exclusionary readings of the nation.

The critical field

It is my contention that the critical territoriality currently arbitrating the boundaries of 'Sri Lankan' literature falls into two distinct but related categories. While significant measures have been taken to counter critical territoriality – notably in the development of critical analyses foregrounding hybridity, such as the essays in Neluka Silva's edited volume *The Hybrid Nation*, the proliferation of literary translations (in which Halpé *et al.*'s *A Lankan Mosaic* stands as significant example) and institutional support for translational activity,[82] as well as the diasporisation of literary culture evident in canonising texts such as Yasmine Gooneratne's *Celebrating Sri Lankan Women's Writing*[83] and the publishing policies of the dynamic new publishing house of Perera Hussein[84] – these efforts to hybridise, dialogise and diasporise the critical boundaries of Sri Lankan writing need to be assessed against the background of the hegemonising forces of critical exclusion that work to define the field. Indeed it could be argued that the full significance of such counter-territorial manoeuvres can only be measured by identifying the critical constituents and cultural and political drives underpinning the hegemonising prescriptives they appear to challenge. The two modes of critical territoriality demarcate different trajectories rather than exclusive and contained critical forms, outlining broad tendencies in a spectrum of discursive practices that may be invested in to different degrees. Like all typologies they are, by definition, reductive, and my scripting of them is inevitably formulaic. Yet I use them, compromising as they are, to identify a fundamental tension in the evaluation of Sri Lankan literature in English: a tension that, I argue, demarcates the key coordinates of a critical matrix from which culturally hegemonising evaluative criteria in Sri Lankan literary criticism have emerged. My definition of these forms is modulated by an exploration of their articulation in critical texts in order to reveal more fully the cultural and political implications they contain.

The first mode of critical territoriality is directed by what I call *patrician* literary criticism: a mode of analysis that derives its authority broadly (but not exclusively) from a Leavisian approach to literature. Patrician literary critics privilege specific literary values. They engage in a universalising, humanist reading of culture, assessing literary texts on their ability to enhance 'Life' so that aesthetic criteria are connected to a text's perceived human importance. Their relationship to textual analysis is essentially paternalistic, marking an investment in their role as guardians of national culture. In their search to find the 'best' in literary culture, they operate in an implicitly hierarchic model of the world, but their position, within the postcolonial context, is a culturally unstable one. Drawing both implicitly and explicitly from European models of literary culture in their evaluation of textual products from a postcolonial location, their authentication of national culture is based upon a borrowed aestheticism that destabilises the boundary of the 'national' that they seek to protect. The Leavisian lament on the decline of national culture has, therefore, in this postcolonial context, a neo-colonial basis, as the evaluations of the patrician critic are based on cultural criteria and authenticated products from the imperial centre. Theirs is not the 'oppositional humanism' described by Benita Parry, a humanism that works in the service of anticolonial resistance and decolonisation, but rather a hegemonising humanism that works to stabilise the dominant cultural order.[85] The patrician deprecation of modern 'ills' such as alienation and anomy marks a communitarian ideology[86] – a factor that helps to situate their cultural politics. The emphasis here is on approval, authentication and legitimation. Critics that follow a patrician line of evaluation feel most secure when undertaking a socially dispersive reading of texts, place an emphasis on literary history, class dynamics and 'community', and favour realist representation.[87]

The second form of critical territoriality is directed by a *nativist* critical approach. Nativist critics undertake a subaltern politics of cultural reclamation and irredentism that often leads them to reject the Western-orientated models of authentication promoted by patrician critical practitioners. They follow an isolationist cultural logic – one premised on the notion of cultural difference and dictated by the cultural politics of decolonisation – and undertake a form of critical territoriality that places value on a writer's place of residence, on origins and on 'tradition'. Their emphasis is on the indigene whom they perceive as institutionally marginalised, not only by the international critical community but also by the local critical establishment. Nativist critiques rely on a reading of the nation as a site of natally determined primary affiliation, as outlined by Raymond Williams in his observation that: '"Nation" as a term is radically connected with "native". We are *born* into relationships which are typically settled in place. This form of primary and "placeable" bonding is of quite fundamental human and natural importance'.[88] They share the patrician critic's interest in canon formation, but they aim to construct an alternative canon – one that privileges local, resident and culturally authenticated expatriate writers. There are two polar forms of nativism: one that emphasises inclusivity and one driven by a politics of exclusivity. Inclusive nativists are driven by the desire to transform the canon by incorporating hitherto marginalised writers from within the country; exclusive nativists focus more on filtering the work of writers resident outside Sri Lanka, assessing them on the basis of their viability for inclusion in the canon. Underpinning the evaluations of all nativists is a primordialist hierarchy of value that underscores indigeniety, domicile and authenticity. Nativists have a tendency to label texts that fall short of their authenticating criteria as 'exotic' and 'orientalist' – terms that tend to be used by non-Sri Lankan critics in a more nuanced form to critique literary alienation or the dominant critical trajectories in metropolitan centres[89] – and are particularly alert to various forms of 'stereotyping'. Their evaluations are largely based on a representationalist assessment of a text – in other words on how an author appears to represent the country and its people.

These two modes of critical territoriality appear to contain diametrical approaches to cultural authenticity. Patrician critics, drawing as they do upon European literary and critical models in their evaluation of texts, appeal to a metropolitan base that works to undermine culturally exclusive readings. Nativist critics, on the other hand, follow a centripetal logic in which cultural boundaries are determined by a putative national centre and appeal to a notion of the 'authentic' Sri Lankan voice. Yet both patrician and nativist critical practitioners clearly invest in a project of cultural guardianship that can – especially within the context of the cultural nationalism generated since Independence and the contestatory dynamics generated by political conflict – work towards a form of critical boundary marking that reinforces specific readings of the nation. Homi Bhabha's analysis of representation in the colonial text reveals how such convergence can come about and is therefore worth considering in detail.

Bhabha's essay initially focuses on the collaboration between historicism and realism, both of which engage with 'the familiar quest for an origin that will authorize a beginning'.[90] He draws attention to the representationalist basis of both discourses and the fact that their '"unmediated" and sequential progression to truth, the originality of vision – what Leavis would call the wholeness of their resolution – are historical and ideological productions [. . .] necessary fictions that tragically believed too much in their necessity and too little in their own fictionality' (p. 97). 'Their practices' he claims 'can be seen to be unmediated and universal because the unity of tradition lies in an absolute presence – a moment of transcendent originality' (p. 97). The collusion between historicism and realism constitute what Bhabha describes as a 'Leavisian Universalism' (p. 99) which privileges the 'Transcendental subject' and the origin of writing as linear time consciousness (p. 98).

Bhabha's central argument rests on drawing correspondences between critics espousing Leavisian methods, or 'Universalist' critics, and the work of 'Nationalist' critics both of whom, he claims fight 'on the same aesthetic ground' (p. 99). In a scrupulous evaluation of the representationalist basis of both these critical discourses he reveals how Leavisian standards have been propounded by one of the foremost Caribbean critics (at a time when postcolonial studies were in their infancy) in his evaluation of Caribbean texts. Universalism is, in Bhabha's terms, fundamentally content-based and privileges representativeness or 'the correctness of the image' (p. 100). It is a mode of analysis in which 'the text as a *form of recognition*' is the central term, one in which the text is 'not seen as *productive* of meaning but essentially reflective or expressive', marking a preference for realist signification (p. 100, original italics). It prepares the way for 'a form of intuitionism of moral values'[91] which valorises specific political and social values under the guise of pure criticism (pp. 102 and 103). Given Leavis' parochialism, the use of universalist methods are 'imbued with an ideological and cultural reference that would make its use critically prescriptive with a marked neo-colonial emphasis' (p. 103). Its appropriation by 'Nationalist' critics clearly internalises colonial representationalism because, in this case, the critic is 'caught in the problem of image analysis, speaks against one stereotype but essentially, and inevitably, for another' (p. 105). In a passage whose relevance to the field of Sri Lankan literary criticism will shortly become clear, Bhabha is unequivocal in outlining the stultifying effects of such a critical discourse:

> The demand that one image should circulate rather than another is made on the basis that the stereotype is *distorted* in relation to a *given* norm or model. It results in a mode of prescriptive criticism which Macherey has conveniently termed the normative fallacy, because it privileges an ideal 'dream-image' in relation to which the text is judged. The only knowledge such a procedure can give is one of negative difference because the only demand it can make is that the text should be other than itself. [p. 105, original emphasis]

This analysis of the inscription of universalism within nationalist criticism reveals not only its prescriptive basis – the reading of 'character' in terms of the transcendental subject, the scripting of time and history in relation to linearity and origins, the privileging of realist inscription over postmodern play – but also, crucially and provocatively, the reactionary, neocolonial underpinnings of putatively resistant (that is anticolonial), nationalist readings of culture. It reveals how the boundary marking of nationalist criticism can serve to reinforce rather than challenge the lines of cultural inclusion and exclusion endorsed under colonial rule.

Bhabha's evaluation exposes the ways in which the neocolonial drives of universalist criticism are closely connected to nationalist imperatives. Furthermore, by identifying the specific ideological underpinnings of these two critical modes – their investment in specific readings of history, subjectivity, agency and representation – he reveals the extent to which they promote a hierarchy of value that provides a sanctioned space for the 'authentic'. His critical paradigm allows us to see not only the fundamental connections between universalist and nationalist criticism but also the ways in which they can work to reinforce each other in ways that prescribe how the 'nation' and 'culture' should be represented. Within the boundary marking of Sri Lankan literature, then, the universalism of patrician critics and the nationalism of nativists can be seen to work towards the same project of cultural reclamation. A detailed comparative evaluation of instances of patrician and nativist critical territoriality can serve to illustrate this. These are presented as instances – moments of connection with these critical trajectories. The cited examples are not meant to present complete embodiments or self-sustaining representations of critical territoriality – containing all the elements outlined in my broad definitions of patrician and nativist modes – but, rather, fluid and fluctuating formulations that substantially intersect with them in ways that reveal the broad tendencies of each.

Some of the clearest and most consistent examples of the patrician mode can be found in the work of one whose contribution to Sri Lankan literary studies can be measured by a career devoted to anthologising, documenting and contextualising the field in ways that have done much to bring the work of resident writers to international attention and chronicle the nation's literary history.[92] This life-long investment in the field, mediated by universalist critical standards borrowed from the metropolitan centre, has resulted in a repeated lament that it is not worthy of critical attention. 'The history of Sri Lankan literature in English' this patrician claims 'and especially of the novel – is so unrewarding that it gives new meaning to F.R. Leavis' comment that "Literary history is a worthless acquisition"'.[93] Illuminated by Leavis' vision and adopting the diagnostic moralising of his mentor, Sri Lanka's failure to produce a great tradition is, it is suggested, a result 'of a defectiveness of the novelists' sensibility and their alienation'.[94] The patrician critic identifies class as a key factor in limiting the social vision of anglophone writers, and in other instance claims that they, even during the period of unprecedented violence marked by the war, 'seem to write for one another, for the local critics, for a few readers of their own class, and for a corresponding class in the developed world rather than for those actively engaged or involved in the struggle'.[95] These reflections on the social and cultural insularity of writers are in alignment with the claims of local journalists such as Rajpal Abeynayake who have long insisted that Sri Lankan literary circles are 'incestuous'.[96] The difference however between these claims and those of the patrician is the basis on which they are made. While the claim of inbreeding and social exclusivity is presented by journalists as one of the means by which a self-appointed group of writers and critics maintains power (establishing a hierarchy of aesthetic value and promoting the work of friends), the patrician critique is based on a specific reading of national literature and the writer's role, which feeds into the very exclusionary dynamic that the journalists object to.

A striking example of the way political ideology affects the evaluation of texts in patrician criticism can be found in the essay 'Sri Lanka's "Ethnic" Conflict in its Literature in English', an essay that purports to situate the literature in its political context. Having contentiously asserted that the 'Tamil minority enjoys a much better position in Sri Lanka than most minorities in other countries' – a stand that effectively works to minoritise the Sri Lankan Tamils[97]– and citing K.M. de Silva's claim that the Tamils are 'a minority with a majority complex',[90] this patrician evaluation then proceeds to dissociate writers from the turbulence of war:

> [W]riters in English are obviously on the sidelines, sensitive souls responding to a situation engendered by politicians, who are not likely to consider their viewpoints, and by militants and soldiers who do not read the language in which they write and in any case would not be influenced by either the pity or the propaganda of a comfortable and cushioned class who share neither their privations nor their perceptions.[99]

We have an instance here of the way in which Leavisian universalism is scripted to serve specific readings of the nation as the majority–minority dynamic is used not only to naturalise Sinhalese hegemony but also to interpellate anglophone writers as outsiders.[100] It is an act of critical territoriality that effectively sections off and demarcates a sanctioned space for Sri Lankan literature in English while simultaneously silencing its political registers. This manoeuvre marginalises as it memorialises so that the *political* import of work by writers such as Carl Muller, who wrote an article that led to his incarceration in prison, and Jean Arasanayagam, who has devoted herself to projecting the violence of war since her displacement, is suppressed or displaced. Thus under the guise of claiming that all writers are 'on the sidelines', this critical evaluation enacts its own form of sidelining. What is more, its hierarchic evaluation of writers in relation to their engagement with 'Western traditions' and its call for writers to present the 'actual conflict in all its complexity' is informed by a totalising universalist impulse that works to obscure the contingency of its own cultural location.[101]

The patrician approach is fraught with paradoxes. The plea for a socially engaged vision is informed by a historically and culturally transcendent universalism that resists such social engagement. Within the context of Sri Lankan political conflict this can result in the presentation of politically prescriptive readings of the nation that appear to emerge from an evaluative space outside the domain of the political. Hence it is striking, but not surprising, that the patrician-led editorial reviews on Sri Lankan writing in the *Journal of Commonwealth Literature* in 1983 and 1984 – the only journal that regularly documents Sri Lankan literary developments for an international audience – make no direct mention of the anti-Tamil violence of 1983 and, simultaneously, reserve qualified praise for Colin de Silva's flagrantly nationalist epic *The Winds of Sinhala.*[102] Succeeding reviews register the marked increase in literary production by clearly detaching it from the social and political context that activates it. In 1989 – the year in which an escalation of extrajudicial killings led to an estimated 30,000 disappearances – we learn that 'the cultural scene was remarkably active *despite* the turbulence and unrest in the country'[103] (my emphasis). Two years later we are informed of the extrajudicial killing of one of the country's most prominent writers – which shocked a people already inured to political violence[104] – in terms that effectively obliterate the writer's political and social role: 'Richard de Zoysa had mastered words, acquired skill and craftsmanship, but had not come into his strength as a poet when he was murdered'.[105]

The emphasis on literary quality and its dissociation from the political reveals another paradox in patrician evaluation: the analysis of writing in terms of its ability to successfully incorporate elements from 'Western traditions' and the denigration of literary work on this very basis. Thus the patrician critical study, monumentally entitled *Sri Lankan English Literature and the Sri Lankan People 1917–2003*, can on the one hand propose that 'the artistic weakness of [Sri Lankan] poetry is [. . .] because our recent poets do not draw upon the Western traditions available to them', and on the other claim 'the sensibilities of several English writers remain remote from Sri Lankan realities and remain Western. The anglicized Punyakante Wijenaike, James Goonewardene and Romesh Gunesekera in *Reef* see the villagers as not like their sensitive, educated selves, but as much the Other [. . .] as the natives were to the sahibs and the bwanas'.[106] The patrician does not distinguish between writers on the basis of domicile as the nativist does – here resident and non-resident writers are drawn into alignment – but rather engages in an antinomian scripting of anglicisation to mark boundaries of belonging in ways that reveal the profound uncertainty underpinning the project of cultural identification. A patrician line of reasoning is trapped in the logic of its exclusion, thus it is able to claim of one Sri Lankan poet, in terms that problematise the very reading of cultural difference, 'she masters an alien language and alien forms in her poetry with no problems being caused by their alienness'.[107] The West is here a negotiable marker of difference that is invoked in the cultural arbitration of texts, scripting their legitimacy in ways that can deny or grant entry to the Sri Lankan literary canon.

The ideological imperatives underlying patrician reasoning come out forcefully in the positioning of Jean Arasanayagam, a writer of Burgher descent, married to a Tamil, who experienced rejection by both the Tamil community she married into, on account of her Burgher ancestry, and by the Sinhalese community, on account of her marriage to a Tamil. Despite the assertion of the accommodation of ethnic pluralism in the country, she is introduced – in the same paper – as part of 'the smallest and most Westernised community in Sri Lanka, *very different from the mass of the people*' (my emphasis). We are then told:

> Thus it is wholly natural for her [. . .] to feel herself an alien in *our* society and to be preoccupied with exploring her identity and heritage, adopting an anticolonial stance. She married a Tamil, and [presents. . .] the problems caused by the hatred directed at her by her husband's family because she belonged to a different community. Still, she identifies herself with her husband's community to the point of being partisan on their behalf in her presentation of the 'ethnic' conflict. [my emphasis][108]

The patrician mode thus serves to sanction an exclusionary model of the nation – one that outlaws difference and alterity – and simultaneously champions aesthetic criteria drawn from the metropolitan centre, seemingly unaware of the contradictions of its own location. Worse, it works to efface the very experience of marginalisation expressed by Arasanayagam – a position she has described as being 'divided among the divided'[109] – by subscribing to a model of authenticity that positions *it* as partisan. The claim of bias is coeval with the aesthetic evaluation of her work as 'high-pitched' rhetoric and allows it to be aligned with the mass of literature that is 'very openly and simply an attempt to express and generate pity and horror'.[110] As Vasuki Walker has claimed, in terms that expose the way in which the humanist imperatives of patrician criticism are compromised when working in the service of a specific politics, 'It is surprising that "shock" and "horror" are regarded as human reactions but not legitimate material for artistic creation'.[111]

I have devoted extensive attention to these elements of patrician criticism to reveal the ways in which its terms of aesthetic evaluation can be deeply implicated in the production of exclusionary models of the nation and to show how the putative objectivity of universalism does not so much mask but rather masquerades as a form of politically 'correct' cultural guardianship. Universalism here is a moral and ethical corrective, policing the boundaries of belonging in ways that serve specific readings of cultural legitimacy. It enacts a form of discursive territoriality that has much in common with the nativist critical approach, even though the latter openly engages in cultural reclamation in its provincialisation of the 'Western' literary and critical models selectively championed by patricians. Indeed the examples of nativist readings that I will now explore all, in their different ways, mark a form of cultural agoraphobia – a fear of the space outside constructed cultural borders.

The nativist approach is a direct by-product of the nationalist impulse for cultural reclamation. Symptomatic of the process of decolonisation and national emergence in all postcolonial countries, its Sri Lankan variant is marked by a post-Independence, anachronistic assertion of cultural difference in terms that register not only external but also internal cultural boundaries.[112] Nativism in Sri Lankan literary criticism does not only delineate the boundaries of belonging in relation to the nation as a whole, but also works to delineate a highly selective reading of the subject constitution of the native itself. It thus has an ontological rather than an epistemological basis, and it is scripted by a reverse discourse of cultural development as a return to roots and origins. There are, as I have indicated, diametrically opposed tensions in the nativist approach: one drawn towards a reclamation and rehabilitation of the indigene and the other directed more towards a politics of exclusion. Both of these have as their premise an implicit or explicit investment in the 'authentic', which is demarcated from the 'alien' on the basis of a variety of factors: 'truthful' representation (in particular of rural and village life) marking an investment in what Bhabha referred to as a 'representationalist' approach,[113] use of vernacular or localised idiom or evidence of perceived proximity to Sri Lankan English, a writer's class background and place of residence, and – in many cases – the presentation of a culturally affirmative or positive representation of the country. Indigeneity is granted a positive value in the autochthonous inflections of nativist critiques so that texts that lie outside the boundaries of a constructed notion of national culture come to be critically expatriated and perceived in a negative light. There is evidence of overlap between the nativist approach and that of the patrician in the attention paid to perceived anglicisation, but whereas a patrician evaluation may register a contradictory pull between connection to Western forms and culture and resistance to it, the nativist registers anglicisation more emphatically as a cultural loss.[114] The nativist aim is to promote that which is 'distinctively Lankan', that is writing that 'remains very Lankan in subject matter, theme, method and texture', and to distinguish between such work and the work of those who 'try to make themselves as "native" as they can, seeking out this nativeness in some kind of "pure", essentialist traditional reality which they presume pre-exists outside the realities they find themselves in'.[115] Oblivious to (as this quote suggests), or at the very least inattentive to, the essentialism underpinning their own enterprise, nativists tend to denigrate such 'false' representations of experience and ally them with the colonising imperatives of the Western Other.[116]

Such cultural discrimination is often made on stylistic or linguistic grounds. Hence James Goonewardene is chastised for his formal English idiom and his apparent detachment from 'the living expression of the rhythms of Ceylonese life'.[117] The attention paid to idiom marks a form of critical evaluation of the texts in relation to a hierarchy of authenticity – one in which linguistic codes themselves are perceived to grant cultural legitimacy – which can effectively serve to marginalise or silence the work of those who seek to write outside its borders. It enacts a form of boundary marking in which aesthetic, ethical and political considerations coalesce to exclude work and ex-patriate writers. Thus Goonewardene, in a somewhat vague and self-contradictory nativist evaluation, comes to be positioned as an exemplar of 'negative writing' which, we are instructed, 'is *just not a valid style* for writers of English in Ceylon, *it is not true to their experience*, which has a positive aspect' (my emphasis).[118] Another critic who also denigrates Goonewardene's work on the basis of his formal prose chastises him for his inability to write English in a style suitable for his subject.[119] The nativist search for authenticity thus leads towards a critical hierarchy in which linguistic connection to a putative national centre is a central criterion. Given the central role language has played in the development of cultural nationalism in the country and the fact that linguistics has for some time constituted a key component of English literary studies at degree level in Sri Lanka, this is not altogether surprising. Hence a critic who rejects the work of Burgher writers Rienzi Crusz and Michael Ondaatje on the basis of their perceived failures to address the local, can claim of another writer that 'the feature that makes Weersingha [sic] a "Sri Lankan poet" in my opinion [. . .] is his attempt at the rhythms and the rhymes of Sinhalese poetry'.[120] While this may appear, at first, to be a relatively straightforward process of searching for equivalence between literary language and local idiom, the assumed cultural 'centre' on which this comparison is made bears scrutiny: in a troubling conflation between the national and the communal, we are told in the same piece that Rienzi Crusz is 'no closer to being *Sinhalese* or *Sri Lankan* than Ondaatje' (my emphasis). The precise cultural coding of this critic's evaluation of Sri Lankan writers is manifest in the explicit consideration of their work in relation to 'Sri Lankan historicity, sensibility and [. . .] worldview', emphatically defined as 'a 2000-year old Buddhist culture, literally, esthetically, culturally, socially, economically, politically and spiritually'.[121] These comments collectively endorse Michael Roberts' observation that 'for some time in the modern era there has been a tendency among some Sinhala ideologues to subsume the category "Ceylonese" (or "Lankan") with the category of "Sinhalese" [. . .] I suspect that the equation of the Lankan with Sinhalese has been widespread at all levels of the Sinhala-speaking population. So one of the tasks for social science inquiries today is the investigation of the degree to which this occurs and the evaluation of the implications thereof'.[122]

The exclusionary dynamic informing the nativist approach clearly shares many of the features of patrician criticism, converging here with its patrician counterpart in its homogenising and hegemonising drive to read the nation as, at base, a place in which Sinhala dominance is both natural and inevitable. It is a process in which the cultural dynamics of decolonisation are firmly linked to the politics of majoritarianism. In the case of those who do indeed try to acknowledge or accommodate cultural pluralism, the terms of inclusion can still serve to endorse a highly selective reading of affiliation on the basis of indigenisation. This is evident in a critique cited earlier that attempts to define the responsibilities of those who are engaged in the shaping of the emergent canon and to which I will now pay more detailed attention:

> the responsibility for that part of the post-colonial struggle which involves the making of the Lankan canon in English falls very squarely on bi-culturals who more obviously than most others are characterised by their symbiotic natures. These biculturals [sic] are called upon to engage with the relationships/ tensions between the two aspects of their symbiotic personalities in a manner that allows what can be felt to be an authentic contemporary Lankan experience to emerge with conviction. For this, the two (or more) originally separate cultural voices that interact within them need to negotiate the relationship between (among) them in some kind of mutually satisfying way, not exclusive of their maintenance in creative tension or even antagonism with each other. *A major danger that these bi-culturals face* and one that is illustrated in [Romesh] Gunesekera's writing among other writing discussed [. . .] *is that too often the formerly alien Euro-Americanized voice makes to overwhelm or negate or invalidate the other, originally indigenously rooted one. If a writer does not find this necessary to resist*, it is her/his prerogative; but *the resulting work will probably not qualify for inclusion in the Lankan canon in any significant sense.* [my emphasis][123]

This passage registers the contradictory drives of the nativist conscious of the unsettling drives of hybridity that lie at the heart of anglophone writing from a postcolonial nation. On the one hand it attends to the 'bi-culturalism' that informs the literature, on the other hand it insists that this indeterminate cultural coding is split between 'alien' and 'indigenous' drives and demands that one should work in the service of the other to qualify for inclusion in the emergent canon. Such a reading is not only prescriptive, but it is also actively resistant to the very negotiation of belonging with which writers, as I have shown, engage. Further, it assumes the primacy of a single cultural centre of gravity to which these writers should feel drawn, a pull that their mediatory texts – situated betwixt and between diverse and different cultural modalities – may well resist. Many anglophone writers from both inside and outside Sri Lanka draw upon a pluralist, diasporic, international or intranational cultural register; the context from which they write, particularly in recent years, is one in which the legitimacy of indigeneity is actively contested. To insist that literature must privilege an indigenous cultural voice not only assumes that such a voice can be retrieved through the polyphonic registers that inform the work of Sri Lankan writers in English but also, of course, that it exists in the first place. The process is one that appeals to the accommodation of cultural difference only to regulate it and require its sublimation within the terms of a dominant order. It delineates a process to be found in patrician criticism too, but, in the case of nativist evaluation, the basis of cultural legitimation is more insistently coded in terms of indigeneity with the result that 'expatriate' – or migrant – writers come to be subject to particularly close surveillance.

The negative critique of migrant literature contained within some nativist readings is partly due to perceived inequalities of reception in which the privileging of the work of migrant Sri Lankan writers in the West, where access to local Sri Lankan literature is curtailed, has led to an emphasis on their role as cultural representatives. It assumes, with good reason, that such writers are 'viewed as preferred insiders and initiated informants on the affairs and culture of the East' and also, but rather more problematically, that a Western readership perceives 'their expatriation has conferred upon them the writerly virtues of detachment and objectivity'.[124] In other words the nativist critic can all too often assume that the representationalism contained within their own approach is in fact shared by readers outside Sri Lanka.[125] It is an assumption that underpins recent evaluations of Romesh Gunesekera's work and the frequent charges of 'exoticism' and 'orientalism' to which his work and that of other migrant writers has increasingly been subject. Such evaluations – the claim that Gunesekera's *Reef* is 'guilty of recuperating and of perpetuating certain myths and stereotypes about Sri Lanka in its often jaundiced depictions of character, class and politics' and that the novel is 'an example of "expatriate activity" which is somewhat "destructive of [. . .] Sri Lankan national culture"'[126] – work not so much to silence a text's complex mediation of belonging but rather to ex-patriate or banish it ('*ex*+ *patria:* to drive a person away from his native country; to banish'), situating it clearly outside the borders of legitimate cultural representation.

The negative criticism of the work of Romesh Gunesekera and Michael Ondaatje (in contrast to the generally more favourable reception of fellow 'expatriates' Shyam Selvadurai and A. Sivanandan) also rests in some measure on the formal properties of their texts which work to unsettle or actively deconstruct the realist representationalism favoured by nativists. These realist prescriptives are partly directed by critical familiarity and formal accessibility, and partly informed by the social and political conditions of the times. As Joe Cleary has shown, in situations of violent repression and cultural turmoil 'social realism seems to answer more directly to the exigencies of political commitment and protest writing than more experimental or modernist literary modes'.[127] This wide range of interconnected factors that work to culturally dissociate writing from a putative national centre requires us not only to attend to the very terms of the ex-patriation of texts from both inside and outside Sri Lanka – their implicit contexts and criteria of affiliation – but also to resist use of the term 'expatriate' literature, which implies a context of writing within the ambit of the ex-patriot: the fallen, former native.

It is for this reason that I refer to *migrant* writing and writers and quarantine the term 'expatriate' literature by placing it within parenthetical speech marks. While the former term certainly has its limitations, it does have the advantage of insisting upon a politics of mediation, of negotiation betwixt cultures that might render the boundaries between them both porous and transactional in a way that allows for the kind of debates and dialogue with which writers are already engaging. Thus my use of the terms *resident* and *migrant* does not assume a polarised dynamic between them, nor does it privilege a hierarchy of place – both of which this study explicitly contests. Rather it is used more broadly and directly to distinguish between different contexts of production and reception. The division in this study between Part II and Part III, distinguishing between resident and migrant writers, is intended to honour this material difference and also to enable the kind of transactional, comparative analysis that opens up the boundaries of the national imaginary, to facilitate movement across borders. It is enabled by an engagement – foregrounded in the final section analysing the migrant writers – with post-stucturalist critical approaches which have been repeatedly resisted by critics within Sri Lanka.[128] Poststructuralism, or 'postmodernism' as is it is more often called by such critics, is they contend complicit with the hegemonising imperatives of dominant, alien, Western powers and is therefore, at the very least, politically suspect. The fact that these critics also draw on intellectual traditions borrowed from the West, that as a postcolonial nation Sri Lanka has a long history of vigorous and dynamic cultural interchange that problematises notions of cultural purity and authenticity and the kind of cultural distance that critical territorialists assume exists, and that political trajectories themselves are not necessarily determined by cultural and historical 'origins', serves to call into question the basis on which some of these charges are made. Certainly as a postcolonial, post-structuralist engagement this study is complicit with the ideological and cultural assumptions underpinning theoretical approaches that are most closely affiliated with metropolitan intellectual bases. Yet the distinction between such metropolitan centres and the margins of the postcolonial nation are not fixed or absolute; inequalities of power operate not only between these sites but also within them; and within the culture of contestation that arbitrates the boundaries of belonging that determine the Sri Lankan nation, it is possible to find in the discursive space of writing an effort at the exploration, mediation and reconciliation of difference that has repeatedly failed on the political level.

By unyoking spatial configurations in Sri Lankan literature from a polarised discourse, I make a case for reading it within the context of an emergent border culture shaped by multiple terroritialisms, a culture in which 'cultural syncretism takes place both at the margins and between the margins and a changing mainstream'.[129] This is not to efface the specificities of social, historical and cultural contexts of textual production, or to argue for any easy political correspondences across differently fractured spaces, but rather to realign locational differences so as to be able to discriminate, as Shohat has put it, 'between the diverse modalities of hybridity, for example forced assimilation, internalized self-rejection, political co-optation, social conformism, cultural mimicry, and creative transcendence'.[130] Such a reading of Sri Lankan literature engages in a 'rooted cosmopolitanism' in which the diasporic and global are read through the registers of local knowledge so that existing hierarchies of power can be effectively identified and contested. It is a negotiation of boundaries that is attendant to both the situatedness of diverse knowledges and to the creative possibilities of dialogue between them, to the national and the diasporic registers within and between texts.

Part II

2 James Goonewardene

Allegorical islands

> They buried James Goonewardene at Kanatte on Monday. It was not raining but the sky was suitably overcast. The gathering was not big. They were either family associates from the days of the old Radio Ceylon or friends from Kinross, a milieu he had vividly re-created in his penultimate novel.
>
> But novelists I did not see that day although James Goonewardene was primarily a novelist and it is as such that he will now join the poets Lakdasa Wikkramasinha, Patrick Fernando and Richard de Zoysa in the roll of the literary departed.
>
> A. Samaranayake, *Sunday Observer*, 25 May 1997[1]

Any evaluation of James Goonewardene's work has to take into account his isolation from the Sri Lankan literary establishment. Invoked as a literary founder and pioneer who – along with Punyakante Wijenaike – 'almost alone kept fiction [in English] going in the late 'sixties', he was nevertheless subject to 'scathing reviews of [. . . his] best work',[2] the full impact of which remains subject to conjecture. Despite having published more English novels than any other writer in Sri Lanka and becoming the first Sri Lankan writer to be published by Penguin,[3] his work has not been substantively evaluated to date. Invoked, after his death, as 'poor James' by one who addressed the novelist's critical isolation,[4] Goonewardene died in penury[5] in 1997 having received 'little or no recognition' for the significant role he played in the development of the Sri Lankan novel in English.[6] He was by then, according to Jean Arasanayagam, 'a broken man'.[7]

Goonewardene's work and critical reception provide an important index of the extent of the alienation and isolation of Sri Lankan writers in English and the discursive forces of 'legitimising agents'[8] such as critics that shape their work. Writing in English in the wake of the nationalist fervour of the 1960s and the JVP insurrection of 1971, Goonewardene's 'cultural treachery'[9] in his choice of medium appears to be compensated for in his choice of subject in his early novels: the rural milieu and an exploration of indigenous culture. Yet this was clearly – like the kaduwa of the English language itself – a double-edged sword: on the one hand, as D.C.R.A. Goonetilleke pointed out in his coded evaluation, it allowed anglophone writers to try 'to capture a *truly national, authentically Sri Lankan*, experience, and find roots in the soil' (my emphasis)[10] and, on the other, it exposed their very distance from their subject, the fact that they are in fact 'anglicized'. What is more, as Thiru Kandiah has made clear in his review of one of the rural texts, this very engagement with urban alienation excludes the text from authentication by the cultural centre for it 'is just *not a genuine, significant one* for writers and readers of English fiction in Ceylon' (my emphasis).[11] Kandiah's fluently written, negative review – steeped in charges of anglicisation and negativity against the author – works to silence the voice of the internal exile, threatening to deepen their alienation further. It also reveals how nativist territoriality colludes with the universalism of patricians for the 'failure' of Goonewardene's work, we are told, is 'not merely a failure with language, it is the larger failure of taste and sensibility'.[12] Underpinning the charge of anglicisation lies what Rushdie has called 'the bogy of Authenticity'[13] and the charge of cultural collusion with the former imperial power. As Goonetilleke has contended, 'the sensibilities of [. . .] anglicized [English writers such as] Punyakante Wijenaike, James Goonewardene and Romesh Gunesekera' 'remain remote from Sri Lankan realities and remain Western'. Such writers 'see the villagers as not like their sensitive, educated selves, but as much the Other (inarticulate, violent, irrational, sex-ridden, cunning yet mindless) as the natives were to the sahibs and the bwanas'.[14] While Goonewardene's presentation of the village community is – in the main – hierarchic and condescending, his social vision cannot so readily be aligned with a 'Western' reading of rural and village life. Rather it reflects a concern for evaluating cultural development from a more open internationalist perspective. It is Goonewardene's failure to find a literary language to accommodate such a perspective – his inability, in other words, to transcend the binary discourse of the very nationalism that he seeks to subvert – that leaves him open to charges of elitism.

The negative evaluations of Goonewardene's rural texts are informed by differently inflected but politically connected forms of critical territoriality. They are also informed by the hierarchic and essentialist discursive registers to be found in the texts themselves. A more nuanced contention is that Goonewardene may himself have been a victim of the nationalist demand for celebrating 'some sort of indigenous ideal [. . .] however artificially expressed',[15] caught, in other words, between the demand for affirmative representations of rural tradition and the difficulty of relating to this very milieu. As Yasmine Gooneratne observes, Goonewardene 'writes as if he were honour-bound to provide' such excursions into rural life.[16] This would account for the double-coded nature of his early work, which presents the village as a retreat from the corruption and commercialism of city life while exposing its inadequacies. Indeed these texts are not so much informed by the postcolonial convention of cultural reclamation of rural and village tradition but revealing of the contradictions inherent in such a reclamation by Fanon's native intellectual.[17] As Nihal Fernando has contended, Goonewardene's rural romanticism is constrained by his emphasis on disenchantment with both the urban and rural communities,[18] an expression of alienation that represents a disaffection from the key social bases of the national imaginary.

Yet Goonewardene's work goes further than this: it registers a passionate critique of nationalism itself and of the cultural investment in it. In this respect his work offers us a compelling example of the honest efforts of a resident writer to find an enunciative site of resistance to nationalist discourse, the very discourse that directs the evaluations of many of his critics. As Yasmine Gooneratne has observed in her sympathetic evaluation of one of his best known stories:

> The permanent value of Goonewardena's [sic] writing lies in its honesty and courage in exploring themes related to the injustice and disharmony created in Sri Lankan society by political opportunists who irresponsibly bend the nation's divided interests to their own advantage.[19]

Drawing upon the psychoanalytical theories of Erich Fromm, Goonewardene developed a literary discourse for cultural evolution that was politically informed by both the post-Independence 'Sinhala Only' Act and, crucially, the JVP insurrection of 1971. Just as the 1983 ethnic riots served as a catalyst for political awakening in the work of Jean Arasanayagam, the 1971 insurrection registered a heightened political resolve in Goonewardene's work that almost amounts to intransigence. This Marxist revolutionary movement of educated rural youth, inspired by the guerrilla campaign of Che Guevara, unsettled the anglicised urban elite. As Lakshmi de Silva has observed, the JVP insurrection 'shook not only our complacency but our conscience'.[20] For Goonewardene, it crystallised his deep misgivings of the nationalist course the country had taken and generated some of his most powerful texts – 'Sow a Storm'(1979), *The Awakening of Doctor Kirthi and Other Stories* (1976) and *One Mad Bid for Freedom* (1990) – as well as work that appears to be crippled by the very intensity of his convictions, such as *An Asian Gambit* (1985) (an extension of his novel *Acid Bomb Explosion*) and *The Tribal Hangover* (1995). His early 'rural' texts thus serve to register the limits of the nationalist retrieval that are satirised, lambasted and even lampooned in his later work.

In drawing upon psychoanalytical theories for his representation of cultural evolution, Goonewardene develops a moral register that inverts rather than transcends the hierarchies of nationalist discourse. The populace, or 'mass' as he calls them, are positioned at the bottom of an evolutionary pyramid on whose summit stands the independent thinker. Yet, as I will show, the mass are not so much identified as a social class as an intellectual order, and it is the failure to identify this fact that may explain some of the cultural misreadings of his work. The extent to which critical responses to Goonewardene might be conditioned by what appears to be his elitist ideological and political stance – as well as his own open defiance of what journalists have referred to as 'the incestuous literary elite'[21] – is open to conjecture. What is clear, however, is that his tone becomes increasingly more strident, and his representation of the country and the people increasingly more polarised and essentialist, in the course of his career, and that this development superceded crude and clumsy evaluations of his early work and short stories. Simultaneously praised for his rugged realism and pilloried for the 'escapism' of his rural representation,[22] the most damning indictment of all is related to one of his strongest texts: in 'Kirthi', as Wijesinha points out, Goonewardene was 'attacked for not writing perfect English'.[23] One of these attacks was couched in such ponderously pompous terms that it is little wonder that Goonewardene turned on his critics.[24] The diminution of the story as little more than 'formal expository prose [. . .] which relies on extended grammatical structures for its effects'[25]– a claim that seems much more applicable to the review than to the story itself – reveals an underlying anxiety over the cultural coordinates of literary criticism in Sri Lanka. It forms the basis of Thiru Kandiah's nativist attack on Goonewardene as a writer whose 'commitment to the academic norms is so great that he rejects not only "broken English" [. . .] but also many of the more normal features of Ceylon English' as well as 'the rhythms of actual English speech' resorting instead to 'the debased romantic journalism in vogue among the Victorians'.[26] Taken to task for his alienated discourse and apparent elitism, Goonewardene is simultaneously ridiculed for shortcomings in his use of English by fellow Lankans who purport to have mastered it in his stead. The critical reception of Goonewardene's work thus reveals how resident writers in English can be trapped in an exclusionary logic of cultural differentiation that delights in denigrating them as either too anglicised or not anglicised enough. It also exposes the postcolonial ambivalence of identity inherent in Bhabha's observation that 'to be Anglicized is *emphatically* not to be English'.[27]

I have opened this chapter with a consideration of Sri Lankan evaluations of Goonewardene's work to reveal the multiple fault lines and cultural fractures in which his work is positioned *and* its exclusionary basis. Goonewardene's early novels were all published in Sri Lanka (and one serialised in a Sri Lankan journal), indicating that, like almost all his literary contemporaries, his target audience was a local one. In contrast his last novels were published by Penguin India,[28] and are uncompromising Manichean allegories. As such they are set in a 'field of diverse yet interchangeable oppositions between white and black, good and evil, superiority and inferiority, civilization and savagery, [. . .] self and Other, subject and object'.[29] They mark a decisive development in narrative position, commodifying the nation for an external readership. The morally coded reading of national space, distinguishing between the country and the city, the insider and the outsider, the enlightened individual and the uncritical 'mass' found in his early texts gives way, in the later work, to the deterministic logic of allegory in which these socially situated elements are essentialised. In the process the cultural and historical registers that inform the ethical evaluation of place are lost and negative evaluations of his last novels become more understandable.

Manichean texts, as Todorov has pointed out, tend to generate Manichean interpretations 'with good and evil simply having switched places'.[30] Like Arasanayagam, who has also been marginalised on extraliterary grounds, Goonewardene fails to achieve a hybridised or syncretic vision. His spatial idiomatics replicate his concern with isolation and the outsider and are connected to a shifting evaluation of nationalist geopolitical productions of space. His oeuvre marks a shift from an engagement with a nationalist cartography, demarcating the traditional village and the modern city, to a postcolonial preoccupation with the trope of the isolated island. A literary iconoclast and satirist in his later years, his rebelliousness was evident even in early novels such as *A Quiet Place* (1968) and *Call of the Kirila* (1971), where his challenge to the dominant pastoral mode of many literary nationalists took the form of an interrogation of the social schisms underlying the apparent harmony of village life. His work also foregrounds the plight of socially marginalised characters who are outcasts on the basis of their unconventional thinking and independence of action rather than for their social station. In his last novels, *One Mad Bid For Freedom* and *The Tribal Hangover*, Goonewardene directs his attention to the social and cultural demise of the country since the civil war by drawing upon the notion of island identity. This allows him to project a more totalised vision of the country and comment upon cultural developments in sweeping terms. Two different models of the island emerge in these novels: an entropic depiction of the island as a discrete social organism, out of time and distinctly out of place, and an externally projected representation of the island as a trading post or port of call. The former is central to the polemic of *One Mad Bid For Freedom* and the latter is foregrounded in *The Tribal Hangover*. Both depend on a specific reading of human psychology and social evolution based on Fromm's theories on violence, community and freedom.

Goonewardene's evaluation of island identity is also closely connected to the internationalism propounded in his articles 'A Blueprint for a Writer's Dream', 'Becoming a writer – the agony and ecstasy' and 'Nationalism and the Writer in Sri Lanka'. Indeed, the last of these presents one of the most prescient and persuasive readings of the dangers of cultural nationalism ever written by a resident writer.[31] Along with his representation of the island as a beleaguered space – a representation informed in part by Fromm's *Anatomy of Human Destructiveness* and in part by nationalist discourse – it is central to an informed critical understanding of his work. My own engagement therefore integrates a consideration of nationalist constructions of place and its relationship to Goonewardene's social theory with an analysis of spatial idiomatics in his work. I begin with a consideration of Goonewardene's representation of the island as a socially contingent space, territorially bounded by nationalist readings, and then move on to examine the ways in which his efforts to develop a discourse outside the binary readings of otherness buckle under the exigencies of migrant experience in *The Tribal Hangover*. Goonewardene's Manichean presentation of the social order encodes colonial discursive strategies in nationalist imperatives and bears testimony to the power of exclusionary discourse to not only inform but also to restrict and constrain those who might seek to challenge it.

The beleaguered island and the 'mass mind'

Sri Lanka is often invoked as an island nation, one that is territorially constrained and set apart from its neighbours. Such spatialisation brings to bear specific readings of cultural and national identity which, as Éric Meyer has observed, are fundamentally antinomian. 'The paradox of an island' according to Meyer 'is to be at once isolated from, yet open to the rest of the world'.[32] Goonewardene's last novels engage with this paradox, broadly marking a shift from the representation of the island as a marooned space to one that is caught in the cultural maelstrom of globalisation. They are also informed by a specific reading of the natural world that carries an allegorical resonance in his work. This world is cited as a space where 'ordinary things [. . .] acquire fantastic meanings [. . .] Everything seemed to get magnified, even the silence and the feeling of peace, and even death. A dead man seemed deader than in other places'.[33]

Meyer's survey of the nation, written for Western consumption, focuses on what he calls the Sri Lankans' 'unique insularity, an insularity that becomes a refuge',[34] and their inability to step outside the territorial prescriptives that nationalistic cultural isolation engenders. This nationalist reading of territory is informed by the notion of the island as a beleaguered space, subject to threat not only from the outside but also from within. It is also central to an episode from the *Mahavamsa* which presents the island as a limited space that is being encroached by resident Tamils. This recounts the story of Prince Gemunu (or Gamini) – the future Dutugemunu who united the country under Sinhala rule – who is too disturbed to sleep because of the perceived threat from neighbouring Tamils:

> [Gamini] went to his bed, and drawing in his hands and feet lay upon his bed. The queen came, and caressing Gamini spoke thus:
>
> 'Why dost thou not lie easily upon thy bed with limbs stretched out, my son?'
>
> 'Over there beyond the Ganga [river] are the Damilas [Tamils], here on this side is the ocean, how can I lie with outstretched limbs?' he answered.
>
> When the king heard his thoughts he remained silent.[35]

Wilfrid Jayasuriya, who, in his reading of this passage has re-scripted the Tamils as externally resident, has noted that 'this way of expressing the dilemma of a people living in a small island with a sub-continent as neighbour from which invading hordes would push the native Sinhalese "into the sea" has sunk deep into the consciousness of the Sinhalese'.[36]

Goonewardene's work is replete with representations of the island as a beleaguered space but is articulated from a very different perspective. Far from focusing exclusively on the encroachment of the alien outsider, it foregrounds instead the dangers of collective or 'mass' isolationism that works from within the Sinhala mainstream. These dangers seem to be amplified by Goonewardene's emphasis on overpopulation in the island – a preoccupation shared by Carl Muller[37] – and on ecology, both of which draw attention to interdependence, cultural relativity and functional rather than hierarchical social relationships. In 'Nationalism and the Writer in Sri Lanka', published in the wake of the first JVP insurrection and almost ten years before the outbreak of military conflict, Goonewardene draws attention to the long-term consequences of mass or collective cultural isolationism and the attendant calls for cultural purity. Littered with evocative registers of entropic disintegration with references to 'insulating', 'inbreeding' and being 'marooned in an island', it exhorts us to 'recognise that art has no national barriers' and urges us to 'strive for a creed of internationalism in art', while drawing specific attention to the plight of the Sri Lankan writer in English who is an 'exile in his own country'.[38] Directly addressing his Sri Lankan readership he warns of the dangers of 'stultification and sterility' attendant on historical revivalism, citing the Kandy Perahera as a ritual that is 'hoary with age and ponderous with feudal meaninglessness', and argues that 'if unchallenged, we are in danger of being effectively cut off from all contact with the rest of the artistic world'.[39] The essay ends with a reflection on the importance of individual salvation and the Buddhist ideal of selflessness, indicating that Goonewardene distinguishes between the uncritical belief in cultural revival and the philosophical doctrine which it promotes.

Goonewardene's readings of what he termed the 'mass mind'[40] are informed by both this resistance to JVP nationalist fervour – what one analyst has called their 'blind faith' and 'uninformed nature'[41] – and his engagement with Fromm's theories on violence. Goonewardene cites Fromm's *Anatomy of Human Destructiveness* in the preface to his autobiographically inflected novel *Dream Time River* (published in 1984; begun in 1978), and he mentions Fromm's work once more in his penultimate novel, *One Mad Bid For Freedom*.[42] Indeed the significance of Fromm's thinking to Goonewardene's work can be seen in the way it intersects with the latter's inversion of nationalistically coded discourse of the resident and outsider. In an ethically coded register that sanctions self-exile, it is the situated community or 'mass' that is found wanting in his texts. Goonewardene's early novels follow the lives of male city dwellers who seek refuge in the village or town and come into conflict with those who live there. Romantic attachments to village women are idealised so that the texts are easily subject to reductive readings as rural idylls. The village or rural community – representative of three-quarters of the population[43] – form the geographic heartland of nationalist cultural retrieval and Goonewardene's negative critique inverts the hierarchies of nationalist discourse in favour of the alienated suburbanite.

The perspective is uncompromisingly that of the outsider: villagers are superstitious, ignorant, 'ill-bred illiterate[s]', 'evil [. . .] in their foolishness', 'bound together by a rigid patter of custom and practice' and they are presented as 'not having a strong critical faculty'[44], leading the protagonists to conclude that the 'village no less than the city was full of cant and hypocrisy'.[45] This denigration of village communities does not, however, register a belief in the inherent backwardness of the poor for there are many moving representations of socially displaced outcasts in Goonewardene's work: the eponymous hero of 'The Hunchback', the pickpocket in 'Podi Roba Lends a Hand', Tamil refugees in 'The Dark Journey'[46] and a plethora of lower-middle-class folk in *Dream Time River* to name but a few. Rather it registers concern over the development of a form of communal, collective consciousness that results in blind violence – a development, it could be argued, marked by the insurrection. As the narrator of *One Mad Bid For Freedom* observes, 'what was commendable about the people of the island was their endless capacity to be fooled' (p. 33).

It is a social vision in which the independent thinker stands as an itinerant self-exiled man (Goonewardene's work invariably presents us with a male perspective) in opposition to the unthinking, geographically situated community. Within these terms the early rural texts are not so much escapist as explorations of the limits of escape. It is significant that the only effective refuge 'free from bondage to place and time' (p. 183) depicted in his novels are the remembered 'private worlds [of the] imagination' in *Dream Time River*.[47] Characters who leave the city – a site represented as a repository of middle-class values and commercialism such as 'respectability [. . .] the electric cooker and the Mercedes Benz'[48] – find that the village is subject to its own collective pressures. What complicates the hierarchies underpinning this vision of social (dis)order is a lurking hope that the village might offer some sort of salvation from the inequities of urban corruption – a vision that seems to be informed by Fromm's contention that 'the more primitive a civilization, the less wars do we find' and that the development of technical civilization may be responsible for the increase in political violence.[49] Yet, just as Orwell's declamation that 'hope [. . .] must lie in the proles'[50] is weighted with middle-class condescension and fear, Goonewardene's presentation of the noble savage is multiply inflected. It draws upon morphological registers of physical backwardness – the 'un-puckered, open faces' of the villagers of Purantota,[51] their 'anthropoid' features (p. 68) that lead them to 'shed their human character' (p. 65) – that are duplicated in even the most poignant of his texts, rupturing their emotional integrity.[52] Innocence and ignorance are shown to make a dangerous combination – subject to manipulation – and culminate in Goonewardene's strident reflection on the communalism of 'tribalism' endemic in Sri Lanka in his last novel.[53] When cultural development is biologically coded it gives moral weight to cultural difference and grants both writer and reader the kind of 'surplus morality' alluded to by Jan Mohamed in his study of Manichean allegory.[54] Goonewardene, however, chooses to detach himself from the English-speaking elite of his readership. In his later novels this class too is biologised, leaving such 'surplus morality' in the hands of the writer and others who might share his specific perspective.

Goonewardene's formulation of 'the mass mind' – based on the social and political realities of the insurrection – has both psychoanalytical and social underpinnings. It is homologically linked to Fromm's analysis of what he called 'group narcissism'. The formulation is based not on an elitist rejection of the masses but on a desire to understand the collective violence to which the country was being increasingly subject. The Sinhala Buddhist resurgence of the late 1950s drew upon working class support and, in particular, on the support of indigenous cultural practitioners such as Ayurvedic doctors, teachers and Buddhist priests. Under the JVP it was reformulated first as a 'revolution through class struggle' in 1971, and later as a 'liberation through patriotic struggle' in 1987.[55] Goonewardene read the political import of this development through the violence it engendered and based his social vision on a belief that 'what goes on in Sri Lanka as insurgencies are not spontaneous eruptions but manipulated disasters – manipulated by outside forces'.[56] Such boundary marking – dependent on a specific reading of the beleaguered island – reflects a belief in the integrity of that which is resistant to external manipulation. Yet the 'outside' referred to is not simply that which is external to the nation – though Goonewardene does present it in these terms as well[57] – but that which threatens an individual's personal freedom, a concept central to Fromm's analysis of violence.

The desire for freedom is, according to Fromm, 'a biological reaction of the human organism'; when the desire for freedom is thwarted or redirected, he contends, it leads to frustration – one of the main causes of violence. Violence, Fromm emphasises, is not innate, but the product of social circumstances. Sadism, for example, is 'more frequently to be found among frustrated individuals and social classes who feel powerless and have little pleasure in life [. . .]. It is also to be found in ruling classes that feel threatened in their dominant position and their property or in suppressed groups that thirst for revenge'.[58] This classless basis for the causes of sadistic violence goes some way towards explaining why Goonewardene's work appears to ubiquitously damn all sections of society: from the village communities of his early novels, to middle-class workers in *An Asian Gambit* and urban professionals in 'Kirthi', presenting a totalised, anthropomorphologised social critique of the Sri Lankan people which was likely to offend all sections of the population. The JVP therefore are presented, in *An Asian Gambit*, as a generation rather than a class, revealing the extent to which Goonewardene is keen to foreground in his work the social and historical conditions of violence over class dynamics.

It is through his formulation of group narcissism that Fromm's theories have most informed Goonewardene's social vision. 'Group narcissism' claims Fromm 'is one of the most important sources of human aggression, and yet this, like all other forms of defensive aggression, is a reaction to an attack on vital interests.' It 'plays a considerable role', he argues, in the mass massacres of Indian Partition and the Indo-Pakistani war, as here we are dealing with 'virtually the poorest and most miserable populations anywhere in the world'.[59] The cultural coding of Fromm's discourse – its hierarchic differentiation of the West from the poor, miserable people of the Indian subcontinent, and his psychoanalytical investment in socio-pathological registers – informs Goonewardene's own double-coded discourse of connection and disassociation from his society and lends itself to the kind of exclusionary critical readings to which his work has come to be subject. Yet Fromm's evaluation, hierarchically coded though it is, offers Goonewardene a persuasive explanation for the violence underpinning Sinhala cultural nationalism, providing a rationale for the development of uncritical patriotism in those who are frustrated in life:

> The assertion that 'my country' (or nation, or religion) is the most wonderful, the most cultured, the most powerful, the most peace-loving, etc., does not sound crazy at all; on the contrary, it sounds like the expression of patriotism, faith and loyalty. It also appears to be a realistic and rational value judgment because it is shared by many members of the same group. This consensus succeeds in transforming the phantasy into reality since for most people reality is constituted by general consensus and not based on reason or critical examination. [. . .] Even if one is the most miserable, the poorest, the least

> respected member of a group, there is compensation for one's miserable condition in feeling 'I am a part of the most wonderful group in the world. I, who in reality am a worm, become a giant through belonging to a group'. Consequently the degree of group narcissism is commensurate with the lack of real satisfaction in life.[60]

The denigration of collective political activism in the name of the group, the critique of social conditions that generate poverty, and the championing of intellectual freedom and independence all form the basis of social critique in Goonewardene's texts. What gives 'Sow a Storm', 'Kirthi' and *One Mad Bid For Freedom* their power is that these elements are politically and historically contextualized.

Goonewardene's reading of Fromm works to emphasise the deleterious effects of group narcissism on the intellectual life of the country. In 'Kirthi'[61] we are reminded of the 'lack of resources in a small country' (p. 1) and that 'the island was too small a place to permit the squandering of human talent and skill' (p.19). The short story, which focuses on what can be colloquially termed the 'brain drain' that has affected the country since Independence, stresses the fact that the country 'had no material wealth worth speaking about; it had only people with whatever skills and talents they possessed' (p. 2). Recounting the disillusionment and eventual emigration of a conscientious and dedicated Colombo doctor, it reveals the way in which the educational system, subject to linguistic nationalism and a new quota system that positively discriminates in favour of rural and village islanders, effectively disenfranchises some of the most talented people in the country. The effectiveness of Goonewardene's critique lies in his ability to construct a totalising account of national decay and corruption by developing the minutiae of an individual's life. Linguistic and cultural nationalism form an external register of internal corruption and decay and are carefully integrated into the everyday experience of the doctor responsible for educating his students:

> 'Are you dumb or can't you understand what I am saying' he would shout at them. Only later would he realize that the students handicapped by a language difficulty, were not responding as quickly as they did in his time as a student. This was a new generation of youth being forced into moulds of the making of the crudest forms of nationalism. He didn't know it then, but he did as time went. Things did happen that drew attention to all this. It was, at first, a simple back-sliding in the administrative machinery – shortages here, shortages there, things not brought up in time for an operation, the blood bank running dry, instruments not sterilized properly, equipment neglected and allowed to rot. It was like the slow deterioration of a car – the tuning not right, the plugs getting oiled up, the clutch sticking. [p. 8]

This 'simple back-sliding in the administrative machinery', which results in the death of a patient, is made possible by the nepotism and negligence of the ruling class and the corruption of increasingly militant trade unionists. Both the working and the professional classes are thus indicted; both are victims and perpetrators of the 'mass mind'. The story registers the moral decay of the country in a poignant register of physical degeneration as Kirthi's erstwhile 'belly-aching' colleague is left like 'a limpet on a rock stuck fast in one position [. . .] Why did one have to move around when one could be happy, staying still in one position, only moving about a bit, now and then, to exercise one's limbs [?]' (p. 33).

The use of biological and morphological discourse to link moral degeneration with physical and cultural decay moves into 'burlesque'[62] in *One Mad Bid For Freedom.* Here nationalist imperatives are resisted by the scientific discourse embodied by its main protagonist, the naturalist, Korala, whose inflatory rhetoric serves to decimate the spurious rationalism underpinning nationalist drives.[63] Described as a 'sage' (p. 139), a 'prophet' (p. 33) and an 'unreal creature of land and sea' (p. 98), Korala's insistence on 'freedom of thought and free inquiry' (p. 136) sets him 'going upstream, against the current, against the tide, against the mass will, against the crazy, whooping, looping, carolling, frenzied, delirious, happy-go-lucky mass of people' (p. 72) and is passed off as 'madness' by visiting journalists. The pseudoscientific register of the text, which draws on the psychopathological registers of Fromm's work in its description of nationalist leaders as 'creatures suffering from various forms and degrees of necrophilia, paranoia, [and] narcissism' (p. 36), is used to devastating effect. The discourse of *One Mad Bid For Freedom* is sedimented with biological registers and is used to lambast cultural purists who control educational standards. These are the:

> scholarly, erudite, distinguished men of letters, who were dedicated to the proposition that all men were born equal and that no artistic creation or work of scholarship could ever be deemed to be accommodated in the national, cultural grid unless its creator had passed the seminal tests for purity of race, language and blood, and that meant blood tissue and blood cell, as well as purity of bone structure. [p. 46]

In a passage that goes on to satirise the significance of

> the bone structure of the cranium and the pelvis, along with the other bones of the skeleton, all of which were of capital importance when considering the importance of racial types who had involved themselves in the cultural resurgence the island was witness to

Goonewardene highlights the absurdity of the racially discriminatory discourse of such cultural resurgence by inflating the logic of scientifically coded racial rhetoric from the sublime into the ridiculous. The need to analyse the 'muscles, the biceps for instance, and the flexors of foot, hand and mouth, along with the sphincter muscle of the anus' thus results in an inevitable explosion of scatological data as the reflections of these scholars are shown to disable the capital's sewage system.

Goonewardene does not end there. Later in the novel he goes on to set up a contestatory dynamic that politically positions pseudoscientific discourse in a way that deflates nationalist investment in the foundational myth of the Sinhalese.

After his death Korala's evolutionary theory, based on the evidence of cultural degeneration in the country, finds itself the subject of attack by cultural nationalists who believe that:

> an extremely dangerous anti-national movement, in the guise of advancing the cause of science, was attempting to foist a decadent, western-orientated pseudo-scientific theory on the nation, and bring into disrepute time-honoured and sacred records, documents and other historical treatises which had proved beyond doubt that the original ancestor, progenitor and creator of the first Sri Lankan man was a brave, courageous and undaunted lion of enormous proportions. [p. 114]

The dead naturalist, it appeared, had attempted to challenge these 'time-honoured' myths by promoting 'the notion that the Sri Lankan man had evolved from the ape, the gorilla, the chimpanzee, and other primitive forms of life, and had even gone so far as to trace the first Sri Lankan man to a nocturnal creature called the Tarsier, which was just eight inches long, and had a tufted tail, a flat face and enormous eyes, and also had a highly developed smell organ' (pp. 114–15). Through this hyperbolic rendition of the pseudoscientific basis of national myths of origin, Goonewardene ridicules a central plank of cultural nationalism enshrined in the *Mahavamsa* and debunks those scholars who have enabled and promoted theories of racial superiority. He thus not only inverts the hierarchies of culturally exclusive discourse – revealing the tyrannical forces underpinning what appear to be democratising influences of the majority – but also creates an inflationary rhetoric that deconstructs the monogenism underpinning one of the core mythological structures that create the group identity of the majority populace. The strength of his satire lies in his ability to encode the very terms of discrimination – culturally discriminatory pseudoscientific historicism – into his critique.

Cultural purism is thus evident not only in 'national purification ceremonies' but also in the 'new witchcraft' of 'space and science fiction and planets and apes' promoted by science-fiction writer Henry Sparkes (p. 31). This caricature of resident writer Arthur C. Clarke as 'the great white wizard' (p. 32) who 'wanted the chimpanzees to build spaceships when they were hard put to build habitable cages for themselves' (p. 31) reveals that Goonewardene is attentive to the way nationalist discourse gains currency from scientific formulations that are drawn from seemingly alien cultural centres. *One Mad Bid For Freedom* presents us with the cultural detritus of a postcolonial country 'suddenly erupting in different directions' (p. 26), and it reveals the ways in which cultural nationalism is closely connected to the multicultural forces and economic imperatives of globalisation. Sri Lanka is thus positioned at the interstices of competing and contestatory forces, caught between:

> this Sparkes character [. . .], trying to convince the people of the importance of the spaceship, while this Siriwadu character, was striving to take the people away from him, back to the time of the dandumonara, Hanuman,

> hooniyamm, pothe gura, kendara karaya and other traditional and sanctified things – and, of course, in between these two were the cassette and video deck maniac and motor-cycle riders and motor vans and heroin peddlers, card-sharpers, swindlers, brigands, hired assassins. [p. 73]

The novel thus serves as a diagnostic register of cultural isolationism within the context of globalised cultural capital. On the one hand the linguistic registers of marine biology and biological determinism are used to present an entropic register of the island as subject to internal decay: an idea drawn from de Chardin's thesis that 'many species through centuries of physical, spiritual and cultural inbreeding often become extinct' (p. 124). On the other hand Goonewardene presents scientific discourse as itself an invasive presence in the cultural mainstream. He thus uses colonially inscribed scientific conceptions of 'race' to undermine the rationale or scientific status of myths that sanction cultural exclusivity. In doing so he fails to transcend the hierarchies of such discourse, but does reveal the extent to which nationalism depends upon both colonial prescriptives and globalised modalities for its logic of cultural retrieval.

Goonewardene's attack on cultural nationalism is contained within a teleological model of culture that reads political violence within the context of social evolution. By using morphological characteristics to distinguish between the 'mass' and the independent thinker, he collapses cultural difference into physical difference replicating the biological essentialism and determinism underpinning colonial discourse. He 'biologizes culture', as Anthony Appiah puts it, and in doing so partakes in a transvaluation of values that integrates colonial codes into his antinationalist directives.[64] His presentation of cultural development is teleologically inflected and evolutionary carrying specific implications. As Patrick Brantlinger has pointed out in the context of colonial nationing, 'evolutionary thought seems almost calculated to legitimize imperialism'.[65] Yet while the novel follows the hierarchic differentiation symptomatic of allegorical satire and is encoded with the same evolutionary registers that can be found in colonial texts, its social and historical coordinates ground it in the political present of competing, resurgent Sinhala and Tamil nationalisms. Thus Goonewardene's literary representation of Fromm's model of group narcissism is granted precisely the kind of socio-historical basis that Fromm himself provided in his structuration of it. The same cannot be said of *The Tribal Hangover*. In this novel the paradoxes inherent in Goonewardene's critique of cultural nationalism – his investment in critiquing it from within its own culturally exclusive registers – break down when subjected to the discourse of migration. The inscription of the outsider as a Sri Lankan emigrant marks a dissociation from the social and cultural registers that provided an enabling critical framework for Goonewardene's formulation of the mass mind.

Manicheism and migration

The Tribal Hangover marks Goonewardene's most dramatic investment in an exploration of exilic experience. While his other work focuses on the alienated self-exile within the boundaries of national experience, this novel explores the experience of an illegitimate Sri Lankan who has been sold for adoption to Australian neo-Nazis and is thereby rendered an unwitting emigrant. Registers of migration are hammered home with insistence but they are always forced through a grid of culturally fixed binaries. The ex-patriation of Goonewardene's critique of cultural nationalism, its relocation to a place outside the native land, serves to divest it of the social and historical registers that empowered it in his other texts. It is not simply that the critique is shown to come from outside national boundaries that disables its interventionist potential; it is rather that the expatriation of Goonewardene's Manicheism *transforms* it from being an internally codified cultural critique, expressed from within the confines of alienation, to being an exteriorised evaluation of the island that generalises the nation for external consumption. Registers of residence that connect the depiction of the island to specific cultural and political developments are missing, jettisoned in favour of a generalised critique that borrows from the very hermeneutic register that Goonewardene pilloried in his penultimate novel. The effect is to dehistoricise and desocialise the formulation of the 'mass mind', petrifying it into a transhistorical marker of national identity. Here 'tribalism' is not dramatically informed by the plot or the development of experience, but is instead extemporised as the subject of debate. It is almost as if Goonewardene has succumbed to the logic of self-exile explored in his novels and chosen to completely disconnect himself from any semblance of cultural connection or investment.

The novel charts the efforts of its central character to form a new identity for himself 'with no loyalties to any flag or nation' (p. 52).[66] Harindra relinquishes his adoptive surname for 'X' but his desire to find out more about his parentage weights this quest narrative with the baggage of cultural reclamation. Siegle's brief analysis of this novel as a 'romance of recovery' claims 'the novel wills him from rags to riches, from isolated exile to reintegrated native', but that 'the prose and narrative form creak and groan under the strain of imposing a Hollywood idyll upon material that refuses to so easily untangle its contradictions'.[67] There is much to substantiate Siegle's argument that the novel is symptomatic of the postcolonial writer's efforts to address the effects of globalisation on a postcolonial nation, but the basis of this argument requires a closer analysis of the text's mediation of the migrant sensibility through the discursive imperatives of nationalism.

The text's spatial idiomatics are central to this antinomian presentation of exilic recuperation of fixed identity. Its mobilised presentation of Australia offers a dramatic contrast to the situatedness with which Sri Lanka is represented. Even the discourse of migration is differently inflected in relation to the two countries. In Australia, Harry, a one time taxi driver, is shown to be always on the move; his romantic liaisons are forged on bus journeys and on walks and in the transitional spaces of hotels. Along these journeys, distant Sri Lanka, the land of his birth, is fetishised as an object of desire, a nodal point of reference in his unstable existence. Yet the mediation of such knowledge – in the form of debates with friends in Australia – reveals that such knowledge can only grant him Foucauldian ownership rather than kinship. In a laboured conversation with a Sri

Lankan emigrant, Manique, that takes up almost twenty pages, the island is presented as, variously, 'a vulnerable little piece of land' (p. 77), 'a country that is being starved of living space' (p. 80), 'a small island, lying directly across the sea-routes of older times' (p. 86) and subject to 'invasions [which. . .] certainly have prevented an uninterrupted growth of a single homogenous race' (p. 81). While much play is made of the fact that the island's population is made up of a long history of migration, trade and invasion, the discourse in which this representation takes place is uncompromisingly exilic and situated. The national narrative is condensed for ease of consumption and presented before the questing exile as a dish to be sampled:

> 'It's quite astounding.' Harindra had a look of amazement and pleasure in his eyes. 'You have been able, it seems, to have condensed an experience of an island – its story, as it were, into the space of a couple of hours.'
>
> 'I myself don't know how I did it, but there you are, Harindra, the island of Sri Lanka is set down before your eyes.' [p. 92]

This external perspective informs the depiction of pack mentality or 'tribalism' in the novel. No longer a socially contingent expression of cultural evolution, the 'mass mind' here is registered in 'waves of tribalism' that are connected to both the 'fascist' JVP insurrection and unspecified ethnic violence (pp. 76, 77). These events, described at third hand by Manique as subjects drawn from a collective memory, are now cited as social aberrations within the context of 'an island that had preached *ahimsa* and self-negation for two thousand years' (p. 77).

The disconnection from the socio-historical basis of nationalism clearly weakens Goonewardene's social critique of cultural nationalism. It is further complicated by his investment in critiquing overpopulation which carries a different moral register to that found in his penultimate novel. Whereas *One Mad Bid For Freedom* forged a link between biological and historical determinism, here the emphasis on overpopulation slips into a eugenicist bias, and the evolutionary paradigm of natural selection found in the earlier novel is replaced by one of social regulation. There is a clear rationale for this in the narrative: Harindra's adoption raises the issue of why and how children are made available for foreign adoption in Sri Lanka. Yet instead of focusing on the socio-economic conditions that allow him to be 'sold like a package' (p. 20) to neo-Nazis, the novel's insistence on overpopulation as one of the root causes of violence (p. 131) serves to endorse a eugenicist rationale that seems to be encoded within the very fascist doctrine it rejects. The result is an alienating discourse in which Harindra's exiled perspective loses moral credibility; he asks himself 'What was there in [the island] that seemed to be leading to the creation of so great a number of mentally and physically dwarfed human beings. [. . .] [D]id the island have the right to breed human creatures at the rate and on the scale it was doing [?]' (p. 133). In the 'frenzy of self destruction and hate'(p. 133) that now marks the 'mass mind', Goonewardene divests biological determinism of the historical and cultural basis he gave it in *One Mad Bid For Freedom* so that it repeats and endorses the codifying strategies inherent in pseudoscientific discourses of race. The outsider's perspective of the exiled emigrant provides the enabling framework for this disconnection.

The text's critique of political violence thus draws on a volatile mix of eugenically informed racist discourses that not only subvert its antinationalist imperatives but also appear to endorse a racially coded line of reasoning. Harindra's alienation from the people of Sri Lanka is marked by racial discourse, the extent of his unbelonging marked by his racial links to resident Sri Lankans as he looks on the brown throng about him 'bonded to him by genetic origin [. . .] with race memories that should have been his' (p. 203). Similarly his relationship with Anna is marked by the difference in their 'genetic heritage' (p. 149), and his encounter with Nimali, who is 'typically Asian [. . .] as if she had been steeped in Buddhist rituals [. . .] with beating drums and thumping elephants'(p. 231), registers an aesthetically enforced resolution of racially marked cultural difference. Harindra's meeting with a Buddhist monk is preceded by a reflection that harks back to the myth of Aryan heritage so central to Sinhala Buddhist nationalism, revealing the extent to which Goonewardene's critique of cultural nationalism is compromised by his inability to speak from outside its registers:

> He had a particularly distinguished face, well-nourished and evenly shaped and several shades fairer than the sun-blackened faces of the peasants around him. [. . .] If it were true that the people of the island were of Aryan origin, this monk certainly bore out the claim. One might even say that the face was faintly Caucasian, as distinguished from many of the faces that seemed to have had, at some point, a Dravidian or Malaysian or even Negroid mixture. [p. 206]

Of course it could be argued that Goonewardene's aim here is to convey the inability of the emigrant to relate to his native land, but the use of racial registers, when set within the context of Goonewardene's long-standing engagement with biologising culture and critiquing nationalism, is clearly corrosive. There is no 'moral surplus' available here. The narrative perspective is one that defies valorisation: it is instead subject to self-erasure, effaced by endorsing the very registers of racial exclusivity it seeks to critique. Tribalism itself is now no longer presented as the outcome of 'artificially aroused tensions and feelings' as it was in 'Sow a Storm',[68] no longer encountered as an experientially mediated product of specific social and cultural conditions; rather it is commodified into a fixed and invariable core characteristic of the national psyche, so that the country itself appears beyond redemption.

It is a model which precludes the possibility of intervention or alteration; its dystopian drive reinforced by the inflexibility of the boundaries it presents. It suggests that in this last novel Goonewardene has exhausted the possibilities for dissent found in his earlier self-exilic texts; has drained the linguistic registers available to him from within the culturally exclusionary discourse of nationalism. This very possibility is anticipated in the moving conclusion to his penultimate novel. Invoking the forest monasteries of Ritigala – one of the sites that is granted symbolic weight in Ondaatje's *Anil's Ghost* – the narrative suggests that the most significant 'eternal truths' are not carried in the written word but through the oral traditions of ordinary people and monks, who had the ability to 'grow wise in silence' (p. 138). The foundational literary myth of the *Mahavamsa*, it suggests, is not only a reductive presentation of the past made palatable for popular consumption, but also an active distortion of history that ignores the lives of ordinary people and their discontents: a popular text that excludes the populace. Against this, an alternative historical register has survived 'passed on by word of mouth and by example' (p. 139). The truths of the island, exemplified by 'one of the greatest humanitarians born into the world',[69] thus escape written inscription:

> The truths the Buddha gave to this island were preserved not by the great Dagobas but by these silent witnesses who disappeared, leaving no record of themselves. You discover the truths about them, and you discover the truths about this island . . . [p.138]

Loyal to the last to the 'Buddhist' ideal of intellectual independence,[70] Goonewardene's oeuvre registers a sustained and uncompromising effort to strain an alternative message from the exclusionary cultural registers of nationalist discourse. His failure to find a literary language for the internationalism propounded in his essays does not only bear testament to the power of such discourse to constrain those who wish to dehegemonise it, it also provides us with a cautionary reminder of the complex ways in which antinationalism can be internally coded to work in the service of precisely that which it seeks to subvert. Thus while it is clear that Goonewardene's Manichean allegories have indeed leant themselves to Manichean interpretations, it is in our resistance to engaging in such binarist readings that we come closest to reaching an understanding of the alienation of which he writes.

3 Punyakante Wijenaike

Spectral spaces

> My body is everywhere: the bomb which destroys my house also damages my body insofar as the house was already an indication of my body.
>
> Jean-Paul Sartre, *Being and Nothingness*[1]

In 1977 Alastair Niven claimed that Punyakante Wijenaike was 'one of the most underestimated fiction writers currently at work in the English language'.[2] Thirty years later she still remains almost unknown in the West. Yet in her writing we find some of the most powerful registers of the relationship between identity and place, belonging and homelessness in Sri Lankan literature in English. What is more, her exploration of a subjectivity under threat of erasure in a shifting landscape bears direct correspondences with political and demographic changes that have taken place in the country over the past fifty years. Unlike Arasanayagam, whose literary resurgence is directly linked to the start of the civil war, Wijenaike's work spans forty years and registers a wide range of cultural shifts, all of which are mediated through an exploration of the link between the individual, the home and the land. As a result it is possible to read her work in a multitude of ways: as nationalist inscriptions of belonging and exclusion, as psychological studies of the effects of dislocation, as feminist affirmations of women's claims to inheritance and as literary explorations of the uncanny or the unhomely. The strength of her work lies in the fact that it invites all these readings while being resistant to appropriation by any one of them, demanding a fluid and flexible reading strategy that is informed by the political events of the time of writing. A spatially mediated study of her work not only accommodates the multiple approaches, allowing movement between them, but also simultaneously reveals the ways in which literary responses to demographic and geopolitical changes serve to create and reconstitute the connections between cultural and territorial boundaries over a significant length of time. As will be seen, hidden behind Wijenaike's ephemeral construction of 'home' lurks the contestatory and materially inflected discourse of territorial control and land rights.

Through an extensive oeuvre that encompasses five novels as well as novellas, children's books, autobiographical pieces and over a hundred short stories, Wijenaike's focus has remained on the individual's relationship to his – or, most usually, her – dwelling place, and she has unsettled the construction of 'home' by focusing on the individual's displacement within it. Her first novel, *The Waiting Earth* (1966), explores the estrangement between a peasant farmer and his wife and represents their eventual rehabilitation through physical resettlement. In later novels identity is even more firmly located in domestic space. In *Giraya* (1971) and *Amulet* (1994) the walauwe, or family manor, and the urban ancestral home (both of which are patriarchal, intergenerational domestic spaces) constitute a central character – a formidable, spectral presence that excludes and alienates the main protagonists. In many of her texts homes determine the boundaries of human experience while, at the same time, absorbing the mental and physical energies of their occupants; they contain both forbidden zones and family secrets, such that Wijenaike's exploration of home is configured by that which is unhomely, unhiemlich or uncanny.

The spatial configurations of these textual homes are replicated in the formal compression, episodic fragmentation and temporal density of her work. In *Giraya*, for example, events are temporally segmented into the form of an annual journal and spatially confined to a walauwe, and in *An Enemy Within* (1998) the collective home of the city of Colombo is spatially reconfigured through multiple narratives that map the city in a telescoped spatio-temporal zone of a single morning in 1996 at the Central Bank of Colombo. Much of Wijenaike's writing also contains elements of melodrama – a feminine, domestic genre[3] characterised by 'emotion, immobility, enclosed space, and confinement'.[4] It registers a claustrophobic configuration of space that serves to test and menace the limits of social order. Mental illness, incest, homosexuality, child abuse, suicide and murder all lie secreted in the homes of a fading aristocracy and an emergent upper class – a space in which a woman, often a new bride, serves as the unwitting interloper. She is an outsider in her own home – a paradigm of an 'unhomely home', which is used to dramatic political effect in the novella 'An Enemy Within'. Thus, as will be seen, Wijenaike's work, more than that of any other anglophone writer, explores Freud's formulation (borrowed from Jenstch) of the uncanny or unhomely as the manifestation of an absent presence that serves to menace the represented order.

Wijenaike is also notable in being the only anglophone writer of her generation (and perhaps of later generations too) whose work has gained regional mainstream popularity. Her novels have been translated into Sinhala and Tamil (as well as Russian) and *Giraya* has been made into a popular teledrama by Sri Lanka's leading film-maker, Lester James Pieris. The unembellished prose, emotional intensity and dramatic charge of her work have certainly been important factors in contributing to this popularity, but these elements alone – evident in all too many anglophone texts – do not set her work apart. Rather it is in her spatialised representation of otherness, of what Anthony Vidler has called 'the architectural uncanny', that reveals Wijenaike's keen sensitivity to cultural changes and her communication of a broader social malaise and anxiety. For the uncanny or unhomely, as Vidler has shown, is a 'psychoanalytical and aesthetic response to the real shock of the modern' arising out of the transformation of something that seemed homely and familiar into something that is definitely not so. It is, he suggests, a product of postindustrial culture, reflecting the insecurity of a newly established class that is 'not quite at home in its own home'.[5]

When relocated to postcolonial Sri Lanka, the exploration of the unhomely in anglophone writing can be seen, through Wijenaike's work, to register the cultural dislocations suffered by the privileged class whose loss of material wealth was marked by loss of land and by a series of territorially inscribed government policies. The colonising resettlement projects that took place from the 1940s to the 1960s, the land reform movement of the 1970s, rural development and urban expansion, and the civil war itself, serve as the social and political backdrop to Wijenaike's texts linking the shift in class relations to the reterritorialisation and deterritorialisation of the times. Indeed the development of her work, charting as it does a movement from a parable of rural life set in an unspecified location, to personalised fictions of the metropolitan capital where Wijenaike lives, delineates the restless search for habitation of an alienated, female, disenfranchised subjectivity. A chronological consideration of her four main texts thus reveals the ways in which literary representations of subject–space relations reflect, re-evaluate and feminise territorially inscribed cultural transformation.

The lust for land

When Wijenaike wrote *The Waiting Earth* in 1966 the literary preoccupation with rural life was still flourishing.[6] Like her Lankan contemporary James Goonewardene, and her Indian precursors Raja Rao and Kamala Markandaya, she sought in rural life and traditions the models of being and thinking that would authenticate the experience of living in a newly independent nation – a concern that might in turn serve to ground and legitimate her writing in English and thereby obviate possible charges of 'cultural treason'.[7] Yet despite this thematic link, *The Waiting Earth* cannot be read as a nationalist novel in the way that Rao's *Kanthapura* and Markandaya's *Nectar in a Sieve* can. There is no sustained, self-conscious effort to indigenise the language or develop a political consciousness as there is in Rao, and neither does Wijenaike engage in the polarising presentation of East–West relations that serves to situate and define the nation in opposition to its former colonial master as Markandaya does. In addition Wijenaike does not simultaneously endorse and interrogate rural life in a bid to focalise the nation's gaze on nationalism in the making, as her counterpart Goonewardene chooses to do.

Instead, Wijenaike's novel draws on the unhomely state of landlessness to define and legitimate a model of territorial ownership that has direct bearings on our reading of the spatially situated discourse of otherness that has gained currency since the war. While for most postcolonial writers village or peasant life serves as marker of pan-national experience – one that integrates the life and traditions of the rural majority of the nation with the knowable communities of the novel – Wijenaike presents rural life as an ambivalent state of disinheritance in which landless peasants are denied the right to own the land they live and work on. It is a manoeuvre which, as will be seen, has serious repercussions when translated into the politics of the present – a step that Wijenaike has already taken in her writing of a short story sequel to the novel, 'Living on the Edge' (2002). Drawing upon a clearly defined moral terrain, *The Waiting Earth* subtly distinguishes between legitimate and illegitimate ownership. When set within its historical context of peasant resettlement, a symptomatic reading of the novel reveals the contradictory political drives of ethnically engineered socialism – a central plank of the ethnic nationalism that emerged in the late 1950s. In this sense the novel, at once moving and measured in its lyricism, persuasively endorses controversial territorial measures.[8] The unhomely takes two forms in the novel. First it is characterised by the disorientation and uncertainty of the central characters and is abstracted into an historical condition in which the impact of modernity (in the form of the erosion of class barriers, women's independence, consumerism and Western modes of behaviour and dress) is gradually being felt, along with the material insecurities and cultural uncertainties attendant upon the homeless condition. More specifically, however, the unhomely constitutes the condition of landlessness itself, in which the desired and absent land becomes obsessively fetishised and destabilises the mental equilibrium of the central character, alienating him from his wife and family. Thus while it is important to recognise and applaud Wijenaike's socialist sympathies and humanitarian impulses in foregrounding the grinding poverty and homeless condition of the landless peasant, it is equally necessary to analyse the implications encoded in the ways in which such homelessness is resolved and the unhomely domesticated.

The Waiting Earth narrates the story of a landless farmer, Podhi Singho, and his wife, Sellohamy, and the former's desire to own land in his native village. This desire expresses a need for security, the fulfilment of which would serve, according to Podhi Singho, to legitimate his belonging to the village; he wishes for

> A small piece of land with roots running deep within it, a piece of earth whose yields will belong to us by right and on which, perhaps, a small house too, a house the wind of misfortunes cannot blow away, because the earth on which it stands is mine by right. [p. 65]

Owning any other land would be to him 'like living with another man's wife' (p. 66).

Yet Wijenaike directly challenges the legitimacy of these 'natural rights' by presenting Podhi Singho's desire for land ownership in his native village as a sexual obsession – one that affirms his need for male sexual mastery in the face of his increasing, but entirely unfounded, distrust of his wife:

> he filled his mind with thoughts of the land and the land alone which Rappiel Appu would get for him. This one thing he had yet to live for, this dream to keep him sane. He made his mind see this land now, made it lie open and naked for him and he saw his own body bend over it and his hand thrust the seed into the waiting earth; felt the warm brown moistness against his flesh as it received the seed with a hungry mouth. He even felt the sweat of his body as he worked and then his pleasure and his pride as he watched the first sprouting of

> the seed he had sown and the great joy he would feel in the final reaping. This land was his and his alone and it would remain so, for always, faithful to him and him alone. It would never turn and twist this way and that with the change of the wind. Unlike a woman, whatever way the wind blew this land of his would lie flat and straight and always in the same place. [p. 190]

The unspoken obsession drives husband and wife apart, leading directly to his loss of control and rape of Sellohamy – 'it was the land that had driven him to her' (p. 220) – and to her sense of competing with the land as with a mistress, an 'evil that possessed his body' (p. 264). Podhi Singho's land lust is thus not merely linked to his poverty; his desire to own land is, in a curious reinscription of the patriarchal forces of colonial territoriality which feminised the alien landscape in order to control it, associated with his desire to achieve mastery over his wife. (It is also aggravated by her own landlessness as her unendowered state upon marriage serves to fuel his obsession (p. 27).) Thus Podhi Singho's land lust is both ethically and territorially coded, inscribed into a model of patriarchal, colonial territoriality that serves to de-legitimate it.

Against this compelling personal drama is set the government land distribution programme of the 1960s, which offered gifts of uncultivated land in the dry zone to landless peasants on the understanding that they clear and work the land themselves and pass it on, undivided, to a single family heir. It was a program that involved significant demographic and cultural shifts: the rupture of settled communities, the division of families, the migration of southerners to the east, the relocation of Sinhalese to land that separatist Tamils laid historical claim to on the basis of ancestral occupation, and new rights of inheritance that effectively enforced long-term occupation by the Sinhalese in these areas. It is a programme described by Farmer as 'an imposed solution [to poverty and landlessness] which has not grown from indigenous society'.[9] Podhi Singho's resistance to the government offer registers the cultural schism caused by resettlement as it is made on the basis that this alien soil would be akin to marital infidelity (p. 66). By setting up a contrast between Podhi Singho's irrational lust for ownership over local land and his rationalised rejection of alien territory on the basis that it is not legitimately his, Wijenaike reinscribes the connection between territorial boundaries and marital rights and makes a compelling case for the legitimacy of the colonisation scheme. The scheme comes to be justified through the text's neutralisation of Singho's land lust within the ambit of government policy.

His views are directly challenged by a fellow villager who has chosen to accept the offer; the latter claims that not only will resettlement on new land end his poverty but also that the legal ownership ties him to the land in perpetuity in a blood bond stronger than marriage:

> A man can be parted from his wife, aiya [older brother], but not from this land. A promise I made that when I die this land must go to my wife, or if she too dies, then to my eldest son and if he too dies, to the second son. If all my sons die then it must go to my eldest daughter and so on down the line. [. . .]

> This land has been so closely tied to my blood that nothing can part it from me. I also had to promise that I would neither sell nor borrow on this land even if my seven children lay starving during a bad time. [p. 151]

The novel thus not only legitimates the colonising policies of the newly Independent nation but openly acknowledges the ways in which internal colonisation is naturalised, adopted land indigenised, made native and 'tied to blood'. The movement of the novel, charting Podhi Singho's reconciliation to the government project and his corresponding reconciliation with his wife, serves to justify this government policy of Sinhala resettlement and internal colonisation; Podhi Singho, we are told, 'could send his old roots into the new soil without fear of their dying' (p. 321).

It is a perspective that Wijenaike seems to continue to endorse. In 2002 she published a short story sequel to the novel, 'Living on the Edge', in which she depicts Podhi Singho's life some forty year years on. The correspondence between Podhi Singho's perspective and the narrator's suggests that Wijenaike does indeed share her central character's views. Podhi Singho's home is now under attack from Tamil Tiger rebels, Sellohamy (whose moral courage and resilience in the novel elevated to her to a symbol of female endurance analogous to the motherland itself) has been killed by terrorists and the possibility of dispossession looms. The legitimacy of the colonisation programme is comprehensively affirmed:

> Even though this new land was dry and hard it was his own through the colonisation scheme. [. . .] The giant water tanks built by his own Kings of the past, stood by to irrigate his new land pulled out of the jungle. [. . .]
>
> The 'tigers' they called themselves and came to drive him from his own land claiming it as theirs by right.[10]

While the novel's claims to territorial legitimacy and ownership of the new land were endorsed through the socialist message that the ownership was, in part, gained through the peasant's physical investment in it – a message reiterated in the claim that 'the land should belong to those who work on it' (p. 68) – the short story disinvests in such political niceties. By 2002 there appears to be no need to question the historical rights of the Sinhalese to these lands; the legitimacy of the colonisation scheme is unquestioned and the land is further reclaimed through a direct link with the ancient irrigation system of Sinhala kings – one of the nation's historical treasures – which stands as an enduring physical marker of ancestral control and ownership, sanctioning Podhi Singho's settlement in the region. While historical evidence does indeed suggest, as this story does, that the appropriated land was neglected and going to waste, 'pulled from the jungle' and tamed, the ideological imperatives of Wijenaike's story suggest a specific political affiliation when situated within the context of war. The overassertion of territorial legitimacy in the later work corresponds to the territorial unease of a nation in which land rights are being violently contested by armed force. Wijenaike's story also powerfully registers how the landless who have been resettled are themselves victims of land disputes and are threatened with dispossession once more. With no counter-narrative of Tamil dispossession to balance it, the unhomely in Wijenaike's representation of rural life can thus be seen to register the cultural and social ruptures attendant on an ethnicised national politics – a social vision that is telescoped into a reflection of class dynamics in her novels *Giraya* and *Amulet*. In these novels, as will be seen, Wijenaike shifts the site of the unhomely from the deterritorialised land to the defamiliarised house.

Unhomely homes

> The uncanny would always, as it were, be something one does not know one's way about in. The better oriented in his environment a person is, the less readily will he get the impression of something uncanny in regard to the objects and events in it.
>
> Sigmund Freud, *The Uncanny*[11]

> I grew up in apprehension, always anticipating something to happen. What exactly would happen, I did not know. Sometimes the fear would grow into such large proportions that I would be compelled to seek the safety of my bed.
>
> Punyakante Wijenaike, *A Way of Life*[12]

In the opening page of her memoir, *A Way of Life* (1987), Wijenaike attests to the influence of her childhood home in shaping her personality, wondering 'whether it is the house that played the most important part in molding people who lived in it' (p. 1). Raised in a sprawling urban mansion run by an affluent Christian grandfather and a Buddhist grandmother, the home disorientated as much as it fed the imagination. Regularly terrified by a sadistic personal ayah who 'practices different kinds of torture, knowing I will never tell on her' (p. 20), Wijenaike sought refuge in a dream world in which 'long winding verandahs turned into streams of water along which I could swim or paddle my own boat [and] the open balconies, three in number, turned into sea beds [where I would lie] believing myself a beautiful mermaid with a long tail and golden hair' (p. 19). The memoir constitutes a reminiscence of a lost and leisured way of life at the heart of which stands the unhomely home, one which promises security but is open to intrusion and terror thus allowing for the development of phobic tendencies such as spatial fear, 'house-bondage' and the desire to create sanitised, safe zones.[13]

All these elements are to be found in *Giraya* and *Amulet*. *Giraya* is set during the time of the land reform movement of the 1970s (a fact not mentioned in the novel but which Wijenaike draws attention to in her preface: 'Land Reform was knocking on the door of people accustomed to living on inherited wealth') and *Amulet* registers the development of urbanisation and the subdivision of inherited property and land characteristic of the 1970s and 1980s.[14] The novels offer complementary and contrastive readings of the unhomely in their anthropomorphistic representation of home and detailed consideration of agoraphobic sensibility, but they do so within a clearly defined social context. The unhomely was, according to Walter Benjamin, born out of the rise of the great cities, where 'what was once walled and intimate, the confirmation of community [. . .] has been rendered strange by the spatial incursions of modernity'.[15] In Sri Lanka, where land reform served to drastically undermine the economic power of the landed class,[16] urbanisation was linked to radical social and demographic shifts. Migration to the city, for example, was exacerbated by the loss of ancestral lands, and the rise in an educated but often unemployed working class undermined the power and status of the feudal landlords of ancestral estates who lived in walauwes – dwelling places that figure prominently in both novels. *Giraya* uses anthropomorphic markers to register social change, siting the unhomely or uncanny in the social reincarnation of the times, in its opening description of the walauwe:

> The Walauwe, the old manor house, waits in silence. Is it awaiting death with courage? Why must anyone need courage to face death? Surely death is but another change and are we not accustomed to that in life as well? The walauwe may be pulled down, brick by brick, and then it will rise again with new bricks and new tiles. It will live again under a new name, a new coat of paint and a new way of life. [. . .]
>
> Yes, a house retains its personality only so long as its inmates live within its walls. When they die, or run away, the house must change. If it is not pulled down, it must at least assume a second personality. It must be reborn. Like a human being a house must die before taking life again. The old ebony furniture will be sold as valuable antiques and the yellowed lace curtains pulled down. The old walauwe will die, but the house will live on. [p.1]

These changes to the walauwe that mark a 'new way of life' are grounded in a gothic tale in which an educated woman from a farming background (a member of the rising middle class) increasingly becomes alienated from her dwelling space and its principal occupants – her silent husband Lal, the heir apparent, her mother-in-law Adelaine, a distant matriarch, Manel, her sister-in-law, and the sinister maid Lucia Hamy. The house itself constitutes a central character, its labyrinthine sequence of sealed interconnecting rooms embodying both the frustrated communication between its occupants and the complex relationships of blood and marriage between them. Its panoptic gaze extends beyond its physical confines to the estate itself so that the narrator feels perpetually under surveillance. The house contains several family secrets that are not divulged until the end – Lal's homosexuality and illegitimacy directly imposing the threat of dispossession and homelessness on the narrator. Perpetually on the threshold, outside locked doors or standing by a partially drawn curtain between rooms, she occupies a liminal space, neither mistress nor servant. This social indeterminacy is also registered by changes taking place outside the home: the building of the biscuit manufacturer's mansion that rivals the fading opulence of the walauwe, the construction of a new road to link two villages that divides the estate in two and the clandestine affair between the estate superintendent and Manel, all of which presage the gradual erosion of power of the landed gentry and further destabilise the social positioning of the narrator.

Indeed it is in the strangeness of personal and social relations – their uncanny manifestation – that much of the power of this novel resides. The appearance of wealth, status and legitimacy, is revealed as just that: an illusion of power and privilege. The logic of ownership and possession is undermined on more than one level and it is this layering of appearances, their doubling, that gives density to duplicity in the text. Indeed the opaqueness of this novel lies not only in the powerful representation of spectral space in the labyrinthine, unhomely walauwe, but also in the slippage and gaps in the narrative itself, between the epistemologically driven unfolding of plot in the disjointed journal that constitutes the text and the ontologically based construction of events of which this plot forms a part – between in other words, the narrator's quest for meaning and the writer's construction of it in the text. The former involves the presentation of Adelaine as a dominant matriarch, owner and mistress of the walauwe, who is dependent upon her female servant – the sinister custodian of the giraya (areca nut-cutter) – and Lal, her effeminate son, for support. Such narrative emplotment presents the instability of feudal power as the primary social framework for the text, and it simultaneously locates the feudal system of inheritance and patronage as the model through which social relations are mediated and negotiated. The inevitability of its demise and the uncertainty of precisely what will replace it unsettles the narrator who, reflecting on her husband's snobbery, is prompted to locate herself in opposition to him:

> The day will come when you will have to step down from your walauwe and walk among us the common people. How will you fit in Lal? If you do not make yourself change now, you may in the future stand in a position that is lower than that of the man who now stands humbly before a table loaded with your money, receiving his pay. [p.110]

Such 'intellectual uncertainty' is fundamental to the structuration of the uncanny according to Freud[17] and the reader's experience of this uncertainty replicates and reinforces the loss of orientation of the narrator.

This intellectual uncertainty is exacerbated when, at the end of the novel, the full extent of Adelaine's powerlessness is revealed. Adelaine and Lal, we learn, are only keeping up appearances – conforming to a model of legitimate feudal ownership. Adelaine, it is disclosed, had an affair with a cousin and therefore her illegitimate offspring, Lal, will not in fact inherit the walauwe – this will pass instead to Manel and her lover, the socially inferior estate superintendent. The threat of dispossession that haunts both the central characters in *The Waiting Earth* thus manifests itself in a new form, that of upper class female dispossession and homelessness, but with an important twist: the very basis of class legitimacy is called into question. Not only is the heir apparent now revealed to be nothing more than an apparent heir, but the estate workers themselves are presented as the product of the numerous affairs of Adelaine's late husband. Blood lines are confused and the very legitimacy of the landed class is subject to scrutiny.

Within this context, the position of the narrator, as the resident outsider, the social interloper who has married into the old feudal order, is uncannily legitimated and centred by the author. A farmer's daughter married to the illegitimate son of the wife of a feudal landlord, her ambivalent social position acquires, at the novel's end, a normative status and her homelessness is neutralised. Unlike her in-laws, she is able to converse with servants in a language they recognise, and her easy appropriation of the accoutrements of modernity (such as powdered milk and imported medicine) serves, in the reversed social logic of the text, to legitimate her position. The duplicity of social perspective – the mediation of a feudal order from the perspective of a social outsider – produces an uncanny dislocation of space and residence in the text. It is impossible to locate 'home' in the mobilised presentation of class confluence and class conflict. It is a world in which the individual perspective gains supremacy, where the temporal is mediated through mental states and fluctuations of the lunar calendar (the journal that constitutes the text is written on *poya* – or full moon – days) and where the spatial is constructed through the imaginative mapping of unhoused domesticity. Thus the mobile social positioning of the unhoused narrator serves as more than just a marker of social change; it also embodies an ontological condition whereby displacement and homelessness prove to be embedded in the very structure of social relations. The narrator, Adelaine, Lal and Manel are all socially unfixed. Far from having nothing in common, they have all transgressed, breaking, variously, class, community and sexual codes, and, what is more, are known to have done so. The walauwe that accommodates them is thus a spectral presence, a construction of spatialised otherness, whereby the inhabitants are rendered strangers not only to one another but also to themselves as they try to maintain the appearance of conformity:

> Here in the walauwe, despite iron bars, Alsatian dogs, padlocks and gates we have to lock room doors as well. And here we lock them, not against people who come and go, but against those living within its very walls'. [p. 75]

As a defamiliarised symbol of the ruling class, the walauwe is destined to die, but, as the opening lines of the novel remind us, 'the house will live on'. Wijeniake's dramatic mobilisation of social relations in this text serves to clear space for new ways of dwelling on the borderland, and in *Amulet* she returns to the theme of the unhomely home in order to reveal the ubiquity of defamiliarised dwelling by focusing her attention on an urban house. The fact that in this later novel the walauwe is presented as a place of light and freedom, 'spacious and cool', where 'birds flew freely in and out of the centre courtyard' (p. 8) and 'people had been free to come and go' (p. 29), indicates that a reading that privileges the walauwe *per se* as the embodiment of the unhomely is misplaced. Rather Wijenaike's work demands that we consider the way in which dwelling itself is negotiated in relation to space, and the ways in which space is resconstructed as a series of displacements in her work.

Amulet was written in response to the popular demand for Wijenaike to produce a sequel to *Giraya*.[18] Set in an old Colombo house, the novel is, in many ways, haunted by its predecessor. Like *Giraya*, *Amulet* is a first-person, temporally segmented, narrative, that focuses on the experiences of a newly wed woman, Shyamali, married to a relative stranger from a different background and class.

The house in which they live is also dominated by servants (including a particularly unpleasant female servant) and contains family secrets that are gradually divulged as the narrative unfolds: the physical abuse of the narrator's husband, Senani, and his sister, Anula, in childhood, incest between Senani and Anula, the suicide of Senani's mother, and Senani's murder of his sister. These secrets are partially revealed in Anula's diary, which Shyamali discovers in her retreat to the attic, and gain physical presencing in the form of Anula's restless, unhoused spirit.

It could be argued that family secrets here, as in *Giraya*, constitute that which has been repressed, for Freud's formulation of the uncanny, drawing upon Schelling's idea that the '*unhiemlich* is the name for everything that ought to have remained . . . secret and hidden but has come to light',[19] claimed that the unhomely constituted 'the return of the repressed'.[20] It could also be claimed, as Wijenaike has herself done, that the focus on taboo subjects such as incest and homosexuality constitute 'a confrontation with reality'.[21] Incest, in particular, is rarely addressed in anglophone literature and Wijenaike has focused on it twice.[22] In Sri Lanka, incest is not just a social phenomenon, it is both a symbolic structure of moral violation that has helped to regulate kinship ties[23] and a central element of Sri Lankan mythological history. In foregrounding it in the context of mobilised class and community relations (the incest between Senani and Anula is after all induced by their nanny), Wijenaike reveals the link between transgressive social and sexual relations.

Amulet intensifies the key themes of the earlier novel by duplicating symbols, situations and characters internally in the text, thereby creating not only the haunting attendant upon intertextual referentiality with its predecessor, but also the recurrent presencing of key ideas and events within the text itself. Duplication abounds in several forms: first, the uncanny doubles of some of the characters (the servant Pinchamma is strategically linked to Nonchi, the nanny who was responsible for child abuse; Anula's spirit – itself a double of her earthly self – inhabits Shyamali's body); second, the correspondences of circumstance and situation (both Shyamali and her husband had unfaithful fathers and belong to divided homes; both fathers had illegitimate offspring; both Shyamali and her mother are dispossessed, physically constrained in their own homes and finally ejected from them; both Shymali and Anula are denied an inheritance); third, the repetition of events (Shyamali is thrice dispossessed: first in being disinherited from her family home, then in her loss of authority and control in her marital home where a servant 'seems the mistress and I, a house guest' (p. 68), and finally in being unhoused when her husband decides to destroy the home; Senani's murder of his sister is replicated in the ominous confrontation with his wife that ends the novel); fourth, the textual replication (Anula's diary repeats and revises the narrator's script); and finally the dual narrators (Shyamali and Senani). This duplication is entirely in keeping with both the structuration of the uncanny[24] and the legal dilemma that underpins the text: the issue of joint ownership – the issue, in other words, of a duplicated occupation of space, the mutual sharing of living room, which foregrounds the question of territorial control. Thus while disinheritance is central to the narratives of her earlier novels, in *Amulet* the issues attendant upon the disinheritance of the female narrator from her family home and her displacement in and from her marital home are replicated by the conflictual dynamic embedded in joint ownership. Shyamali's exclusion from the family legacy is shown to create as many problems as the legacy of joint ownership inherited by Senani and his sister. What is more, by focusing her attention on the ownership of the home (rather than land ownership as in *The Waiting Earth*), Wijenaike is encoding her reading of the unhomely within a specifically (but not exclusively) female space. For a woman, as one object relations analyst has shown, the home can reflect an expanded boundary of the self.[25]

Here then, once again, dispossession, and more specifically the gendered homelessness of women, is foregrounded. The Deega system of marriage (in which a newly married woman goes to live in her husband's home) is analysed as a trope of both physical estrangement and cultural situatedness through the experience of Shymali and her mother in *Amulet*, the narrator of *Giraya*, and Sellohamy in the *Waiting Earth*. It is a system that mobilises women's identities in relation to their dwelling place and marks an area of experience rarely considered in English literature from Sri Lanka.[26] In *Amulet*, however, Wijenaike goes further in naming it and comparing it with the alternative of joint ownership. Both are found wanting. Shyamali is effectively disinherited by her parent's decision to write the ancestral property to her brother – a man who clearly does not work for a living though he is qualified to do so – on account of the need to keep it in the family name; and the joint ownership of Shyamali and Senani is presented as an embodiment of an unnatural relationship cemented by their incest, a corrosive arrangement that can only lead to family division and estrangement. The only feasible alternative to these two modes is, the text suggests, the creation of separate dwellings, a proposition that Senani – an architect who claims 'I had structured my marriage like I structure buildings' (p. 91) – puts into place. But this marker of modernity destabilises the social conventions under which an earlier generation of women live and effectively serves to unhouse Shyamali. Like the walauwe in *Giraya,* the old Colombo house and the intergenerational family are synonymous, the very structure of dwelling space informing the structure of relationships. Its destruction and replacement with separate dwellings and 'a concrete fortress, a block of apartments [that] will sit heavily on the past so that it will never rise again' (p. 134) presages a fundamental, irreversible shift in interpersonal relations, a radical change in the structuration of community in terms of separation and segregation.

In linking the social conditions of uncanny experience to their psychological effects, Wijenaike's work clearly draws attention to the 'disturbances of identity, time and place'[27] generated by the disjunctive temporalities of a society that, while tied to traditional beliefs and customs, is also registering the disintegration of traditional social bonds. The social, cultural and personal alienation attendant upon this shift is increasingly gendered in her work as women – the narrators in *Giraya* and *Amulet* – are shown to gain their identity through and from their dwelling space. If, as Bachelard claims, 'the house image would appear to have become the topography of our intimate being',[28] then Wijenaike's exploration of the unhomely home registers the difficulties of settling into new modes of being and dwelling in the world. Old structures of living are shown to cohabit the present, haunting and unsettling the sites of regeneration and expansion so that territorial security is rendered impossible. This is true of all Wijenaike's work, but what gives *Amulet* the edge over its predecessors is its clear investment in the uncanny: not only in the doubling and repetition noted earlier, nor in the spectral spaces of dispossession informing experience, but also in two other elements that are not present in *Giraya* or *the Waiting Earth*. The first is its focus on what Hamid Naficy has described as a 'phobic partner' and the other is the intellectual uncertainty that pervades the ending.

According to Naficy the experience of the unhomely leads the victim to draw comfort from '"phobic partners", such as a trusted person, or object (such as an umbrella and a suitcase)'.[29] While Wijenaike does focus on an uncanny object in her earlier novel, the giraya which gives the book its name, it is presented as an alien and alienating instrument that diminishes rather than empowers the narrator, who feels herself caught between its blades. It is a symbol of exorcism which, in the hands of Adelaine and Lucy Hamy, threatens to divide her from herself. In *Amulet*, however, multiple phobic partners present themselves: Anula's diary (and the spirit of Anula contained herein) and the amulet itself which Shyamali fingers when she is uncertain. There is also a space that offers Shyamali sanctuary – the attic – separate from the house and yet attached to it, which constitutes what Naficy would describe as a 'safe zone' but one constantly under threat of intrusion.[30]

In addition the ending of the novel, with its impending confrontation between Shyamali (now emboldened by her communication with Anula and wearing the amulet) and Senani (who is intent on 'destruction of Shyamali, destruction of house' [sic] (p. 132)), carries the reader to the edge of resolution, the cusp of connection and a kind of suspended logic with the final lines: 'I knock. Shyamali opens the door to me' (p.134). Senani, who has been propelled by images of the future to seek out his wife – 'I can already see in my mind the beautiful new building towering over the two small houses of my children' (p. 134) – is also confronting the future in his wife, who feels protected by the uncanny amulet and is 'prepared for whatever or whoever is coming up the stairway' (p. 88). Her communication with Anula, or rather the spirit of Anula, reconfigures her identity into a doubling of selfhood, a presencing of a simultaneous past and future, for as Royle notes (in relation to Derrida) 'ghosts don't belong to the past, they come from the future'.[31]

It is this haunting of an unstable present by an uncertain future, a present that registers the impact of rural displacement, gendered dispossession, class migration and urban emigration, that gives potency to the representation of psychological disturbance in Wijenaike's work. Through historically and socially situated reflections on the unhomely, *Giraya* and *Amulet* offer a reading of the way in which migrations across culture, class and territory affect and influence the structuration of identity, and they reveal how identity itself comes to be spatialised and mobilised in its search for bearings and a home. As Rapport and Dawson have noted, as home becomes more mobile so it comes to be seen as more individuated and privatised.[32] Wijenaike's spatialised structuration of gendered identity carries us to the threshold – the open door of *Amulet* – where transformation occurs. Yet in 'The Enemy Within', Wijenaike retreats from this position. Here, in a novella that explores the experience of death in the city, the alienation of the protagonists is ethnically and politically coded and boundary marking is foregrounded once more.

The fortress city

In 'An Enemy Within',[33] 'home' constitutes the city of Colombo, conceived by its residents as 'a fortress' that grants immunity from the war. The text is part of a collection of the same name comprising two novellas and two short stories, and it focuses on the experiences of the victims of a major suicide bomb attack of January 1996 that extensively damaged Sri Lanka's business centre – in particular the Central Bank, the target of the attack – killing over 90 people and wounding some 1400 others. For the first time in her long career, resident space is both fragmented *and* sanctified, and place is explicitly shown to be socially and communally (de)constructed. While her earlier novels registered a nostalgia (a word that literally means 'homesickness') for settlement and security, this novel is at pains to demonstrate the close connections already existing between the city dwellers, presenting the city as an active and thriving community of individuals and the very hallmark of modernity. Buildings are animated by the activity they engender, and the multiple narratives that structure the text are narrated from above, at and below ground level, creating a powerful, spatialised sense of community and connection. The eight narratives of the novella are themselves fragmented; but this fragmentation does not describe an alienated subjectivity as it does in her earlier work, rather it works towards a collective mapping of urban life in Colombo. The spatialised presentation of the city as a network of human relationships is contained and constrained by the temporal linearity of narrative emplotment that focuses sequentially on events prior to, during and after the bomb blast. The collectivity of voices thus promote a compelling image of security in residence, of homeliness and of individuals at home in their own narratives.

Yet in focusing her attention on a real political event that took place in her home city, Wijenaike's own political persuasions come to the fore, resulting in a personal response to ethnic violence that inscribes boundaries in the process of appearing to interrogate them..[34] The 'enemy within' refers to both the terrorists living in 'safe houses' – ironically the only houses that appear safe in the text – to the trauma induced by the blast itself.[35] Unlike her earlier powerful evocation of the uncanny or unhomely as a marker of social and cultural displacement, here the uncanny is personalised and politicised, given material shape in the insidious form of the Tamil suicide bomber. This personalisation of the uncanny occurs in and through a corresponding anthropomorphisation of the city which 'like a traumatised person [. . .] awaits re-building' (p. 49). Indeed the depiction of Colombo is symbolically saturated, both masculinised and feminised, as military fortress (the dominant metaphor in the text) and maternal nurturer, both mobile and situated – elements that compete for authority in the following passage:

> Colombo in the past, had, from time to time, been a beleaguered city. The Dutch, the Portuguese attacked and raped her virginity. During World War II when she lay in submission under the British, she had been turned into a fortress. But apart from an air raid or two, a bomb or two dropped from the air into the harbour and that too after a warning siren signal, she had not suffered too much.
>
> Today she faced a different situation. The enemy coming from within, from the womb of her own mother. How could she guard against herself? Check-points, cordoning off with barrels and barb wire [sic] how could they stop the earth exploding under her feet? The enemy could not be identified, separated. He moved among citizens, he lived among the people of Colombo. [p. 49]

This excess use of metaphoric and symbolic registers to describe a territorially defined space substantiates Featherstone's observation that a geographically bounded space is 'sedimented with symbolic sentiments'.[36] Here community is constructed by the sharing of this symbolic space, whose very excess of registers resists easy categorisation. Rather it is through a clearly defined structuration of belonging that the city gains coherence and definition in Wijenaike's text, for, as Sibley has contended, social space is shaped by our sense of belonging – who does and who doesn't.[37] The contradictory pull of registers siting the city as fortress and maternal source reveals an uncertainty in Wijenaike's placing of the Other. The Other or 'enemy' has both a blood bond to the city and a clear wish to ravage or 'rape' it as the colonisers had done earlier, thus placing him as both insider and outsider, both native and alien. Such uncertainty reflects a fundamental need, in my view, to demonise the enemy through domesticating him; an enemy who, inverting the logic of Wijenaike's earlier texts, constitutes the resident outsider. This ethical elision that grants outsider status through residence has serious ideological implications. As Neloufer de Mel has observed, 'Wijenaike's book shares an ideological affinity with those who cannot/do not wish to separate the Tamil civilian from the militant', foreclosing 'any possibility of reconciliation between the two communities or a just solution to the underlying causes of the ethnic war'.[38] What is more, as de Mel and others[39] have pointed out, Wijenaike's failure to address the issue of army atrocities on Tamil civilians results in a one-sided presentation of the conflict; the 'enemy within' – both suicide bomber and the embodiment of trauma – is clearly an external force that needs to be resisted and overcome, never the Sinhala citizens (and readers) who are complicit in fuelling the war nor the Sri Lankan army itself. What is more, while the novella does present two Tamil victims of the bombing, their deaths serve to heighten the betrayal implicit in the suicide bomber's actions, whose thoughts are included in the collective memory that constitutes the city.

The biomorphic presentation of the city as a bodily organism thus repeats and revises the anthropomorphic presentation of unhomely homes in Wijenaike's earlier work, reversing the presentation of the resident outsider and revealing a dramatic reversal in her reading of subject–space relations. Wijenaike's uncompromising presentation of the resident outsider does not so much destabilise the boundaries of belonging as reinforce them, inviting a univocal and unifocal response. Unlike her explorations of women's private experience within the marital home, Wijenaike's politically situated texts are territorially deterministic, presenting 'human species as self-markers'[40] and reveal the way in which the ethnic conflict has constrained and codified representations of belonging in a writer who has been fearless in her exploration of the cultural repressed. As Don DeLillo has observed:

> What terrorists gain, novelists lose. The degree to which they [terrorists] influence mass consciousness is the extent of our decline as shapers of sensibility and thought. *The danger they represent equals our own failure to be dangerous.* [my emphasis][41]

4 Jean Arasanayagam

Fugitive selves

Jean Arasanayagam has been introduced as a 'poet, painter, short story writer, lino print maker, batik artist and teacher' in a recent volume 'celebrating' Sri Lankan women writers – a catalogue of occupations that effectively, if inadvertently, works to diminish her significant contribution to Sri Lankan literature in its dispersive plurality of qualifications.[1] Indeed this motley list of identity markers reveals the ways in which the instabilities of critical positioning can reflect the very registers of cultural and social indeterminacy that inflect and inform her writing. A writer of Burgher descent whose work has been peripatetically introduced in the opening chapter to this study, her generically diverse oeuvre is marked by its direct engagement with the difficulties of occupying a borderland identity, difficulties brought into focus during the political violence of 1983 when she was evicted from her home on account of her marriage to a Tamil.

This year marked, in her words, her 'regeneration' as a writer, and from this point on, as Chelva Kanaganayakam notes, identity is a central preoccupation in her work.[2] Identity is established as a site of exclusion, of policed boundaries, but it is in the interplay between the recognition of the violence of enforced difference and Arasanayagam's literary mediation and efforts to create a grammar that contests and transcends difference that her work gains its power and conviction, its complex syntax of resistance. From the exploration of her Tamil mother-in-law's rejection of her on account of her being an 'outsider' despite commonalities of gender experience, so that, as Alka Nigam has claimed, the 'oppressor ends up being an outsider herself',[3] to her evocative representation of victimhood and culpability in ways that distance themselves from ethnic markings and relocate them in terms of moral and ethical codings, Arasanayagam's work effectively and emphatically insists on a relocation of the boundaries of difference and belonging into a moral terrain in which the arbitration of inclusion and exclusion is determined by humanitarian prescriptives: an exercise in boundary marking that requires an acknowledgement of the violence underpinning its enforcement in the cultural, social and political spheres. Indeed the movement from an emphasis on externally manifested temporal and spatial Manicheism in the allegorical representation of the country as a childhood 'Eden', to the fluid mediation of difference in terms of internalised, personal registers scripted in relation to split subjectivity in the poetic present, reveals the extent to which land, place and the fugitive self are saturated with moral significance in her work. More than any other Sri Lankan writer to date, Arasanayagam's mediation of selfhood in relation to landscape enacts both the natural world's power to entice and nurture and, simultaneously and significantly, the nation's power to eject and extrude those who occupy its social and cultural borders.

Jean Arasanayagam's work almost insists upon spatial and territorial readings. Not only does her poetry and autobiographical fiction draw upon a plethora of sensuous, spatialised registers – from the lush garden of her childhood, the fecundity of forests, hills and rivers of her hometown of Kandy, and the contrastive limestone, seas and palmyrah groves of her husband's birthplace in Navaly – but also her very negotiation of belonging has come to be encoded in territorial tropes and metaphors. After her political displacement in 1983, when she was forced to seek shelter in a refugee camp, the metaphors of boundaries, territoriality and policed space have become central to her imaginative world and repeatedly appear both in her imaginative writing and in interviews, public talks and personal communication with critics.

Her work charts the development from a personal to a public voice, and a corresponding development in spatial register as the mergence of an apparently unified self with landscape is abandoned for a stark territorially bound discourse in which selfhood is clearly fractured. It is a development she is conscious of and has commented on:

> In the past I was also a painter and my poetry reflected this – words, visual impressions, whole landscapes, were brushstrokes in my mind and then became words [. . .] I painted everything I saw on tremendous canvasses flooded in colour. Nature always had dimensions for me that went beyond a supra reality. Colour, shape, form, sound, constantly formed patterns and vibrations in my mind – all was wrought into an overall cohesion [. . .] into something final.
>
> The landscape was unmarred until 1971.[. . .] The river over which the white kokas flew now had bodies which casually drifted down river – the bodies of the insurgents of 1971. Even here, I was the watcher on the hills, untouched virtually by what was happening around me.
>
> With the events of 1977–1983 I found myself moving into history and becoming part of it. I think this was the beginning of my moving away from the old landscape. I began to explore a new climate of experience [. . .] [In 1983] I stood together with the minorities on the other side of the barrier. I began to see myself as one who could possibly be unacceptable in a society in which I feel I had always belonged.[. . .] I began to explore my own identity – the really serious question began to arise 'Who was I?' Identity meant Race – my racial identity. I write endlessly on this theme – the colonial inheritance – and the landscape keeps changing, changing all the time. Being a writer today means also being committed not to oneself but to the social and political changes around one. 1983 was the year of my regeneration.[4]

The close correspondence recorded by Arasanayagam here between the changing social and political landscape and her own evaluation of a racially defined identity has been central to critical evaluations of her work to date. Neloufer de Mel, in a spatially orientated reading of Arasanayagam as a 'cast-away', has contrasted the pastoral, Edenic gardens of her early work, which offer safe sanctuary to the poet, with her later presentation of 'destroyed, unpeopled landscapes'.[5] Arasanayagam's focus on developing a subjective speaking voice has also led Neluka Silva to observe that her work reflects the 'search of a lone individual, struggling to find a meaning in nature for a condition relating to and engendered by human realities'.[6] Both de Mel and Silva identify a tension between Arasanayagam's romantic sensibility and the social and political events she attempts to record. De Mel goes on to identify alienation even in Arasanayagam's first collection of poetry where the city-dwelling poet stands apart from those whose connection with the land is the outcome of their physical investment in it – those for whom 'with earth and growing / there is no separateness'.[7]

My aim here is to consider the ways in which alienation in Arasanayagam's work gains expression through spatial idiomatics. I show that while Arasanayagam herself has presented her development as one from an overall cohesion between self and landscape towards a rupture between the speaking subject and society, the imaginative trajectory of her work reflects a more complex negotiation of belonging: one which through its exploration of interstitial subjectivity works to relocate the bordered dwelling space as a site not only of real or potential dislocation but also of indigeniety and moral authority. Her oeuvre resists reductive ethnically marked readings in several ways. The generic range of her work – which includes poetry, short stories, (auto)biographical fiction and plays – is compounded by shifts in cultural register (drawing upon Sinhala, Tamil, and Burgher beliefs, languages and traditions) and the construction of multiple perspectives and fluid subjectivities. Her accommodation of a wide range of literary forms, social perspectives and cultural registers reflects not only a hybrid perspective but also presents us with a comprehensively pluralist vision, one that reflects a restless search for dwelling in several locations and her desire, as she puts it, to 'play [. . .] with the chequer board of different genes'.[8] As will be seen, the presencing of this culturally pluralist self is shown to be concomitant with its dislocation, exile and erasure, and it provides compelling evidence of the stark territorialism present in the nation. It also effectively reveals some of the literary, social and cultural coordinates of what Radhakrishnan has described as 'post-colonial hybridity' – a form of hybridity to be distinguished from its comfortably transnational and celebratory metropolitan counterpart in its 'frustrating search for constituency and a legitimate political identity', its presencing as 'an excruciating act of self-production by and through multiple traces'.[9]

The disjunction between the ceaseless search for belonging and the painful experience of rejection provides political impetus to Arasanayagam's work. Her oeuvre explores and articulates different forms of alienation – personal, cultural, social and political – which become increasingly defined in territorial terms after her political displacement. Thus, as I will show, her work, through its complex negotiation of a multiple forms of displacement across a range of differently marked borders, emphatically validates Bakhtin's observation on culture:

> One must not [. . .] imagine the realm of culture as some sort of spatial whole, having boundaries but also having internal territory. The realm of culture has no internal territory: it is entirely distributed along the boundaries, boundaries pass everywhere, through its every aspect [. . .]. Every cultural act lives essentially on the boundaries: in this is its seriousness and its significance.[10]

Her literary exploration of these multiple, overlapping boundaries involves the creation of a poetic discourse that centres the peripheral, disturbs ethical distinctions, and engenders resistant readings, effectively creating its own frontiers by dividing readers into cultural insiders and outsiders. Her work – which has attracted a small but growing international readership and has been translated into five languages – thus has the potential to demarcate and remap the national imaginary through the juxtaposition of culturally and politically differentiated readings. As her readership widens, differently situated evaluations of Arasanayagam's presentation of landscape might serve to, in the words of James Duncan, 'defamiliarize the relationship between [. . .] landscapes, dominant ideologies, and political and social practices'.[11] My reading attempts to promote this enterprise by revealing the ways in which the spatial tropes of the garden and refugee camp serve to promote specific readings of selfhood in her work. I begin with an analysis of the construction of identity in relation to landscape in Arasanayagam's poetry and poetic fiction and then move on to consider the spatial idiomatics that structure belonging in her short stories and her unpublished play *The Captain has Come.*[12] I show how her poetic construction of a textual self and home successfully situates itself outside the boundaries of a territorially marked discourse while the dialogism of her prose works is inscribed by a territoriality that simultaneously serves to redraw the boundary between insiders and outsiders, dwellers and refugees. The rhetorical devices through which Arasanayagam establishes a dialogue between implied author and implied reader, and between textual selves, are integral to the construction of identity and nationhood in her work.

Landscapes of desire

Arasanayagam's work reveals a self-conscious construction of a poetic identity or textual self in and through landscape. This landscape, while regionally based (primarily in the central hill-country province of Kandy and the northern town of Navaly), is systematically flattened into an abstraction through a metaphoric impulse that mobilises it as a vehicle for self-discovery. In situating the construction of self through an abstracted landscape, Arasanayagam is able to draw upon a trope that transcends social, political and ethnically bounded constructions of identity. Landscape serves as a culturally transcendent metaphor for belonging in her work, one that simultaneously allows her to mark her close connection to the country of her birth while releasing her from the constraints of social identification. Two significant exceptions to this rule are to be found in her poem 'Nallur '82' and the collection of short stories *Peacocks and Dreams* (written in 1984; published 1996) – a mythopoeic reconstruction of her husband's childhood in Navaly in which sensuous imagery is used to evoke the young boy's spiritual ties with his birthplace in order to register the harshness of its later loss and destruction. In both cases Hindu mythology is central to the articulation of a culturally defined and differentiated landscape. Yet for the most part Arasanayagam's extensive oeuvre – in particular her poetry – eschews local identification. 'The land', is evoked in one short story as a place 'where the spirit was released of its constraints and found true freedom'.[13] Abstraction takes the form of metaphoric registers, most notably through reference to gardens and in particular through evoking the paradisiacal Garden of Eden. As Neloufer de Mel has pointed out, the Garden of Eden serves as a 'safe sanctuary' for the poetic self, 'its primeval cyclical temporality stand[ing] against the linearity/fracture' of the violent present.[14] In a poem on the 1971 insurgency Arasanayagam registers the impact of political violence in the country as an incursion into or destruction of this landscape:

> Blue foliage trembles in the pelting rain,
> Trees disappear in thick mists,
> Now there are no mountains
> Only falling rain
> And bloated bodies
> Casually drifting downriver.[15]

The garden is incorporated into the broader lexical landscape of a primeval natural world, beyond temporal and spatial limitation. In the short story 'The Witness', in which a gardener murders his two elderly female employers, the garden variously represents childhood innocence, a forgotten or lost paradise and the island nation itself. The landscape in which it is placed is not only deterritorialised – a place without boundary, where land and sky merge – but is also allegorised as it is shown to contain the seeds of an evil that is initially imperceptible to the narrator in her childhood, a veritable Garden of Eden. This mergence of a fixed Manichean morality with a timeless, generative temporal cycle is in danger of mythologising the island nation into the site of original sin – historical and political context become supplementary investments required of the reader:

> Valleys and hills merged into a peerless sky with no brushstrokes to separate or divide the world. There was no dichotomy in that landscape. Time had no laws. Only daylight and dark. Flowers opened out like poems. It was only later that the discovery of the flies, the insects entrapped in the viscous fluid of the deadly nightshade, were discovered. Too late for rescue. The early preoccupation with death began there in that discovery, listening to fairy tales that enchanted you with magic and sorcery. The entrance to a hidden world which contained the greater truths of good and evil. Knowledge could not be denied.[16]

This passage reveals the problematic use of an 'unpeopled' landscape as an index of both social and political change and personal development. Like the Garden of Eden – a symbolic register of lost innocence – the landscape serves as a marker of dissemblance and illusion, poisoned at inception from within. The narrator's initiation into the adult world of a bifurcated moral order – one split between Good and Evil – is related in clear, unambiguous terms, but the exact correspondence between this Manichean morality and the social and political coordinates that shape personal development remain unclear, in particular to cultural outsiders less familiar with the history of political violence in Sri Lanka. While those familiar with the genesis of the nation may well be able to read this tainted Eden through their knowledge of the post-Independence call for Sinhala supremacy and the rise of Tamil nationalism, others may well see in Arasanayagam's use of the trope a negative logic that rationalises the violence of the present through asserting its inevitability.

The escapist impulse in Arasanayagam's presentation of landscape – a fact evident in the passage in the narrator's desire for 'rescue', and by references throughout Arasanayagam's work to the search for refuge – can also serve to weaken the hermeneutic connection between the development of political violence and the narrator's own loss of innocence, while simultaneously investing greater moral urgency in the power of the narrative voice: 'for me, as a child, the garden was an unspoilt place until sin, synonymous with knowledge, entered'.[17] This metaphoric correspondence between an allegorical, morally saturated landscape and a naturalised, organic selfhood grants both moral authority and indigeneity to the narrator, furthering Arasanayagam's project to serve as the conscience of the nation. As she has made clear, her aim is not merely to write the nation but to rewrite it from the margins, and by so doing to speak the 'truth': 'As a writer I cannot expect to be partisan. My responsibility and commitment is to report and document the truth – whether it be massacres of minority or majority ethnic groups. I speak for humanity. [. . .] I speak for the victim, the sufferer. [. . .] My voice is the voice of minorities everywhere'.[18]

Thus, it could be argued that in melding moral and Edenic boundaries through a discourse of alienation and exile, Arasanayagam is able to decentre an originary hierarchy of monocultural authenticity and create a post-national textual self – a process that depends upon rendering landscape into a locus not only of growth, and regeneration, but also of ejection, expulsion and exile. Eden, an originary site of enforced expulsion, is a logical trope for the Christian-educated Arasanayagam to use in her bid to articulate her sense of rejection from the landscape through which she gains her sense of selfhood. It also serves to foreground her outsider status (as a minority Christian and product of colonial rule) and comes close to affirming a stance that is both 'orientalist' (Sri Lanka as the Garden of Eden) and nationalist (the idealisation of, and identification with, the land), revealing the overlapping of cultural boundaries (European and Sri Lankan), the connections between apparently opposed ideological perspectives (colonial and nationalist) and the simultaneity of historical registers (pre- and postcolonial), exposing the contradictory impulses that inform her work.

Expulsion and ethical uncertainty

An understanding of Arasanayagam's mythopoeic construction of landscape is thus central to an analysis of alienation in her work. The spiritual and emotional sustenance provided by the early identification with landscape is strongly conveyed in autobiographical passages where the physical delineaments of landscape and the corporeal self converge, such that 'within the oasis of the body [. . .] the trees fruited and nature procreated'.[19] In her autobiographical work Arasanayagam repeatedly provides a topography of selfhood in which self and landscape are affirmed as one: 'I touched my face and felt the ocean and the island in all its lineaments. The map had all the imprints of the self-made cartographer'.[20] Arasanayagam extends the metaphor of land as self in her poetry by exploring expulsion as a literal 'uprooting'. In 'Defeat' uprooting is materially inscribed as a physical expulsion from the womb of the earth, a form of deracination that links birth with death, burial with ejection, and which powerfully conveys the instability of belonging:

> This is where I stand
> Feeling the firm earth give,
> Sinking into the treacherous
> Hollows of shifting
> Sands,
>
> This was my territory
>   Once
> My roots were here
>   But plucked with bloodied hands
> Flung aside and scattered
>   Only the soil disturbed
> And wounded shows
>   The emptiness[21]

In 'Aftermath', another poem from the same collection, Arasanayagam reveals how the soil which had 'half ingested' her expels her as if it were impossible to absorb her whole:

> It seemed
> I knew this earth too well to feel
> Its heave and its revulsion
> Expel my half ingested being
> From its twisted guts[22]

This reference to being 'half ingested' suggests the instability of her borderland identity, an identity that is, paradoxically, partially produced by her very negotiation of belonging though landscape. As Robert Crawford has pointed out, 'Identity (including, I would contend, the poetic identity which allows a poet to identify with a particular territory) always lives through and is determined by a "debatable land", a shifting, dynamic, border territory'.[23] Here belonging, registered through the visceral rooting in the land, is ruptured by a metaphorically rationalised marker of her hybrid identification in which, as a Sri Lankan of mixed heritage, she is only half-absorbed into the country.

Within the context of the social and material devastation of war, the destruction of towns and villages (some of which Arasanayagam had seen for herself) in a land contaminated by violence and her own displacement and exile, the logic of Arasanayagam's chosen trope of landscape as the metaphoric register of belonging and identity can lead her to only one conclusion: the destruction of self itself. Hence the social and cultural rejection that culminated in her physical ejection from her home in the riots of 1983 gains literary articulation through the exploration of both alienation *and* physical obliteration. *Out of Our Prisons We Emerge* (1987), a later collection of poems written in exile in Scotland, explores this dual eviction from self and landscape:

> There could never now be a return
> to that garden I so fondly imagined
> to be real how can a ghost go back
> to walk in sunlight
>
> even the leaves will not stir
> as I pass through and the light
> hardly quiver, the shimmering reptiles
> will not now recoil from me but slither
> between the stones that do not feel
> the glide of my diffusion[24]

Here, as before, rupture from an imagined landscape serves as a marker of loss of selfhood but with one key development: the interiority of the earlier landscape is acknowledged and serves to magnify the physical presence of a new landscape contaminated by 'shimmering reptiles'. In an increasingly territorialised land, Arasanayagam's experience of being 'divided among the divided'[25] leads her to the stark conclusion (in a poem published four years later) that 'I have no country now but self'.[26]

Expelled from the land, Arasanayagam's nebulous construction of a liminal textual identity disintegrates into what Chelva Kanaganayakam has described as an 'orchestration of voices' where 'the literal merges with the metaphoric, the formal with the colloquial and the solemn with the comic'.[27] It is often discordant, recording, according to Norman Simms, not so much 'the precise poetic statement, the well-turned phrase or well-made metaphor' but rather the 'new discourse of poetry traumatized by massacres, bombs, disruptions to normal life' 'a condition where normal (normative) discourses must be held under erasure'.[28] Neloufer de Mel has questioned the extent of Arasanayagam's linguistic innovation, claiming, in my view correctly, that some of her work is overwritten;[29]

yet both Simms and Ellen Dissanayake have emphasised the fluid, protean energy of her poetry, with its cascading lines and 'slippery syntaxed lavishness'.[30] It is as if in playing the chequerboard of different genes Arasanayagam has dismantled more than the barriers of historically contingent ethnic identities and transgressed the proprieties of lyrical expression – the overwriting so obvious in her poetry, a product of her untrammelled desire to find habitation in a country that lacks the will or desire to accommodate her. It is an expression of selfhood that substantiates Radhakrishnan's claim that postcolonial hybridity is marked not only by extreme pain and agonising dislocation but also by the need to compile 'a laborious "inventory of one's self" in order to gain political legitimacy for a complex genealogy.[31]

Hers is a poetry of excess,[32] one that fully explores and reveals the interconnections between boundaries – ethnic, linguistic, historical and spatial – showing us, in Bakhtin's words, that in 'the realm of culture [. . .] boundaries pass everywhere'. The force of Arasanayagam's poetry lies in the way it compels Sri Lankan readers in English – including members of the ruling class – to address their own boundary marking. By throwing the reader into a dehistoricised, deterritorialised, fluid landscape mobilised by violence alone, these readers experience a loss of bearings that can only be recuperated by an act of negotiation with the subjective speaking voice. In 'Bullets that Smash Through Screens' Arasanayagam uses pronominal slippage to draw the reader into a garish scene of bullet-ridden bodies and then proceeds to unsettle the boundaries between victim and aggressor. The subtle slide in subject positioning from victim to Tamil militant (identified by a cyanide capsule) to anonymous citizen and potential aggressor and finally – with force – to a composite identity melding victim and militant, compels the reader to negotiate a morally unstable world in which the only certainty remains the reality of brute violence and inevitable death:

> we carry poison
> round our necks to sweeten death
> rather than let the ear scream with
> the pain of cracking bone and searing flesh
> we carry poison in us, so that we can hate
> that which betrays our humaness (sic) [. . .]
> we are the walking
> shadows of our fleshless souls
> our voices brief the bullet cuts off
> tongues that utter words but taste
> the final sorrow of death's bitter feasts[33]

The violence within the poem has no edges. The boundary between victim and aggressor is always blurred, and the poem has a nomadic moral perspective that demands a constant renegotiation and redefinition of responsibility, agency, suffering and – ultimately – identity itself. Even the spectral presence of the suicide bomber emerges ('the walking / Shadows of our fleshless souls') in and through the form of the living dead. Identity is mobilised through a tortuous chain of connections but the deferral of identity does not lead to the redemption of survival. There is no easy dichotomy of good and evil in this poem, no simplistic reduction of the complexity of violence. Rather, Arasanayagam is articulating what might be called the poetics of complicity – a sense in which the readers, whatever their ethnic or political affiliations, are at once victims and oppressors. In itself, this might seem unremarkable, but within the polarised context of Sri Lankan cultural politics it is deeply subversive.

Arasanayagam's work thus challenges narrow nationalist inscriptions in key ways: her sensuous response to landscape is both a critique of the reification of territory and a register of her physical presence and belonging to the landscape. Her right to be there is inalienable as belonging is emphatically asserted through being and becoming. Within such a context the dissolution of self stands an index of cultural disintegration as the nation's inability to accommodate her is registered as central to its rupture. While her work resists ethnically marked readings it has, as indicated earlier, been consistently so positioned by some critics, who analyse her mediation of Burgher and Tamil identity with little attention to the broader dynamic of a subjectivity struggling against the erasure imposed by such territorial markings. The constant shifts in subjective speaking voice found in her work describes a restless search for formal resolution, for finding the right expression for her subject, and are evident in her repeated return to the same subject from different genres. The need to renegotiate her identity, to 'find again / New brightness from a self created firmament',[34] results in a self-interrogation that is reflected in the formal properties of her writing.

Her construction of a poetic textual self involves a form of internal dialogue, such that she has described her own work as 'a kind of self-questioning a [. . .] private dialogue with myself'.[35] Poems such as 'Medusa' and 'Narcissus' register what Bakhtin has described as the 'nonself-sufficiency' of the self in which 'a person has no sovereign internal territory, he is wholly and always on the boundary; looking inside himself, he looks *into the eyes of another* or with *the eyes of another*'.[36] In 'Medusa' Arasanayagam plays with the boundaries of self, destabilising markers of difference and alterity by directly addressing her readers, reflecting their alienating gaze in ways that require its internalisation: 'It is your own fear, not fear of me / that turns you into rock'.[37] In 'Narcissus' the registers of incestuous self-absorption – 'where self entwined with self becomes / Its own inamorata' – are shown to be impossible to maintain. The poem explores the split subjectivity of both the implied author and the implied reader resulting in a doubling of identity so that the gaze of the implied author is refracted and reflected through the eyes of the reader, splintering to reveal 'a myriad faces' and dislocating desire ('Friends that are ghosts and lovers strangers'), before the final rupture:

> No longer the image in the mirror
> Teases thought, enamoured by incestuous passions
> Where self entwined with self becomes
> Its own inamorata, now the mirror shows

A myriad faces and through their eyes
Appear a thousand others to tantalise
And set ablaze the frozen fire of silver vein.
Time reveals to a heart estranged
Friends that are ghosts and lovers strangers.
Suddenly the pool grows black
The eyes that watch, close
Blind in darkness and the mirror cracks.[38]

Arasanayagam's self-questioning unsettles the Manichean model of the world found in her originary Garden of Eden and compels her to explore the permeability of moral boundaries. 'Personae' follows a sliding moral trajectory as the overtly reprehensible crime of murder is paralleled with the seemingly softer crimes of silence (in which the silence of the oppressor is horrifyingly melded with the silence of the murdered victim) and wilful blindness, culminating in the shocking gratification of seeing the death:

Have you ever killed, tell me?
Or burnt or slashed?
Does the bullet speed away from you
Like a bird takes wing to nest
Within a body warm with blood
[. . .]

Have you ever killed, tell me?
Or burnt or smashed or axed
Hated a stranger one like you
Turned his face into a searing mask
And watched his eyeball
Like a whirling comet
Drowning in sockets of blood?

Have you ever been silent tell me?
When words you must speak out
Choke you and clog your throat
To drink the bitter gall and vomit
Till your guts twist and writhe
With the poison of guilt and hate.

Have you ever turned away from those
Tell me, who once were friends
Avert your gaze from ruined homes
And piled up bodies licked by flames
Or have you gazed and gazed
With eyes of lust upon the dead
The dying and the burning.[39]

Here the power of direct address compels resident readers and those close to political events in the country into an awareness of their own imbrication and complicity in crimes of war. The interpellation results in the presencing of the reader within the arena of conflict, transforming each witness to murder into a perpetrator, one who is subject to the cosmically comprehending gaze of the dying victim within the pornography of violence. Reading her work is an uncomfortable experience, particularly for those who have remained silent witnesses to war, and does much to explain the distance or disapproval of some resident critics to her work. In later poems, such as 'The death carvers', 'The stubborn image' and 'Interrogation', Arasanayagam uses the comfortable and inclusive 'we' to seduce the reader into sharing a perspective that is morally uncertain:

> We talk as if it is another country
> The harsh rock of flesh hacked with hatchets
> The secret men with masks who belong to bloodnights
> The death carvers, but no blade is delicate enough
> To chisel something that gives like moss
> What adheres can be scraped off with fingernails
> Someone has to wipe the blades clean
> Remove the smell of blood[40]

Here, as elsewhere, the collective pronoun serves to draw the reader into a sense of community before the moral dissociation from the death carvers is ruptured by the acknowledgement that the guilt for the killings cannot be contained by those who wield the knife; the moral weight of the crimes exceeds, spills over and cascades beyond the boundaries of identification onto the reader whose visceral connection to the flesh 'that gives like moss', collecting under the fingernails, is powerfully brought to bear onto an identification with the intractably anonymous 'someone' who wipes the blades clean.

Arasanayagam's work thus creates its own boundaries of belonging – to understand her work, to identify with it, requires a cultural and political awareness that offers immediate and direct access to a moral domain demarcated by victimhood. Her work resists easy assimilation by the political ingénue or the cultural outsider who are likely to be confused by the play on borderless decontextualised subjectivities. Instead it is directed at those who are all too aware of the political violence in Sri Lanka; to be admitted entry into it automatically results in an interpellation that thrusts upon the reader a moral responsibility and social conscience, enforcing an understanding of the borderlessness of political agency. What is more, the moral integrity of a victim subject is itself unsettled by the guilt that accompanies surviving where others have died: 'my fear is that escape / From martyrdom makes our complexion and / Our stature, coward'.[41]

Such poetry is richly hybridised and dialogised, creating connections and dialogues across social communities by drawing upon a shared history and shared cultural and moral norms, but its very hybridity also effectively makes it countercultural in its refusal to grant moral or agentive autonomy to subjectivities differentiated by armed conflict. While all readers are admitted to the authorial audience, privileged access is only granted to those who reside within the context which made armed conflict possible, creating a hierarchy of readership that is determined by moral responsibility. The borderless world of Arasanayagam's poetry thus serves to generate its own borders – ones based upon political and cultural contiguity with a clearly defined historical terrain. It is a mode of representation that contrasts dramatically with the cultural geography of many of her short stories and of her play. In these, as I will now show, Arasanayagam blatantly registers the search for sanctuary in a territorially defined land.

Territoriality and the refugee

A land becomes a territory through the imposition of political power. Arasanayagam's work registers this fact in three collections of short stories written since the outbreak of war, *All is Burning* (1995), *In the Garden Secretly* (2000) and *The Dividing Line* (2002), and in an unpublished play, *The Captain has Come*. In these Arasanayagam explores the experience of political displacement, centralising it and in so doing reveals, in the words of Daniel Sibony, every place to be 'a potential of displacements'.[42] It is a position that has revolutionary potential, paralleling as it does James Clifford's observations, noted by Karen Fog Olwig, that cultural sites are created through the interplay between 'dwelling and traveling, presence and absence, localizing and globalizing' and are defined by human relations.[43] In other words, Arasanayagam's focus on displacement within a territorially bounded landscape has the potential to present displacement (a form of dwelling *in* travelling) as a generative site for the construction of new social relations and the creation of new contexts of belonging. As will be seen, her stories and play explore this possibility but do so in terms constrained by the discourse of territoriality.

While, as has been seen, Arasanayagam's emotional affiliation with the land is registered through a morally channelled connection with the natural world, a place that is emphatically *not* a social space lying outside the boundaries of a geographically bounded territorial discourse, her political affiliation with the land is marked by her historical sense of 'tenantship' in the country – a condition that, as Neloufer de Mel has observed, is related to her Burgher ancestry.[44] Such tenantship invokes a notion of temporary residence, of mobile accommodation rather than fixed and certain ownership – a mode of dwelling made all the more precarious by the alienated mode of being that is central to her construction of subjectivity. The mobile habitat and subjectivity so central to Arasanayagam's mapping of land and self in her poetry are starkly territorialised in most of her short fiction and in her play. In my view this is related in large measure to the formal constraints Arasanayagam is subject to. Unlike lyric poetry, which allows for the gradual unfolding and expansion of the textual self into a limitless territory of metaphoric resonance, the realist form of the short story and play chosen by Arasanayagam demand social and historical situatedness and individuated subjectivity. Context matters, characters count, and Arasanayagam is compelled to bring to bear on her autobiographically centred vision an external register of belonging that accommodates the language of ethnic differentiation and political division. Thus, in contrast to the effusive excess of her poetry, Arasanayagam's prose is journalistic and disjointed, in which 'the stunted, even stunned, quality of the language mimic [. . .] brutalisation'.[45] It is also significant that most of Arasanayagam's poetry on her experience of being a refugee is uncharacteristically spare.[46] In a speech delivered at the British Council in 1987 she has articulated this sense of division by drawing directly on her experience of the refugee camp:

> I see the whole country being divided into camps – some of the barriers being visible, others invisible [. . .] Majority and minority ethnic groups find themselves in an ever widening territory of refugee camps [. . .] as well as military camps. [. . .] There seems hardly room for a man to walk outside of these camps – it engenders a feeling of 'nomadism'.[47]

Thus while gardens are the principal register of bounded landscape in her poetry, camps are the central trope of contained dwelling in her prose. Further, while gardens are encoded allegorically, offering a multilayered writing of landscape that is open to multiple meanings, and successive rewritings and overwritings, the refugee camp is a synecdochic marker of national space, particularising the experience of political expulsion. This shift in the narrative encoding of land and space marks a corresponding shift in the encoding of identity; Arasanayagam's explicit assumption of the discourse of territoriality in her short stories reveals a desire to situate the narrative subject as a politically scripted body, for as Ericksen has shown, 'the concept of territorial determination takes on meaning only to the extent of understanding human species as self-markers'.[48]

'The Dividing Line', 'Fear: Meditations in a Camp' and *The Captain has Come*, all draw upon Arasanayagam's experience as a refugee in 1983. All of them are fragmented in form, offering vignettes that present multiple experiences of displacement, resisting any overarching allegorising of displacement as a singular condition. By this means displacement is presented not so much as a universal human condition (a presentation that might allow for a mobile structuration of national space) but as a historically situated consequence of war – a socially fracturing experience that does violence to the victim, effacing individual identity into collective anonymity. The texts dramatise the way in which territoriality is self-generating and can escalate exponentially, perpetuating itself by further deterritorialising and reterritorialising social and cultural space. The refugee camp is a place where 'demographic maps were being set up',[49] a place that is partially domesticated by the women, who gather to wash clothes and cook food, but nevertheless a place of estrangement, of enforced intimacy and new barricades, a 'no man's land where [. . .] the victims themselves had set their boundaries'[50] and 'chairs were arranged like a stockade to give them privacy'.[51] This gains expression in the territorial discourse and segregated spatial arrangements of the play *The Captain has Come*. Here internal social divisions within the Tamil community are evident as the hierarchy of caste divides refugees further: some Tamils refuse to share the communal water tap while others acquiesce (p. 49), fracturing time-honoured social customs and serving to create the basis for new connections and divisions. The failure of these connections to create a community is central to the dynamic of despair activating the text, repeatedly revealing the way in which the individual is further fractured by the experience of physical constraint:

> Space is restricted here [. . .] but from day to day your needs become less and less. There isn't enough space to stretch out your limbs, so you learn to sit with your legs drawn up to give someone else a little extra room. . .lie crouched up so your legs don't touch someone else's head. [. . .] You can't create private islands in a camp. [. . .] somehow it seems wrong, morally wrong to be able to stretch out your limbs here, encroach and not share whatever little space the other has.[52]

The logic of territorialism and territoriality permeates these texts. Arasanayagam does not offer any alternative discourse, but rather explores spatial constraint as a catalyst for spiritual regeneration. The refugee camp is, significantly, situated in a school, and Arasanayagam uses this symbolic space to re-vision the territorialised nation as a site of learning and individual growth; the refugees' rehabilitation in their new identity is shown to mark an initiation into knowledge. Unlike the Garden of Eden, however, the politicised 'sanctuary' of the refugee camp serves to offer rebirth into a clearly nationalised identity, one that is simultaneously inside and outside the boundaries of political legitimacy:

> What then was the practicality of becoming and surviving as a non-person? One's needs had to create a space, even minimal, that would accommodate the physical body. A staked out territory with invisible walls. [. . .] One would learn to live within the limitations imposed on oneself so as not to impinge on the territory of others. So one would lay out with as much precision as possible, the sheets of newspaper or the single cotton sheet on the measured square feet of one's abode. It would become not merely the reprieve from the battlefield but a striving to attain nirvana, that desired world of non-being.[53]

There is a subtle paradox at play here: the 'non-self' referred to is at once the person denied individual rights on account of lying outside the boundaries of the legitimating national narrative (and thereby granted a confirmation of identity on this basis – becoming a refugee, as Arasanayagam herself has pointed out, confirms one's outsider status[54]) *and* a condition of existence that grants direct entry and acceptance into the national narrative of Buddhist hegemony in which Nirvana is a spiritual ideal. That incorporation into the Sinhala Buddhist cultural order is only possible by a process of self-immolation remains the ultimate irony.

Yet several of Arasanayagam's stories resist such culturally constrained readings. In 'Fragments from a Journey' and 'The Crossing', migration across territorial boundaries registers a spiritual transition or samsaric journey involving a shedding of negative emotions and human desires[55] – a metaphor linking Buddhist and Hindu cosmologies – and 'Exodus' makes forceful connections with the Biblical episode from which it draws its title.[56] These multicultural connections extend Arasanayagam's reading of expulsion, displacement and migration beyond a politicised national space into the spatially and temporally transcendent context of the global diaspora. The discourse of territoriality is central to her rationale for exceeding the bounds of cartographic constraint, projecting the human body as more than just a marker of politicised place but as a sanctified land or sanctuary that lies beyond the national narrative:

> I had only the country of myself to return to where no flag of conquest would ever fly. The territory of my uninvaded self. Where I would finally discard that archival documentation from an identity scrawled in hieroglyphics of blood. Nameless. Anonymous. Dismissing the archaic language of that identity, no longer duped by history's forgeries of name and lineage. This was the final truth. The choice of route. Maneuvering the vessel of myself to voyage out, explore, discover, but never, never to lay claim to or acquire territory or set up boundaries.[57]

Here Arasanayagam returns to and reverses the colonial trajectory inscribed in her ancestral history, erasing imperial conquest by replacing the divisive discourse of territoriality with the mergent scripture of migration. The recourse to privileging the integrity of an 'uninvaded self' reconciles the political with the allegorical, the territorial reclamation of the physical body as a self-marker with the allegorical impulses of fractured poetic subjectivity, and presents the displaced subject as a creative agent in the construction of new cartographies and new routes. The reification of territory that has dominated the discursive production of the nation since the start of the civil war is thus not simply rejected by allegorical evasion (as it is in much of her poetry) but here is directly absorbed to define a new cartography – one that acknowledges the internalisation of territorial impositions within the migrant subject so that a refugee camp becomes 'a mental state'.[58] It is a rationale that is absorbed into her definition of the uninvaded subject. Arasanayagam's work powerfully communicates the way in which the landscape and the nation are discursively produced and territorialised, revealing the way in which such territorialisation is imbricated in the construction of subjectivity. As part of an ethnic community 'that is now almost extinct'[59] and linked to another that is struggling for its inclusion in the national narrative, her identity is doubly marked by an erasure which can only be effectively carried out in the wastelands of critical neglect or diminution.

5 Carl Muller

Genealogical maps

Carl Muller is probably Sri Lanka's most versatile anglophone writer. A former signalman in the navy, he went on to become a journalist in 1964, working in newspapers in Sri Lanka and the Middle East and later as a political columnist for the *Lanka Monthly Digest*. He came to prominence with his award winning novel *The Jam Fruit Tree* (1993) and has written a further five novels, three volumes of poetry, short stories, several monographs and collections of essays, experimenting with genre, style and dialect. His work straddles historical novels, satiric poetry, epic saga, personal and political essays, cultural biography and science fiction, encompassing a plurivocity that suggests that he, like Rushdie's Grimus, is trying to find a suitable voice to speak in. It repeatedly transgresses the boundaries of fact, fiction, and myth, personal and public history employing, in his Burgher trilogy, a mongrelised Sri Lankan English idiom that is explicitly related to his own hybrid status as a Burgher of mixed ancestry. Yet despite the virtuosity of his linguistic excess, most evident in *The Jam Fruit Tree* and *Children of the Lion* (1997), and the generic multiplicity of his oeuvre, a clear and consistent method of explicating the past is evident in his texts – one that, despite his self-professed ambition to be a 'dig in the universal rib',[1] appears to contain reactionary and even nationalist implications.

This paradoxical melding of carnivalesque linguistic subversion and ideological conservatism – its double-codedness – is central to my reading of his work. For the very 'flaws' in his writing – their inconsistencies, excesses and paradoxes – register the very intransigence of cultural taxonomies that determine the terms of national affiliation. Unlike Arasanayagam – whose work clearly registers the need to find new terms of belonging in her capacity to claim for herself the ethnicity of another – Muller reveals a sneaking respect for inherited categories of belonging evident in his preoccupation with legitimacy, ancestry, historical succession and pedigree. This preoccupation does not merely check but also, as I will show, informs, directs and determines the very form and expression of his more radical impulses. One of the most interesting paradoxes in his work – and one central to this chapter – is that while it explicitly explores the construction of cultural, racial and ethnic difference, it simultaneously assumes and exhorts the value of gender difference. This difference is fundamental to his social vision, the single certainty in an unstable present. Boundaries in his work thus play along the margins of a biological difference that has ideological affinities with colonial constructions of 'race', such that sexual differentiation is central to the negotiability of cultural interchange providing the very basis upon which a distinct cultural or racial group gets defined and legitimated.

Muller's varied textual strategies serve to open up key 'discursive spaces', to use Scott's felicitous phrase, in the writing of the nation. His significant investment in discursive hybridity delineates an alter-native linguistic register that marks a dislocated space in the national narrative. What is more the ideological tension in his work replicates the contrasting ideological impulses – assimilationist and dialectical – of what Young, after Bahktin, has described as organic and dialectical hybridity.[2] Organic hybridity, according to Young, is broadly assimilationist in its cultural logic whereas dialogic hybridity is dialectical. These forms are, of course, not mutually exclusive – the difference is one of degree rather than of kind – but the distinction remains a useful one as it reveals the close connection between discourse and constructions of place, the way in which language marks out alternative dwelling places in literature. Organic hybridity, for example, is central to the idiom, the socio-historical context and the representation of genealogy in *The Jam Fruit Tree*, a novel set in the hybridised space of a Colombo suburb. As in Kureishi's *The Buddha of Suburbia*, the novel is propelled by an assimilationist cultural logic, marking out a transgressive space of excess occupied by those who cannot or will not be contained by the regulatory dynamic of a normative metropolitan centre. Conversely, dialogic hybridity in Muller results in an explicitly hierarchical representation of subject–space relations. His representation of Colombo, in his biographical anthropomorphisation of the city in a 'novel' of the same name,[3] is clearly divided between a diurnal space of commerce and a nocturnal underworld.

Yet despite this apparently playful engagement with hybridity in discourse, race and culture, Muller's affirmation of cultural pluralism is contained within a broader discourse that endorses Sinhala cultural and political hegemony marking an insertion of difference that disturbs but does not disrupt the dominant narrative of Sinhala Buddhist hegemony. It reaches its culmination in his monumental epic, *Children of the Lion*, a novel that explicitly endorses Sinhala Buddhist nationalism within the cultural logic of accommodation. The text is generically a pastiche, juxtaposing a variety of discourses in a totalising, inclusive gesture of national reconstruction and cultural reclamation. Written in the wake of R.A.L.H. Gunawardana's seminal essay 'People of the Lion' it marks both a continuity and a break from its predecessor, emphasising the historical continuities affirmed by the former while simultaneously suggesting possibilities for alternative discursive paradigms. Ultimately the teleological, hagiographic thrust of the novel magnifies the nationalist rhetoric which fuels it, serving to endorse a unique, differentiated 'Sinhala' identity.[4] Yet Muller's overt mythologisation, his emphasis on text as performance, marks a radical break from Gunawardana's presentation of history as an objective representation of the past.[5] It is this double-coded nature of Muller's work that opens up what Scott has called a 'problem space' for new questions to be asked of nationalist discourse in Sri Lankan literature. For like Gunawardana, Muller grants:

> in principle, a natural or necessary link between past identities and the legitimacy of present political claims[. . .], grants in principle that consciousness can have an 'age' reiterable or changeable across the self-succession of time [. . .] grants in principle that a politics of the present can be wagered on a reconstruction of what community might have been in the past[6]

while, at the same time, revealing those very communal identities to be hybridised products of specific discursive strategies. Muller's text thus marks a significant shift in contemporary literary discourse on ethnic identity and nationalism in its implicit resistance to the uncritical application of contemporary categories of identification – such as ethnicity, race and religious affiliation – onto historical events which were shaped and informed by prior taxonomies of belonging *and* its simultaneous endorsement of these terms in its promotion of Sinhala claims to sovereignty.[7] As Scott succinctly reminds us, 'History appears to us today in Sri Lanka [. . .] as the natural and sovereign horizon of adjudication for rival claims about community'.[8] Muller's epic reveals the evolution and contingency of ethnic identities and inserts them into a historical continuum of communal development that, paradoxically, grants them historical and political legitimacy.

Almost all Muller's work follows a linear, teleological logic: the picaresque biographies of Sonnaboy and his family in his best known novel *The Jam Fruit Tree*, the collapse of empire in *Colombo* and the emergence of a unified Sinhala nation in *Children of the Lion*.[9] In mapping the country historically, connecting place with ancestry and lineage, Muller succeeds in spatialising and personalising history, constructing a genealogical map of the nation that is rooted in the politics of the present. The preoccupation with genealogy and lineage is shared by other Burgher writers: Ondaatje's *Running in the Family* and Arasanayagam's self-conscious interrogation of her Burgher past in *Inheritance* and *A Nice Burgher Girl* testify to the fact that for Burgher writers the relationship to the land is mediated by blood ties. History for these writers is a question of genealogy, perhaps because their genealogy itself is so open to question, revealing a spectrum of responses that span a movement from what Radhakrishnan has referred to as the comfortable transnationalism of 'metropolitan hybridity' to the agonistic self-production of 'postcolonial hybridity'.[10] In a country where ethnic affiliations have become rigidly encoded (and simultaneously contested) in relation to ancestry, the position of the Burghers – the only group whose identity is based upon explicit hybridity – is an embattled one. The response of Burgher writers to this position has varied from comic acceptance of the radical uncertainty of ancestry in Ondaatje's *Running in the Family* to the well-researched self-inventory and agonistic evaluation of the political implications of the colonial inheritance found in Arasanayagam's work. Muller's response is rather different. As will be seen his engagement with genealogy is mediated by an acute anxiety *for* ancestry, a desire to affirm seemingly legitimate connections in the face of the apparent illegitimacy marked by his own hybrid status, and it is marked by its displacement into a historical register that works towards affirming a homogenous reading of culture.

What is more genealogy is patriarchally inscribed in Muller's work. His insistence on patrilineal bloodlines results in a discourse that affirms a gender hierarchy which is used to simultaneously mask and unmask other markers of identity, such as ethnicity and language. Women's bodies mark the boundaries of racial, ethnic and national affiliation; they are territories whose invasion and occupancy determine male national allegiance. In a corresponding logic, there is an implicit assumption that men's role is to regulate female behaviour and that women's virtue is central to determining the moral well-being of the nation. As a result, textual hybridity in Muller's work serves to simultaneously deride and uphold the value of racial purity.

Liminality in Muller's work is limited and provisional: restricted to those areas that do not directly challenge the grand narrative of legitimated Sinhala supremacy. Thus it is possible for Muller to emphatically insist that Sri Lanka is Dhammadipa – the land of the Buddha's teaching – and simultaneously assert that it is a country where Burghers belong, for both these configurations present an assimilationist model of the nation – one that inscribes hybridity *in* hierarchy. This anomaly is discussed in Chapter 9, my conclusion to this volume, but for now I wish to consider the specific repercussions it has on how belonging gets negotiated in Muller's work. For the Burgher writer, whose main language is English, is both privileged and compromised by having a comprador's relation to colonialism. The ambivalence of being a member of a once privileged (but now culturally disenfranchised) minority results in a curious affirmation of compromised belonging – an element that Charles Sarvan has drawn attention to in his analysis of Muller's Burgher trilogy:

> The Burghers were essentially apolitical. Where Ceylon itself was concerned, they were 'distressed' by independence and the departure of the British (*Once Upon a Tender Time*, 193), for their wish was that colonial rule would continue indefinitely. Still, Muller paradoxically insists that the Burghers knew how to belong, that they had 'accepted, centuries ago, that Sri Lanka was their land [as well]' and were 'as native as the most strident Sinhala native' (*Jam Fruit Tree*, 137). There was no going back for the Burghers; they would never be outcasts (*Yakada Yaka*, 229). And yet the Burghers had cast themselves out by staying within their group, ignoring rather than mastering the Sinhala language, rejecting Sinhalese culture. So it is that, contradictorily, and despite assertions about being 'native', the characters in the trilogy, unaware of [the] implications, see the Sinhalese as the 'true people' (*Jam Fruit Tree*, 27) to whom the country belongs. The implication is that the Burghers themselves, despite the centuries, are outsiders, that Ceylon is not their true home – though it is the only home they have ever known. The discourse is contradictory: in Althusserian terms, a problematic which needs to be probed.[11]

It is a 'contradiction' that goes some way to explaining the empathetic, if revisionary, affirmation of Buddhist culture and thought in Ondaatje's *Anil's Ghost*. In the case of Muller, a writer who is more openly political than Ondaatje, it results in a tension between the affirmation of Burgher identity as a site of hybridity and cultural intermixing, and the celebration of Sinhala Buddhist hegemony found in *Children of the Lion*. Between Burgher hybridity and Sinhala Buddhist hegemony can be found a complex cultural taxonomy that is based upon a notion of exclusivity that is central to the discourse of hybridity itself. Muller, who considers himself a 'third class Burgher', draws upon a protean range of linguistic registers to communicate his own ambivalent status.[12] His affirmation of the degenerate Burgher in the trilogy implicitly affirms moral values, such as sexual abstinence and tee-totalism, identified with (but of course not necessarily followed by) the Sinhalese Buddhist majority. When it is impossible to accommodate Burgher ex-centricity, for example in a text that eulogises Sinhala identity, Muller replaces organic linguistic hybridity where 'the mixture merges and is fused into a new language'[13] with dialogic linguistic hybridity. Thus in *Children of the Lion*, his most ambitious text to date, Muller abandons the organic hybridity and linguistic syncretism of the trilogy for a dialectical, double-coded discourse that contrasts the elegance and sophistry of religious and courtly epic with the explicit sexual invective and gratuitous salaciousness of pornographic literature.

Muller uses both forms of linguistic hybridity to foreground the link between transgressive sexual desire and compromised bloodlines. This is entirely in keeping with the ideological underpinning of hybridised discourse and reveals the full extent of Muller's investment in it. For hybridised discourse – in all its permutations – is indissolubly linked to the material and cultural reality of racial hybridity or miscegenation. As Robert Young has pointed out in his study of the colonial encounter, 'the historical links between language and sex were [. . .] fundamental. Both produced what were regarded as "hybrid" forms (creole, pidgin and miscegenated children), which were seen to embody threatening forms of perversion and degeneration'.[14] Young goes on to offer an explanation for the political polarities in Muller's work in an astute observation on the ideological paradox that lies at the core of hybridised discourse. Hybridity, he claims, can be 'invoked to imply contrafusion and disjunction (or even separate development) as well as fusion and assimilation'.[15] The duality of Muller's prose, its seemingly contradictory logic, is explained here. I will now develop this notion of contradictory impulses in hybridity to explore the ways in which they come to be neutralised and contained in Muller's controversial representation of female sexuality.

Hybridity: gender and genealogy

> Hybridity as a cultural description will always carry with it an implicit politics of heterosexuality.
>
> Robert Young, *Colonial Desire*[16]

Carl Muller's work has elicited both critical acclaim and outrage for its bawdy presentation of sexual relations. A self-confessed rebel who was expelled from three schools and briefly imprisoned for disorderly behaviour when working as a signalman in the Royal Ceylon Navy,[17] Muller deliberately challenges normative sexual codes, playfully celebrating sexual excess, transgression (such as homosexuality, incest, underage sex and, in *Children*, bestiality) and linguistic ribaldry. The energy of his prose relies in large measure on this focus on the sexual activities of his characters. He first made his mark recounting the hedonistic lives of the von Bloss family in *The Jam Fruit Tree.*[18] The novel was written in direct response to Penguin India's claim that they were looking for 'a Burgher book, like Michael Ondaatje writes'. Muller's decision to give them 'what they wanted with knobs on'[19] led to family dissension (the story was loosely autobiographical) and critical acclaim in the form of the first Gratiaen award. In the novel the connection between linguistic and sexual play is strong. For example the banter after Anna's marriage to the Sinhalese Colontota fuses the desire to test sexual, racial and linguistic boundaries:

> [. . .] a bunch of ladies huddled in the bedroom to watch the bride change and finger the lace and feel the satin and say ooh and aah and giggle and whisper. Mavis Lappan couldn't contain herself. 'So what you do when he coming to sleep in the night?'
>
> Anna turned scarlet. '*Chee*, men, as if you don't know.'
>
> 'Yes,' said Lalla Boniface, 'but Sinhalese fellows have black ones, no? And long also.'
>
> 'So never mind. Anyway, Mister Colontota not so dark,' said Anna.
>
> 'That's sure, quite fair he is. Must be doing same way like Burghers, no?'
>
> [. . .] Dora Marwick sighed and said, 'I also feel like going with Sinhalese boy. Or Muslim'
>
> '*Chee*, now Anna marry Sinhalese, everybody getting mad or what?'
>
> 'Burgher boys nice, men. But when marry only want to drink and do. Can see, no? Even Mama say can't with Papa. Only last week she telling that she tired of going to maternity home and Papa don't know when to stop.'
>
> 'Yes, men. And when coming home drunk won't even eat and sleep. [. . .] Whole time squeezing his thing and saying where's your mother. No shame, men.' [pp. 56–57]

Hybridity is written palimpsestically here: the physical and material otherness of gender difference is used to unmask the culturally constructed otherness of race, colour and ethnicity. The language follows a syncretic impulse of creolisation, enacting a subversive politics by marking a decentred discourse that destabilises the dominant culture through its very differentiation. The 'delicious titbits' (p. 57) that make up much of the narrative constitute an alternative linguistic register whose boundaries of acceptability are informed by the 'shame' of the moral majority represented by the Sinhalese.

At the heart then of Muller's linguistic subversion and presentation of sexual anarchy is a reactionary affirmation of Sinhala cultural dominance. Neluka Silva has taken this point further and claimed that Muller's presentation of Burgher sexual promiscuity subscribes to an essentialist logic that endorses the colonial stereotype of the Burgher as the 'degenerate outsider',[20] a person who occupies the moral margins of the national narrative. She takes Muller to task for his depiction of women in particular, claiming that he ignores the historical realities of pioneering professional Burgher women of colonial Ceylon. While it is hard not to concur with Silva here, it is, in my view, both necessary and salutary to consider whether the gendered racial essentialism to be found in *The Jam Fruit Tree* and its successors might not itself be a by-product of the form of hybrid discourse to which Muller subscribes. In other words, the anarchic emphasis on Burgher breeding, inbreeding and cross-breeding, where 'every blood infusion and transfusion made them stronger, more virile' (p. 29), depends for its definition on the antithetical notion of a fixed, stable and unified cultural homogeneity. The overtly contestatory notion of hybridity is thus always provisional, contained within a dialectical logic of otherness. In these terms, Muller's essentialist presentation of Burgher women is carrying the logic of hybrid discourse to its inevitable conclusion; in presenting them all as sexually active agents of the procreative impulse he is simply inverting the logic of colonial desire which seeks to situate them as sexual subjects of procreation. Hybridity is presaged on an essentialised discourse of gender identification, its very construction based on the assumption of normative heterosexual reproduction.[21] Muller's subversion then is *inevitably* dialectical rather than deconstructive, an inversion of the colonial presumption of subaltern passivity of the colonial woman that is contained within a logic of opposition that requires that women and their bodies bear the burden of racial representation.

Thus it could be argued that linguistic syncreticism in *The Jam Fruit Tree* (evident in the creolised, corrupted, colloquial English used in dialogue) is defined and contained within the cultural boundaries of an isolated and readily identifiable Burgher community, and that the gender essentialisation of Burgher women is a by-product of Muller's reading of the nation in these racially differentiated terms. Muller's reading of national culture thus bears out the contradictory impulses of both assimilation and disjunction, fusion and contrafusion identified by Young, and his presentation of the Burgher community is correspondingly defined by its occupation of a space of uncertain pedigree on the margins of the national narrative – of sprawling family trees (of which the jam fruit of the title stands as an enduring symbol),[22] mixed liaisons and unrecorded private histories. Burgher women's sexuality – their biological fecundity and sexual energy – are a performative index of the hybridity of their community. In this economy of sexual desire men hold an uncertain place for, while their virility and fertility is never in doubt, their paternity and parenthood is. It is for this reason, I believe, that masculinity and male sexual prowess are overasserted: it compensates for the lack of certainty in Muller's gendered genealogical reading of the cultural space of Burgher hybridity. The Burgher male occupies a constrained position in Muller's national narrative marked as he is by both an unrestrained fertility *and* uncertain lineage and paternity. Cecilprins' dismay at the profusion of granddaughters and his delight at the birth of his first grandson, Carloboy (the author's fictional nemesis), are clearly registered in relation to the need for a patriarchally inscribed genealogical security. What is more, unlike the birth of all the granddaughters, Carloboy's birth is historically marked: 'the new generation was well on its way and the island of Ceylon surely held its breath. Here was new life in a new time'

(p. 156). Patriarchy, paternity, filial succession and national history converge here to endorse a highly conservative reading of a Burgher culture and community marked by sexual licence and transgression.

In contrast to the linguistic syncretism and emphasis on miscegenation in *The Jam Fruit Tree*, the discourse of hybridity in *Children of the Lion* is dialogised and dialectical, affirming the value of ancestry and pedigree.[23] This massive novel – it is nearly 1000 pages long – is a polyphonic text that rewrites the events chronicled in the first part of the national chronicle, the *Mahavamsa*, covering several hundred years of the country's history.[24] A 'grand narrative' in every sense, the novel is encyclopaedic in its range and register – incorporating historical myth, literary fable, religious discourse, cultural and anthropological criticism, popular song, folk tale and authorial commentary. It is painstakingly referenced, and has detailed family trees charting the genealogy of the Buddha and Vijaya to reiterate the narrative's claim that the founder of the Sinhala nation has kinship ties with the Buddha.[25] Significantly however the *Mahavamsa* itself is repeatedly cited without references and stands as a sourceless, authorless, transhistorical text aspiring to both the sanctified status of a religious edict and the undisputed authority of a reference book – a position validated in the preface by the senior Buddhist monk who vouches for the novel's account of events.[26] Thus Muller's totalising gesture marks an assimilationist impulse, a desire to be all inclusive and incorporate multiple discourses and histories, high and low cultures, *and* contain these differentiated discourses within a narrative that, in line with its literary antecedent, presents the history of the island as concomitant with the history of Buddhism.[27] Taking his cue from this urtext of Sinhala nationalism, Muller presents the development of Buddhism and the development of Sinhala identity as indissolubly connected. In contrast discourse is dialogised, ranging from the heroic to the mock epic as it spans the public realms of religious and courtly ritual to the private world of human relationships and intimate connection. The latter contains lurid accounts of sexual congress. It thus constitutes a seemingly subversive secular subtext that punctuates the religious idealism and heroic drama of the main narrative.

Liberal critics who are drawn to the heightened drama of the novel may well be tempted, as I was initially, to embrace Muller's graphic depictions of sexual activity as a necessary part of his inclusivity – his desire not exclude anything and to confront the raw, human reality underpinning historico-mythic events. It could even be claimed that these episodes spice up a narrative that would otherwise read as one long succession of military conquest and religious conversion. Bestiality, incest and parricide are, after all, essential components of the *Mahavamsa*, and Muller's direct engagement with these issues can be seen as a refreshing change from the delicate, muted handling of these concerns in the original. But Muller goes much further than confront these issues directly: he indulges in a troubling celebration of female subjugation, a salacious depiction of child sexuality and a problematic portrayal of female physicality that collectively endorse a sadistic pleasure at the violation of women and – most troubling of all – of young girls. Muller's secularisation of the *Mahavamsa* leads him to present all mythical women (with the exception, as one critic has pointed out, of the Buddha's mother)[28] as sexual agents. Even the princess Sanghamitta and Vihara Maha Devi, women who occupy a sanctioned place in Sinhala Buddhist mytho-historiography, are sexualised and, simultaneously, infantilised. Muller takes most licence in the mythological first half of the book.[29] While nobody could doubt that a secular rewriting of the story of a mythical princess who left home and mated with a lion, thereby creating the future line of Sinhala kings, might legitimately involve a playful consideration of her unusual sexual tastes and predilections, there seems no basis whatsoever for the presentation of her as a self-professed 'slut' who is sexually promiscuous from infancy, lacks a hymen (described as 'a badge of her virginity' 'a lock to prevent the entry of man' (pp. 8, 7)), is permanently sexually available and enjoys genital mutilation. Here is Muller's description of the aftermath of the bestial union:

> Such a strange consummation, panting, back to back, each heaving, each knowing a supreme satiation as none of beastkind, humankind had ever known. When the lion had finally drawn free, it turned to sniff, lick at the blood of her ravaged vagina and Sihavathi, after a deep breath, laughed. [p. 11]

This reading of bestiality as a sadomasochistic engagement is presaged on a specific reading of women's bodies as a dangerous site of rampant sexuality that demands male mastery. Without a hymen, the court ascetic deduces, the young Sihavathi's 'body must be the vehicle of great and terrible offspring' (p. 8). Like Kuveni, the Yaksha queen and first mate of Vijaya who seduces him under the guise of being a sixteen-year-old girl, Sihavathi's sexual power is connected to her ambiguous status as child-woman and presented as a threat to male autonomy. This motif of infantilised female sexuality and promiscuity runs throughout the novel. Indeed the virgin–whore dichotomy is central to Muller's reading of female sexuality as a whole here. In the middle of an explicit account of Vijaya's first, mutually satisfying, sexual encounter with Kuveni, who contorts herself to pleasure him, he observes that she is 'So small [. . .] so tight [. . .] it clutches me, as a chamber of a child' (p. 126). Similarly Vijaya's descendant Gamini (the future warrior-king Dutugemunu) delights in claiming a 'nymphet' whose 'eyes held much pain as he rode her, heaved into her, uncaring as he thrust in and out in her blood' (p. 789). Despite such violence, we are told, 'she found lovemaking a game, an art, an unceasing desire' and is so consumed with lust that she offers him oral sex. The novel is littered with salacious accounts of sadomasochistic sex with virgins or virginal women and of the yearnings of sexually mature girls. It comes as little surprise then that child rape itself is legitimised. Muller infantilises a woman who, according the *Mahavamsa* drove men mad with desire, and, in an entirely invented account of her story, describes her violation. The rape of princess Citta, an eight-year-old who is 'tall and willowy for her age' (p. 240) (but in a curious reversal after the rape is described as 'too small to look out [of her tower-room], even on tiptoe' (p. 243)) is shown to be endemic to her natural sexual awakening: she recovers promptly after the event and is left 'full of questions' (p. 243). Even Viharamaha Devi is written into this narrative of virginal sadomasochism (p. 607), and is presented as one who is both 'truly woman' and still 'but a girl' (pp. 617, 612), her 'singular piety' moderated by her sensuality (p. 617).

While feminist critical readings of Muller's work have, understandably, staged robust denunciations of his representations of women, I believe that the dramatic difference between the presentation of female sexual agency in *The Jam Fruit Tree* and *Children* reveals that his representation of women – as of men – needs to be read in relation to his hegemonic conception of Sri Lankan national identity. The representation of sexuality, sexual intercourse and gender is presaged upon an ideological investment in genealogy and legitimacy here. For Muller, sexuality is scripted by a specific reading of the nation as a racially segregated space that accommodates but does not endorse hybridity. Thus *The Jam Fruit Tree* draws a clear correspondence between female (and male) fertility and genetically confused bloodlines. This is in striking contrast to the preoccupation with female virginity in *Children* – a novel that rewrites the founding myth of the nation and works to affirm the certainty of origins. The graphic accounts of the violation of, and sexual pain experienced by, child-women thus serve as an inscription of *certain* paternity, a physical confirmation of pedigree, an affirmation – in a novel that seeks to rewrite Sinhala history – of Sinhala lineage and 'purity'. This preoccupation with virginity reveals a fundamental fear of women's sexuality that is also to be found in early Buddhist teaching which, according to one analyst, promotes wifely duty and fecundity over spiritual development.[30] This is not, of course, to excuse Muller's blatant celebration of male sexual domination, but rather to show that his chauvinism is based upon prejudices that exceed those of gender. While Neluka Silva has drawn attention to the links between his representation of women and the fact that 'ethnic homogenizations are endemic in his profile',[31] she, like others, has tended to contain the reading of ethnic difference in a reading of gender difference. I believe this logic needs to be reversed, for Muller's textual hybridity – both the organic hybridity of *The Jam Fruit Tree* and the dialectical hybridity of *Children* – is contained, as I will now show, within a hegemonising discourse that situates the Sinhala Buddhists as the rightful owners of the island.

Hybridity: race, ethnicity and Buddhist hegemony

In *Children of the Lion*, Muller's gendered reading of genealogy works to sustain a notion of the legitimacy of the new rulers of the land within a specifically Buddhist, Aryan model of the nation. Drawing upon the *Mahavamsa*'s narrative cartography of the island as a unified sacred space, consecrated to the promotion and development of Buddhism, Muller invests in a rich topography of a mythologised landscape that subscribes to both Buddhist scriptural dynamics, which encode the island as a holy land marked by the Buddha's visits, and a contemporary geopolitical prescriptive that attests to the need to assure the unity and territorial integrity of the island. Past and present merge in the continuities of geographical presencing: mythical stories of, for example, a principality of serpents, a meeting place of demons, a river of gems, vast elaborate gardens, and mountain ranges of magical herbs that form stepping stones of a monkey god, are named and placed (examples taken from pp. 129 and 246) in a meticulously mapped account of events that takes care to situate specific fables in relation to the contemporary cartography of the country.

Muller of course is taking his cue from the *Mahavamsa* in his mythological spatialisation of the island, but he deviates from the chronicle in a number of important ways. The novel charts the complex formulation, negotiation and crystallisation of Sinhala identity in relation to the prior taxonomies of Buddhist and Aryan identities, drawing upon the nationalist scripture of the *Mahavamsa*, but in the process it enacts both an intervention in and a reinscription of ethnic difference. In his cultural taxonomy Muller thus rewrites, but also serves to partially endorse, contemporary readings of these categories. His investment in an immutable notion of Aryan racial identity and an assimilationist model of Buddhism are the most dramatic signs of his rewriting of the chronicle to serve the needs of present; they collectively influence his reactive inscription of Tamil residence in the land and the mapping of the island as a sacred space. It is imperative therefore to explore the construction of racial and ethnic difference in his genealogical reading of the island's spatial history before revealing the ways in which territoriality itself is addressed.

Kinship structures in the *Mahavamsa* are primarily based on clan, caste and region. Even the Buddha himself, described as 'Sambuddha the pure, sprung of a pure race' in the opening page of the chronicle,[32] is genealogically absorbed into a convoluted succession of several thousand kings belonging to the Sakya tribe.[33] Muller departs from this genealogical model in his explicit emphasis on Aryan ancestry, thus drawing upon a colonial reading of race that has currency in contemporary constructions of ethnic difference. The difference can be seen in a comparative reading of a key event: the choice of a suitable wife for the first consecrated king of the island. This is how Vijaya's decision to choose a royal bride is explained in the chronicle:

> When they had founded settlements in the land the ministers all came together and spoke thus to the prince: 'Sire, consent to be consecrated as king.' But, in spite of their demand, the prince refused the consecration, unless a maiden of a noble house were consecrated as queen (at the same time). [p. 59]

In striking contrast Muller argues that Vijaya's consecration as king is only viable upon his marriage to an Aryan princess (p. 146), a manoeuvre that erases the agency of the king affirmed by the chronicles and substitutes for it a formal code of kingship. What is more, a wife from a suitable 'noble' background is presented as a prerequisite for not only the legitimacy of royal rule but also the very structuration of Sinhala identity. In Muller's text the fact that all Vijaya's followers marry 'royal ladies and maidens' from the same region is encoded in a discourse that celebrates Sinhala racial purity: as one of Vijaya's followers observes, 'the people of the lion have wives who are of the true blood of our ancient home. Now therefore will they be Sihala [Sinhala] and their children Sihala and their numbers will fill this land from the coasts to the mountains' (p. 168). Whereas Aryan identity in the

Mahavamsa forms the basis of a mutable register of belonging, covering meanings as diverse as 'noble', 'outsider' and 'South Indian',[34] Muller's reading is polarised around the binary structuration of contemporary cultural discourse and openly serves to distinguish between Aryan and Dravidian peoples. In a detailed passage, Muller claims that Vijaya's royal bride was of 'fine Aryan stock' and that – despite evidence to the contrary – she came from a region where there 'was no Dravidian connection'. He then proceeds to engage in an explicitly racist discourse, claiming that Dravidians can be distinguished by 'their dour faces, their splayed nostrils and thick lips' (p. 149).

This early investment in the value of Aryan ancestry seems to peter away in the course of the novel as Muller's depiction of the growing population of the island accommodates the heterogonous multitudes that make it up so that his focus shifts to an evaluation of the position of Tamils in the island. (It could also be argued that the overemphasis on racial purity and Aryan heritage in the early part of the novel could be Muller's way of addressing the very monstrous beginnings of a people spawned by the union between man and beast.) As the island becomes increasingly populous, Muller's emphasis shifts to address and accommodate racial and cultural hybridity (see pp. 228, 374, 593, 903 for strong examples of this), so that he even claims – in a passage citing the island-long journey of an envoy – that 'for the most part, the Sihalas and the Damilas were indistinguishable from each other and each spoke the other's tongue' (p. 727). Having asserted the Aryan ancestry of the Sinhala people, Muller now seems to play with the boundaries of racial and ethnic difference, invoking 'race' to cover a multitude of identity markers such as caste, ethnicity and clan which get fused in a hybridised account of the nation: 'Indeed, Ruhuna was ruled and peopled by the bravest mixture of *races* – Sihala, Sakya, Naga and Shatriya' (my emphasis) (p. 611). What is more, in belated defiance of the stereotypes affirmed earlier he claims that Aryans were 'barbarians' who 'did not bring with them any forms of advanced civilisation, for they were mostly nomadic or belonged to pastoral societies. They came to conquer an ancient and elaborate civilisation [in India], and reduce it to naught' (p. 881).

The scripting of race and ethnicity takes place at the intersection between a range of discourses, from spuriously authoritative anthropological observations (the cited passage on the Dravidian's 'dour faces' is one example of this) to conversational exchanges between characters; from self-reflexive observations on the work of cultural historians to direct, unmediated citations from a range of texts. What emerges is a presentation of the human invention of, and intervention in, the taxonomy of difference. The text is a cultural performance, an enaction of hybridised discourse, engaging in a form of intentional hybridity in its polyphonic juxtaposition of a wide range of dialogised voices. From a hermit's observation that all the early settlers in the island are 'all Aryans [. . .] all of the great dynasties of the sun' (p. 187) to the omniscience of the epic historian's observations on racial and cultural connections between Sinhalas and Tamils over centuries (pp. 454, 457, 615), the text presents hybridity in hierarchy, diversity and pluralism within a model that asserts the importance of pedigree, of authenticity, of assured origins, and it draws upon Sri Lanka's relationship with India to justify this. In a move characteristic of the colonial erasure of the indigene, Muller presents India as the original 'father' of the island nation's people (pp. 339, 367–68) so that Sri Lanka emerges as nothing less than 'a beautiful butterfly from the Indian chrysalis' (p. 368).[35]

This model of belonging, of unity in diversity, does have the potential to unsettle some of the established paradigms of identity. In presenting caste, ethnic and racial difference as emergent, processual and historically provisional, Muller calls into question the very fixity of racial discourse, revealing it to be mediated and constantly under construction. The novel registers the gradual evolution of Sinhala identity, its construction as a discursive category of identification, and does so through a negotiation of (and investment in) established taxonomies. What is more, Muller registers a significant riposte to the *Mahavamsa* mentality[36] of his times in his tantalising claim that Elara, the very symbol of Tamil domination, was not a Tamil at all but a Yemeni Jain.[37] (It should be noted however that the subversive potential of the claim is somewhat weakened by it being withheld until the very end of a long novel, where only a dedicated minority of readers might come across it.) Muller follows the lead of the *Mahavamsa* in presenting Elara as a defender, though not a follower, of Buddhism, but extends it to stress that Elara was crowned at the explicit behest of the Sinhala people and that he ruled with their consent and support (p. 507). In Muller's portrayal Elara is a passionless man of uncertain origin (until the final disclosure on the last page), an outsider from the cultural mainstream of emergent Sinhala identification, and a peaceful, democratic king who promoted pluralism (p. 513). Yet it is this very pluralism which Muller problematises as Tamils are shown to resist the assimilationism propounded by the novel and be exclusive, caste-ridden, territorial and anti-Buddhist (pp. 481, 768, 801).

It is here that Muller's positive presentation of a hybridised nation, of unity in diversity, breaks down and he succumbs to the ethnic prescriptives and narrow nationalism of his time. Elara's reign is registered as an index of failed assimilation not so much by the Sinhalese but by the Tamils, who see him as one of them. In a curious rewriting of the *Mahavamsa*'s chauvinist inscription of Elara as an alien Cola, Muller reverses the racial dynamic of rejection and ascribes it to the Cola-based Tamils themselves, claiming Elara's mistake was to try to be 'a Sinhalese in a Sihala land now swamped by the Damilas [Tamils]' (p. 596). The Tamil Colas are shown to see themselves as a 'master race' who 'looked on the Raja Rata [Lanka]' as theirs. Sinhalese chauvinism is thus deftly deflected and replaced by a model of Tamil intolerance and territoriality. What is more, in the logic of racial pedigree and royal legitimacy inscribed in the text, Elara, however peace-loving and tolerant (a model, some might say, of Buddhist pacifism), is without question an illegitimate king – his reign unendorsed through his failure to become a Buddhist.[38]

Muller's hybridity thus has a political resolve above and beyond the assimilationist impulse noted earlier. Far from being a gesture of open accommodation of difference, the very tolerance and inclusivity that it enacts are used to project a contrastive model of Tamil territoriality and economic greed. This is particularly striking given that Vijaya's conquest of the island forms an act of colonial occupancy. As Kemper has shown in his illuminating study of the *Mahavamsa*, Vijaya was 'the foreigner who gives Sinhalas grounds for thinking of themselves as natives'.[39] His control of the land is legitimated by a discourse that scripts his actions as preordained by the Buddha, a reading of history as divine destiny that effectively erases human agency. The island in turn becomes a gift to the Buddha (p. 658), a process of consecrated territoriality that literarily eradicates the original inhabitants – referred to as other-worldly beings with magical powers – conveniently voiding the island of human presence. In contrast, then, to this legitimated occupancy of the newly created Sinhalese people, the Tamils are presented as invaders who threaten the security of the peace-loving Sinhalese:

> [T]hroughout their history, from the most ancient times, whenever the government was weak, parties of Damilas invaded the island and either despoiled it, or seized upon and exercised for some time the supreme power. It is astonishing how easily these marauders established themselves, and how patiently the Sinhalese submitted themselves to, or accepted their domination . . . seeing that the frequent invasions by their Tamil neighbours were the cause of all the worst disasters that lay before their splendid industries, the persistent neglect of their national defences was the most remarkable, especially as they had not a long line of exposed boundary to protect [. . .] but only a few points along their coasts. [. . .] They [the Sinhalese] were ever a domestic, not a political people, and so continue to be to this day. People of this disposition fall almost necessarily under the subjugation of any resolute power, and become the servants, if not virtually the slaves, of those who wield it. [p. 480]

While some readers may suppress their surprise on learning that the Sinhalese were never 'a political people', it is impossible not to register that Muller's presentation is alarmist in the extreme, drawing directly from the current discourse of contested territorial rights. (Notice how Muller shifts from historical to contemporary discourse, replacing 'Damilas' with 'Tamils' here.) The performative gives way to the pedagogic as historical 'invasions' – which themselves are constructed by the notional assumption of prior legitimated Sinhala settlership and domestication (replicated in Muller's emphasis that the Sihalas are a 'domestic' people) – are directly related to the politics of present-day Tamil occupancy.

Tamil territoriality is firmly repudiated – read not simply as a desire for regional political autonomy but in its more extremist form as a colonising expression of the desire for outright subjugation of the majority Sinhalese. While Muller is clearly comfortable not only to accommodate but also to argue for the need to see the Tamils as racially allied to the Sinhalese, in other words to invest in a hybrid reading of racial and cultural identity, it is clear that the notion of Tamil territorial autonomy provokes him to respond in a way that allies all Tamil claims for territorial control with separatism and military and cultural supremacy. The novel thus marks the way in which an investment in territorial discourse (through a unitary reading of the island as the sanctioned land of Sinhala Buddhists) lends itself to an exclusionary spatial politics that works to silence and suppress the territorial claims of others. It marks an overdetermination of spatial discourse akin to the condition described by political geographers as the 'territorial trap' in which the state-centred account of spatiality overdetermines the links between power and territorial sovereignty.[40] The effects of such an investment are particularly striking in the case of a writer who has done so much to explore the discursive politics of cultural hybridity and inclusivity. It is but a small step before Tamil residence itself comes to be assimilated into this territorial logic. As 'marauders' and invaders (from however distant or mythological a past) their presence by definition constitutes an evil 'infestation' (p. 659) that threatens Buddhist hegemony. Muller argues that Buddhist hegemony, far from being a divisive force (which the current political climate might suggest is the case), constitutes 'the greatest binding factor' (p. 418) in the country. Buddhism is scripted teleologically and monologically in the text, leading Muller to take a paradoxical stand which suggests that in defence of such a tolerant and pacifist religion any military action is justified: 'it was the function of the king to protect Buddhist doctrine. He could do so with the sword if needs be. . .and none would fault him!' (p. 659).

Muller's discourse becomes increasingly rhetorical, energised by exclamation marks and direct address when writing on territoriality and the defence of the nation, alerting us to the need to critically distance ourselves from his polemical stand. In a direct attack on Tamil claims to a homeland in the north he urges his readers 'to make no mistake about what we say. The north *was* truly Sihala. . .*and* intensely and intensively Buddhistic!' (p. 475). These assertions are made in the name of a threatened Buddhism, yet in choosing to write the past through the contestatory, polarising discourses of the present, a present in which Buddhism in its institutional form is fiercely promoted and protected by the state, and in resisting any engagement with a counter-discourse that might question the ethno-nationalist polemics exhorted and extolled in the novel, Muller falls into the trap of subscribing to an exclusionary cultural logic.

While it could be argued that the very exaggeration of nationalist invective appears to *parody* the discourse of ethno-religious nationalism, in other words that the novel works to defamiliarise such rhetoric and compel us to question its politics, the very absence of a counter-discourse, or of any critical or ironic interjection in a novel that delights in plurivocity and cultural pastiche, emphatically works to project a unitary model of belonging that endorses a specific reading of cultural legitimacy. It further – and perhaps inadvertently – subscribes to a cultural logic, described by K.M. De Silva, which interpellates the Sinhalese as a majority with a minority complex.[41] Muller's rewriting of the founding myth of the nation articulates this complex within a discourse that strains under the teleological burden of attempting to legitimate the need for a continuous and contiguous history of Buddhist presence in the land while acknowledging the need for revising it. Muller thus repeatedly refers to the persecution of Buddhists in India, which justifies the protection of the faith in the sanctioned 'home' of Buddhism, Sri Lanka (pp. 173, 191), while simultaneously presenting us with a modified reading of Dutugemunu's victory over Elara: arguably *the* mythico-historical event that endorses Sinhala Buddhist hegemony in the island. In Muller's mediation of secularisation within hagiography, of the human within the divine, Dutugemunu's actions are presented as both a preordained, divine destiny – in the teleological thrust affirming the need for a unified Buddhist state in which '(t)erritorial incorporation was the greatest achievement of all' (p. 864) – *and* the result of human agency: Gamini's deliberate use of Buddhist myth to reinforce his power, sparking 'the process of ethnicization' that 'places the Sinhalese and Tamils in bitter conflict even in this day and age!'(p. 760). This double-coded discourse enacts the tensions of trying to simultaneously promote hybridity and Buddhist hegemony. Muller's approach to the Buddhist chronicle is thus reformist rather than revolutionary, motivated by a secularising impulse that is attentive to, and respectful of, the missionary spirit in which the chronicles were written. Thus while he directly challenges the *Mahavamsa*'s heroic presentation of Dutugemunu's victory he does so in order to present a specific model of Buddhist identification. He moderates and secularises two events from the chronicles that have been invoked in recent years to justify state military engagement – the use of a Buddhist relic in Dutugemunu's spear and the *Mahavamsa*'s explicit erasure of Dutugemunu's Tamil victims:

> We have recorded how he [Dutugemunu] placed a Buddhist relic in his spear, just as one would have, in the myths of old, carried a magic talisman. His war was a 'holy war', and such a war is counter to the Buddhist doctrine. He made his declaration of this intent before his assault on Jambu; would not the old storytellers look on this as a 'magic spell'?
>
> Later, when he sat upon the lion throne of Anuradhapura, grieving for the millions he had slain, was he told by the monks that since he had slaughtered the unbeliever, this was no crime. No greater statement of sheer intolerance had ever been made in Lanka's long history – a statement that showed complete ignorance and defiance of the Buddha's first precept! [p. 863]

This is a slippery passage. The narrator seems to slide between the registers of other anonymous chroniclers, between the 'myths of old', the tentative considerations of the views of past storytellers, and the more assured claim to knowledge of Buddhist precepts. It is also unclear whether the nominative 'we' referred to in the opening line refers to the narrator's own recording or the inheritance handed down to the present generation by the original chronicles. What does come across, however, is that Muller is engaging in a process of historical secularisation, evacuating the spear relic of its religious significance by interpellating it as 'a magic talisman', and calling for a return to a reading of Buddhism as a religion of non-violence and tolerance, fundamental precepts of the doctrine. Muller thus endorses and promotes an assimilationist model of Buddhism – one that bears comparison with Ondaatje's hybridised presentation of Buddhist practice in *Anil's Ghost* – that in the hierarchical, hagiographic thrust of the narrative as a whole necessarily excludes all those who lie outside the boundaries of this religious identification. Within such a rationale the Tamils are outsiders not so much because of their racial or ethnic ties (which Muller has shown to be linked to the Sinhalese) but because they are not Buddhists. They worship 'foreign gods' (p. 490) and pillage Buddhist temples (p. 481). Muller's rewriting of the chronicle thus invests in a moderated presentation of the island's past: one that both endorses Sinhala Buddhist hegemony and promotes assimilationism and tolerance, and which advocates fusion while acknowledging the indissolubility of the boundaries of religious difference.

For one who delights in unsettling orthodoxies, this is hardly a revolutionary stand, but given his fluid and flexible engagement with linguistic and cultural hybridity and his complex investment in national unity, it is perhaps the only logical one for Muller to make. For those who occupy the tenuous borderland of compromised belonging and confused bloodlines, the choice to belong and lay claim to a singular inheritance would seem to require either a colonial reclamation that wilfully flies in the face of postcolonial realities or an investment in hegemonic identification and an espousal, albeit modified, of its main ideologies. Thus the contradictions and paradoxes in Muller's work enact the difficulties of finding a register that accommodates difference within the mainstream, of both the need to find, and the difficulties of mobilising, new categories of identification.

Part III

6 A. Sivanandan and Shyam Selvadurai

Border dialogues

The boundary is that from which something *begins its essential unfolding.*

Martin Heidegger, 'Building, Dwelling, Thinking'[1]

It is by living on the borderline of history and language, on the limits of race and gender, that we are in a position to translate the differences between them into a kind of solidarity.

Homi K. Bhabha, 'DessemiNation'[2]

Political exiles do not merely live on the borderline of history and language, but owe their ruptured lives to the simultaneous intransigence and transgression of its limits. As exiles, their lives are mediated by the experience of geographic and political expulsion, the intractability of different boundaries. For them then the 'borderline' alluded to by Bhabha is a site not merely for the potential translation of difference but, as significantly, for the exploration of the very translatability of difference, the (im)possibility of mediation across and between cultures and identities. The terms that construct 'the limits of race and gender' and other exclusionary identities are, for them, weighted with the reality of their active enforcement: exclusion and expulsion enacting a spatial, temporal and ideological distancing from the site once identified as 'home' so that 'difference' becomes a marker of both alienation and belonging. Within this context the borderline is simultaneously the site of potential translation, the site of unfolding, and the site where 'certitudes of belonging'[3] index both a resistance to and a radical assertion of policed identities.

It is within the context of this notion of the borderline as simultaneously a liminal and an interstitial site of resistance, intransigence and potential translation that I propose to analyse the work of Ambalavener Sivanandan and Shyam Selvadurai. Exiled during the politically crucial years of 1958 and 1983 respectively, their work explores and enacts the social, cultural and political boundary marking delineated by discourses pertaining to race, ethnicity, class, language, gender and sexuality in Sri Lanka from their residence in England and Canada. Sivanandan, the son of a Tamil postmaster, left Sri Lanka (then called Ceylon) for England with his Sinhalese wife after the race riots of 1958; Selvadurai, of mixed

Tamil and Sinhalese parentage, left Sri Lanka for Canada with his family in the wake of the race riots of 1983.[4] The sheer range of intersections between the different discourses explored in their work cannot be comprehensively addressed in this chapter. Rather I attempt here to delineate some of the points of connection and difference between the writers and their novels by focusing on the way discursive boundary marking in their texts intersects with the performative construction of lived experience whereby individuals serve as touchstones for broader social and political truths. My aim here is to create the conditions for creative and critical dialogue across different discursive boundaries, furthering the deconstructive, interruptive project of attempting to create new modes of affiliation found in the texts themselves. While the novels of Sivanandan and Selvadurai have not been subject to expatriation by resident Sri Lankan critics in the way that the work of Ondaatje and Gunesekera has, the basis of their inclusion within the emergent canon both within and outside Sri Lanka has not yet evaluated the intersecting marginalities that forms a central hermeneutic in linking their work.[5]

Both Sivanandan and Selvadurai are broadly 'realist' writers who draw upon their own experience of socio-cultural relations to foreground the discrepancy between lived experience and social and political prescriptives. Both of them appear to have forged their identities and goals in exile: Sivanandan's 'double baptism of fire',[6] in which he left the race riots of Sri Lanka only to enter the race riots of Notting Hill, leading to his political awakening, and Selvadurai finding his racial and sexual identity in Canada.[7] Their texts are dialectical, highlighting social contradictions through carefully revealing the way in which class, ethnic and gender distinctions are promoted and maintained. There are some structural correspondences to be found in their texts too. Selvadurai's *Funny Boy* (1994) and Sivanandan's *When Memory Dies* (1997) are both first novels made up of discrete but interlinking sections: *Funny Boy* is, we are told, 'a novel in six stories', and *When Memory Dies* is a novel of epic proportions which consists of three 'books', each focusing on a different member of the family and a different historical period. All their novels are temporally linear, focusing on cause and consequence, affirming a need for continuity and coherence in the face of increasing social fragmentation; and they are ideologically congruent in their sympathy for the Tamil struggle for emancipation. Furthermore, their first novels have a polemical bias that has been used to promote specific causes. *Funny Boy* was read by the Sri Lankan President and prompted a national debate on the need to repeal the anti-sodomy law in the country;[8] and *When Memory Dies* was conscripted by the Tamil Tigers for propagandist purposes on their website.[9] These novels enact the double narrative movement described by Bhabha, in which the 'powerful master discourse' of both colonial and national narratives is countered by a recursive and repetitious narrative of interrupted address in which 'the people' are constructed and constituted in the performance of narrative.[10] As I will show, this temporal split between the 'pedagogical' and the 'performative' culminates in a full and complex literary exploration of the performative in the form of mimicry in Selvadurai's second novel *Cinnamon Gardens* (1998). Here the instability of enunciation offers a playful but radical counterdiscourse to the nationalist narrative of cultural reclamation and originary history, as identity is shown to be both culturally displaced and subject to deferral in relation to the project of nationing.

Yet despite these formal, structural and ideological correspondences there are significant differences between their texts – differences that signal contrasting perceptions on the form and role of history, on individual and collective agency and on subject constitution. Sivanandan, an influential Marxist cultural analyst, whose critical interventions on race and class have been acclaimed by activists and ideologues alike, is, as Chris Searle points out, 'an interrupter'.[11] His political project in *When Memory Dies* is to 'interrupt' the Manichean, hierarchic historicisation of the nation as a zone of conflict between essentialised identities and reveal an alternative past of inter-ethnic working class solidarity in Sri Lanka. As the title of his novel suggests, the revisionism underpinning this manoeuvre is addressed in terms of the need to accommodate memories that are in danger of being lost. The novel is an act of historical retrieval and political recuperation, interrupting the culturally exclusive nationalist narratives of both Sinhala and Tamil nationalisms, and sets out to transform hegemonic prescriptives that provide the enabling context for racial and ethnic division and dissent. In it individuals are sites of cultural contestation and conflict for, as Sivanandan has claimed in one of his essays, 'every shard of the self is a social movement'.[12] Sivanandan's searingly direct attack on the academic theorising of post-Marxism is relevant here. It takes the form of an inversion of one of the central aphorisms of the times and its replacement by the assertion that the political is personal:

> the personal is the political [. . .] has tended in practice to personalise and fragment and close down struggles. [. . .] The personal is the political is concerned with altering the goal posts, the political is personal is concerned with the field of play. The personal is the political may produce radical individualism, the political is personal produces a radical society. The personal is the political entraps you in the self-achieving, self-aggrandising life-style of the rich, the political is personal finds value in the communal life-style of the poor.[13]

This attack on 'the personal politics of the subject'[14] reveals that the performative basis of Sivanandan's text is constructed on the basis of its relationship with an *alternative* pedagogy rather than in the deconstruction of the pedagogical *per se*, rendering the novel, in the words of one critic, 'a work of creative pedagogy'.[15] Yet this marks, in my view, not so much the compromising of Bhabha's performative temporality, but rather an emphasis on its symbiotic relationship with the pedagogical so that the temporal disjunction or split between the pedagogical and the performative comes to be discursively enacted within the text. If individuals constitute 'shards' of social movements, then the creative scripting of an hegemonised Sri Lankan history in relation to the socialist past is necessarily carried out in the terrain of overlapping temporalities of the performative (repetitious, recursive and interruptive) and the pedagogical (continuist, accumulative and historically sedimentary),[16] registering the '*instability* of cultural signification' at the heart of Sivanandan's political enterprise.[17] Such instability, as I will show, draws attention to the extent to which political formulations are rendered less secure when mobilised in the service of creative fiction.[18]

In contrast, Selvadurai's strong investment in the performative is conducted on the basis of a discrete and static rendering of the pedagogical. *Funny Boy*'s foregrounding of an adolescent's perspective and the ambiguity of sexual identity is mediated through the essentialisation of ethnic identities. The narrator's transgression of gender codes and roles in the game of 'bride-bride' and his resistance to 'becoming a man' within the strictures of the colonial Queen Victoria Academy are enacted through the performance of staged identities against which the discourse of fixed ethnic identification serves as a counterpoint. In narrating events through the eyes of a political ingénue who is dependent on adults for information on the past, history is rendered both mobile (in the act of transmission) and fixed (weighted and coded by their prejudices). The intransigence of pedagogical, continuist, accumulative temporality alluded to by Bhabha is foregrounded by such performative temporality. In *Cinnamon Gardens* Selvadurai goes further. Here he ambitiously confronts the cultural effects of colonial mimicry by narrating a critical period of the pre-Independence past – a time of national emergence when the role of ethnic minorities and women were subject to political debate and constitutional reform – from within the discourse of the nineteenth century English novel. Narrative authority is constantly unfixed within such blatantly mimetic discourse so that meaning is generated 'within determinate institutions and systems of representation – ideological, historical, aesthetic, political'.[19] It is a process, as I will show, in which performativity works towards the 'unseating of the Transcendental subject'[20] so that the central characters, Anna and Balendran, are rendered *beyond representation*.

Thus, a comparative analysis of the work of these writers can offer us insight into the differential dynamics of historical and cultural representation and subject constitution that are under debate on the borderlines of belonging, the edge of expulsion. My analysis begins with a consideration of the discursive construction and deconstruction of multiple borderlines in the representation of subaltern history, ethnic hybridity and coexistence in *When Memory Dies*.

Performative and pedagogical readings of the past

When Memory Dies[21] charts the history of working class struggle over an eighty-year period in Sri Lanka by relating the story of three generations of a peasant family from Jaffna. Sivanandan wrote the novel in his early 70s in an effort, he claims, to address the 'hollowness' that resulted from his departure from his native land some forty years earlier. Having devoted four decades of his life to contributing to the antiracist struggle in Britain, he felt the need to make 'a contribution to my own country and my own people' and 'the novel came out of that'.[22] The novel constitutes an impassioned plea to reclaim the forgotten history of working class solidarity and its transcendence of ethnic difference. The erosion of this memory is initially marked as a product of the violent rupture enforced by the alien presence of the coloniser, disabling the country's capacity for regeneration:

> There is no story to tell, no one story anyway, not since that day in 1505 when the fidalgo Don Laurenço de Almeida, resplendent in gold braid and epaulettes and hat plumed with all the birds of paradise, landed on our shores and broke us from our history. No one story, with a beginning and an end, no story that picks up from where the past left off – only bits and shards of stories, [. . .] for there was no staying in a place or in a time to gather a story whole, only an imagined time and place. [p. 5]

Here memory, fragmented and processual, is shown to be recuperative; migration made concomitant with exile. The development of the Tamil Tiger movement is shown as a logical outcome of this loss of historical narrative – as Para, the narrator's uncle, observes: 'the British took away their past, the Sinhalese took away their future. All they have is the present. And that makes them dangerous' (pp. 334–35). Fictional events are thus fleshed with the substance of historical fact, while simultaneously memory is shown to be mobile and mobilised in the service of historical narration. Brought together in this way they work to mark the disjunctive temporalities of the pedagogical and performative. Thus, unlike Selvadurai, who chooses to focus on monumental history as an externally defined context or grid in which individuals serve as hapless victims or passive onlookers, Sivanandan presents history as an open-ended arena of contestation, with individuals functioning as active agents in its construction.

The novel, though chronological in its structuration, repeatedly signals its own enterprise of historical retrieval and reclamation,[23] most notably in the epigrammatic exchange that lends the text its title:

> 'When memory dies, a people die', Uncle Para broke into his reverie and Vijay, [. . .] remembering his experiences of the past few days [. . .] asked, 'What if we make up false memories?'
>
> 'That is worse', replied the old man, 'that is murder'. [p. 335]

With the aim of reclaiming the suppressed past Sivanandan presents us with a genealogy of hybridity in which characters' racial histories are, on the one, hand subsumed within the history of inter-ethnic friendships, and, on the other, confused by intermarriage. By invoking the community in familial terms, the novel allows for 'unconventional lines of affiliation'.[24] The first book for example focuses on the experience of Sahadeven, born into a Tamil family but adopted into a Sinhalese one. His friendship with Tissa, a Sinhalese, sets up the pattern for the other two books, in which the primary relationship is a male bond between members of the two different communities. It is a world in which all the central characters are bilingual and connected through their practical and ideological commitment to working class struggle. The differences between them are not presented as ones of ethnicity, religion, language or culture, but are based upon differences of praxis, as they argue over the means and methods required to achieve their socialist goals. Indeed ethnic difference, far from being discursively essentialised and historically rationalised as it is in *Funny Boy*, is presented as a strategic construction deployed by political opportunists. Lalli's rape and murder by Sinhalese thugs, and Vijay's killing by his own cousin, a Tiger leader, constitute the culminating fictional incidents of racial intolerance in the novel, and they are problematic and unsettling precisely because they constitute an assault on those who have lived without a sense of difference.

What is more these incidents echo the ending of the first book, when a Muslim boy, Sultan, is killed at a political rally by police in the service of the British. By ending all three books with an event that marks the violent outcome of racial and ethnic intolerance, Sivanandan sets up a tragic climax to the pattern of inter-ethnic bonding that precedes it. This pattern of iterative recurrence – the forging of inter-ethnic bonds that are then subject to the violence of intolerance – serves as a performative index of the way communal history is remembered and then itself subject to rupture by the assertion of the pedagogical. For the official narrative of the nation is scripted by what Suvendrini Perera has called 'the will to partition' in which 'areas of cultural, linguistic and religious overlap [. . .] are overwritten by the organisation of a various population into distinct racial/ethnic categories, hierarchically positioned in the space and time of a single national history'.[25] This official narrative that works in the service of dividing communities is espoused by both Sinhalese and Tamil extremists.[26] Perera's excellent analysis emphasises the need to retrieve and acknowledge forgotten histories of coexistence which she sees as 'a necessary first step towards an active *politics* of co-existence, a politics that involves unmaking the anti-historical absolutism of the present, and remaking – or "re-membering" – other understandings of the past'.[27] It could be argued that the dense network of inter-ethnic relationships charted in the novel go even further than promoting a politics of coexistence. They reveal not only the 'quotidian transactions within shared spaces, both symbolic and physical', 'the parallel and intersecting trajectories of everyday desires', 'the daily proximities of people who have lived together over centuries'[28] but also the fundamental *interdependence* of these communities, the fact that they bear a constitutive relationship with one another.[29] The fratricide that concludes the novel – when Vijay is killed by his half-brother – is a stark assertion that the bonds between communities are bonds of blood that can only be ruptured by its spilling. Such an emphasis on interdependence and the constitutive relationship between the communities would make the 'necessary first step' towards a politics of coexistence even more of a necessity.[30]

The novel's aim to affirm an alternative pedagogy reveals the extent to which the performative – in the form of the dialectical and dialogic construction of a subaltern history and memory – intrudes on the pedagogical in the text. The tension between these disjunctive temporalities is evident in Neil Lazarus' claim that 'Sivanandan's prose is essentially performative. To read him is to be made aware of oneself as reader, [. . .] that the writing represents a staging, that it is *occasioned* (motivated, situated, context-dependent), that the writer – Sivanandan

– is engaged'.[31] The novel's refrain, reminding readers of the need to remember and reclaim a forgotten past of working class, intercommunal solidarity,[32] serves as a performative index of recursion that interrupts the hegemonising prescriptives that constitute 'official narratives of partition'[33] in an interventionist pedagogical manoeuvre that seeks to instruct its readership. The instability of memory thus appears to be steadied by its encoding within a project of subaltern truth-telling.

Given this aim of exposing a hidden history of coexistence and challenging the prescriptions of official history by asserting communal truths, why does Sivanandan appear to engage in the deliberate and unmarked falsification of historical fact? Regi Siriwardena has drawn attention to this citing several instances of Sivanandan's distortion of historical events, the most notable of which concerns the seminal event of the killing of thirteen soldiers in Jaffna which preceded the communal riots in Colombo in 1983.[34] Here is the contentious passage:

> 'What's happened in Colombo then, Mother Know-All?' inquired Vijay.
>
> 'I don't quite know. But somebody high-up put out the rumour that Buddhist priests had been killed in Jaffna and Sinhalese mobs went on the rampage, killing Tamils.'
>
> 'And was it true the story about the priests?'
>
> 'Oh no. It turns out they were soldiers, young recruits, volunteers probably, some thirteen of them, killed in a guerrilla ambush. But the government is bringing their bodies home for a state funeral.' [p. 381]

Siriwardena, a literary critic resident in Sri Lanka and a long-standing socialist campaigner for human rights, is unambiguous in his response to this piece. His critique of this passage raises important issues on the politics of reading and writing Sri Lankan historical fiction, and I therefore cite it in full:

> In the historical actuality of 1983 there was no rumour of Buddhist priests being killed in Jaffna; the public knew that thirteen soldiers had been ambushed and killed, and the fact was so reported and headlined prominently in the papers. And the rioting followed, not preceded, the aborted arrangements for the bodies to be given a funeral under state sponsorship. Of course, it could have happened the way the novel describes it in some imaginary fictional world. But why use the detail about thirteen soldiers (a figure that is etched indelibly in our contemporary memory) if you are going to play about with the facts in this way? And why construct a version that unintentionally, no doubt, softens the reality? A slaughter resulting from a mass misconception that Buddhist monks had been killed would have been, though not defensible, mitigated by being an outburst of outraged religious emotion. The reality, with its planned pogrom and state connivance, was much more horrible. Isn't Sivanandan guilty, in his own way, of 'making up false memories'?[35]

The discrepancy between historical fact and fictional recreation can only be identified as such if the reader has a prior and fairly detailed knowledge of the events described. The passage, if read from such a position, can then be placed within the context of Sivanandan's opening assertion of the rupture of the historical past and could be seen as an indication of the susceptibility of historical events to distortion, as well as the fallibility of memory. It could also be read in relation to Sivanandan's political project: a displacement of a historical landmark that works to unsettle the collective memory of the pogrom from its mythic status, creating the conditions for the mapping of subaltern histories by enacting a tactical rupture to the Sri Lankan grand narrative. Yet this passage reveals that the extent to which the project of subaltern truth-telling, which gains – in the case of *When Memory Dies* – part of its legitimacy from affirming the deconstructive, fragmented and partial nature of its enterprise, might be compromised when it simultaneously appears to try to project an inclusive monumental history of its own. A significant factual slippage such as this one thus serves to expose the *internal contradictions* at work in the act of re-membering the nation. The slippage creates an interpretative gap for readers 'in the know' – a gap already evident in the disjunctive temporalities of the performative and pedagogical as they are mediated and deployed in the text. It also raises issues relating to the role of the exiled political writer who scripts an alternative past for an international readership many of whom are likely to be less than fully familiar with the facts. Siriwardena's important critique thus *activates* the internal contradictions within the text in ways that work to promote the text's broader aims; it effectively 'renews the past, refiguring it as a contingent "in-between" space, that innovates and interrupts the performance of the present'.[36] Read in terms of such a critical paradigm, the passage can be seen to register the instability of cultural signification through which 'national culture comes to be articulated as a dialectic of various temporalities – modern, colonial, postcolonial, "native" – that cannot be a knowledge that is stabilized in its enunciation'.[37]

Clearly the clash between the imperatives of performative deconstruction and pedagogical reconstruction suggests that Sivanandan's fictional text is internally marked by contradictory impulses as he enters what Timothy Brennan has described as 'a rhetorical world where polemic cannot be'.[38] This can also be seen in the way that, despite its significant success at blurring ethnic boundaries, *When Memory Dies* does subscribe to a logic of difference: that of gender difference. In contrast to *Funny Boy*, which, as will be seen, mediates homosexual identity against the normative inscription of heterosexual relations, exploring the liminal space between gendered identities, Sivanandan's novel focuses on the primacy of male friendships in which women stand as sexualised outsiders. Key women characters – including independent, individuated women such as Manel, Mrs Bandara and Meena – are invariably big-breasted, wide-hipped or lush-thighed. Maternal figures such as Sahadeven's mother and his foster-mother achieve historical transcendence in their depiction as 'a sort of aura that surrounded them all but had no life of its own' (p. 35) and a woman who 'was for all time and all places' (p. 28). Bodily imagery is used not only in the physical description of them but also invested in their very articulation of themselves, constraining them further within a sexually differentiated discourse. Lalli's mother's invective against her enforced separation from her grandson, Vijay, is articulated in the transcendent language of the natural and elemental – 'You kill us in our wombs, you men.' 'You never let a thing lie and grow and put forth in its own season' (p. 242) – and similarly Devi's reasoning is bound by a temporal logic that negates the possibility of human agency and intervention: 'everything was karma for her. . .no history. . .no determination. . .just a cycle of birth and death and birth again [. . .] "We give birth to you and you destroy what you make us give birth to; what could be more topsy-turvy than that?"' (pp. 390–91). While Sivanandan does present their gendered perspective as a valid and valuable alternative to the confrontational and historically contingent discourse of men, and does present exceptions – such as Padma – to the generality, his main objective is to present women in a supporting role to his male characters' historically situated quest for social emancipation. As Sharanya Jayawickrama has shown, this representation of women fundamentally contradicts Sivanandan's political writing, in which the 'power of the revolutionary act of everyday existence' is asserted.[39]

Such internal contradictions reveal the extent to which the 'staging' of writing referred to by Lazarus is situated at the interstices of affiliation, that the 'context' the writer addresses is less than secure, and the engagement of which he, Lazarus, speaks is subject to slippage under the pedagogical and performative exigencies of the text. Sivanandan's political writing expresses a concomitant positional flexibility that can be seen in the discrepancy between his evaluation of the disruptive effects of colonialism on Sri Lankan society and culture and his description of the impact of these on himself. His political writing is uncompromising in its emphasis on the social and cultural contradictions generated by colonialism, which 'divided in order to rule what it integrated in order to exploit. And it raised a class of administrators, suckled on English language and culture to reconcile the contradictions'. This is extended in his evaluation of colonial capitalism:

> Colonial capitalism creates nothing and destroys nothing. Instead, it distorts, disfigures, disorientates. It develops the productive forces only to stifle them in the service of the 'mother country'. It engenders new social relations and social classes only to suspend them between the past and the future: the bourgeois temperament remains feudal, the proletarian mind unreleased from the land. It creates a hybrid culture only to frustrate its finest flowering.[40]

The disjunctive temporalities alluded to by Bhabha are clearly evident in Sivanandan's emphasis on the disorientating cultural effects of a system that enforces new social relations 'suspended' between the past and future. Yet Sivanandan, while alert to the social and cultural contradictions generated by his own up-bringing and education,[41] seems keen to try and belittle the disruptive effects these might have had on himself. He explicitly rejects exilic status, taking issue with the term, and takes care to historicise the ruptures enforced by his own multicultural education into a specific narrative of reclamation.[42] Although both his political and creative writing are, as Lazarus points out, indebted to Western political philosophers and 'dense with allusion to the "great tradition" of English literature',[43] Sivanandan's own description of his university education insists that his teachers worked to 'nativise' English authors, 'to appropriate them so as to enrich, not to be a substitute for, our own' so that they 'localised Chaucer while still leaving him in England'.[44] His scripting of his colonial education is correspondingly selective – 'it was the progressive, anti-colonial, subaltern aspects of British culture, not the dominant aspects of British culture, which influenced me'[45]– suppressing the cultural disruptions that form the basis of much of his attack on colonial capitalism by resisting acknowledgement of the multiple, contradictory and unpredictable effects of colonial lines of influence on his own thinking. Might this impulse to suppress the ruptures of hybridity in the scripting of his own personal narrative reflect a lurking respect for the 'bogy of Authenticity'?[46] And if so, how might this affect our reading of interethnic relationships in *When Memory Dies*? To what extent, in other words, does the thwarting of cultural hybridity (referred to in the passage cited earlier) affect Sivanandan's own scripting of it? Such questions in no way diminish or undermine the significant achievement of Sivanandan's text in radically realigning Sri Lanka's social and cultural history through its subaltern reclamation of a suppressed past and in articulating a 'practice of co-existence' that has the potential to generate a 'politics of co-existence'. Rather they open up for consideration a space for debating the extent and effects of the very social and cultural contradictions of which Sivanandan writes by revealing how they might, indeed, have been rendered internal to his own discourse. It is perhaps through such symptomatic readings that the disjunctions and disruptions that drive his poetics, his politics and his polemics can be fully articulated, addressed and negotiated.

Staged identities: performance, mimicry and historical narration

In contrast to Sivanandan's work, Shyam Selvadurai's novels explore the disjunctions between the pedagogical prescriptives that inform the 'powerful master-discourse' and the performative in their explicit exploration of staged identities.[47] Selvadurai's emphasis on performance works in different ways: in *Funny Boy* – as well as his recently published novel for young adults *Swimming in the Monsoon Sea* (2005) – it works to undercut and reconstitute the grand narrative in ways that endorse what Sivanandan calls 'the personal politics of the subject'.[48] In *Cinnamon Gardens* – a novel that self-consciously mimics the discourse of canonical nineteenth century realist texts – textuality itself serves to rupture the inscription of the subject, revealing the disruptive effects of colonial mimesis in ways that appear to call into question some of the assumptions implicit in Sivanandan's claim that his experience of colonial education effectively worked to 'nativise' canonical texts. Of course, one of the key distinctions between the writers rests in their class affiliations – a distinction evident in Sivanandan's scripting of the nation through the rural working class and Selvadurai's focus on the lives of urban, affluent, upper-class Tamils. Their divergent scriptings of ethnic difference in the mapping of the nation could be related as much to this distinction as to their different approaches to the politics of the subject.[49] It is a distinction that finds expression in spatial representation: Selvadurai's novels which, as will be seen, deploy the discourse of territoriality and are firmly situated in the respectable heart of Colombo, the metropolitan centre, clearly enact a corresponding discourse of ownership and control, whereas Sivanandan's novel mobilises multiple 'stories of small places'[50] in its regional coverage of the land and the landless. Both writers reject and rupture a nationalist cartography but from radically different sites of enunciation.

In *Funny Boy*,[51] Selvadurai reveals the border as a site from which the subject begins its 'unfolding' in ways that draw a distinction between pedagogical and performative temporalities. The novel enacts the disjunction between the two by clearly distinguishing between externally imposed categories and the transgressive, desiring body as the mediation of emergent homosexuality is played out through foregrounding the mobility of the desiring self across clearly defined territories. From its opening story on the cross-dressing boy narrator, Arjie, who gravitates to the 'girls' territory' during playtime, to the final story of his homosexual relationship with a Sinhalese school friend, Shehan Soysa, it is clear that the cultural coordinates of identity in the novel are marked along exclusionary lines determined by ethnicity and gender identification. It seems that Selvadurai positions desire as an unpredictable force field which threatens both to disrupt the established order of an ethnically divided society while simultaneously offering it its only means of redemption. The love affairs of Radha Aunty, Aunt Doris and Arjie's mother and father cover a wide a range of ethnic and cultural pairings (Tamil–Sinhala, Burgher–Tamil, Tamil–English), substantiating the boundary-crossing of Arjie's homosexual relationship with his Sinhalese friend, but, just as in Arjie's case, they are all shown to fail as a result of the collective investment in maintaining ethnic difference. Thus while all the affairs are presented from Arjie's point of view – a boy's politically naive perspective – their imbrication within the pedagogic marks the nationalist discourse of ethnic essentialisation which reinforces cultural difference.

This difference is shown to be not only externally imposed (by the increasing racism in the country) but also internally policed by Arjie's family. Such policing is brought into sharp relief after Arjie has overheard his grandmother's heated exchange with Radha Aunty and reflects upon her response:

> The intensity of Ammachi's reaction had shaken me. I wondered why Anil's being Sinhalese upset her so? I was in a Sinhala class at school and my friends were Sinhalese. My parents' best friends were, too. Even our servant was Sinhalese, and, in fact, we spoke with her only in Sinhalese. So what did it matter whether Anil was Sinhalese or not? [pp. 58–59]

Arjie's surprise at ethnic intolerance is repeatedly foregrounded in the novel, and is emblematic of his idealism and naivety in the face of the increasing ethnic polarisation going on around him. Although he himself speaks Sinhala and knows no Tamil, his identity as a Tamil is asserted at home and reinforced by the bullying he receives at school. As a result his emotional investment in the romance and intrigue of ethnically mixed relationships becomes a mark of his innocence, something that will inevitably have to be shed as he grows into adulthood and develops an awareness of political contingency and the inflexibility of social prescriptives.

Arjie's political naivety is also marked by his limited grasp of historical 'facts' in ways that reveal the erosion of registers of intercommunal existence in the construction of a grand narrative of partition that essentialises ethnic difference. The single historical event that marks his awareness – the killing of his great-grandfather in the race riots of the 1950s – works to reinforce his increasing awareness of ethnic polarisation in the increasing communalism of the late 1970s. In the absence of alternative histories of intercommunal exchange, ethnicity is not so much presenced as a strategic identity, but is conscripted in the service of the pedagogic as an immutable and transhistorical essence. As a result the increasing racial violence in the country – marked by the attack on Radha Aunty in Jaffna, the abduction and murder of Daryl, the victimisation of Jegan in the South and the final explosion of violence in Colombo in which Arjie's grandparents are killed – is in danger of appearing as the natural by-product of an intractable social malaise, a kind of cultural pathology. This is in stark contrast to *Where Memory Dies*, where it is consistently presented as a politically orchestrated enterprise.

The fixity of ethnic boundaries is given material resonance in the novel through spatial configurations. *Funny Boy* charts a clearly segregated terrain of permitted spaces and forbidden zones, and it is the negotiation, invasion and violation of these spaces that occupies much of the novel. Physical space is politicised, gendered, socially stratified (into the family residence and servant's quarters), legitimated and policed. Its contestation stands as a metaphor for the larger struggle for territorial control in the country. Selvadurai invites such a reading at the outset when, in the opening pages of the novel, children's play is articulated in the discourse of spatial contestation:

> [W]e had developed and refined a system of handling conflict and settling disputes ourselves. Two things formed the framework of this system: territoriality and leadership.
>
> Territorially, the area around my grandparents' house was divided into two. The front garden, the road, and the field that lay in front of the house belonged to the boys, although included in their group was my female cousin, Meena. In this group, two factions struggled for power, one led by Meena, the other by my brother, Varuna [. . .]
>
> The second territory was called 'the girls', included in which, however, was myself, a boy. It was to this territory of 'the girls', confined to the back garden and the kitchen porch, that I seemed to have gravitated naturally [. . .]
>
> For me, the primary attraction of the girls' territory was the potential for

> the free play of fantasy. Because of the force of my imagination, I was selected as leader. [p. 3]

It is significant that Arjie's physical mobility is linked to his youthful desire to indulge in such imaginative play. His ability to move to the girls' territory, his acceptance into his mother's bedroom (he is the only child permitted to enter it) and his artful navigation of permitted space into both forbidden zones (crossing the boundary back into the girls' space in 'Pigs Can't Fly' after his eviction, for example) and conflictual but open public spaces (such as the rehearsal hall in 'Radha Aunty'), all lead him into conspiratorial engagement with illicit activity. Selvadurai's mapping thus remains precise and unintrusive, emerging naturally within the context of social events and personal relationships within the novel.

The focus on furtive spatial negotiations prepare the ground for the climactic end to the novel, when Arjie and his family go into hiding during the communal riots in Colombo. The celebration of physical mobility driven by the 'free play of fantasy' gives way to the nightmare of enforced eviction. It is now clear that Selvadurai's reliance on the construction of segregated space is necessary to his enterprise, as space and place define the illegitimate activities they promote. Activities such as the illicit liaisons of Radha Aunty and Anil, Arjie's mother and Daryl, Arjie and Shehan, Jegan's liaison with his terrorist comrades, and even Arjie's practice of eavesdropping, define and are defined by the clearly marked spatial structures Selvadurai maps for us. They follow a complex choreography and collectively work to naturalise the final, precisely plotted escape by Arjie and his family. At the end of the novel Selvadurai signals loss of home through the breakdown of physical boundaries as Arjie's house is burned and left exposed to the elements. As Pradeep Jeganathan has pointed out, the pogrom in which Arjie's home is destroyed did indeed lead to the renegotiation of space and the domestication of differential power dynamics.[52]

The emphasis on essentialised ethnicities and segregated physical space allows – as I indicated earlier – Selvadurai to focus on the relative fluidity of relationships and the physical mobility of his central character. They provide a context of constraint that allows us to witness the process of emergence of a bordered sexual identity. Arjie's cross-dressing replicates Bhabha's notion of mimicry as menace and, in Judith Butler's words, 'implicitly reveals the imitative structure of gender itself – as well as its contingency'.[53] The narrative *I* in *Funny Boy* is both coherent – there is no postmodern play on fragmentation here – and fluid. Therefore, the reason, in my view, Selvadurai essentialises ethnic identities is because his primary interest is not so much in contesting these categories (though by overdetermining them he may be doing this too), but in revealing the emergence of the decentred, 'queer' subjectivity of his central character.[54] (It is significant that Arjie is not called 'gay' or 'homosexual' in the text, but 'funny', indicating the instability of his subject-positioning.) The overdetermination of both ethnic and gender identities provide the material and ideological conditions for this emergence.

It is a position that can be reformulated in terms of the models of subjectivity presented in queer theory. In *Gay and After*, Alan Sinfield has distinguished between the model of a decentred hybrid self and one that draws upon an ethnic affiliation. An 'ethnic' mode of identification in queer theory is a strategic one that allows gays and lesbians to position themselves as a political minority with rights comparable to those of other ethnic groups. It is exclusive and contestational, and contrasts with the model of decentred, hybridised subjectivity presented by Selvadurai. Indeed *Funny Boy*'s emphasis on the process of self-discovery, of a sexual identity in the making, foregrounds the process of 'coming out', which Sinfield has identified as central to gay identity, an identity that is in process and always incomplete:

> The lesbian or gay person is poised at the brink of a perpetual emergence, troubling the straightgeist with a separation that cannot be completed, a distinction that cannot be confirmed. It makes it hard for us [gays and lesbians] to know, even to recognise, ourselves. It is a kind of reverse diaspora that makes our subcultures hybrid.[55]

The difference between the model of a decentred and processual queer identity favoured by Selvadurai and the model of ethnic identification defined earlier foregrounds contrasting experiences in identity formation: the former is exilic or transmigratory, articulating the incompleteness of connection, and the latter is a model of belonging, expressing fixed affiliation. For Selvadurai, the queerness of Arjie as a 'funny boy' is therefore mediated through his status as an outsider, a migrant, a subject on 'the brink of perpetual emergence' from the borderlines of belonging. It is interesting to note that this has a structural correspondence with Selvadurai's own experience of sexual emergence, which took place in exile in Canada and marked a radical break from a sense of originary identity, for 'the pure sense of being Sri Lankan was based on rigid heterosexual and gender roles'.[56] As Patton and Sánchez-Eppler observe, 'when a practitioner of "homosexual acts", or a body that carries any of many queering marks moves between officially designated spaces – nation, region, metropole, neighbourhood [. . .] – intricate realignments of identity, politics and desire take place'.[57] Therefore Selvadurai's foregrounding of the mobility of 'funny boy' Arjie, when set within the context of Sri Lankan ethnic conflict, not only enables but perhaps also requires the reinforcement of constructed, essentialised ethnicities and the clear demarcation of 'officially designated spaces', marking a disjunction between performative and the pedagogic.

Yet territoriality, gender identification and ethnic essentialisation are not the sole agents of boundary marking in the text; language too, as Sharanya Jayawickrama has shown, serves as an important agent of cultural difference. The segregation of education into Tamil and Sinhala streams after the 'Sinhala Only' Act effectively narrowed lines of communication between the two communities, and the novel replicates this process by moving from 'a situation of linguistic multiplicity and syncreticism where the English language medium in which the novel is written serves to draw attention to the implied crossings between languages' to a situation of increasing linguistic segregation between individuals.

Jayawickrama has observed that Sinhala is not simply presented as the language of power and heteronormative identity but is also the language of survival in the text, and has suggested that Arjie's lack of knowledge of Tamil is linked to his sexual innocence. She focuses on Arjie's final, retributive performance – his deliberate mangling of English verse at the prize-giving ceremony – describing it as 'an act of subversion from *within* a structure of control'.[58] Such a reading, linking sexual maturation and personal survival with the borderlines of language, reveals the extent to which the performative functions as an index of personal transformation in the text.[59] Arjie's emergent sexuality draws upon a range of sources from popular culture – such as Sinhala love comics and film icons – as well as close observation of his mother and the evolving romances about him, culminating in his ritual enactment of 'bride-bride' at weekends. All of these sources involve a staging of identity – a performative index of the ambivalence of presencing, its partiality and incompleteness – that threaten to unhinge pedagogical prescriptives of gender and ethnic essentialisation by revealing that they too might be 'roles' that serve competing desires and interests. The historical mediation of essentialised identities that informs pedagogical temporality in the text is thus under threat. Arjie's fantasies of identity have the potential to call into question other scriptings of identity by revealing their performative basis. They work to foreground the inherent instability of all 'signifying processes of cultural identification'.[60] Such a staging of identities relies, however, on the concomitant and clear structuration of intractable and intransigent pedagogically inscribed boundaries for their effectiveness so that Arjie's 'exile' from childhood (p. 5) can be shown to be an emergence into a *different* space and temporality.

In *Cinnamon Gardens*[61] the emphasis on the fantasy of staged identities is taken further. The novel marks the disjuncture between the inscription of the past – its staging within the pedagogical – and the inscription of the colonial subject through the self-conscious activation of the native as mimic. The parallel narratives of Balendran and Annalukshmi are enacted within the prescriptive logic of colonial discourse and emergent nationalism, revealing the fundamental collusion between these two discourses. Yet this very inscription within the borders of a self-consciously *borrowed* discourse renders unstable the site of enunciation where the subject gains its presencing. Discourse itself is externalised and extemporised into a code of conduct with each chapter opening with a verse from the Tirukkural – a first century doctrinal Tamil text that directs readers towards the path to leading 'the ideal life', in particular on finding happiness in married life. This is then followed by a narrative of cool and constrained prose, weighted with the decorum of nineteenth century English manners and romance, relating the lives of those who, despite appearing to be the very models of respectability, flagrantly fail to fulfil the Tirukkural's precepts of marital fidelity and loyalty to social duty. Annalukshmi's feminism and Balendran's homosexuality are not so much repressed but recoded into the dominant discourse of writers from 'the great tradition' of English literature – writers such as George Eliot, Austen, Dickens, Hardy, the Brontës, E.M. Forster and Shakespeare, whose works are alluded to in the novel. The fundamental discrepancy between the duties of these comprador colonials and their actions, their ability to dissemble and hide their putative misdemeanours, attests to the fragility of the very system that protects the social and material privileges of those who mimic the colonial power.

It is significant that this exploration of cultural hybridity and colonial mimicry is set within the critical period of pre-Independence nationing, a time of the growth of labour unions and emergent Tamil nationalism, when the Donoughmore Commission was debating the question of universal franchise and the rights of ethnic minorities and women. The Commission is no mere historical backdrop – its concerns are formative in the relationships between the key players – and its ultimate failure to change the balance of power (p. 379) registers a lost opportunity for national unity that has its subaltern counterpart in *When Memory Dies*. It is also a novel, as Carmen Wickramagamage has pointed out, that focuses on the female subject in the context of emergent feminism. Her argument that Selvadurai raises the issue of feminism through Annalukshmi's subjectivity – which is shown to be divided between the competing ideologies of 'imperialist feminism and native patriarchy' – only to constrain its active expression so that her autonomy is effectively denied,[62] reveals the extent to which agency is problematised by Selvadurai's scripting of history. I would like to suggest that, and now show how, the scripting of national and cultural emergence in *Cinnamon Gardens* relies upon a corresponding reading of colonial mimesis and mimicry that destabilises notions of the transcendental subject (on which Wickramagamage's analysis is based). I will further show how this marks the radical instability of the very project of nationing, working to undermine prescriptive, pedagogic readings of the past.

The central characters of the novel are all urban, anglicised comprador Tamils who live in the most affluent residential part of Colombo. Selvadurai's meticulous mapping of the area and his careful historicisation reveal not only that this novel is intended to inform and elucidate those who are unfamiliar with this region and period of Sri Lanka (making it readily accessible to Western readers), but also that it is intended to be in alignment with realist prescriptives.[63] This putative realism is, however, recoded within the restrained discourse and mannered idiom of the canonical English text, in particular the high realism of the nineteenth century[64] – the period of dramatic colonial domination and expansion – a manoeuvre, I suggest, that works to create an uncanny space of (mis)recognition for both Western and Sri Lankan readers. The key characters all appear to be anglicised exemplars of Macaulay's mission to create in the Indian subcontinent 'a class of interpreters between us and the millions whom we govern – a class of persons Indian in blood and colour, but English in taste, in opinions, in morals and in intellect'.[65] As Bhabha has shown, however, such efforts are inevitably compromised by the unstable logic of rearticulation resulting in 'a flawed colonial mimesis, in which to be Anglicized is *emphatically* not to be English'. Such a staging of identity in relation to fantasies of colonial emulation effectively works to undermine both realism and historicism, rupturing such discourse and transforming it into 'an uncertainty which fixes the colonial subject as a "partial" presence' 'both incomplete and virtual'.[66] Identity is thereby rendered strategic rather than essential, problematising notions of the authentic and destabilising discourses of originary culture. Within the logic of consciously mimetic discourse, historical events are, correspondingly, staged as discursive constructions, caught not only in the temporal indeterminacy of the time lag between event and narration, but also in the cultural indeterminacy of translation betwixt and between different sites of affiliation.

This reading of colonial mimesis and mimicry reveals a radical instability in the project of nationing presented in *Cinnamon Gardens*. Set in the metropolitan 'centre' of political reform and in a critical period of national emergence,[67] the displacement of cultural authority evident in the novel's self-consciously borrowed idiom is translated into the construction of the colonial subject as a 'partial' presence – both incomplete and virtual, in Bhabha's formulation. Their liminal status does not merely register ambivalence but, equally significantly, hierarchies in hybridity, in which, for example, Jayaweera's truncated speech (see pp. 126–28, 321–22) serves as a marker of both his status as a member of the impoverished, rural Sinhala community and his difference from the anglicised urban elite.[68] Characters do not appear to be conscious of their own alienation, and Selvadurai relies upon the discursive saturation of dated English literary idiom and careful mediation of perspectives to reveal the ironies underpinning their cultural displacement – Balendran's reflections on his Indian-born nephew's anglicisation serving to highlight his blindness to his own:

> Seelan's clothes spoke of an affluence that equalled his own or that of any Cinnamon Gardens family. Like the son of a Cinnamon Gardens family, Seelan carried himself with a sense of importance. In fact, Balendran thought, as he looked at the rakish angle of Seelan's hat, his nephew was quite a dandy and, judging from his British intonation, an anglophile as well. How strange this was, how unexpected. [p. 264]

While Balendran's surprise is largely mediated by his assumptions of Seelan's impoverished circumstances, his shock upon hearing Seelan's 'formal, almost oratical tone, the British intonation to his voice' (p. 263) registers the ruptures of cultural disjunction deployed in mimesis, the vicissitudes of alienation and self-alienation that construct the colonial subject. A staunch supporter of British imperialism, Seelan's liminality is clearly positioned as a site of disjunction where the aspirations of the impoverished outcast meet the prescriptive ideologies of cultural imperialism: his 'self-important, dandyish manner, his anglophilia was an attempt to bridge, in some way, the space between who he was and who he felt he should be' (p. 283). Balendran's inability to translate the logic of such cultural and social disjunction to his own circumstances as a member of the comprador class reveals that the partiality of identity in the construction of the colonial subject is extended here to include the partiality of class affiliations too. It is Selvadurai's attention to the historical and ideological *production* of the mimetic subject and his corresponding awareness of the multiple psychological, social and cultural *effects* of mimicry that is his major achievement in the novel. The double-coded discourse of the novel effectively dramatises the temporal disjunctions – the multiple zones of belonging – mediated by those who are positioned on the borders of belonging, thus emphatically marking the 'exilic' as internal to the project of nationing.

Yet *Cinnamon Gardens* does not constitute a celebratory retrieval of liminality on the basis of its interventionist potential. While the novel's representation of the cultural instabilities endemic to the project of nationing works to relocate the emergence of Lankan independence in an interstitial space of cultural indeterminacy – revealing the radical instability at the heart of originary notions of identity – there is an equal and significant emphasis on the loss, aporia and silences in the spaces created by such cultural and temporal disjunctions. The narrative trajectories of the central characters mark the victory of dominant codes: Balendran conceding to family dictates and Anna left suspended in indecision while historical events proceed relentlessly, unfolding towards an increasingly unstable future. While the novel explicitly rejects romantic closure, testifying to the constraints of such discourse, its allegiance to redeploying the performative registers of colonial mimesis and mimicry work to reveal what is lost in the translation and resettlement of colonial idiom and codes of inscription. The construction of the colonial subject as mimic thus not only works, as Bhabha has pointed out, to unseat the transcendental subject,[69] but also here registers its very resistance to representation.

Carmen Wickramagamage's emphasis on Anna's absence of historical agency – an element mirrored in Balendran's narrative of ultimate acquiescence – her position as a 'passive by-stander' and 'mere on-looker' at the periphery of key political events is significant here.[70] It marks Anna's marginalisation from political events as well as her exclusion from the discourses of contestatory identities embodied in them. It also registers the way in which the text's self-conscious allegiance to mimetic discourse has served to resist representations of subjectivity that carry authority outside its registers. Wickramagamage's claim that Anna's character is 'over-determined by history' so that her 'autonomy' is denied and her emergent feminist individualism is 'retarded' by multiple socio-political and historical currents[71] is premised on a notion of the transcendental, unitary subject – a positioning explicitly resisted by the radical instability of subjecthood generated by colonial mimesis.[72] Yet what Wickramagamage's search for a feminist voice in the text also reveals is the ways in which the self-conscious staging of mimicry through discursive metatextuality resists the construction of alternative sites of resistance. The subjectivity of the characters – constructed from an overtly borrowed discourse – is not simply 'alienated' from an originary essence. Rather, the problematisation of the originary and the corresponding revelation of the instability of representation dislocates both the fictional and historical in ways that render subjectivity itself beyond representation. By limiting resistance to the horizon of the discursive, Anna and Balendran's compliance with the prescriptive logic of socially constrained colonial mimesis insists upon a silence that eludes translation.

Selvadurai's engagement with the discursive borderlines of belonging – in both these novels – marks the limits of performative resistance. They stand in contrast to Sivanandan's interruptive manoeuvres that work to re-site the performative in an alternative pedagogical register. Between them these political exiles explore areas of cultural hybridity that intervene in a politics of nationing bound to 'the will to partition', revealing the contingency of such nationing in their emphasis on the epistemological limits of belonging. Their work insists on a revaluation of the past as a site of discursive territoriality so that Bhabha's claim that displacement and discrimination render 'political survivors [. . .] the best historical witnesses'[73] carries within it a need to analyse, ever more closely, the enunciative borders that have been negotiated and crossed – as well as those that remain unbreached – if our understanding of the historical past is to invigorate and revitalise the fractured present.

7 Michael Ondaatje

Place as palimpsest

> To speak of unspeakable violation, there must be a safe witness.
>
> Patricia Lawrence[1]

In his seminal study of spatial practice, Michel de Certeau has observed that places drawn from memory render subjectivity precarious. 'The memorable' he claims 'is that which can be dreamed about a place. In this place that is a palimpsest, subjectivity is already linked to the absence that structures it as existence and makes it "be there", *Dasein*'.[2] For Michael Ondaatje, a diasporic Sri Lankan who left the country at the age of nine and first returned after an absence of twenty-five years, Sri Lanka is a site where the ephemeral reconstructions of a remembered past are ruptured and reconstituted by the peripatetic exigencies of travel and temporary habitation. For in the sites of belonging available to those whose mediation of the land is largely determined by their mobile relationship to it, subjectivity itself is marked by its erasure, as the absence of locatedness mobilises shifting registers of affiliation. Place is now a palimpsest, land and territory subject to simultaneous inscription and erasure as the migrant writer moves across multiple sites of belonging, writing betwixt and between cultural narratives and histories in a process of subject constitution.

Such 'postmodern' reclamation does not mark an evacuation of history, rather, as I will show, it is premised on a notion of its diasporisation, its dispersal into a variety of cultural registers and temporal inflections. Palimpsestic discourse impels both an archival critical approach – one that articulates the traces of prior, intersecting stories and discursive spaces – and one that is attentive to the range of narrative framings that are opened up by such inter- and intratextual dynamics. This hermeneutic is crucial to an evaluation of *Anil's Ghost*, a text that anticipates the diasporisation of its own readership and the legitimating strategies of an industry that commodifies information about 'the third world' for an international market. Here the putatively 'postmodern' investment in the indeterminacy of interpretation – a subject central to the emplotment of the narrative itself – is culturally recoded to form the basis of a metacommentary on the spuriously 'Western' reading of the Sri Lankan nation. Ondaatje's work requires the reader to mediate between several discursive levels resulting in what Huggan has described as the 'diasporisation of cultural knowledge'.[3]

My engagement with Ondaatje's Sri Lankan texts thus moves across two diasporic registers: from an inquiry into the relationship between subject constitution and travel in *Running in the Family* (1982) to an evaluation of the way in which different narrative framings in *Anil's Ghost* (2000) reveal the 'heterogeneity of reception' anticipated within the text.[4] As will be seen, in *Anil's Ghost* the central concern is not so much how to bear witness to traumatic events, but how to find 'truth' – or rather truths – in variable and shifting registers of meaning, how to render the act of witnessing 'safe' amidst the epistemic violence of hegemonic and hegemonising constructions of history and culture that provide the enabling context for extrajudicial killings and terrorism.

The richness of Ondaatje's work is largely derived from its lyrical intertextuality and intratextuality. Painstakingly researched, plurivocal and self-avowedly 'communal', it invites readers to look for sources while simultaneously mocking their search for an originary textual centre or writing subject.[5] In this palimpsestic rendering of identity and experience the difficulty for most critics has revolved around how to place Ondaatje; on identifying through the shifting layers of interpellation what Said has called 'the strategic location' of the author. Ondaatje's status as, first, a distinguished Canadian writer and, more recently, an international celebrity has complicated and compromised his positioning as a Sri Lankan writer to the extent that one notable Sri Lankan critic has felt impelled to insist that 'Michael Ondaatje is not Sri Lankan, and has not been Sri Lankan for years' and maintain that the politically situated *Anil's Ghost* is in fact 'a highly wrought orientalist' text.[6] Yet it is perhaps through this process of relating his Sri Lankan texts to political, cultural and literary developments in his native land that we can come closest to understanding the social and cultural coordinates that shape the very migrant sensibility he is so lauded for abroad. It is clear that the spatio-political registers in these texts bear imaginative and ideological affinities with the work of resident writers: the cultural investment in Buddhism in *Anil's Ghost* serves as a radical critique of the political bias found in the work of a number of Sri Lankan writers, including fellow Burgher Carl Muller; and links can be drawn between the spectral spaces of Wijenaike's novels, which are related to anxiety over class dynamics and social mobility, and the decentred, haunted narrative spaces of Ondaatje's work. Most significant of all, perhaps, the connections between the evaluations of the Sri Lankan art historian Ananda Coomaraswamy and Ondaatje's own aesthetic ideals offer invaluable insights into the structuration of the 'postmodern' sensibility that characterises his work. Such contextualisation serves not so much to root his work in an originary myth of natal cultural affiliation, but reveals instead the very fissures within such mythologies by routing it through multiple channels of cultural affiliation.

Reading Ondaatje as a Sri Lankan writer not only highlights how contexts are invented rather than found, but also foregrounds the hidden hierarchies that structure cultural affiliation, thereby raising 'invidious questions of "eligibility"'.[7] It comes as little surprise that Ondaatje's Sri Lankan texts are his most controversial, provoking critical responses that are informed by evaluative strategies that, in seeking to locate his site of cultural enunciation, come to be mediated by a polarising discourse marked by postcolonial and postmodern readings of Otherness. These evaluations often tell us more of the strategic positioning of critics than the diasporic constituents of the cultural registers found in the texts. Written almost twenty years apart, Ondaatje's Sri Lankan texts have ended up being subject to the radically divergent charges of 'orientalism' and 'nationalism' – subjects central to my analysis. These charges reflect more than the shift in emphasis in Ondaatje's oeuvre – from the secular spaces of the cartographic in *Running in the Family* to the iconographic representation of spiritual awareness in *Anil's Ghost,* and from the personal odyssey of the former to the political transactions of the latter – that inevitably requires a resettlement of the authorial subject. Rather they mark ways in which internationalism, or the diasporisation of cultural registers, threatens the legitimating strategies of those who invest in homogenous readings of culture and nation. To understand the vicissitudes of Ondaatje's internationalism it is first necessary to come to grips with his engagement with the much more thorny issue of nationalism. As I will show, *Running in the Family*, a text published a year before the escalation of ethnic conflict in 1983, readily lends itself to a postmodern reading that abstracts it from the context of contemporary Sri Lankan politics. In contrast *Anil's Ghost* marks a major investment on Ondaatje's part in Sri Lankan cultural politics. It can be read, on the one hand, as a revisionist text that not only strategically locates his own affiliation with the country but also – even more ambitiously – comes to relocate a cornerstone of Sinhala Buddhist nationalism by actively dismantling some of the unitary orthodoxies underpinning culturally exclusive nationalist readings of the past. On the other hand, it can be read as a text that undermines the certainties of such political coding in its persistent negotiation of incommensurable territories of knowledge. My aim is to move across the discursive levels of both texts to reveal the ways in which Ondaatje rewrites origins, both personal and national, into a mobile and provisional, alternative scripture of heterogeneity and hybridity.

'Rumours of topography' in *Running in the Family*

Running in the Family is perhaps Michael Ondaatje's most problematic and paradoxical text to date, both formally and ideologically.[8] A generic mix of journal, travelogue, memoir, biography, oral narration and poetry, it also contains photographs from family collections and public archives and a map, foregrounding a kind of textual hybridity that replicates – as Neluka Silva points out – the provisionality of ethnic boundaries.[9] The text's mediation of the Sri Lankan context however is openly autobiographical, leading to readings that invest in the challenge of defining the political biases of the writing subject. The openly autobiographical impulse and personal investment in recovering and reclaiming a homeland from the position of the returning native stranger has left Ondaatje open to a charge made by admirers and antagonists alike: that of exoticising his homeland. Even David Leahy's subtle negotiation of a range of readings concludes with a statement that attests to what he sees as a colonial bias in the text;

'It is difficult', he observes, 'not to read Ondaatje's masculine identified emphasis upon his anti-heroic father as eclipsing the heroine-ism of his mother; as partially recapitulating or re-internalizing the oldest colonial discourse'.[10] Daniel Coleman, who in contrast argues that the text celebrates interdependency and challenges a traditional masculinist perspective, nevertheless concurs with the charge of cultural exclusivity in claiming, at some length, that the text subscribes to the dominant discourse of 'exoticised Orientalism'.[11] And one of Ondaatje's most vociferous early critics, Arun Mukherjee, has claimed that Ondaatje's focus on family life made him guilty of indifference to 'the sordid realities created by centuries of colonial exploitation' and his own 'family's exploitative relationship to Sri Lanka', drawing attention to his seemingly uncritical stance on class dynamics in the text.[12]

These views have been amply supported by Sri Lankan critics, one of whom – referring to the exodus that took place after the ethnic riots of 1956–58 – has claimed that the lack of political and cultural engagement in the text clearly indicate that Ondaatje was, by dint of his Burgher and middle-class origins, 'the colonizer'.[13] In a rather more nuanced and sympathetic reading, Chelva Kanaganayakam points out that Ondaatje's failure to engage with public history reflects the country's own wilful blindness to social and political realities[14] – a view that effectively situates the nostalgic reclamations underpinning constructions of the 'exotic' squarely within Sri Lankan shores. Yet the approach of the first critic appears to be more closely aligned to that of the critical establishment in the country, even though it might be articulated rather more robustly and contentiously. In a move that directly connects Ondaatje's exilic status with critical expatriation and nationalist exclusivity he contends that Ondaatje forms 'part of an English-speaking, (sort of) Sinhala-hating and culturally ignorant bourgeoisie that fled the revolution'.[15] It seems that the personal odyssey charted in *Running in the Family* has directed attention to the writer's own position as the positioning of the writing subject and the identity of the author are identified as contiguous.

Yet *Running in the Family* does not so much delineate a colonising impulse or an act of postcolonial reclamation and recuperation, but rather reveals the instability and permeability of the migrant self. To confine it to the domain of colonial discourse forms an act of epistemic violence based on a misrecognition of its spatio-temporal registers. *Running in the Family* was written after two visits to the country, the first in 1978 and the second in 1980. It is first and foremost a nomadic text of interrupted journeys and broken connections that tries to chart the emotional map of Ondaatje's parents and their time through a narrative of travel. This attempt is, like all attempts at historical retrieval, only successful in imaginative terms, and Ondaatje highlights this fact. Within this context of self-reflexive metafictionality, the apparent 'orientalism' and 'exoticism' identified by so many critics is not a marker of difference substantiating a hierarchy of knowledge, but rather it registers alterity itself as the basis for mediating a range of cultural knowledges. In these terms, Eleanor Ty's observation that Ondaatje's 'exoticization' of landscape works to displace otherness onto places rather than people marks a useful distinction that works to situate the politics underpinning

Ondaatje's scripting of the itinerant stranger.[16] Through the use of real and metaphorical maps of the place and its people the text attests to the incompleteness of both colonial ownership and postcolonial reclamation, creating a liminal space of identification – one in which Ondaatje can claim in self-annihilating terms 'I am the foreigner. I am the prodigal who hates the foreigner' (p. 79). The spatial configurations in the text are closely connected to the process of storytelling and the construction of identity. While one critic has claimed that *Running in the Family* is 'a picture without a frame',[17] it would be more appropriate to claim that the text's many narratives have *too many* frames, and that the mapping of space and story is dependent upon slippage between the two.

I would like to start my consideration of the text – as Ondaatje does – with reference to maps. Michael Ondaatje's objectives in writing *Running in the Family* are self-avowedly cartographic. He has told Linda Hutcheon that his aim was 'to establish a kind of map; I wanted to make clear that this was just part of a long tradition of invasions [. . .] So the map and the history and the poetry made a more social voice, became the balance to the family story'.[18] The cartographic impulse to map the territory and construct a 'social voice' has a direct bearing on the way stories get framed in the text. *Running in the Family* opens with a map of Sri Lanka – a country Ondaatje consciously refers to as 'Ceylon' in the book. (The use of the colonial name for the country, which changed its name to Sri Lanka some twenty-four years after Independence, is one of the many means by which Ondaatje asserts a disjuncture between past and present and simultaneously reveals that he is conscious of the implications of his own act of interpellation.) The distance between signifier and signified gains resonance in this unnamed map, which is marked only by the names of a few towns, two national parks (which, boundaryless, seem to float free on the page), the fault lines of three named rivers and loose circles of unidentified lakes. This map of an as yet unnamed island faces two epigrams that offer contrasting perspectives. The first, by Oderic, a Franciscan friar from the fourteenth century, is openly fantastical: 'I saw in this island fowls as big as our country geese having two heads . . . and other miraculous things which I will not here write of'. The second, by Douglas Amarasekera, written contemporaneously to the text, offers an ironic commentary on the arrogance of Western mapping of other peoples' realities: 'The Americans were able to put a man on the moon because they knew English. The Sinhalese and Tamils whose knowledge of English was poor, thought that the earth was flat'. Together these epigrams unsettle the fragile certitudes of the map on the opposite page, suggesting the impossibility and inappropriateness of mimesis and gesturing towards the disjunction between the colonising imperatives that inform cartography and the illegibility of the territory it claims to represent. The reader is invited to consider this before coming to the title page and the second of Ondaatje's own 'maps' – the table of contents.

Ondaatje's consideration of cartographic discourses highlights the way 'the map [. . .] becomes a subject of a proposition rather than a statement of fact'.[19] He goes further than this however in questioning the reliability of all representative systems, visual and linguistic, through the ironic juxtaposition of photographs and stories. He thus constructs a textual dynamic in which different kinds of 'mapping' unsettle the authority of all systems of representation. The photographs preceding each section are deliberately difficult to decode and interpret, forcing the reader to share the writer's role of observer and participant in the construction of meaning. A couple of them – such as those of his parents pulling faces and of members of his community in fancy dress – focus on disguise and dissimulation. Others, such as the panoramic shot of Galle Face Hotel taken from the end of the mile-long promenade, force the observer to strain to make sense of their subject. Signs – map and photographs – collectively operate as a grid, providing loose visual coordinates for the stories themselves. Unlike the grid of Said's orientalism,[20] which filters and thereby transforms the subject into a representation of Otherness that consolidates the power of the Western observer, Ondaatje's grid serves to unsettle the colonialist enterprise, offering the reader unstable points of reference that frustrate the possibility of establishing a totalising, hierarchical system. In these terms the cartographic impulse in *Running in the Family* is typically postcolonial, foregrounding what Graham Huggan has described as 'the discrepancy between [the map's] authoritative status and its approximate function'.[21] The very fixity of the map and photographs thus becomes, paradoxically, Ondaatje's means of presenting an historical context that is shifting, provisional and contingent. Other frames of reference – such as the wide range of textual citations from writers as diverse as Edward Lear, D.H. Lawrence, the Sigiriya poets of Sri Lanka and Lakdasa Wikkramasinha – serve to foreground the sense of a surplus of context rather than a dearth of social commentary. What Ondaatje is articulating here seems not so much the 'desirous epistemologies of the Occident'[22] but rather the instability of the cartographer's experience in which all contexts are relativised and are equally valid before inscription. Within these terms *Running in the Family* is, as John Thieme has claimed, not a deconstructed text but one which foregrounds the problem of arriving at any kind of construction at all.[23]

The articulation of different family stories within this fluid and unstable historical context serves to present discourse as the only viable dwelling place. In a world in which the concept of home has become increasingly mobile, plurilocal and an act of performance, people's search for home increasingly comes to rest in the narrative of their lives. As John Berger has claimed, people are now more at home in 'words, jokes, opinions, gestures, actions, even the way one wears a hat'.[24] The stories of the exploits of the Gratiaen and Ondaatje families, their love affairs, cross-hatched careers, colonial (dis)connections, ambitions and achievements, are all overtly exaggerated as the emphasis on oral narration – on story as performance – is foregrounded. This theatricality, as Neluka Silva has shown, serves to conceal and mask their social marginalisation as Burghers,[25] so the reader is left – to borrow Huggan's useful term – with 'staged marginalities' whose histrionics serve to disguise their own interpellation in the narrative of the nation.

For Ondaatje is at pains to efface the identity markers of speakers. He does this by removing quotation marks from cited passages (blurring the distinction between different acts of storytelling), repeatedly using unascribed passages of speech (guaranteeing anonymity to his sources) and standardising the speech of his different interlocutors, further obliterating differences between them and conflating their stories with his through using the same linguistic register when slipping into his own account of the narrative. This technique of constructed anonymity, of presenting a tale (itself made up of multiple tales) without a teller, is highlighted in the section entitled 'Eclipse Plumage' where the reader is presented with an unstable narrative space that is made up of multiple contested territories of narrative. The identity of individual speakers is deliberately blurred as the act of narration takes precedence. The passage is followed by an overtly magical and cartographic account of his grandmother's death, which is presented as the ultimate spatialising act, her 'last perfect journey', as she floats across Nuwera Eliya race course, park and bus station, 'travelling [as fast] as Vere's motorcycle' (p. 128). Lalla gains a cartographer's synoptic view as she floats over the maze, 'its secret spread out naked as a skeleton for her', gazes down on the symmetrical flower beds and sees 'the drowned dogs of the town. Cattle, [. . .] men on roofs fighting with each other, looting' (p. 128); but it is a survey of surfaces and surreal transformations. Her death, which occurs a year before Independence, has been read as a representation of the end of imaginative licence before the period of indigenisation.[26] Yet this text, written long after cultural nationalism had taken its toll, resists such historical fixity through its retrieval of such fantasies of mobility – spatial and social – through reconstituting narrative through the migrant self. Here home is, as John Berger has observed, 'no longer a dwelling but the untold story of a life being lived'.[27]

It is this presentation of place and story as both situated and mobile that locates the author's position in relation to his former homeland, his 'strategic location', as that of a migrant rather than a colonial, exile, or even a native Sri Lankan Burgher. It is a position of self-erasure and annihilation, for in presenting being as an outcome of discursive practice 'the subject or self has no ontological or epistemological priority'.[28] This act of foregrounding discourse over authorial presence may perhaps have led some critics to assume that Ondaatje is endorsing the privileges of the cartographer without declaring his responsibility – an act of self-erasure that can lend itself to an 'orientalist' reading of the text. The very invisibility of the author-narrator is carefully maintained by the obliteration of identity markers in speech acts and through the repeated use of pronominal slippage – the collapse of third- to first-person narration on the opening page for example, and at moments of intense identification with Mervyn Ondaatje's story. It is this very invisibility that makes the narrator simultaneously the producer of the written text, the participant in the events described and the addressee at the dinner table, someone who not only creates but also bears witness to events. Furthermore it is a position that impels the reader to be implicated in the process of mapping both land and story. The discomfort some critics feel about the text may also, therefore, be the result, not so much of witnessing a postcolonial writer adopt an apparently colonial or 'orientalist' approach to the country of his birth, but rather of having to themselves engage in what they perceive as the colonising process of cartographic construction of an 'other' land.

But, as I have shown, the cartographic impulse in *Running in the Family* disturbs colonial imperatives. Orientalism, Said has claimed, depends upon a 'flexible *positional* superiority', and while Ondaatje's work presents us with positional flexibility it does so by exposing the incompleteness of reclamation.[29] The maps reveal 'rumours of topography, the routes for invasion and trade, and the dark mad mind of travellers' tales' (p. 64), and the stories tell us 'nothing of personal relationships', of the 'exchange of gift and character', leaving the narrator still searching for the 'intimate and truthful' in all of this (pp. 53, 54). Neluka Silva, in her invaluably detailed contextualisation of *Running in the Family*, has claimed that these stories serve to register the destabilisation of identity for the mixed raced Burghers in the transitional era of decolonisation. The arbitrariness of these multiple narratives, she contests, mimics the unfixity and provisionality of their history and lineage.[30]

Yet detailed historical contextualisation can, even while (as in Silva's case) working to deconstruct homogenising cultural prescriptives, serve to 'fix' this travel narrative within the very framework of nationing that the text's dispersive discursive registers seek to resist. The spatial present of the questing travelling narrator converges with the fluid past of his mobile and evasive subjects enacting a dispersal and diasporisation of spatio-temporal registers, connecting each individuated act of reading into a globalised network that reconstitutes the island diasporically. Retrieved stories meander through interrupted and broken journeys that cover the length and breadth of the island. The chaotic, drunken travels of his father in the Ford; the car breakdown on the way to the wedding; his father's last train ride, where the 'train kept shunting back and forth, never reaching Kelaniya, because [. . .] my father was absolutely certain the Japanese had mined the train with bombs' (p. 155); and the morning drive to Colombo where Mervyn and the writing subject become one (p. 185) – all these disrupt the spatial fixity of hierarchic cartographic representation. They foreground the fact that, while maps are authorless and fixed, all cartographic mapping is based on the contingency of travel and the proclivities of the individual traveller.

Ondaatje's investment in cartography is directed by an ethical impulse; in *Running in the Family*, as Neluka Silva has emphasised, colonial territoriality is linked to sexual dominance,[31] and in *Anil's Ghost* official maps reveal how spatial particularity can obliterate human beings, the lack of a human scale reinforced by the emphasis on the geography of disappearance (p. 39).[32] The apparent disregard for geographical accuracy and spatial logic of course invites the very charge of 'orientalism' that Ondaatje seeks to disturb. Qadri Ismail's damning critique of *Anil's Ghost* as a putatively racist text points out that Ondaatje is guilty of topographical inaccuracy,[33] and many of the episodes in the novel are linked by circumambulatory journeys that defy logic. Yet these spatial configurations – the disruption of cartographic certainty and the privileging of the process of travel and displaced subjectivity – could be mapped onto a specific politics of location. It foregrounds the idea that writing is itself a journey, a process of travel, so that 'every story is a travel story – a spatial practice'.[34] What is more this configuration can be inscribed into a logic that reveals that the author draws upon paradigms that reflect both a privileged social background and a disadvantaged one. If we agree with the claims of Rapport and Dawson, that the configuration of space is dependent on class,[35] *Running in the Family* can be seen to mediate both the spatial registers of the affluent and less privileged, as the individuated autobiographical impulse works through a series of multiple contested biographies within the context of an unstable and conflictual past.

The text exposes the ambivalence of assumed authority, of the writer as cartographer, through positioning the subjective self of the narrator as an enunciative site in discourse rather than a marker of presence, impelling the reader to share the experience of linking a fragmented contextual surplus with a profusion of tall tales, gossip and rumour. Favourable and less favourable readings of the 'colonial' and 'postcolonial' content of the text can thus be read as an indicator of a reader's willingness to share this experience of creative uncertainty – an engagement which carries specific responsibilities at a time when contexts have increasingly come to be defined for us. The very discomfort that critics register with the perceived orientalism of *Running in the Family* can therefore be seen as an indication of the text's power to enforce a correspondence between the writing and reading subject, of drawing readers into the very dynamics of displacement that is its central theme. As Said has pointed out, 'All cultures tend to make representations of foreign cultures, the better to master or in some way control them. Yet not all cultures make representations of foreign cultures *and* in fact master or control them' (original emphasis).[36] It is this presentation of thwarted and ruptured 'orientalism' through the registers of an open subjectivity that effectively denies readers the essentialising stability of fixed subject positionings. It is a position that might well have particular permutations for readers and critics in Sri Lanka as, in this case, mergence with the instabilities of the apparently exoticised gaze of the itinerant stranger induces a process of defamiliarisation that estranges the familiar landscape of 'home' and dislocates it into otherness, compelling those for whom settlement in Sri Lanka might well appear to be organic and autochthonous to experience an ontological displacement that unsettles their sense of who they are and where they might belong.

Re-siting Buddhism in *Anil's Ghost*[37]

Of course this mediation of migrancy as a site of displacement and deferred subjectivity resists direct political readings. While it is possible of course to read the postmodern evaluation of narrativity itself as a political act,[38] such an approach appears to invest in what Sangari has argued is a Eurocentric cultural logic that serves to disable interventionist textual dynamics in postcolonial texts, appropriating them in a kind of poststructuralist reclamation of marginality.[39] Yet Ondaatje's postmodernist (de)constructive drive is neither Eurocentric nor exclusively 'Western' in its basis; it also bears a striking affinity to the model of aesthetic understanding proposed by Ananda Coomaraswamy, a prominent scholar of Asian art upon whom Ondaatje draws heavily in *Anil's Ghost.* Like Ondaatje, who claims that 'the last thing a writer should be preoccupied with, when writing a book, is representing himself. The books I distrust – they could be memoir, fiction, poetry or criticism – are those that are basically advertisements for the self',[40] Coomaraswamy foregrounds the importance of what he calls 'the anonymity of the artist'.[41] In ways that replicate the title of Ondaatje's volume of poetry written at the same time as *Anil's Ghost*, Coomaraswamy claims that in Asian art 'the artist is never consciously exploiting his own personality, but merely leaves in his work the trace of his character in the same way that idiosyncrasy reveals itself in handwriting'.[42] Coomaraswamy's theories were driven by a politics of cultural reclamation that was defined by resistance to modern, secular aesthetic ideals that had its basis in Western theories of art. Thus his notion of the anonymity of the artist was formulated in defiance of what he interpreted as the modern cult of personality, 'our conception of art as essentially the expression of a personality, our whole view of genius, our impertinent curiosities about the artist's private life, all [. . .] products of a perverted individualism [that] prevent our understanding of the nature of medieval and oriental art'.[43] In contrast the anonymous ideal 'belongs to a type of culture dominated by the longing to be liberated from oneself. All the force of this philosophy is against the delusion "I am the doer". "I" am not in fact the doer' he claims 'but the instrument; human individuality is not an end but only a means'.[44]

This is precisely the model of artistic creation represented by Ananda Udugama in *Anil's Ghost*. An 'eye-painter turned drunk gem-pit worker turned head restorer' (p. 168), Ananda represents the artist as truth seeker, and it is *his* fate, according to Ondaatje, that forms 'the central core of the book'.[45] He is the only person to effectively humanise Sailor, the skeleton Anil and Sarath are trying to identify, but does so by imprinting the peace he wishes for his missing wife on the reconstructed head, rendering it useless for identification purposes (p. 185). His method of reconstruction fulfils one of the tenets of oriental art, in which, according to Coomaraswamy, the artist must 'be made over into what he imagines, remaining only potentially himself',[46] so that a portrait shows the essence of the subject and not anatomical accuracy.[47] It foregrounds the notion of artistic creation as a process of intuition – one that is echoed in the epigraphist Palipana's exegetical research – which is itself grounded in the conception of experiential egolessness foregrounded in Buddhism. One analyst has gone so far as to claim that it is in fact a key characteristic of Mahayana Buddhism, in which the conception of ego is experiential and intuitive, and has distinguished it from the conception of the ego to be found in Theravada Buddhism, which she claims is analytic and scholastic.[48] While the divisions between these two forms of Buddhism are not fixed or absolute, and all religious nomenclature can work to occlude the historically and socially contingent basis of their active, transformative practice, it does appear, as I will show, that Ondaatje works to displace a culturally exclusive reading of Theravada Buddhism (the form sanctioned by the state in Sri Lanka) in his aestheticised consideration of the religion in *Anil's Ghost* by foregrounding both Mahayana Buddhist practice and others that lie outside contemporary institutional structures.

The cultural grounding of the aesthetic values promoted in *Anil's Ghost* reveals the heterogeneity and hybridity underpinning the text's diasporisation of knowledge. This, as I will show, is central to the representation of the eye-painting ceremony that forms the climax of a novel whose central subject is not so much the causes of war but the interpretation of its effects. The novel focuses on a culturally grounded *conceptual crisis*, as Anil, Sarath, Palipana and Ananda are all in search of the 'truth' and causal connections appear radically uncertain. Violence is disturbingly anonymous – neither perpetrators nor victims are easy to identify – so it is registered not so much as a historically produced outcome of specific political conditions but as a condition of disjunction and disconnection, in which the very question of 'origins' is shown to have little currency. It is thus not ethnic conflict or extrajudicial killing that is the focus of the novel but rather the contested terrain of hermeneutics, between epistemologically based and ontologically driven forms of knowledge and understanding, with forensic anthropology, archaeology, epigraphy, visual art and the plastic art of sculpture introduced as different channels of awareness. Regular discussions between the principal protagonists on the nature of 'truth' require the reader to arbitrate contestatory interpretative strategies generating a sense of interpretative indeterminacy that gains expression in both the formal slippage from a broadly 'realist' political drama to a postmodern metaphysical narrative, and the cultural diasporisation replicated in the text itself. In a manner that replicates Palipana's own intuitive methods of deduction which invent facts in order to prove a broader truth (pp. 81–83), the circumstances of Sailor's death are proven through the use of a different skeleton: false 'origins' are used to prove his identity, showing how the displacement of originary histories may be a necessary precondition for the retrieval of meaningful registers of identity.

The ending of *Anil's Ghost* is contentious partly because it seems to replicate such interpretative indeterminacy in the very act of presenting an epiphanic insight. Critics have variously praised it as a 'healing vision' that offers 'a peace that *encompasses* understanding' (original emphasis)[49] or either attacked it or dismissed it as a literary gloss. In terms that replicate Althusser's formulation of art as an aesthetic resolution of political conflict, John de Falbe has claimed that this epiphany 'uses an easy poetic image to evade a problematic conclusion to the novel'.[50] Fans have claimed that it is 'a tour de force' linked 'with the redemptive act of writing', while Qadri Ismail, in a vituperative attack on Ondaatje's 'casual racism', has claimed that it indicates that Ondaatje is clearly 'on the side of the enemy or Sinhala nationalism'.[51] In terms that endorse Obeyesekere's observation that any affirmation of Buddhism within contemporary Sri Lanka is read to imply an affirmation of Sinhalese ethnic identity,[52] Ismail contends that the chapter is 'clearly a metaphor for restoring *a pure Buddhism* in war torn Sri Lanka' (my emphasis).[53] Even Radhika Coomaraswamy in her defence of the novel on the basis that it promotes a humanist side to Buddhism has concluded that the novel 'does not aim to foster a multicultural alternative for Sri Lanka'.[54] While both latter critics may have grounds to be concerned with the (under)representation of Tamils in the text and the representation of violence perpetrated by them, Ondaatje's political focus in the novel is not on an evaluation of Tamil militancy but rather of its more insidious Sinhala counterpart in the form of Marxist-nationalist JVP insurgents and their suppression, which led to extra-judicial killings and the disappearance of an estimated 30,000 people. The radically different views of critics reflect conflicting approaches to the placing of Buddhism and reveal dangerously reductive readings of what 'Buddhism' as a cultural and political entity stands for in the text. While Radhika Coomaraswamy is therefore – in my view – quite right to claim that Ondaatje is appealing for a humanist reading of Buddhism, she is, I believe, mistaken in denying the novel's multicultural drive. For the Buddhism of *Anil's Ghost* is not the grand assimilationist vehicle of national pride and unity found in Muller's mythopoeic epic, *Children of the Lion.* It is not the Buddhism of state pageantry and patronage, the monastic order, or scholastic doctrine, but is instead represented in its subaltern, unofficial, communal, hybridised and democratic forms as distinctly non-nationalist in basis. This is the Buddhism of the nētra mangala ceremony, of bodhisattvas, of statuary at the Sanxi Province and Buduruvagala, 'of forest-dwelling fraternities [. . .] monks who opposed rituals and luxuries' (p. 86) and of a theistic conceptualisation of the Buddha. This is the Buddhism invoked by the aesthetic idealism of Ananda Coomaraswamy, for whom 'every work of art is [. . .] potentially a "support of contemplation"; the formal beauty of the work inviting the spectator to the performance of a spiritual act of his own, of which the physical work of art has been merely the starting point'.[55] Even the emphasis on burial in the text could be seen to be an expansion of Sri Lankan Buddhism beyond the confines of a narrow, officially sanctioned, ethnicised and increasingly nationalist Theravadic orthodoxy.[56] To understand Ondaatje's reading and inscription of Buddhism it is therefore productive to recognise that he has moved beyond the confines of Sri Lankan Theravadic traditions to incorporate core elements and perspectives from the related but doctrinally distinct Mahayanist tradition.

As a number of scholars have made clear, Mahayana Buddhism is broadly distinguished from Theravada Buddhism in a number of significant ways. It emphasises universal rather than individual enlightenment, and intuition rather than analytical speculation.[57] In it, the Buddha is transcendental, eternal and absolute, and the ideal is embodied by the bodhisattva (or Buddha-to-be) – who strives for the emancipation of all – rather than the arhat, who strives for individual salvation.[58] This form of Buddhism, found predominantly in North and East Asia, lessens the distinction between monk and layman,[59] wresting power from the clergy.[60] It emphasises the connection between beings, promoting the 'theory of universal, indissoluble interdependence' with 'all creation sharing a common karma to which every individual contributes for good or ill'.[61] In keeping with Ondaatje's emphasis on communal experience and the blurring of boundaries between selves, the notion of a common karma is invoked in *Anil's Ghost* through the words of Robert Duncan: 'The drama of our time is the coming of all men into one fate' (p. 203). While for Sinhala Buddhist nationalists the notion of historical destiny has territorial implications, the thrust of Ondaatje's reading of collective karma is curiously agentless and boundaryless. What is more, as Theravada Buddhism is more insistently soteriological whereas some forms of

Mahayana Buddhism have communal elements,[62] Ondaatje's emphasis on the communal could be seen to mark a subtle but significant re-siting of the religion. It is an emphasis that results in a specific reading of historical determinism. As I have shown elsewhere, Ondaatje's work is marked by a dissociation of cause and effect so that the emphasis lies on multiple potential and the random relationship between events.[63] This model of understanding uses the rupture of history and narrative to reconstruct the continuum of space and time so that the miraculous and mundane can coexist. The model of community presented in *Anil's Ghost* – a motley group of war refugees living in an abandoned space – replicates that found in *The English Patient* but is emphatically democratic. While Ondaatje has called this a 'very celibate book'[64] – a term that has a distinctly monastic ring to it – the classless connections between the national swimming star/expatriate forensic anthropologist, the government archaeologist, and artist-miner are striking given the hierarchies of Sri Lankan society. The walauwe they inhabit is here the site of the very social mobility that informs the uncanny representation of the ancestral home in Wijenaike's texts.

This emphasis on the communal, on mobility across social boundaries, is symptomatic of the hybridity that could be seen to inform the scripting of Mahayana Buddhism. It also marks an assertion of multicultural agency in religious practice. This is not to suggest that there are no multicultural or syncretic elements in Theravadin practice – one of the most illuminating findings of Gombrich's research is that the religious effect of the political ethnicisation of Buddhism in Sri Lanka is its hybridisation in the form of Hinduisation[65] – rather that the text militates against a culturally purist scripting of Buddhism that works in the service of an ethnicised and exclusionary cultural politics. As Jonathan Walters has shown, an emphasis on 'multireligion' works to dislocate religious nomenclature from exclusionary, ahistorical readings of culture and foreground both human agency and moments and sites of cultural syncretism.[66] The political interpellation of Theravada Buddhism, which has been granted 'the foremost place' in the Sri Lankan constitution since 1972 (a position reaffirmed in 1978), has been used not to simply displace but to actively resist its Mahayanist counterpart in Sri Lanka; attempts to establish a Mahayanist centre in the country were thwarted as recently as 1990, while Theravada Buddhism was granted political representation in the form of a Ministry of Buddha Sasana during the same period.[67] Ondaatje's investment in a syncretic, hybridised, pluralist Buddhist aesthetics, philosophy and practice – when situated within the specific registers of Sinhala Buddhist nationalism at the time the text is set – can thus be seen to carry a distinctly revisionist bias.

Ondaatje's focus on eye painting is central to this project of re-siting Buddhism. While many critics have drawn attention to the significance of the nētra mangala, or eye-painting ceremony, that concludes the novel, the aesthetic implications and the precise cultural basis of Ondaatje's interpretation of this ritual have been overlooked. Set in Buduruvagala, the most significant site of Mahayanist Buddhist sculpture in Sri Lanka, the reconstruction of the ancient Buddha statue culminates in the eye-painting ceremony of another, newly built one. The process of eye painting is, earlier in the text, described as one in which 'the artificer brings to life sight and truth and presence' (p. 99). In his impressively long list of acknowledgements – a paratextual device that supplements the diasporisation of knowledge found in the novel – Ondaatje credits Ananda Coomaraswamy with his interpretation of the ritual. In the book sourced by Ondaatje, Coomaraswamy explicitly claims that this ritual is in fact Hindu in origin.[68] The idea of the Buddha as a god, which dominates the depiction of Buddhist statuary in *Anil's Ghost*, and the idea of the image as a medium between worshipper and god is, according to Coomaraswamy, Hindu too.[69] Indeed the whole casting of the Buddha as a cosmic deity has been read as an indication of the influence of Hinduism on the religion.[70] Ondaatje – indebted to Coomaraswamy's analysis of this ritual – is undoubtedly aware of this fact. His deliberate centralising of this subaltern form of Buddhism (subaltern, that is, in Sri Lanka) is therefore contentious and draws upon a time when Hinduism and Buddhism were not seen as distinct religions but rather as 'two aspects of one faith'.[71] It is also a perspective endorsed by the multireligious practice evident in a vast number of Buddhist temples in Sri Lanka today[72] and militates against what Rajasingham-Senanayake has shown to be the discursive consolidation of religious categories along ethno-racial fault lines.[73] Ondaatje's choice of the Mahayanist site of Buduruvagala and the south of the island for the ritual could thus be read as a deliberate assertion of Sri Lanka's hybrid history and cultural practice in the face of the essentialising manoeuvres of Sinhala and Tamil nationalisms and constitutes an insertion of a disjunctive, alternative past (and present) into the contemporary landscape. Southern Sri Lanka, which – within the context of the JVP resurgence in which the novel is set – serves as the political heartland of Sinhala Buddhist nationalism, is also, according to Douglas Bullis, the place where aesthetic hybridity is most manifest and where 'people [. . .] have taken the most liberties with Buddhist imagery'.[74] If 'place-names represent the geographical limit of historical consciousness',[75] the politics of Ondaatje's mapping of Buddhism constitutes a major dislocation of Sri Lankan historiography from its nationalist base.

The emphasis on burial and excavation, mining and reconstruction, on hidden histories and lives, also offers a metaphoric register for Ondaatje's aesthetic enterprise of retrieval and recuperation of forgotten ways of knowing. What is more, it turns away from the rationalist, epistemological and empiricist understanding of 'truth', promoted by Anil and Sarath, towards one that links the human and the divine in terms that deliberately marginalise state power. As Palipana, whose intuitive logic parallels Ananda's methods of reconstruction, observes when describing the ceremony:

> Coomaraswamy points out that before eyes are painted there is just a lump of metal or stone. But after this act, '*it is thenceforward a God*'. Of course there are special ways to paint the eye. Sometimes the king will do it, but it is better when done by a professional artificer, the craftsman. Now of course we have no kings. And Nētra Mangala is better without kings. [original emphasis, p. 97]

The value of dissociating spiritual leadership from monarchic and state power – which runs counter to the basis of Sinhala Buddhist revivalism as embodied in the *Mahavamsa* and the increasing politicisation of the Buddhist clergy in the present day – could not have been made clearer.[76]

The extent of Ondaatje's critique of nationalism is not only evident in this syncretic scripting of Buddhism and his emphasis on forest-dwelling fraternities within the text – both of which lie outside state institutionalised structures in contemporary Sri Lanka – but can also be measured in his dramatic inversion of several elements of a story which appeared in *Channels* (one of the few regularly published journals of Sri Lankan writing in the English) two years earlier.[77] Written in a style very similar to Ondaatje's, Uthpala Gunethilake's short story 'Continuity' offers a striking contrast to Ondaatje's presentation of Buddhist statuary. It describes the experience of the sculptor who carves the eyes of the Aukana Buddha, the most celebrated statue of a standing Buddha in the island. Standing forty-two and a half feet high, its only rival in terms of size is the less-frequented Buduruvagala statue, which at fifty-one feet high is now one of the tallest standing Buddha statues of the ancient world – since the destruction of the Bamiyan statues by the Taliban. Both the Aukana and Buduruvagala statues face east, as is the custom, and it is the Aukana or 'sun-eating' statue that is central to Gunethilake's story. Here is how it begins, quoted at some length to give an indication of the extent of Ondaatje's revisionism:

> *Archaeological evidence proves that the Avukana Buddha statue in Anuradhapura was constructed during the reign of King Dhatusena (5th Century* AD*). But a legend buried deep in the Kala-Oya valley confers this honour on King Dutugemunu (2nd Century* BC*).*
>
> The world was all blue and green. Nothing but blue and green that poured down at him from the deep still sky, and shot up from the dark, tough wilderness beneath him. Perched on a wooden gallery on top of a massive rock that emerged from the sea of moving green forest all around, he could feel the green and blue crashing and exploding midway in the air around him, exploding with the exultant force of life. The brown fingers holding the hammer and chisel shook for a second before they chipped away the last piece of rock from the chin of the statue. Then the fingers set the tools in motion, back and forth, rhythmically smoothing the sharp, raw edges of the rock.
>
> Now, only the eyes remained to be carved and shaped out of the rock.
>
> The sculptor laid down his tools and sat back. The tension left his body in a long deep breath. Yes, only the eyes were left. Yet it is the hardest part of his work. For what expression can he create in those eyes of stone? How could he give life to those eyes, those eyes of the Buddha, the one who saw it all? And the meaning he carves out in those eyes should harmonize with the nature of the rock, just as the rest of the statue did. It should be something that lives with the hard, rough, rock, not something which lives apart from it.
>
> The sun was moving slowly behind the statue, lengthening the shadows to the east. When twilight slips away into night, he needs to descend from the top of the rock, and leave the stone figure to merge with the life around it. For

> at dawn the next day the troops must resume their march to Anuradhapura. Nearly two full-moons had passed since they had had to halt here, in the dry forest between Anuradhapura and the hamlet of Sasseruwa. After the tremendous victory at Vijithapura, the strongest fortress of the Tamil king Elara, the Sinhala troops marched north-east towards the Kala-Oya. [original emphasis][78]

The sculptor then reflects on Dutugemunu – the celebrated ruler who united the country under the aegis of Sinhala Buddhism – in the 'last stage of his battle against Tamil rule' (p. 58), observing that while Dutugemunu knew the Tamil king to be 'a noble ruler', 'the destruction caused by his subjects was unpardonable' so that 'he [Dutugemunu] knew that many rulers long after him would have to repeat his act [of war]' (p. 58). Mention is made too of the sculptor's unfinished Buddha statue at Sasseruwa and of the need to present a homogenous image, for 'it would be an insult to the Buddha, to carve him as something apart from the nature of the rock [. . .] for the Buddha and nature were one' (p. 58). Finally the sculptor finishes the work, reflects on the fact that this dawn-facing statue would 'always be a symbol of renewal and life [. . .] a symbol, not of eternity, but of endurance; not everlasting glory, but of resilience that is of Sri Lanka itself [. . .] a symbol of the creative force by which the people thrived [which] shall be dormant at times, but alive and ready to catch fire at any moment' (p. 60). The story then ends with a reaffirmation of this symbolism by a self-conscious reflection on its relevance to the present day: 'The writer laid down his pen and walked out. He stood, gazing northwards where history was being re-enacted. And he hoped that this soil would still prove alive with resilience' (p. 60).

This story is a strong example of the *Mahavamsa* mentality, whereby the myth of national unity is celebrated in relation to Sinhala Buddhist rule and the religion itself is invoked in terms of the right of 'the people' to fight in its name. The binary reading of the nation – enabled by scripting Tamils as the ancient enemy – is sanctified by connecting visionary awareness with a panoptic view of the land that is forged out of spatio-temporal continuity. The political message of the story is thus – literally and metaphorically – naturalised as the composite vision of the Buddha statue, the sculptor, and the writing subject are related to the permanence of rock that constitutes the natural world. Despite such naturalisation, the opening lines make it clear that the writer wishes to foreground the fact that he is playing with historical records to suit his purposes, so that the demands of the present 'where history was being re-enacted' clearly determine the writing of the past, and 'legend buried deep in the Kal-Oya valley' has aesthetic precedence over mere 'archaeological evidence'.

In contrast to 'Continuity', the epiphany in *Anil's Ghost* – entitled 'Distance' – is at pains to centralise the hybridity of Buddhism. Drawing on the Hindu-based ceremony of eye painting the emphasis is on a fictional 120-foot tall reconstructed statue in the South whose fractures give it a 'quilted' appearance (p. 302). It has been destroyed not out of religious rivalry or spite, but by Sinhalese thieves looking for treasure in its body, 'trying to find a solution for hunger or a way to get out of their disintegrating lives' (p. 300). The destruction of the statue is therefore a result of a breakdown in social order and is committed by those who are followers of the religion that it represents. Unlike 'Continuity', which foregrounds the 'small solitary figure [of the sculptor] standing by the recumbent stone' (p. 60), Ondaatje emphasises that the reconstruction of the Buddha statue is undertaken collectively, drawing together a wide variety of people: villagers (many of them trying to avoid military detention or having to serve in the army), engineers and local women. It is a communal, agentive act – dissociated from war – which serves to link people across class. Notably no 'foreign specialists' or 'celebrities' (p. 301) – like Anil – are involved.

This reading of the destruction and reconstruction of a fictional statue at the fabled site of Mahayana Buddhist worship serves to dislocate Buddhism from the mythologically inscribed centres of ancient Buddhist worship in the North and relocate it in the South, a place where the bodies of victims of extrajudicial killings are taken to be burned and buried. As I mentioned before, while there is no doubt that the novel condemns Tamil militancy, the main political focus of the novel is not Tamil violence but the violence committed by the Sinhalese upon each other. Both Ondaatje's fictional statues break with convention and face north. The promotion therefore of Hindu inflected Buddhism, and its relocation in the site of internecine Sinhala violence, effectively serves to dismantle both the homogeneity and hegemony of institutionalised and ethnicised Buddhism and insist on an alternative 'vision' of events in the North. It is significant that the cracks are left to show on the quilted statue as Ananda chooses not to 'homogenize the stone, blend the face into a unit', but to 'leave it as it was' (p. 302).[79] The importance of laying bare the process of reconstruction relates to the need to make visible the heterogeneity, fragmentation, inconsistencies and human practices underpinning the history of the religion represented.

While the reconstructed statue seems to represent the historical evaluation of Buddhism, the replacement statue is related to the practice of Buddhism in the present day. It is this statue that Ananda consecrates in the Nētra Mangala ceremony and which draws villagers to worship. Whereas 'Continuity' used two historical statues – the unfinished Buddha statue at Sasseruwa and the Aukana Buddha – to emphasise both the aesthetic and spiritual *links* between time past and time present, the two fictional statues of 'Distance' are used to create an alternative foundational myth that *differentiates* between the historical construction of a Buddhist past – one riddled with cracks and bound by the molten iron veins of war – and a creation of a communal, hybridised, pluralistic Buddhism in the present day. It is thus not spatio-temporal continuity but the differential dynamics of historical rupture and cultural fusion that form the basis of Ondaatje's presentation of Buddhist statuary. The broken bones and bodies of the 'disappeared' and the broken limbs of Buddha statues are markers of real political violence and also of the generative potential of social and political breakdown. The implications of this have been explored by Marlene Goldman, who has, drawing on the work of Kapferer, shown how the blurring of spatial and temporal horizons is fundamental to the nationalist myth-making project in Sri

Lanka, and how in the novel 'the danger associated with blurring the difference between past and present is [. . .] illustrated by the contemporary practice of burying victims of late-twentieth century ethnic warfare in ancient graves located in sacred sites'.[80]

The process of reconstruction and construction of the statues take place simultaneously but they form separate acts within the novel. The consecration itself takes place at dawn (in contrast to the late evening in 'Continuity'), emphasising the fact that this new image promises a new start. All these elements reveal an insistence on the need for a re-evaluation of Buddhism as a cultural entity and its encoding in literary criticism – a need that seems pressingly urgent in the light of critical affirmations by some Sri Lankan literary critics who increasingly use Buddhism as a marker of exclusivity and exclusion. Suwanda Suganasiri's claim that expatriate writers such as Ondaatje fail in their duty in not laying claim to a Sri Lankan culture that is 'a 2000-year old Buddhist culture, literally, esthetically, culturally, socially, economically, politically and spiritually',[81] and Qadri Ismail's diametrically opposed reflection that Ondaatje's reading of Buddhism clearly puts him 'on the side' of Sinhala Buddhist nationalism, reveal how reductive, hegemonic conceptions of a singular and exclusive Buddhism are used to demarcate the boundaries of belonging and acceptance and how literary texts are caught in these exclusionary cultural registers.

Why – given this – does Ondaatje fight shy of acknowledging the full political implications of his aesthetic enterprise? When quizzed by an interviewer on the 'withholding of overt political material' from the novel, Ondaatje claimed that he wished to write a novel that 'wasn't "politically verbal" but where everything had a political light'.[82] This very elusiveness is, in part, an idiosyncrasy of the private writer, who feels 'over-revealed and dangerously self-conscious'.[83] It also corresponds with Ananda Coomaraswamy's ideal of the anonymous, intuitive artist who deflects attention away from his personal biases and predilections and instead insists on the autonomy of art and its openness to interpretation. In both *Running in the Family* and *Anil's Ghost* Ondaatje has used a palimpsestic rendering of the past to negotiate multiple discursive levels, compelling readers to link archival, epistemological modes of understanding with ones that are sensitive to art's transformative potential and its subjective logic, working their way to discovering their own 'truths' through multiple layers of meaning. Yet in *Anil's Ghost* Ondaatje has gone further, suggesting another reason for the silencing of overt political commentary in the text. In a passage resonant with high irony he reveals the way in which readings of political events in Sri Lanka are subject to the epistemic violence of commodification for a Western audience. Gamini's observation to Anil, whose status as a Westernised expatriate celebrity of course mirrors Ondaatje's own, serves as a metacommentary on the novel's status as cultural witness to political events:

> American movies, English books – remember how they all end? [. . .] The American or the Englishman gets on a plane and leaves. That's it. The camera leaves with him. He looks out of the window at Mombasa or Vietnam

> or Jakarta, someplace now he can look at through the clouds. [. . .] [T]he war, to all purposes, is over. That's enough reality for the West. It's probably the history of the last two hundred years of Western political writing. Go home. Write a book. Hit the circuit. [pp. 285–86]

The need for trust, so powerfully conveyed in the silences that inform Anil's relationship with Sarath and the dramatic conclusion to their investigation, is here extended to encompass the tacit contract between a writer and the readership that legitimates and sanctions his work.

Within this context the layers of discourse that serve to diasporise the text into a range of cultural and interpretative registers do not so much conceal the politics that underpin Ondaatje's strategic location but are instead constitutive of it. Ondaatje's revisionism is not just palimpsestically coded, it rewrites the conventions of the political novel set out in the passage just cited to assert alternative truths that are unavailable to those who insist on reading from outside its registers. 'Witnessing' is not possible to those who insist on homogenous readings of national culture. This may not appear to be a particularly contentious claim on Ondaatje's part, but given the prescriptive readings to which his work has been subject – from both inside and outside Sri Lanka – it may indeed be radical. In an interview Ondaatje, reflecting on Anil's position as 'the returning stranger', offers a telling insight into the politics underpinning his own strategic location:

> You have someone who is part of the country, and in a way, has to betray it. It's an odd state to be in, blowing the whistle on your home country. What exactly is the morality? What is your responsibility to the place you come from? Obviously that is something that concerns me.[84]

From his first Sri Lankan text that broadly unsettled the fixity of map-makers by prioritising the migrant's experience of travel, it seems that Ondaatje has come, in this second Sri Lankan work, to meander conclusively into the very eye of the political storm.

8 Romesh Gunesekera

Past paradise

> Exotic: alien; introduced from abroad, not indigenous; drawn from outside; foreign; hence outlandish, barbarous; of foreign extraction.
> Exoticism: a tendency to adopt what is exotic; a foreign idiom or expression.
>
> *The Shorter Oxford English Dictionary*

Exoticism is – along with *orientalism* – one of the most commonly used terms of cultural exclusion in the critical evaluation of Sri Lankan literature. Its formulation, as Graham Huggan reminds us, is part of a symbolic system or 'semiotic circuit that oscillates between the opposite poles of strangeness and familiarity [. . .] recoded to serve different, even contradictory, political needs and ends'. Huggan's seminal study focuses on the marketing of postcolonial writers within the Western mainstream and emphasises the duality inherent in the transaction, on the way exoticism serves as 'a control mechanism of cultural translation which relays the other inexorably back again to the same'.[1] Yet the contradictory political drives of exoticist readings of literature can also be seen in the contrastive means by which texts are scripted as exotic from different postcolonial locations. The different evaluations of Michael Ondaatje's *Running in the Family*, for example (discussed in Chapter 7), show how the scripting of apparent exoticism can reflect different shades of marginalisation from the cultural mainstream: readers and critics from outside Sri Lanka tend to use exoticism as a marker of both marketable domesticated difference and a writer's alienation from his or her native land, whereas critical evaluations from within Sri Lanka tend to script exoticism as an unequivocal indicator of compromised belonging and, more poignantly, of unbelonging, based upon a form of false consciousness allied to Western interests. To describe a text as exotic therefore is, particularly within the boundaries of evaluation set by Sri Lankan critics, a critical manoeuvre that works to disable its political registers, evacuate it of cultural import and relevance to the country being 'exoticised', and throw serious doubt on its ethical drives. Within this exclusionary critical discourse, the text's own scripting of belonging is in danger of getting obscured or reconstituted to serve a radically different purpose to that which might have been intended. As Huggan's text pertinently demonstrates, exoticism is in the eye of the beholder, a by-product of a form of surveillance that seeks to disguise its own objectives. There is a need therefore to return the gaze and scrutinise what is gained and lost by such readings, while simultaneously undertaking an evaluative critique of the cultural positionings with which the text actually engages. As Huggan presses us to consider through his African figure of Tintin, '"so you find me exotic; and what does that say, my friend, about *you*?"'.[2]

Critical evaluations of Romesh Gunesekera's novels have been entangled in this invidious scripting of exoticism in a multitude of contradictory ways. His texts have been read to be in the service of exoticism, to work to subvert or redeploy exoticist impulses, and to affirm a displaced or deferred exoticism in its perceived representation of the nation as a past paradise. The invocation of Sri Lanka as a 'paradise' itself bears further critical scrutiny, covering as it does a multitude of registers – from the mythological and fabular to the stereotypic discourse of (predominantly) Western media and tourist brochures – all of which work to commodify the country in Manichean terms. Paradise is, after all, the Garden of Eden, 'the abode of the blessed', 'a region of supreme bliss', 'a state of supreme felicity', a pleasure ground[3] – a sexy and spiritual sell.

The argument therefore that Gunesekera presents Sri Lanka as a former paradise – that he indulges in a kind of displaced or temporally deferred exoticism – is especially interesting, for it is here that the inherent contradictions of the cultural positioning of the displaced writer are most strikingly manifest. The scripting of displaced exoticism in critical evaluations of his work takes two forms: it manifests itself through the direct recoding of the representation of the nation in his work as a 'poisoned paradise',[4] or indirectly through an evaluation of the effect of this representation on the reader. The first is central to Walter Perera's evaluation of Gunesekera's work and is the focus of much of this chapter. As John Thieme has shown, Gunesekera's scripting of the nation as a past or fallen paradise is self-conscious, as the distance between characters' Utopian vision and the impossibility of sustaining such perspectives is foregrounded.[5] Paul Binding's review of Gunesekera's second novel, *The Sandglass* (1998), serves as a good example of the second form. While recognising that the novel may be reaching for a more subtle critique of the nation, he advances the idea that the text makes clear one 'emotional truth', that is that:

> Sri Lanka compels the leaving of it. Not for nothing is it 'tear-shaped', fecund and beautiful, it is the putative site of the Garden of Eden, of the paradisiacal Atlantis, from which humanity was exiled. Even those who stay there are forced, by the uncertainties and cruelties of its unflagging war, to live in a kind of exile.[6]

The notion of displaced exoticism, both in relation to the self-conscious representation of the nation as a former paradise and in relation to the emotional registers provoked by the text (which in itself is the product of the critic's own reading of the country as potentially Edenic), poses particular challenges for those wishing to address cultural codings in Gunesekera's work. On the one hand it serves to register his apparent alienation from his native land, on the other it directs the reader to the fact that the critic's consciousness of the aesthetic value of cultural difference in his work is held *in suspense* by the cultural codings to be found within the text itself. It results in the kind of temporal indeterminacy that has prompted Walter Perera to argue that 'a writer who uses the metaphor of a fallen paradise to describe a country should provide some idea about paradise before the fall'.[7] This argument alerts us to the need to ask: in what 'past' is Gunesekera's putative paradise located? If, as Gāmini Salgādo contends, 'all paradise is paradise lost',[8] then there is no necessary logic in confining the concept of paradise to a linear, historically bound and teleological framework in the way that Perera's reading implies.

Before proceeding therefore it is worth noting the basis of Gunesekera's expatriation by some Sri Lankan critics. Referred to by a resident Sri Lankan critic as arguably the most controversial Sri Lankan expatriate writer writing today,[9] his critical expatriation is based on a range of factors referred to by Thiru Kandiah: his 'distortingly stereotypical anglicized, middle class élite perception of what the rural Other in the backwoods' is like; his 'blanket of tropicalism [which is] presumably intended to invest the situation with a certain exotic "oriental" charm'; his presentation of political events within a 'feeble and debilitating free-floating nostalgia, which opens no insights into the specific human tragedies'; and his 'gross distortion of [. . .] actual historical happenings [which] causes the pernicious race and class attitudes that are really responsible for the tragedy to be radically misrecognised, in such a way in fact as would, in spite of the writer's own personal decency, facilitate their legitimisation'.[10]

Gunesekera's cultural legitimacy is called into question here largely on the basis of several 'distortions' – a basis that contains a universalising representationalist assumption of mimesis, authenticity and truth-telling in its reading of fictional representation. What is more, the charge of cultural illegitimacy is based upon a further assumption – one that as Ruvani Ranasinha's observations reveal – transpose these very representationalist values onto the Western readership for which Gunesekera largely writes: 'Gunesekera and other expatriate Lankan writers have been viewed as preferred insiders and initiated informants on the affairs and culture of the East, and their expatriation has conferred upon them the writerly virtues of detachment and objectivity. The acclaim these writers receive legitimizes and maintains the authority of stereotyped, unchanging ideas about the Orient'.[11] I would argue that such a reading is both reductive and – to an extent – misleading. Reductive because it fails to understand that the very nostalgia, exoticism and 'stereotyping' which critics such as Ranasinha appear to see in Gunesekera's writing in fact serve to signal the radical uncertainty of cultural reclamation at the heart of his work. Misleading because it assumes that readers outside Sri Lanka are equally bound to a purely representationalist reading of the text. As Gautum Kundu has shown, Gunesekera has been lauded by critics outside Sri Lanka for the quality of his prose, its elegiac lyricism and formal complexity[12] – terms of analysis that are notably absent from the evaluations of those Sri Lankan critics who work to expatriate his texts. Indeed the reading of exoticism in his texts by critics outside Sri Lanka – unfair but perhaps inevitable, as Kundu suggests[13] – is largely undertaken on the understanding that the exotic functions as a modulated and mediatory marker of personal exile and alienation rather than a blanket statement on the country, an understanding that is central to Kundu's own critique. What is more, whereas the depiction of Sri Lanka as a lapsed paradise is regularly used to expatriate Gunesekera from authenticated status in the Sri Lankan canon, Jean Arasanayagam – who, as has been seen, also draws upon the image of Sri Lanka as a lapsed Eden to communicate alienation and exile – has notably *not* been subject to critical expatriation on this basis. There is clearly a need, therefore, to engage in a critical dialogue that mediates the modulated registers of migrancy in Gunesekera's work in terms that address both the complexity of his texts and the representationalist concerns of certain Sri Lankan critics.

Criticisms pertaining to inappropriate, misleading or inauthentic representations of Sri Lanka are of course not only reserved for migrant writers – James Goonewardene too was subject to similar attacks. Kandiah's implicit assumption that Goonewardene subscribed to a form of 'negative writing, a writing of rejection and failure' which is 'just *not a valid style* for writers of English in Ceylon, it is *not true to their experience*, which has a positive aspect' (my emphasis),[14] effectively serves to invalidate the efforts and experiences of this internationalist writer to convey alienation from within Sri Lankan shores. In addition to critiquing such 'negative' writing, Kandiah also attacks the 'negativism' of what he calls 'post-modern thought'. Reading the latter in terms of a form of 'reductionist relativism', he firmly locates such thinking within the metropolitan centres and dismisses all 'that ambivalence, indeterminacy, fragmentation, unrealization, negativism and so on of the dark hued *angst*'.[15] Such strategies of exclusion that serve to legitimate one form of literary and critical writing by denying authority to another in order largely to champion work that has 'an authentically Lankan English ring [. . .] which helps evoke a recognisably Lankan experience', reveal the ways in which national identity and cultural affiliation are internally policed, prescribed and promoted. In dismissing notions of ambivalence, indeterminacy, fragmentation and negativism, Kandiah essentially misses the significance of Goonewardene's 'negativism' and Gunesekera's spatio-temporal disjunctions and ambivalent cultural reclamation that reveal their attempts to articulate and give aesthetic form to conditions of exclusion and alienation. It is a manoeuvre that effectively marks a double exclusion in which the experience of alienation is itself silenced and erased by critical reception in Sri Lanka.

Gunesekera too has been arraigned for his apparently negative representation of the country and its people. Describing *Reef* (1994) as a novel containing 'chauvinistic attitudes',[16] Walter Perera, one of Gunesekera's most consistent critics, has further claimed that in the novel Gunesekera 'projects a country that is immoral, amoral, exploitative, poorly governed, prone to violence [and] demoralized'.[17] *The Sandglass*, Perera contends, is little better, as here 'no individual or community can be exemplified as offering a positive outlook'[18] and Sri Lanka is presented as nothing more than 'a theatre of war for 365 days of the year,

[. . .] the island has nothing to offer unless the visitor is a pedophile'. Within such brutally representationalist readings it is little wonder that the spatio-temporal disjunctions mediating migrant memory come to be rescripted teleologically so that in *Reef* 'the savagery of the present [appears to be] a natural descent from the "barbarity" of the past'.[19] The expatriation of Gunesekera's work on the basis of his negative representation of the country is not only presaged on an essentialist reading of the authentic but also on a prescriptive notion of what 'positive', culturally validated representations of the nation should be. It calls to mind Naipaul's contention that a key sign of literary and cultural maturity lies in the ability to acknowledge and address the shortcomings that are to be found in one's home country.

There are further similarities between the work of Gunesekera and Goonewardene that suggest that the basis of negative evaluations of their work might rest on some shared political perspectives and spatial idiomatics to be found in their writing. Gunesekera, like Goonewardene, focuses in large measure on a negative critique of the cultural nationalism embodied by the JVP insurrection of 1971, foregrounding the effects of political violence and nationalist prescriptives on the country. Furthermore he draws upon an allegorical trope of the island, investing in an ecological register that focuses on the need for conservation, replicating Goonewardene's investment in a representation of the beleaguered island nation.[20] Both Gunesekera and Goonewardene thus appear to present Manichean allegories that invite, as Todorov points out, Manichean responses.[21] The notion of a lapsed paradise, with its registers of a fall from grace, is one that lends itself to such an inscription.

Yet the Manicheism of Goonewardene and Gunesekera have different temporal bases that serve to reveal fundamental differences in the objectives of these writers. Goonewardene's critique of the mass mind or 'group narcissism',[22] which forms, as I have shown, the basis of his negative representation of the island, is premised on an evolutionary dynamic that attests to the historical development of the more extremist forms of Sinhala nationalism. What is more, his use of ecology is mediated by an interventionist drive that is anthropocentric rather than ecocentric, promoting a notion of a 'whole system ethic'[23] that is in keeping with his call for internationalism. Gunesekera's presentation of violence is unhinged from such an evolutionary basis and instead works from a spatio-temporal dynamic that recodes and displaces the past to serve the needs of a disjunctive, ruptured and misplaced present. His use of ecology is – as I will show – divided between a utilitarian drive that acknowledges the centrality of commercial imperatives and an exploration of its utopian basis through the discursive registers of migrant fantasy. Gunesekera's evaluation of political events is mediated by the migrant's experience of spatio-temporal dislocations in which the incommensurability between different locations and times results in a loss of confidence in the accessibility and knowability of any 'real' environment. Instead of Goonewardene's evolutionary dynamic, we encounter in Gunesekera's work a form of spatio-temporal diffusion in which resolution is constantly deferred and displaced into a horizon of endlessly deferred possibility. As Susheila Nasta has claimed of *The Sandglass*, Gunesekera's work presents us with 'rooms of memory' that 'open like Chinese boxes' mapping 'the interiority of an imaginative territory of desire'. Here 'the tragic epiphanies of individual lives occur in counterpoint with the haunting and beautiful landscape of an island which is not "exoticised" but exists instead as a source of subliminal anxiety *always out of reach*' (my emphasis).[24]

Nasta's evaluation astutely identifies the key problem confronting those who might wish to engage in essentialised, exoticist readings of Gunesekera's work; that is, the problem of identifying the cultural coordinates underpinning the spatio-temporal dynamics in his texts. It is a problem that frustrates and antagonises critical approaches that seek to situate his work in relation to a fixed and knowable Sri Lankan context. The contention that his work reconstructs the nation as a lost or past paradise is predicated on the assumption that the text opens up the possibility of an imaginary retrieval of an idealised essence. While Gunesekera does directly refer to the country in these terms in his novels, the atemporal mediation of landscape in his texts is not determined by the idealism underpinning nostalgic reclamation, whatever its cultural registers, but rather by a recognition of the violent incommensurability of competing realities and truths that render such reclamation impossible. In these terms the scripting of Gunesekera's representation of the island as a lost, or former, paradise marks an acknowledgment of the way in which his texts use the unsettled present to mediate the provisionality of the past and project them into a provisional future foregrounding the allegorical (and therefore metafictional) basis of his representation of the nation. There is a need therefore to distinguish between a reading of his work in relation to the displaced exoticism of a past paradise, which alerts us to this radical spatio-temporal uncertainty (a reading upon which my own approach is based), and a reading that situates such displaced exoticism into a teleological, postlapsarian historical register that the text itself might seek to resist. In doing so it is possible to see how the critical bases of diametrically opposed readings of his work as promoting a negative and essentialist cultural reclamation (found in Perera's and Binding's readings) and as an example of ambivalent cultural indeterminacy (evident in Nasta's critique) are fostered. My negotiation of this critical tension requires me to compare the ways in which critical evaluations of the putative displaced exoticism in his texts is matched by, or contrasts with, the texts' own self-conscious scripting of exoticism. It is primarily by these means that we can come closest to identifying the different ways in which boundaries are marked in Gunesekera's texts.

The mediation of incommensurable space–times results as, Middleton and Woods have shown, in a kind of 'disembedding' in which social relations are lifted from their local contexts and restructured across infinite expanses of time and space.[25] Gunesekera's novels work to 'disembed' Sri Lankan social relations by privileging the migrant's experience of displacement. His novels present historical events through the disjunctures of a displaced present in order to project an imagined landscape that is both out of time and out of place. From the retrospective reach of *Reef* (1994) and the dialogised reconstructions of *The Sandglass*

(1998) to the dystopian fantasy of *Heaven's Edge* (2002), Gunesekera requires us to interrogate the exoticism underpinning commodified representations of the nation, to read through and past paradisaical registers, while simultaneously revealing how exoticism might contain a moral idealism that serves a real social need. The presentation of Sri Lanka as a past paradise is not only recognised as an imaginative construction, but is also shown to be a necessary myth to grant hope for the future. It is a context that alerts us to the fact that the way in which the past is remembered and the form in which it is represented determine its political and cultural import, and that these may be, ultimately, even more important than what is remembered. My engagement with his novels – all written in England where Gunesekera has been resident since 1972 – thus begins with an analysis of retrospective reconstructions of the island in *The Sandglass*. I then move on to consider, in more detail, the ways in which this mediation of the migrant sensibility works both in the service of and to undermine exoticist readings of Sri Lanka as a paradise lost in *Heaven's Edge* and *Reef*. His latest novel, *The Match* (2006), eludes exoticism and marks a move toward a more historically situated scripting of migrant experience and the diaspora, and it is therefore not included in the analysis.

Spatial Manicheism in the *The Sandglass*

The novel forms a retrospective reconstruction of the exploits of two wealthy families, the Ducals and the Vatunases, who become neighbours after the sale of a tract of Vatunas land in post-Independent Sri Lanka. The recollections are assembled after the death of Pearl Ducal in London and narrated almost entirely through interrupted dialogues between Prins (Pearls' oldest son) and Chip (Pearl's former lodger), drawing extensively on recollected conversations between Chip and Pearl. These dialogised narrative strands mediate several different time zones that are telescoped into the span of twenty-four hours, with each chapter marking the progress of a few hours in the build-up to Pearl's funeral, leading to a 'thickening [. . .] sense of simultaneity'.[26] The recollected past of life in Sri Lanka, the immediate past of the characters' experiences as British immigrants, the conditional present in which funeral preparations take place and the unresolved present of writing through which Chip, in transit in a hotel room, opens the novel are all juxtaposed in an intricate and complex mediation of incommensurable space–times that serve to loosen historical narration from spatial and temporal moorings. History is spatialised, levelled into simultaneity, and space temporalised, marked by the vicissitudes of an emergent time, so that both are rendered inherently provisional and unstable. It is a context in which dwelling is permanently displaced, making settlement permanently temporary. Chip, the narrator, is always on the move, his temporary residence with Pearl constantly unsettled by Prins' periodic visits which expel him from his lodgings. Home is therefore not a space that is deferred into the provisionality of the future or past, nor is it merely a mobile habitat, but rather it is located as a dwelling place marked by its imminent loss. It is haunted not by the ghosts of a knowable past, but by the spectre of inevitable loss in a way that projects the future proleptically into the present. The condition of predictive loss is reinforced by a narrative trajectory in which disrupted histories are shown to refuse to relinquish their secrets: the exact circumstances surrounding Jason Ducal's death and Prins' disappearance remaining unknown at the novel's close. It is a context that serves to present memory as 'a material force' in the mediation of competing temporalities.[27]

In reconstituting memory as a material force in its construction of exilic space, Gunesekera's novel powerfully registers the imaginative basis of his inscription of the island nation. It is clearly an allegorical reclamation of Sri Lanka, with the fate of the symbolically named Ducals and Vatunases signalling the interlinked destinies of those who passively endure suffering and are compelled to inhabit idealised spaces of the imagination and those who actively engage in territorial boundary marking in order to develop their family fiefdoms.[28] The morally lapsed or 'fallen' Vatunases represent a feudal territoriality for whom 'the land [. . .] was the result of a deep and intense relationship between the sleeping earth and the ambitions of a line of modern dynasts' (p. 22). In contrast to the exoticist colonial fantasy of 'Arcadia' in which the Ducals live, the Vatunas land that encircles them is defined by an erotic reconstitution of territory in which the family tree is used to make 'procreative sculptures' out of the property so that the estate is carved to reproduce sexual organs such as testicles, vulva, lingam and swollen glans (pp. 27, 28). This 'lewd land-map' (p. 28) is akin to a form of commodity fetishism that veils the material circumstances that generate the conditions of its realisation by sublimating them into a territory of desire. Its erotic registers are recoded into distinctly Manichean terms by Esra when he 'described his property as the imprint of a divine hoof as God cantered to heaven from the island' – a metaphor that also draws to mind the image of the devil's cloven foot – 'neatly obscuring the secret lasciviousness of his father's vision' (p. 29).

The reconstruction of the island is thus territorially determined in the contrast and connections drawn between exoticist and erotic inscriptions of land. Pearl Ducal's imaginative reconstitution of her marital home, 'Arcadia', is mediated by both an acknowledgement of her husband's 'colonial' desire for 'place and status – geographical and social' (p. 23) and its place within a migrant's mapping of a lost past. The house, built by an Englishman 'as a kind of homage to a suppurating colonial dream: the dream of a voyage of adventure' (p. 23), is a dwelling place in which the doomed desires of the displaced migrant and the usurped colonial connect, mediating these forms of territorial reclamation through the spatio-temporal idiomatics marked by the mobility of temporary habitation. 'Arcadia' as a pastoral idyll is thus unequivocally situated as the fantasy of the displaced subject, clearly located within an aesthetics that foregrounds its decontextualised, disembedded status. Thus Gunesekera's text resists the exoticising strategy of defining margins[29] and instead indexes the cultural insecurities of connection between colonial, postcolonial and migrant imaginative reclamations of land. The eroticism underpinning Vatunas territoriality, while also mapping a territory of desire, is, in contrast, not merely imaginatively reconstituted but actively marks the material conditions of exploitation. The plantation economy of which

Buttons Vatunas is an exemplar gives way to the rapacious territoriality of his son, who goes beyond the relatively benign cultural mimicry of his peers, so that while they are busy 'transform[ing] themselves into brownskin imperial successors, Esra turned himself into a full-blown emperor' (p. 103). *The Sandglass* thus sets into operation a contrastive dynamic of competing models of territoriality in which the territorial dispute between neighbours has a subliminal allegorical resonance with contemporary territorial debates. By distinguishing between the imaginative reclamation of territory and the material conditions of its effects, Gunesekera splits the scripting of exoticist readings of land into the simulated dehistoricised registers of fantasy, and the active conquest, control and consumption of territory – between, in other words, the spectacle of compensatory retrieval and its active, brute enforcement.

Gunesekera does not alert the reader to the dangers of such a dissociation – the fact that territorial reclamations are presaged on imaginative desire – because his aim is not so much to intervene in historical reconstructions of the past that feed into competing nationalisms, but more to destabilise all historical registers and thereby foreground the spatio-temporal indeterminacy of migrancy. 'Arcadia' as a pastoral idyll is thus subject to the relocations of a Manicheistic allegory that contrast the uncertain gains of spatio-temporal indeterminacy with the situated evils of voracious territorialism. Exoticism is displaced into a provisional past and contained in the imagination. It is marketable as the commodified 'paradise experience' (p. 195) of Prins' tourist business but is – in this form – merely constitutive of cultural denegration, a 'jaggerified' (p. 209) jumble of folk art and handicrafts that have little to do with the creative life of the country. Unlike Goonewardene, who draws comparisons between the commodification of culture and Sinhala nationalism,[30] Gunesekera does not invest in a critique of national culture so much as foreground the ways in which such commodification is the product of the loss of spatial certainty, an outcome of the accelerated self-estrangement which colonialism and postcolonial migration has generated. The celebratory, cosmetic 'boutique' multiculturalism[31] underpinning Prins' enterprise are – within the dynamics of migrant displacement in which they are presented – not registers of alienation from a knowable homeland, but rather a register of a commodified relationship to the past which dislocates and displaces the imagined territory into a site that is beyond historical reclamation.

The negative response to Gunesekera's presentation of Sri Lanka is partly prompted by the Manicheism underpinning his spatio-temporal dynamics. Perera's criticisms are written from a position that recognises the presence of ethical evaluations underpinning the exoticism in the text, but not the multiple inflections of its displaced basis. Hence he attends to the fact that the Sri Lanka of *The Sandglass* is allegorically retrieved and essentialised but realigns this allegory into a teleological trajectory that the novel's temporal spatialising contests. This is clear in his contention that Gunesekera's representation of the island suggests the country 'contributed little in the past, can provide even less in the present, and will offer nothing whatsoever in the future'.[32] Further, he registers the text's spatial Manicheism in his claim that Gunesekera presents England as a 'sort of haven' and Sri Lanka as place of 'violence and anarchy',[33] but does so on the basis of an inverted Manicheism that fails to recognise the mediatory, transnational and ahistorical drives underpinning Gunesekera's imaginative reclamation of territory. The reductive, binary and overdetermined reading of territorial boundaries is precisely what the text's scripting of displaced exoticism serves to critique, but here it forms the very basis of such an expatriated reading which effectively excludes or disqualifies the writer from any claims to cultural legitimacy.

Perera's reading thus constitutes an enactment of critical territoriality that is based on a dislocation of the text's spatial Manicheism from a migratory, mediatory and provisional basis to a situated one. In the process the reading of displaced exoticism in the text is scripted to serve an exoticist and essentialist impulse. His reading of the text's displaced exoticism reifies processual dynamics so that Gunesekera's dialogised and open-ended reflection on the tourist-led commodification of culture (in the passage cited earlier) is reread as a direct attack on tradition itself.[34] The published abstract to the article in which these claims are made throws into sharp relief some of the contradictions inherent in such a relocation of the transnational impulses of the text:

> *The Sandglass* marks an extension to and a continuation of Romesh Gunesekera's *Reef.* The author provides a complex study of the perils of expatriation through the suggestion that assimilation, even marrying into British stock, is the way forward for immigrants. The 'Fallen Paradise' offers nothing but corruption, violence, and chaos. Gunesekera's ambivalence towards Sri Lanka disallows, rather than enables, the creation of sophisticated fiction.[35]

Assimilation is situated as a negative gain in the 'perils of expatriation' whose ultimate manifestation is the miscegenation of 'marrying into British stock'. The birth of Dawn that concludes the novel is scripted in this critical analysis as an epiphany whose material and cultural basis marks an adulteration of a fixed and essentialised culture, an 'ever-diminishing Sri Lankan make-up'; her multicultural inheritance is purged of its pluralist registers into the homogeneity of singular affiliation as one who is likely to be 'English bred in addition to being English born'.[36] Another resident critic, Rajiva Wijesinha, echoes this sentiment in his reading of Dawn's mother as 'essentially British'. His unwittingly paradoxical conclusion that the novel is 'utterly an English novel, albeit without any significant English characters' marks the cultural boundaries mediating expatriated readings of migrant texts.[37] Cultural assimilation is thus drained of its multicultural basis, rejected as external to the basis of a legitimated, authenticated identity as the registers of a beleaguered, imperilled 'Sri Lankan' cultural inheritance are marked by its overdetermination. It is thus clear that Perera's lament that Gunesekera fails to engage in a complex negotiation of identity and Wijesinha's claim that the novel reflects the destruction of identity in the elite Sinhalese are presaged on a notion of the very completeness of 'identity',[38] revealing the ways in which the notion of the transcendental subject can work to reinforce culturally exclusionary readings of migration in which 'ambivalence' is disallowed.

This position reveals how the displaced exoticism of a migrant text can be scripted to meet the logic of cultural difference and authenticity contained in exoticist readings. Clearly a 'hierarchy of authenticity'[39] has been brought into play here, one that polices degrees of cultural affiliation and serves to exclude certain texts on the basis of the models of belonging that appear to be valorised in them. In *Reef* and *Heaven's Edge* the spatio-temporal indeterminacy of migrancy is re-sited to mark an allegorical representation of the nation as a threatened sanctuary. Haunted, in many ways, by Goonewardene's ecological construction of the beleaguered nation, Gunesekera's use of the trope of conservation raises further fundamental issues on the place of memory and historical retrieval in the scripting of the nation as a past paradise. As I will show, the ecological call for conservation and island sanctuaries foregrounds the utopianism underpinning the exoticist impulse, indexing cultural alienation through its inscription in fantasy.

From utilitarian utopianism to ecological fantasy

Both *Reef* and *Heaven's Edge* reveal a preoccupation with the search for a safe space, or refuge, within the context of unpredictable violence. Whereas in *Heaven's Edge* the allegorical spatial Manicheism underpinning such a reading is topographically registered through multiple underworlds and the quest for Uva's self-sustaining farm and an Edenic Samandia, in *Reef* this spatial register is located in the historically contingent world of post-Independence Sri Lanka, and in particular in the events leading up to the JVP insurrection of 1971. Thus whereas the sanctuary of *Heaven's Edge* is symbolically weighted and geographically dislocated to emphasise the idealism underpinning its representation, *Reef*'s political contextualisation culturally positions the ecological message of conservation in a beleaguered island allowing for a more situated understanding of its interventionist drive. From the isolation of Mister Salgado's house, which offers a haven set apart from political turmoil (p. 93),[40] to Salgado's desire to transform the coast into a 'sea sanctuary [. . .] a real refuge' (p. 171), and to the 'refuge' of cooking (p. 24) that serves to protect Triton from Joseph's brutality and ultimately gives him the means to advance himself, the sanctuary in *Reef* is registered as a metaphorical space of sustenance that is not simply imagined but actually realised and occupied. It is not, therefore, so much an imaginatively constructed ideal set in the putative past or provisional future, but more a condition of lived experience. The narrator, whose denial of his history has meant that for twenty years he had been 'protected from the past' (p. 12), is compelled on meeting a Tamil petrol-pump attendant in London to grapple with the conditions that led to his own exile, affirming the fact that this past too is one that constituted a refuge from political violence. It is a temporal mediation that foregrounds the reality of refuge so that his Edenic vision of his former homeland – where he 'could see a sea of pearls. Once a diver's paradise. Now a landmark for gunrunners in a battle zone of army camps and Tigers' (p. 12) – is more substantive than the brute facts of violence that corrupt his imagination.

This historical contingency of spatial representation, its situatedness in the real politics of contemporary Sri Lanka, contains a pedagogic register that disturbs the imaginative investment in exoticism in the novel. Cooking does not merely serve as a refuge for Triton, it is his means of mediating with the outside world. Mango stones become sexual toys (p. 61), polish smells of 'fenugreek and lentils', adrenalin is rendered a 'nerve juice' (p. 89) and eyes contain 'irises packed with ice' (p. 102). Spices also form part of Triton's erotic arsenal against Joseph's sexual advances, with chillies presented as a weapon of revenge (p. 30) and red onions providing a means of protection (p. 36). The sensuous emphasis on the process of cooking spicy Sri Lankan food lends itself to readings that privilege an emphasis on the domestication of difference in the text's scripting of exoticism. Hence Sharanya Jayawickrama has contended that through the focus on cooking 'the author effectively employs markers of cultural difference to create a very palatable product – a novel whose allure emanates from the delectable descriptions centring around food into the imagination of the reader who feels that he is able to grasp hold of a new experience of place and time'.[41]

Such an approach draws attention to the performative role that cooking plays in the text, in which the act of reading is sensuously connected to the preparation of food: 'I could feel the air move when he turned a page, each one catching the lemony light slice by papery slice' (p. 61). Indeed Gunesekera has himself contended that Triton's role reflects that of the artist, whose efforts to express himself by culinary means are analogous to his efforts to find a voice.[42] This subtle metafictional play on the process of producing and consuming a text is one of the pleasures of a novel that confounds those who work to shear it of its strategic metaphoricity and render it extraneous to the novel's message[43] or part of a 'conscious depoliticisation of Sri Lanka'.[44] Yet far from being outside the novel's central frame of reference, the 'strategic exoticism'[45] deployed here is central to the temporal coding of historical reclamation. In a manoeuvre reminiscent of Rushdie's pickling of Indian history in *Midnight's Children*, Gunesekera's sensory overload in the representation of cooking registers the reader's active consumption of the text and its status as a marketable narrative product in which 'taste' is presented as a product not of the mouth but of the mind (p. 97). Such a manoeuvre is only a form of 'depoliticisation' if the 'political' itself is divorced from the subjective framing of the imaginary. By revealing the close connections between imaginative and historical reclamation, Gunesekera allows for a reading of the nation that is both fluid and discursively produced, one that shows how politics itself is a matter of individual 'taste' so that the putative Garden of Eden is rendered a construct that 'panders to anyone's chauvinism' (p. 95).

The differential power relations uncovered by such strategic exoticism are not only those of the postcolonial writer writing back to the imperial centre, but they also reflect the position of the migrant writer working to unsettle the orthodoxies of historical constitution at the national centre which are constructed around the binarisms of Manichean allegory. The novel mediates and merges a 'pre-history' of the natural world – constructed from a nostalgic reclamation of the past home – with a projected ideal for the future. What is more, Mister Salgado's dream sanctuary is multiply inflected as the terrain of future domestication in which the private domesticity of Triton's culinary expertise is granted recognition as a public commercial enterprise. The representation of this sanctuary is contained within a utilitarian model of conservation that is, in its own way, exploitative of nature, prompted by an individualistic work ethic that shows how capitalism might be made more ecological, rather than by the more radical desire to respect nature's laws:[46]

> 'I used to think that in a month or two, next year, I would have a chance to turn the whole bay into a sanctuary. A marine park. I used to plan it in my head: how I'd build a jetty, a safe marina for little blue glass-bottomed boats, some outriggers with red sails, and then a sort of floating restaurant at one end. You could have produced your finest chilli crab there [. . .]. I thought of it like a ring, a circular platform with the sea in the middle. We could have farmed for the table and nurtured rare breeds for the wild. A centre to study our pre-history. We could have shown the world something then, something really fabulous. [. . .]'
>
> 'Let's do it here,' I said. 'Let's open a restaurant here, in London.'
>
> 'That's for you to do,' he said. 'Some day, for yourself.' [p. 187]

The material exploitation of nature is counterbalanced by the ecocentric concern for self-sustainability – in the aim to farm for the table and nurture rare breeds for the wild – revealing how the commercial marketability of the exotic is fundamentally allied in the text to the pastoral ideal. In the real and imagined sanctuaries of *Reef*, utopianism and utilitarianism meet, showing how exoticism in the text is held in an uneasy tension between a strategic critique of exoticism and an apparent collusion with it. It is a manoeuvre that reveals the commodification of utopianism – its utilitarian purpose in a socially divided world – and the transactional processes underpinning its emergence.

This scripting of exoticism from the displaced centre of migrant experience has potentially serious repercussions on how we read cultural authenticity in the text. As Graham Huggan has shown, the exotic can contain rival conceptions of cultural authenticity. These can be distinguished between a 'culture of authenticity', based on 'the ethically driven, historically situated quest for fulfilment', and a 'cult of authenticity' in which the authentic 'becomes simultaneously anxiety-ridden sign of loss and redemptive fetish'.[47] The cited passage could be read as falling victim to the 'cult of authenticity' in which Mister Salgado's nostalgic desires for his homeland are reconstituted through the fetishistic reconstruction of an islanded sanctuary.[48] Yet it is precisely the spatial and temporal scripting of the text that salvages it from falling into an exoticist trap. Mister Salgado's call for conservation, made from the confines of his London home shortly before the 1983 Colombo riots, is not presented as a reactionary plea for the preservation of an idealised past, but instead as an appeal for the construction of *alternative* – and as yet uninscribed – past or 'pre-history' that might pave the way for an alternative future. By presenting this appeal for an alternative past from a context of an imaginative construction of future potential, Gunesekera reminds us that, as James Clifford has pointed out, 'authenticity is something produced not salvaged',[49] and suggests that it is only by revisioning the past that a future free from violence is made possible.[50] It is also significant that the call for the creation of a self-sustaining, ecofriendly centre for marine research is rescripted in entirely utilitarian terms when transposed to the metropolitan centre. Through these means it is lifted from the utopian atemporality of nostalgia and presented as a materially viable response to the 'consuming desire'[51] for the creation of a new home, a new landscape of belonging.

Gunesekera's historically and politically situated representation of a past paradise from a dislocated immigrant perspective, mediated through metafictional registers that play with the reader's appetite for exotic fare, situate the social and historical contingencies of migration, impelling this narrative recreation of a former homeland and grounding the 'authentic' in a displaced site of production. It is a process that disturbs the distinction between the domestic and the savage, between the indigene and alien, thereby registering the social production of the authentic as a *provisional* site of enunciation. The lived refuges of Mister Salgado's homes in Colombo and London, and his imagined sea sanctuary in Sri Lanka, also register the ways in which the domestic moves from being a private dwelling place – a retreat from political unrest – to a site of political and moral engagement. The hope here is that the private refuges of the present might form the basis of a new moral order in which sustainability and respect for life are central. The strength of the novel thus lies in its resistance to any easy accommodation within exoticist registers and its ability to slide within and between different scriptings of the exotic while maintaining a grip on the historical and material contexts that provide the enabling context for such inscriptions. It is a process that effectively plays with the boundaries of strangeness and familiarity, negotiating the distance between past and present homes, real and imagined sanctuaries, without losing sight of the social and cultural coordinates of the production and enunciation of these mediations.

The emphasis on the mediation of clearly defined spaces and times presents a rational view of ecology as a site of resistance against violence. Ecology here works in the service of a critique of a society in which social and political violence threatens the lives of all its members, in particular the weak and vulnerable. Reinforced by the materialist scripting of exoticism in the text, ecological ideals are presented as socially and historically situated with real material results. In this it is comparable to Goonewardene's investment in ecology in *One Mad Bid For Freedom* where the plan to build a marine sanctuary is presented as a potential form of resistance to political violence, social destruction and cultural degeneration. Like Goonewardene, Gunesekera affirms the ecological need to protect endangered species – a model of the world that has its social and political expression in the protection of marginalised peoples. Yet Gunesekera's oppositional investment in ecology is to a large extent undermined by his investment in the exploration of the exotic. Whereas Goonewardene's novel emphasises ecological interdependency and biodiversity in keeping, some might say, with the author's promotion of internationalism, Gunesekera's investment in the exotic, combined with his cultural disembedding, presents us with a much more ambivalent reading. In *Reef* it is clear that the utopianism underpinning the ideal of a sanctuary of self-sustainability is held in tension with the manifestation of real refuges in the text, which are themselves constructed out of the desire for personal space. Gunesekera's sanctuaries, both real and imagined, are like Goonewardene's, anthropocentric, in that they are mediated by social rather than environmental concerns, but it is also clear that they emerge out of the desire to serve the metaphysical needs of the individual rather than the aim of addressing deficiencies in the social order. In *Reef* the desire to conserve is not so much an expression of altruism, but more closely connected to the personal needs of socially alienated and physically displaced characters. In this way it corresponds closely to the desire for rehabilitation that manifests itself in fantasy – a genre especially suited to finding ways of reintegration with the social and natural environment.[52] It is unsurprising therefore that Gunesekera should develop this interest in rehabilitation in *Heaven's Edge*, a novel in which ecology is mediated through dystopian fantasy as a register of alienation. As will be seen, in this novel Gunesekera takes social and cultural disembedding to its limits in his representation of an unnamed war-torn island, out of time and out of place.

Fantasy has been described as 'a mass-produced supplier of wish-fulfilment'.[53] It has the potential to be socially subversive, indexing, as Rosemary Jackson has pointed out, the limits of the dominant cultural order by making up for society's prohibitions through vicarious fulfilment.[54] Such a reading of fantasy as a literature of subversion poses particular difficulties when applied to the migrant text, for it is predicated on a notion of an identifiable social and cultural centre as a counterpoint for resistance. It is not only unclear from Gunesekera's disembedded narrative of the returning stranger in *Heaven's Edge* which dominant cultural order, if any, might be being critiqued, but also the extent to which the exoticism underpinning his engagement with fantasy might itself be constitutive rather than subversive of 'orientalist' readings of the nation as a former paradise. The unnamed island of the novel both is and is not Sri Lanka, its allegorical connection to the nation disturbed by the social and cultural disembedding that situates it as an imagined territory of desire ruptured by the anonymous forces of guerrilla warfare and state control that have divided the land into zones of surveillance, resistance and subversion. The novel is thus not so much postlapsarian as postapocalyptic, as forgotten underworlds, displaced sanctuaries and deferred Edens register the spatial limits of resistance. The illegibility of the forces of violence thus serves to generate a sense of existential angst,[55] resisting rather than inviting political readings.[56] This disembedding is furthered by the form of vicarious fulfilment manifested in the text. The sensuous descriptions of the natural landscape and Marc's erotic encounters with Uva (herself named after a lush region of the country) are frequently articulated in what Thieme has described as 'aphoristic purple prose'.[57] The relationship with both the environment and this local ecowarrior – who literally and metaphorically constitutes a daughter of the soil – promises to rehabilitate the exiled narrator, while the exoticised language that mediates such potential rehabilitation evacuates this possibility. Hence the displaced, strategic exoticism of Gunesekera's earlier texts here gives way to an exploration of the exotic that fails to assert anything outside its registers. In the novel we witness the inscription of the wish fulfilment element of fantastic literature that marks an exhausted exoticism, as displacement – a central characteristic of fantasy[58]– is evicted from conventional spatio-temporal registers. Gunesekera's privileging of the migrant sensibility finds its natural expression in the fantastic, 'an overfull or empty form [that] eludes interpretation, leaving the reader only with the experience of disjunction'.[59] It generates a sense of interpretative interdeterminacy that registers the possibility of dissent as everywhere and nowhere. For fantasy is, as Ursula Le Guin has contended, not antirational but pararational.[60] It works alongside, past or beyond the dominant order, bearing a disjunctive relationship to it. My aim here is to show how *Heaven's Edge* lends itself more readily to a reading of the fantastic as an exploration of a displaced reality rather than direct resistance to a knowable community, and to interrogate the extent to which this investment in the fantastic works to disable the political registers found in his earlier fiction.

Heaven's Edge is a migrant quest narrative that situates the exotic as a mode of aesthetic perception.[61] The narrator, Marc, returns to the island on a mission to uncover the secrets of his father's past, to 'explore an older terrain and discover [. . .] what was best to remember, and what might be better to forget' (p. 5).[62] It is as if, as Nasta has contended of *The Sandglass*, the text reveals 'a preoccupation with the representation of an interior landscape of desire [and] a longing to enter the symbolic as a narrative journey'.[63] The novel constitutes a search for origins that places the narrator as a socially disembedded exile (rather than a socially situated expatriate) whose mediation of the land is controlled by his exoticised and exoticising gaze. His alterity is marked not by displaced or deferred residence, but rather by his mediation of the world in terms of fantasy. This shift is one that focuses on social non-being which, in turn, comes to be endorsed as the legitimate basis for affiliation and connection. It is a manoeuvre that sets up a polarised dynamic in which the alienated individual comes to be marked as not merely an outsider but, more contentiously, as the exoticising foreigner: 'in any country it is only the foreigner who can feel a genuine sense of belonging, of arrival, of arriving home. We become committed: perpetually enchanted or permanently detained' (p. 41).

Here social and personal 'commitment' is scripted as 'enchantment', as migrant memory meets the constitutive exoticism of the 'foreigner'. Idealism is overt, as the pleasure seeker's interpellation of the nation as a potential paradise becomes the performative register of the text's mediation of belonging. The registers of exoticism are evident in Marc's subsequent scripting of his exilic status as a sign of his investment in the place he finds himself in, and in Uva's firm rejoinder that punctures any lofty claims of reclamation:

'Perhaps people like me', I added. 'We feel committed.'
She laughed. 'Desire, my love, is all you feel.' [p. 41]

In this rare instance of explicit irony, Gunesekera alerts us to the idealism underpinning Marc's perspective. Exoticism is not direct but strategically deployed. Yet in unhinging Marc's naivety from a clear contextual base, the novel marks a move from the mediatory, migrant reading of exoticism found in the earlier novels to one that is positioned in an exilic space occupied by the enchanted outsider. The island is rendered 'hallucinogenic' (p. 180) in such a dissociative manoeuvre.

If Goonewardene's pastoral romances registered his urban alienation, then Gunesekera's fantasy of a paradise that lies beyond reclamation or reach marks a disenchantment with all knowable environments. Yet unlike the early novels *Reef* and *The Sandglass*, which attempted to portray a situated idealism within the context of political breakdown, *Heaven's Edge* actively resists accommodation into a social and historical order. In this it subscribes to what Hayden White has described as an anarchist ideological positioning, in that its socially transcendent vision is connected to an idealisation of a 'remote past of natural-human innocence from which men have fallen' and the projection of a potential utopia onto a non-temporal plane which might be achievable at any time if only people would seize control of their own essential humanity.[64] It is primarily a novel of ideas – sharing imaginative affinities with Rushdie's science fiction fantasy *Grimus* – that draws upon the registers of Manichean allegories and myths in order to explore the position of the migrant as a mediator between disjunctive temporalities, a traveller between worlds. Unlike Grimus, however, the migrant self in Gunesekera's novel is compromised not by his marginalisation from the imaginary worlds of the novel but by his interpellation as a 'foreigner' – an interpellation that bears the burden of a prior and situated construction of 'authentic' identification. Thus within the cultural logic of the novel, Marc's desire for habilitation and accommodation *must* remain unrequited for such unrequited desire is necessary to his subject constitution.

The full implications of such a position are made clear when we compare this process of interpellation to the one outlined in Ondaatje's *Running in the Family* – another text that draws on the exotic as a mediatiatory marker of alienation. The travelling subject in Ondaatje's text is a metafictional construct whose interpellation registers a gravitational pull that draws reader and writing subject together. In contrast, the travelling subject in *Heaven's Edge* appears to rely upon stable registers of subject constitution; on the notion, in other words, of a unitary, transcendental subject. The unrequited desire of *Heaven's Edge* stands not so much as a marker of the impossibility of historical and cultural reclamation (as in Ondaatje's text and Gunesekera's early novels), but more as a marker of cultural alterity, of distance, and even, it could be said, of cultural ignorance. Hence Marc is rendered a self-professed 'foreigner', whose identity relies on the endorsement of notions of difference and alterity, marking his collusion with the discourses that seek to exclude him. Eroticism and exoticism – registers of Marc's unrequited desire – thus become a *generative* means of the expulsion as the text appears to subscribe to its own imbrication in a system in which difference is not denied or contested but actively endorsed.

Marc's position as an outsider not only reveals how displacement can register a form of social non-being[65] but also registers his collusion with discourses that are customarily perceived as 'orientalist'. It is here that Perera's charge that Gunesekera is 'guilty of recuperating certain myths and stereotypes of Sri Lanka' seems to bear credence, as the exilic experiences of the narrator come closer to that of the culturally rapacious tourist than the questing migrant in several ways.[66] The novel contains some of the key features of 'tourist' mediations of place. These have been described as an awareness of the terrain in visual, physical and sensual terms, an emphasis on oral pleasure and consumption, the experience of timelessness (a product of leisure), and the 'circular confirmation of self-identity' in which the strangeness of surroundings serve to endorse the unity of self.[67] All these elements can be found in the novel's mediation of time, place and identity.

The novel's spatio-temporal dynamics also register its subservience to a 'cult of authenticity'. The past exists as a personal fetish – in Uva's carved knife and Marc's video, which remind them of their respective fathers – thereby becoming 'an anxiety-ridden sign of loss'. Similarly, the divided and ruptured terrain could be seen as not so much a signifier of the displacement engendered by exilic forces and competing allegiances, but rather a marker of the inaccessibility of the bordered paradise alluded to in the novel's title, its status as an object that is *always out of reach.* Here the authentic as a 'sign of loss' saturates the text's cultural coding, so the reader is required to situate the text's scripting of cultural difference in order to understand the precise basis of such loss.

Yet this very openness to interpretation also allows a space for resistant readings. Does Marc align himself with the 'foreigner' because he draws upon an exclusionary discourse – one that resists mediation – or is it that his travel through deterritorialised and reterritorialised zones precludes him from accommodation into the land? Does such travel endorse or resist the preconstituted subject positioning assigned to him by discourses of the authentic?[68] And does the island's division into multiple zones of surveillance and deterritorialisation constitute a recognition of the land as a space of non-belonging, marking the way in which alienation is enforced by the landscape itself and the fact that war reconfigures the land into an space where belonging is no longer (yet) possible. Spaces generated by the rupture of armed conflict are thus marked as uninhabitable, spaces that (yet) lie beyond domestication and dwelling. Marc is, *in fact*, neither native nor foreigner, but it could be argued that the Manicheistic scripting of territory in the text, of the land as a former paradise, insists that he is habilitated in these exclusionary terms.

Such possibilities suggest that there is a need to look beyond the exoticist coding of the text, to disengage from narrow 'cultural' readings of the work and to accommodate instead a reading more attentive to the novel's interpretative indeterminacy in our evaluation of its exilic status if we are to recognise that behind the Manicheistic registers of a past paradise lies a much more challenging paradigm of regeneration. As Uva acknowledges, her ideal of the past serves a specific purpose: 'We all lived for each other once, not in need of each other [. . .] *You have to believe that, don't you?*' (my emphasis, p. 32). Such a reading would reveal that idealism – self-conscious and overt – is not so much the product of escapist fantasy, but rather is the expression of an urgent need to revitalise and rejuvenate the cultural order. Gunesekera's work reminds us that writing is not simply a place to live – a refuge from the violent clash of incommensurable realities – but also constitutes a regenerative means of addressing social and cultural disjunction. In displacing the past the novel also displaces destiny, opening the door for a future outside political violence in a pararational logic that works *alongside* real political events. For, as André Brink has suggested, 'only by dreaming and writing the *impossible* can life be made possible once again' (original emphasis).[69]

9 Conclusion

Destinations

Long before I became fully aware of the extent to which displacement would shape the course of my life, I was given a poster for my birthday by a friend at school that depicted a lone skier poised at the summit of a curled dune of snow. The words etched on a tantalisingly cobalt sky above the skier read: *Where you come from is not as important as where you are going*. While I had no means at the time of relating in any concrete way to the skier, snow or frosted peak, the words held my attention and haunt me still. They stirred in me a recognition of both the importance of my past – my origins and my natal and familial ties, scattered across countries – and the potential freedom of their disavowal and diminution. They encoded a hierarchy of value, replacing beginnings with the liberatory potential of unknown destinations, showing how 'being' could (and, it suggested, should) be informed by 'becoming', releasing the fixity of situated affiliation into multiple potentiality. The poster suggested an element of choice, but not one that was blindly celebratory or inattentive to material constraints: the skier could choose her path, but she would have to negotiate a terrain as difficult as it was beautiful. The words seem to suggest, when read from a broadly poststructuralist perspective, that it is only by breaking away from the teleological determinism of a prescribed history, of recognising that the value of origins may lie in the ability to transcend (and thereby question) them, that we can truly gain a sense of who we are and where we might rightfully belong.

This message may seem absurdly misplaced after the increased boundary surveillance following the attacks of 9/11, and almost painfully idealistic when set within the context of present-day political violence in Sri Lanka from which I write,[1] but that does not make it any less relevant. Intervention need not (and perhaps even ought not) draw upon the discourses generated by the contexts that demand it. Much of this study has been driven by a conviction that there is need to interrupt, to intervene and to challenge the assumed deterministic link between putative beginnings and potential destinations; to release the unilateralism of a trajectory of origins and destinations into a synchronicity in which destinations themselves mark the potential for new beginnings. These are not fanciful constructs that merely import 'alien' poststructuralist readings of and from the diaspora onto a rooted and situated context. Rather, it could (and I suggest should) be argued that such a history of mixed and unsettled beginnings, of destinations marking origins, is encoded in the very formulation of the originary 'Sinhala' nation: a history marked by the arrival of an unruly Indian prince and his retrograde followers onto these shores (are not all migrants lapsed natives?), marking the founding of a distinct Sinhala 'people'. Opening up this foundation myth to a reading that challenges some of the nationalist invectives of the present day allows us to base it – at the critical moment of Vijaya's apotheosis into the founder of the Sinhala 'race' – on the indigenisation of the outsider, and to contend that our future might be transformed if we were to try and read our past in such terms.

For as I mentioned at the outset, we are living in a time described by Scott as a Gramscian interregnum *after* postcoloniality; that is, a moment of considerable instability and uncertainty when hitherto established conceptual paradigms seem no longer adequate and new paradigms are yet to assert themselves.[2] It is a time when nationalism itself is no longer territorially determined or bounded, but rather crucially diasporic – a development described by Anderson as 'long-distance nationalism'[3] – and when the scripting of the alien outsider is not only formative of nationalist thought but also integral to the mobilisation of migrant subjectivity, estranging the authority of what Nikos Papastergiadis has described as 'certitudes of belonging'.[4] As Peter van der Veer has observed, 'nationalism needs this story of migration, the diaspora of others, to establish the rootedness of the nation'.[5] The interruption of polarised views of settlement and migration, of bounded distinctions between the insider and the outsider and a relocation of critical discourse into terms that reveal the interdependence and overlap between these constructions, works not only to undermine the basis of exclusionary nationalism but also to redefine the very terms of critical debate, revealing the contestatory connections between multiple 'centres' and 'margins' and displacing the assumptions underpinning their singularity, homogeneity and situatedness. As the study of the work of Sri Lankan writers in English reveals, there can be many 'insides' and 'outsides' to the nation. A critical approach that engages with what Iain Chambers has described as *writing as a form of travel*,[6] a movement that marks a trajectory between different sites of placeable bonding and dislocated, migratory subjectivities, can also mark what Bhabha has called a 'hybrid strategy or discourse [that] opens up a space for negotiation where power is unequal but its articulation may be equivocal. Such negotiation', Bhabha continues, 'is neither assimilation nor collaboration'.[7] It is an approach that might help to 'bring us up against the limits of our inheritance',[8] identify the boundaries of belonging and their multivalent sites of contestation and reveal the discursive dynamics that allow for the accommodation of cultural difference, transaction and translation.

Location *does* matter, as the work of internal and external exiles, and some of their literary critics, makes patently clear. It makes available certain discourses but not others,[9] helps socially situate and politically contextualise critical approaches drawing attention to inequalities of power in discursive practice, and provides a spatio-temporal compass alerting us to the significance of material and historical contingency in the construction of situated identities; but location alone is neither a neutral construct nor is it the determining factor in how difference gets mediated in literary texts. What is more, any invocation of location as a discursive basis for the critical mediation of texts requires us to attend to the ways in which boundaries are marked within and between texts, for it is through the discursive construction of such boundaries that we can best identify the moments where cultural difference *resists resolution*. As the work of the writers in this study goes to show, hybridity cannot be uncritically cited as the transactional space for the resolution of difference, and there are clearly hierarchies in hybridity that are not dependent on physical or geographical placement. Hybridity should not be invoked as a neutralising antidote to the dislocations of migration and globalisation: such a coding would work to efface the very cultural differences that mobilise its enunciation, diverting attention away from racialised and ethnicised social relations and material divisions. Invoked from 'outside' Sri Lanka, a decontextualised scripting of the hybridised, diasporic subject stands in danger of reclaiming that which it resists, registering a form of interpellation in which, as Spivak has put it, 'the diasporic stands in for the native informant', combining 'triumphalist hybridism' with 'nostalgic nativism'.[10] Such a neutralising conceptualisation of hybridity (as both discourse and process) rationalises inequalities in a way that leaves social hierarchies intact and works to homogenise and anaesthetise the experience of discrimination, opening up a space for diasporic nativism to slip in under the guise of deconstructive multiculturalism.

Radhakrishnan's distinction between 'metropolitan' and 'postcolonial' hybridity – a distinction based upon power dynamics generated by global processes rather than the static registers of geographical orientation – is worth consideration here. Metropolitan hybridity, according to Radhakrishnan, is 'ensconced comfortably in the heartland of both national and transnational citizenship', characterised by 'an intransitive and immanent sense of *jouissance*' and 'underwritten by the stable regime of Western secular identity and the authenticity that goes with it'. In contrast, postcolonial hybridity 'in a frustrating search for constituency and a legitimate political identity' marks 'an excruciating act of self-production by and through multiple traces' and compiles 'a laborious "inventory of one's self" characterised by 'expressions of extreme pain and agonizing dislocations'. It is important, Radhakrishnan reminds us, that metropolitan hybridity does not speak for postcolonial hybridity, for this would not only silence its political registers but also render its rebellion 'causeless'.[11]

Radhakrishnan's observations offer a cautionary reminder of the limitations of a poststructuralist approach that might work to efface the subject in its scripting of hybridity and marginalise identitarian forms of thinking and belonging that are crucial to the experience of many postcolonial peoples. As the work of Arasanayagam shows, such forms of thinking are a precondition to the articulation of an agonistic hybridity in which the 'laborious "inventory of one's self"' provides an act of literary resistance to the dislocating identitarianism generated by war. Her work offers a stark contrast to both Carl Muller's celebration of creolisation in his Burgher trilogy and to the elision of subjectivity to be found in Ondaatje's travel memoir, both of which gravitate toward a coding of hybridity in its metropolitan form. These different expressions of hybridised discourse cannot easily be mapped onto a general politics of location or domicile – for instance, Arasanayagam and Muller are both resident in the country whereas Ondaatje is not – revealing how readings of the 'metropolitan' and 'postcolonial', exile and resident, need to be closely attentive to alternative lines of influence, critical and textual boundary marking, and the complex historical and social conditions in which inclusion and exclusion are mediated. A detailed historicised reading of exclusionary discursive practice in Sri Lanka belongs in a different book; here – in a manoeuvre that invites a form of contextualisation attentive to the contingent construction of the past and national subjectivities – I have focused my attention on the discursive registers that mediate belonging, determining boundaries within and between anglophone literary texts and the critical reception of them. As I contended in my opening chapter, there is a need to read 'place', space and location territorially, as sites of contested cultural legitimation in both literary and critical production. It is a need not only pertinent to countries in which boundaries are subject to violent dispute and radical realignment, such as Sri Lanka, but also, I would suggest, to those parts of the world in which space is seen as a neutral abstraction or 'given', dissociated from its discursive registers so that boundaries can remain hidden and unchallenged.

The variant scriptings of hybridity evident in both Radhakrishnan's formulation and in the work of writers reveal not only unequal levels of empowerment and divergent registers of diasporic consciousness (including internal migration, multilinguism, political exile and transnationalism) but also a clash of discursive and representational cultures. It is a clash that has been foregrounded in the Rushdie Affair, in which – as Radhakrishnan points out – postrepresentational and representational cultural politics can be seen to confront one another. The argument, he contends, is not between two different identities (Western and indigenous) but between 'two different narratives and their intended teleologies',[12] between – in other words – an emphasis on 'where you come from' and 'where you are going'. Within such a discursive paradigm my own approach may yet appear, not only to diehard representationalists but also to others sceptical of the merits of the poststructuralist turn in postcolonial criticism, to be yet another example of metropolitan critical reclamation and depoliticisation of an agonistic postcolonial voice, an invitation not simply to mobilise locations and subject positionings but to divest them of their contingent political spaces and authenticating criteria.

I would like to respond to such concerns (concerns which I too have shared in the process of writing this book) by considering a statement by a prolific, internationally recognised Sri Lankan critic, whose work has been analysed in the opening chapter and who has done much to chronicle the nation's literary history. In a recent publication of collected essays on Sri Lankan writing, this critic went to some lengths to distinguish Sri Lankan writing in English from postmodernist literature of the 'West', claiming that:

> Western writers have become so disenchanted with, or alienated from, technological society that they have, in effect, made alienation the subject of their

> work. They have attempted to subvert or overturn all our received or traditional notions of what fiction is and what it is about, an expression of the desperate state of their minds. Sri Lankans do not share this condition of mind and it is a moot point whether it is desirable or necessary to adopt or adapt Western experimental modes. Such postmodernism is at odds with the rhythm and realities of Lankan life.[13]

Here patrician and nativist approaches can be seen to be working together to consolidate an all too familiar cultural binarism that differentiates an authenticated and culturally validated 'Sri Lankan' experience from that of alienated 'Western writers'. Indeed the process of cultural validation is based upon its dissociation from the perceived 'alienation' of the West, a process that effectively lays claim to a rooted, settled and culturally integrated conception of the Sri Lankan nation. Not only is alienation itself excluded from this authenticated cultural boundary – one that is determined by a transhistorical reading of culture in terms of 'a condition of mind' – in ways that render invisible the impact of modernisation on the postcolonial nation, but also literary experimentalism and innovation is itself expatriated. It is difficult not to be struck by the parochialism underpinning such a statement and wonder at the impact of such an exclusionary scripting of Sri Lankan writing on the development of Sri Lankan literature and literary studies both inside and outside the country. Given the dramatic political, social, cultural and demographic changes that the country has experienced since Independence, and the need to explore what one reviewer has viscerally described as 'the gut wrenching truths of this country's self slaughter',[14] this attempt to expatriate writing that actively attempts to find innovative literary expression for alienation, cultural displacement and radical uncertainty appears deeply disturbing.

What is more, the ready conflation between 'alienation', 'postmodernism' and the 'West' works to critically disable the political registers of postcolonial hybridity by recoding alienation itself as a marker of Western cultural affiliation, revealing how wholesale resistance to one of the constituent markers of hybridity can work in the service of exclusionary readings of the nation. Indeed this perception that the three concepts are closely connected and mutually reinforcing is so commonplace in literary criticism in Sri Lanka that attempts to question it are likely to be dismissed as the by-product of contamination from 'Western' cultural influences. It is a perception that endorses critical evaluations of texts that arbitrate cultural legitimacy in ways that permit Michael Ondaatje to be presented as 'not Sri Lankan' on account of his perceived orientalism, and allows James Goonewardene to be expatriated on the basis that his style of writing is just 'not valid'. On reading such statements it is hard not to wonder what would have become of English literature if the same criteria were applied to its canonised writers – if James Joyce and D.H. Lawrence had been critically expatriated on account of their residence abroad and literary experimentalism, or if Thomas Hardy's work was assessed on the basis of its correspondence to the dialect or idiom of the communities he purported to represent. Of course both Joyce and

Lawrence did experience considerable critical resistance in their time – a salutary reminder that often the enduring worth of a text can be registered in its ability to challenge the prejudices of its age. However the politically fraught context of Sri Lankan literary production and critical reception requires us to pay particular heed to the potential transformative effects of literary criticism – effects which writers as diverse as Goonewardene and Sivanandan have commented on – and their relationship with cultural and political developments of the time.

Based upon a politics of cultural surveillance drawn from both a violently unstable national centre and the diasporic reaches of metropolitan legitimation, where 'postcolonial' literature is largely arbitrated, the boundaries of 'Sri Lankan writing' in English are largely contested on the basis of nationalist and post-nationalist readings of literary and cultural legitimacy. Any reading of Sri Lankan literature in English needs to be alert to this struggle for critical and cultural hegemony and address the basis of their competing claims for authority. What is more, as my readings of variously expatriated writers have shown, the cultural politics of a text can often be exposed by addressing the critical transactions that work to situate, authenticate, legitimate, habilitate or ex-patriate it. An effort has made here to present an approach that, while consistently attentive to the broader context of these critical claims, has endeavoured not to be constrained by them. I have tried to avoid falling victim to the dictates of critical territoriality by privileging the discursive registers in literary writing and engaging directly with the vital and often powerful interrogation of spatial and cultural boundaries to be found within the texts. It is an engagement that works towards finding an enunciative space – or 'third space' in Bhabha's discursive register – that mediates the national and the diasporic while being attentive to the situated cultural politics of each. It suggests that the division between these formulations is far from clear-cut; that while it is certainly true that 'all hybridities are not equal',[15] there are to be found spaces of representation in literature in which the national can be found in the diasporic, the diasporic in the national, and that the spaces generated by such radical dislocations may not yet have become spaces of belonging. Some critics – including Radhakrishnan – have found such mediatory spaces within the discursive registers of the 'ethnic', but as Kalra, Kaur and Hutnyk have shown, ethnicity (in both metropolitan and postcolonial locations) 'reinstates the nation-state as the legitimate social sphere in which boundaries are made'.[16] To subscribe to the discourse of the ethnic works to identify specific sites of exclusion (and is therefore, I believe, integral to the process of critiquing literary and critical territoriality) but does so at the expense of subscribing to dominant identifications and hegemonic readings of the nation.

I would therefore suggest that the affiliated discourses of migration and diaspora offer a tactical politics of discursive displacement and intervention that works to estrange authority within a context attentive to conditions of political and historical antagonism. 'Migration' is all too easily decontextualised in its theoretical permutations to construct a celebratory rhetoric of travel, and the 'diaspora' has for too long been bound to the teleology of originary histories and one-way migration (facilitated in large measure by its etymological rooting to the scattering of seeds). But a reading of the diasporic as a process of *aleatory* mediation, of *dislocated and emergent* subjectivities, and *interrupted and bifurcated* histories reroutes the diasporic and mobilises it to address new formulations of belonging that accompany the multivalent violence of enforced mobilisation. Such a discourse introduces 'a viral destabilization to classificatory systems' in its anti-essentialist drive,[17] infecting the discourse of nationing in a manner that violently disconnects the interpellated subject from territorially inflected and homogenising readings of national and cultural belonging. It enacts a hermeneutic politics that is heuristic in its inflections; one that, nevertheless, insists upon a recognition of the material and social forces of boundary surveillance while simultaneously requiring the opening up of borders. For, as Salman Sayyid has observed, the diaspora is not so much 'the other of the nation', but is rather 'an anti-nation' since it 'interrupts the closure' of national boundaries: 'The existence of a diaspora prevents the closure of the nation, since a diaspora is by definition [also] located within another nation'.[18]

Read and invoked as *anti*-national rather than alter-native, diasporic and migrant mediations work to reveal the resistance of the nation to openness while simultaneously insisting upon its subjection to transactional practices. In the fields of literary and cultural analysis, such mediations demand a form of deterritorialisation that is based upon our ability to re-situate ourselves – to move into dislocated spaces and find alternative origins and sites of belonging in them. It also requires us to both resist and acknowledge the centrality of closure; to retain an enduring belief that it is both necessary and possible to reclaim our multiple pasts without being claimed by them.

Notes

Introduction

1 J. Perera, 'LTTE Needs to Work Jointly to Rebuild North East', e-mail communication, 3 January 2005.
2 I am referring here to incidents involving the routine killings of security forces in the North and East and the targeting of Tamil civilians by military personnel in December 2005.
3 M. Glasius, 'The European Union and Sri Lanka: Tsunami Response and the Long-Term Policy', Centre for the Study of Global Governance, LSE publication, 14 October 2005, available online: www.lse.ac.uk/Depts/global/2securitypub.htm. This report contends that the tsunami has 'accentuated rather than ameliorated conflict dynamics'.
4 D. Scott, *Refashioning Futures: Criticism After Postcoloniality*, Princeton, NJ: Princeton University Press, 1999, p. 10.
5 D.C.R.A. Goonetilleke, *Sri Lankan English Literature and the Sri Lankan People 1917–2003*, Colombo: Vijitha Yapa, 2005, p. 12.
6 I use the term 'civil war' as a historical marker to describe the period of military conflict following the pogrom of July 1983 in Colombo. It needs to be differentiated from 'ethnic conflict', which has a broader historical reach.
7 D.C.R.A. Goonetilleke has claimed that the cultural nationalism of the 1950s in fact worked to motivate writers to write in English. Others, such as Rajiva Wijesinha, emphasise the diminution of literary output during the 1960s.
8 These include *The Hybrid Nation* edited by Neluka Silva, Neloufer de Mel's *Women and the Nation's Narrative*, Darini Rajasinghan-Senenayake's *Identity on the Borderline: Multicultural History in a Moment of Danger*, Qadri Ismail's *Abiding by Sri Lanka* and several studies by Michael Roberts.
9 T. Brennan, 'The National Longing for Form' in Homi K. Bhabha (ed.), *Nation and Narration*, London: Routledge: 1990, pp. 49–50.

1 Literature and territoriality: boundary marking as a critical paradigm

1 H.K. Bhabha, 'Sly Civility' in *The Location of Culture*, London: Routledge, 1994, pp. 99–100.
2 My use of the term 'settlement' is informed by John Hay's observation that it may be the expression of psychological yearning towards stability; J. Hay, 'Settlement as Displacement: The Narratives of History' in E. Thumboo and T. Kandiah (eds), *The Writer as Historical Witness: Studies in Commonwealth Literature*, Singapore: Unipress, 1995, p. 54.
3 K.M. de Silva, *Reaping the Whirlwind: Ethnic Conflict, Ethnic Politics in Sri Lanka*, New Delhi: Penguin India, 1998, Chapter 1.

4 M. Roberts, *Firstness, History, Place and Legitimate Claim to Place-as-Homeland in Comparative Focus*, Colombo: International Centre for Ethnic Studies, 2005, pp. 2–3.

5 C. Kanaganayakam, 'Dancing in the Rarefied Air: Reading Contemporary Sri Lankan Literature', *ARIEL*, January 1998, 29:1, pp. 52, 57. For a contextually grounded consideration of related issues see C. Kanaganayakam, 'Literature and the Politics of Ethno-Nationalism in Sri Lanka', *The Sri Lanka Journal of the Humanities*, 2000, XXVI, 1 and 2, pp. 29–43.

6 Kanaganayakam, 'Dancing', op. cit, pp. 58, 57, 62 and 57.

7 D.C.R.A. Goonetilleke, 'Sri Lanka's "Ethnic" Conflict in its Literature in English', *World Literature Today*, 1992, 66:3, p. 451.

8 I use the term 'cultural nationalism' in Michael Roberts' sense, to embrace a range of linked concepts such as language, tradition, identity, history and race. See M. Roberts, 'Sinhala-ness and Sinhala Nationalism', *A History of Ethnic Conflict in Sri Lanka: Recollection, Reinterpretation and Reconciliation*, Colombo: Marga Institute, 2001, p. 1. Roberts contends that counteracting extreme forms of Sinhala nationalism has to be effected in and through the Sinhala medium (p. 2).

9 G. Huggan, *The Postcolonial Exotic: Marketing the Margins*, London: Routledge, 2001, p. 173.

10 Wilfrid Jayasuriya has observed that 'it is the possible prospect of an international audience which spurs the energy of writers in English now'. W. Jayasuriya, *Sri Lanka's Modern English Literature: A Case Study in Literary Theory*, New Delhi: Navrang, 1994, p. 102.

11 T. Kandiah, 'Towards a Lankan Canon in English Creative Writing: Subversions of Post-colonialism and the Resisting Representations of Chitra Fernando's Fictional Voice', *Phoenix: Sri Lanka Journal of English in the Commonwealth*, 1997, vols 5 and 6, p. 68.

12 Y. Gooneratne, 'The English-Educated in Sri Lanka: An Assessment of Their Cultural Role', *South Asia Bulletin*, 1992, XII:1, p. 24.

13 Ibid., p. 21.

14 W. Perera, 'Images of Sri Lanka through Expatriate Eyes: Romesh Gunesekera's *Reef*', *Journal of Commonwealth Literature*, 1995, 30:1, pp. 63–77.

15 D.C.R.A. Goonetilleke, *Sri Lankan English Literature and the Sri Lankan People 1917–2003*, Colombo: Vijitha Yapa, 2005, p. 113. Goonetilleke makes this observation in the process of evaluating a literary text that considers the plight of those living in border zones. It is worth noting that there has no been no official recognition of a border zone in the country. According to Darini Rajasingham-Senanayake the government has not admitted to its existence because it would constitute a recognition of the LTTE's partial victory in its separatist cause. D. Rajasingham-Senanayake, *Identity on the Borderline: Multicultural History in a Moment of Danger*, Colombo: Marga Institute, 2001, p. 8.

16 M. Foucault, *Power/Knowledge: Selected Interviews and Other Writings 1972–1977*, edited by C. Gordon, New York: Random House, 1981.

17 E.G. Ericksen, *The Territorial Experience: Human Ecology as Symbolic Interaction*, Austin, TX: University of Texas, 1980, pp. 33–34. In a related vein, Jayadeva Uyangoda has contended that the two central components of foundational myths are centralised sovereignty and fixed border territory. J. Uyangoda, 'Biographies of a Decaying Nation-State' in M. Tiruchelvam and C.S. Dattathreya (eds), *Culture and Politics of Identity in Sri Lanka*, Colombo: International Centre for Ethnic Studies, 1998, p. 176.

18 M.J. Shapiro, *Violent Cartographies: Mapping Cultures of War*, Minneapolis, MN: University of Minnesota Press, 1997, p. xi and Chapter 1.

19 N. de Mel, *Women and the Nation's Narrative: Gender and Nationalism in Twentieth Century Sri Lanka*, Colombo: Social Scientists' Association, 2001, p. 235.

20 D. Rajasingham-Senanayake, *Identity on the Borderline: Multicultural History in a Moment of Danger*, Colombo: Marga Institute, 2001, pp. 21–22.

21 C. Kanaganayakam, 'Literature and the Politics of Ethno-Nationalism in Sri Lanka', *The Sri Lanka Journal of the Humanities*, 2000, XXVI, nos. 1–2, p. 33.

22 D. Rajasingham-Senanayake, 'Identity on the Borderline: Modernity, New Ethnicities, and the Unmaking of Multiculturalism in Sri Lanka' in N. Silva (ed.), *The Hybrid Island*, Colombo: Social Scientists' Association, 2002, p. 47. In a project closely affiliated with the critical impulses directing my study, this essay explores the connections between spatial, territorial and ethnic categories in the context of the political conflict.

23 Rajasingham-Senanayake, *Identity on the Borderline*, op. cit, p. 20.

24 S.J. Tambiah, *Buddhism Betrayed?: Religion, Politics, and Violence in Sri Lanka*, Chicago, IL: University of Chicago Press, 1992, p. 111; N. Serena Tennekoon, 'Rituals of Development: The Accelerated Mahavali Development Program of Sri Lanka', *American Ethnologist*, 1998, 15:2, pp. 294–310.

25 D.R.I.B. Werellagama, L. Herath, J. Manatunga and M. Nakayama, 'Health and Sanitation Aspects of Communities Displaced by the Mahaweli Multipurpose Development Project', available online: www.asiaoceania-conference.org/abstract/HS/2nd%20Round/HS10/58-HS-Ao8o4.pdf; B. Refslund Sørensen, 'The Experience of Displacement: Reconstructing Places and Identities in Sri Lanka' in K. Fog Olwig and K. Hastrup (eds), *Siting Culture: The Shifting Anthropological Subject*, London: Routledge, 1997, p. 142; W. Stegeborn, 'Indigenous Rights in Sri Lanka: Assimilation of the Wanniyala-Aetto (Veddahs)', March 2002, available online: www.cpsu.org.uk/downloads/wiveca_s.pdf

26 S. Kemper, *The Presence of the Past: Chronicles, Politics, and Culture in Sinhala Life*, Ithaca, NY: Cornell University Press, 1991, pp. 133 and 206.

27 R.M. George, *The Politics of Home: Postcolonial Relocations and Twentieth Century Ficion*, Berkeley, CA: University of California Press, 1999, p. 2.

28 Michael Roberts has pointed out that 'questioning this tradition sometimes evokes apoplectic responses of the same order as the apocalyptic fears aroused by striking Tiger successes'. M. Roberts, *Burden of History: Obstacles to Power Sharing in Sri Lanka*, Colombo: Marga Institute, 2001, p. 23.

29 S. Krishna, *Postcolonial Insecurities: India, Sri Lanka and the Question of Nationhood*, New Delhi: Oxford University Press, 2000, pp. 54 and 51.

30 D. Austin, *Democracy and Violence in India and Sri Lanka*, London: Pinter, 1994, p. 61.

31 J.S. Duncan, *The City as Text: The Politics of Landscape Interpretation in the Kandyan Kingdom*, Cambridge: Cambridge University Press, 1990, p. 25.

32 Available online: http://peaceinsrilanka.org/peace2005/Insidepage/Pressrelease/RNG/RNG5thDec.asp Although this phrase was used in the early rounds of peace talks in relation to an agreement on the principle of internal self-determination, the demand for an independent Tamil homeland has remained a prominent part of much LTTE literature.

33 Deleuze and Guattari use this term to describe the position of tribal peoples. See Shapiro, op. cit, p. 196.

34 Krishna, op. cit., p. 72; J. Arasanayagam, *The Captain Has Come*, unpublished play; p. 48.

35 Q. Ismail, *Abiding by Sri Lanka: On Peace, Place and Postcoloniality*, Minneapolis, MN: University of Minnesota Press, 2005, pp. 104–05.

36 It has been pointed out that the only non-Tamils now in the north are Sri Lankan military personnel, who effectively constitute an occupying force. Rajasingham-Senanayake, *Identity on the Borderline*, op. cit., p. 22.

37 R. Cheran, *The Sixth Genre: Memory, History and the Tamil Diaspora Imagination*, Colombo: Marga Institute, 2001, pp. 21, 16–17, and 22. Cheran cites the annual national Tamil calendar, *Thamil Thaay Naat Kaatti* (The Mother Tamil Calendar), issued simultaneously from France, Germany and Canada: 'Hitler transformed a weakened and dishonoured Germany into a powerful state, he aspired to win the world'.

38 For an illuminating exploration of some of these issues from the perspective of a non-resident Sri Lankan writer see Shyam Selvadurai, 'The Influence of Canada in *Funny*

Boy' in N. Silva and R. Wijesinha, *Across Cultures: Issues of Identity in Contemporary British and Sri Lankan Writing*, Colombo: The British Council, 2001, pp. 3–10.

39 Aparna Halpé has pointed out that local presses are largely dependent on state or institutional funding (such as the International Centre for Ethnic Studies or the English Writers' Cooperative) or the beneficence of wealthy entrepreneurs, and that the average print run for a book is about 2000 copies. A. Halpé, 'Inclusion and Exclusion: The Impossibility of South Asian Literature in the Classroom', unpublished graduate paper, University of Toronto, 2003. pp. 2–3.

40 Kanaganayakam, 'Dancing', op. cit., pp. 55–56; D. Coleman, *Masculine Migrations: Reading the Postcolonial Male in 'New Canadian' Narratives*, Toronto: University of Toronto Press, 1998, pp. 105–30.

41 Ibid., p. 63.

42 Penguin India and Indialog are two of the main publishers outside Sri Lanka that publish the work of local writers. Meenakshi Mukherjee has pointed out how few Sri Lankan texts are available in India. M. Mukherjee, 'A Blighted Garden', *The Hindu*, Sunday April 1, 2001. Available online: www.hinduonnet.com/2001/04/01/stories/1301067j.htm, pp. 4–5.

43 This has been described as a condition in which the state-centred account of spatiality intimately links power and territorial sovereignty. See A. Paasi, 'The Political Geography of Boundaries at the End of the Millennium: Challenges of the Deterrotorializing World' in H. Eskelinen, I. Liikanen and J. Oksa (eds), *Curtains of Iron and Gold: Reconstructing Borders and Scales of Interaction*, Aldershot: Ashgate, 1999, p. 10.

44 Krishna, op. cit., p. 77.

45 A. Steen Preis 'Seeking Place: Capsized Identities and Contracted Belonging among Sri Lankan Tamil Refugees' in Olwig and Hastrup, op. cit., p. 86.

46 The choice, as Joe Cleary points out, lies between nationalist homogenisation through cultural assimilation of minorities and the territorial division of the ethnic communities into separate states, which also leads to nationalist homogenisation. J. Cleary, *Literature, Partition and the Nation State: Culture and Conflict in Ireland, Israel and Palestine*, Cambridge: Cambridge University Press, 2002, p. 21.

47 Ibid., p. 193.

48 I am indebted to Joe Cleary's engagement with these genres for my evaluation in this section. Ibid., pp. 112–13 and 120–21.

49 Yasmine Gooneratne has noted the rise in satiric fiction in Sri Lanka and observed that such work invites moral regeneration through ridicule. Y. Gooneratne, 'Making History in Sri Lanka: Comic Modes of Satire and Fiction' in Thumboo and Kandiah, op. cit., p. 378.

50 R. Wijesinha, editorial, *Journal of Commonwealth Literature*, 1998, 33:1, p. 2. Also see R. Wijesinha, 'Sri Lankan Fiction in English' (1989) in *Breaking Bounds: Essays on Sri Lankan Writing in English*, Belihuloya: Sabaragamuwa University Press, 1998, pp. 26–39.

51 D. Sibley, *Geographies of Exclusion: Society and Difference in the West*, London: Routledge, 1995, pp. 39 and 183.

52 R.R. Rao, 'Because Most People Marry their Own Kind: A Reading of Shyam Selvadurai's *Funny Boy*', *ARIEL*, January 1997, 28:1, p. 127.

53 H. Thomas, 'Shyam Selvadurai', Fall 1997. Available online: www.emory.edu./ENGLISH/Bahri/Selva.html

54 Cited in R. Wijesinha, 'Oddities and Excesses: Sri Lanka Substantiated by the *Funny Boy*' in Wijesinha, *Breaking Bounds*, op. cit., p. 85. Wijesinha quotes Maureen Seneviratne's letter: 'Make no mistake – homosexuality is unnatural. It is immoral and goes against all religious teachings as well as civil law [. . .] The very heart of all our religious and moral teachings is at risk, and we would be wanting in our religious duty to future generations of unspoilt children if we were, not only to condone these practices, but also legalize them [. . .] [A] strong stand must be taken against deviants who would worm themselves into and destroy the very fabric of society'.

55 Rao, op. cit., p. 126.
56 Kanaganayakam, 'Dancing', op. cit., p. 61.
57 J. Arasanayagam, 'Ancestors' in *Reddened Water Flows Clear*, London: Forest Books, 1991, p. 25. Neloufer de Mel also comments on the significance of tenantship in Arasanayagam's work. See 'A Question of Identity: Jean Arasanayagam's Landscape of the Nation' in de Mel, op. cit., p. 187.
58 Ibid., p. 163.
59 Goonetilleke, *Sri Lankan English Literature*, op. cit., p. 50; T. Kandiah, '"Kaduva": Power and the English Language Weapon in Sri Lanka' in P. Colin-Thomé and A. Halpé (eds), *Honouring E.F.C. Ludowyk: Felicitation Essays*, Dehiwela: Tissa Prakasakayo Ltd, 1984, p. 117.
60 Ibid., p. 135.
61 The Act, which made Sinhala the sole official language, effectively disenfranchised ethnic minorities (most notably the Burgher and Tamil communities), who were dependent on their knowledge of English for access to employment in the civil service and administrative sectors, and it created a form of pedagogic apartheid in the streaming of education into Sinhala and Tamil mediums.
62 Wijesinha, *Breaking Bounds*, op. cit., p. 73.
63 For a personal reflection on English as a marker of exclusion see Sasanka Perera, 'The Hegemony of Language Imperialism and the Colonization of the Mind' in *Living with Torturers*, Colombo: International Centre for Ethnic Studies, 1995, pp. 37–45. Also Regi Siriwardene's poem 'Colonial Cameo' in R. Wijesinha (ed.), *An Anthology of Contemporary Sri Lankan Poetry in English*, Kelaniya: English Association of Sri Lanka: 1991, p. 114. Aparna Halpé has also observed that the student journal *Kaduwa*, established in 1980, served as an alternative press for radical critics of the times: Halpé, 'Inclusions and Exclusions', op. cit., p. 10.
64 S.G. Samarasinghe, 'Language Policy in Public Administration, 1956–94: An Implementor's Perspective' in K.N.O. Dharmadasa (ed.), *National Language Policy in Sri Lanka: 1956 to 1996, Three Studies in its Implementation*, Kandy: International Centre for Ethnic Studies, 1996, p. 88.
65 Gooneratne, 'The English Educated', op. cit., p. 21.
66 The English literate community constitutes less than 10 per cent of the population, whereas the literacy rate for the country as a whole is over 90 per cent.
67 See B. Ashcroft, G. Griffiths and H. Tiffin, *The Empire Writes Back: Theory and Practice in Postcolonial Literatures*, London: Routledge, 1989, Chapter 2.
68 M. Gunesekera, *The Postcolonial Identity of Sri Lankan English*, Colombo: Katha Publishers, 2005, pp. 24 and 39–42. Gunesekera distinguishes between four types of Sri Lankan English: prestigious Standard Sri Lankan English (based on Sinhalese and spoken by members of the elite, who have been introduced to the language from birth), non-standard Sri Lankan English, Tamil English, and Burgher English, pp. 34–37.
69 T. Kandiah, 'New Ceylon English: *The Call of the Kirala*, a Novel by James Goonewardene', *New Ceylon Writing*, 1971, p. 92; M. Gunesekera, 'Language and Identity: In a Class of their Own' in Silva and Wijesinha, op. cit, p. 84; R. de Chickera, 'Preface', *Kider Chetty Street* by Jagath Kumarasinghe, Kelaniya: Sooriya Publishers, 2005, pp. 7–9.
70 L. Wikkramasinha, 'Note' in *Lustre: Poems*, Kandy: Privately published, 1965, p. 51, cited in Goonetilleke, *Sri Lankan English Literature*, op. cit., p. 49.
71 Wijesinha, *Breaking Bounds*, op. cit., p. 72.
72 M.M. Bakhtin in M. Holquist (ed.), *The Dialogic Imagination*, Austin, TX: University of Texas Press, 1981, pp. 358 and 67.
73 Unusually for Arasanayagam, a glossary is provided; but this is rudimentary and incomplete.
74 J. Arasanayagam, 'Mythologies of Childhood' in *Peacocks and Dreams*, New Delhi: Navrang, 1996, p. 6.

75 C. Kanaganayakam, 'Jean Arasanayagam (1930–)' in J.C. Sanga (ed.), *South Asian Novelists in English*, Westport, CT: Greenwood Press, 2003, p. 17.
76 H. Bhabha, 'Signs Taken for Wonders' in *The Location of Culture*, London: Routledge, 1994, p. 120.
77 See for example 'Destroying the Enemy' and 'Ancestors' in Arasanayagam, *Reddened Water*, op. cit., pp. 15 and 23.
78 Gunesekera has qualified this in claiming that Muller's rhetorical strategies capture the flavour of a variety of Burgher English, a form that is largely a mixture of Portuguese Creole and English. See Gunesekera, *The Postcolonial Identity of Sri Lankan English*, op. cit., pp. 59 and 37.
79 C. Muller, *The Jam Fruit Tree*, New Delhi: Penguin India, 1993, pp. 42–43.
80 Bakhtin has contended that parody is central to heteroglossic linguistic struggle and forms an intralinguistic, intentional dialogised hybrid. See Bakhtin, op. cit., pp. 76–78.
81 See Olwig and Hastrup, 'Introduction', op. cit., pp. 1–14.
82 For example the Gratiean Trust's award of a translation prize and the establishment of Three Wheeler Press.
83 While Gooneratne's text has a diasporic reach, its cultural coding endorses a communitarian ethos.
84 This recently established Colombo-based press already has a number of strong titles by writers resident inside and outside the country and marks, in my view, a significant cultural intervention in providing an enabling context for intercultural exchange.
85 B. Parry, 'Resistance Theory/Theorising Resistance, or Two Cheers for Nativism' in F. Barker, P. Hulme and M. Iversen (eds), *Colonial Discourse/ Postcolonial Theory*, Manchester: Manchester University Press, 1994, p. 193.
86 N. Rapport and A. Dawson make the same observation in 'Home and Movement: A Polemic' in N. Rapport and A. Dawson (eds), *Migrants of Identity: Perceptions of Home in a World of Movement*, Oxford: Berg, 1998, p. 32.
87 The term 'community' is often used euphemistically in Sri Lanka to denote caste difference – a form of boundary marking that deserves further analysis but lies beyond the scope of this study. My own use of the term is broader and more general, and is intended to foreground the practice of discursively creating and generating affilliative ties by alluding to discrete cultural networks.
88 Williams goes on to observe: 'Yet the jump from that to anything like the modern nation-state is entirely artificial.' Cited in M. Featherstone, 'Localism, Globalism and Cultural Identity' in R. Wilson and W. Dissanayake (eds), *Global/Local: Cultural Production and the Transnational Imaginary*, Durham, NC: Duke University Press: 1996, p. 53.
89 For example Arun Mukherjee's critique of Michael Ondaatje's work as orientalist serves not only to align his texts with colonial prescriptives but also to foreground the radical instability of his cultural position as a Canadian author. Mukherjee's argument that Ondaatje misrepresents the past in *Running in the Family* is used to support her case for the need for a more inclusive approach in Canadian literary studies – one that is open to overtly political writing. In making it she draws upon a nativist Sri Lankan critique, thereby revealing how Sri Lankan nativism can be used in the service of a very different cultural politics in the West. See A. Mukherjee, 'The Sri Lankan Poets in Canada: An Alternative View', *Toronto South Asian Review*, 1984, 3:2, pp. 32–45. Similarly Gautam Kundu's critique of Gunesekera's work as 'exotic' is attentive to its place in the dynamics of mediating migration and alienation. Such critical positionings reveal the instability rather than the fixity of these migrant subjects and are attentive to the positioning of the 'exotic' as a marketable producer of domesticated difference. See G. Kundu, 'Romesh Gunesekera (1954–)' in Sanga, op. cit., pp. 93–99. These critical analyses need to be distinguished from publicity blurbs on dustjackets that refer to the exotic, as the primary purpose there is to market the text rather than subject it to literary evaluation.

90 H. Bhabha, 'Representation and the Colonial Text: A Critical Exploration of Some Forms of Mimeticism' in F. Gloversmith (ed.), *The Theory of Reading*, Brighton: Harvester, 1984, p. 96. Bhabha mentions in his first footnote that the essay was written in mid-1980. All subsequent references are to this volume.

91 Bhabha is citing Mulhern here.

92 Many instances of patrician criticism are to be found in literary reviews which do not lend themselves to extended or detailed evaluation. I have therefore chosen to focus on the work of one prolific literary critic in my consideration of this mode.

93 D.C.R.A. Goonetilleke, 'Novel (Sri Lanka)' in E. Benson and L.W. Conolly (eds), *The Encyclopedia of Postcolonial Literatures in English*, Vol. 2, London: Routledge, 1994, p. 1155.

94 Ibid., p. 1159.

95 Goonetilleke, 'Sri Lanka's "Ethnic" Conflict in Its Literature in English', *World Literature Today*, Summer 1992, 66:3, p. 451.

96 Abeynayake's criticisms are addressed not just to critics but to the English-speaking literary community as a whole. R. Abeynayake, 'Gratiaen Award: A Few Owe So Much to So Many', *The Sunday Times*, 10 March 1996. Available online: www.lacnet.org/suntimes/960310/oped/gratiaen.html Ajith Samaranayake also refers to the literary elite in these terms in 'James Goonewardene and the English Language Novel', *Sunday Observer*, 25 May 1997. Also see James Goonewardene's essay, 'Nationalism and the Writer in Sri Lanka', *Journal of Commonwealth Literature*, August 1974, IX: 1, pp. 50–56. Here he cautions against cultural nationalism where 'the ground was being prepared for artistic inbreeding', p. 54.

97 Qadri Ismail refers to this in his consideration of the interpellation of Tamils as a minority in his study *Abiding by Sri Lanka*, op. cit., p. xxvi.

98 De Silva puts it in a rather more counterpoised form: 'The conflict' he argues 'is between a majority with a minority complex, and a minority with a yearning for majority status, a minority with a majority complex'. K.M. de Silva, *Reaping the Whirlwind: Ethnic Conflict, Ethnic Politics in Sri Lanka*, New Delhi: Penguin India, 1998, pp. 303–04.

99 Goonetilleke, op. cit., p. 451.

100 For a political analysis that effectively uses the majority–minority dialectic to reveal the significance of its impact on the scripting of democratic relations in Sri Lanka see J. Uyangoda, *Questions of Sri Lanka's Minority Rights*, Colombo: International Centre for Ethnic Studies, 2001. Uyangoda observes that the denial of the existence of an ethnic conflict by the intelligentsia curtails political pluralism, p. 101.

101 Goonetilleke, op. cit., p. 453.

102 It is described as the 'outstanding novel' of the year, but reservations are expressed on the basis of its divergence from historical accuracy. The piece also refers to Ondaatje's *Running in the Family* in terms that clearly indicate critical discomfort with its postmodernist drive. See D.C.R.A. Goonetilleke, 'Sri Lanka', *Journal of Commonwealth Literature*, 1983, XVIII: 2, p. 139.

103 D.C.R.A. Goonetilleke, 'Sri Lanka', *Journal of Commonwealth Literature*, 1989, XXIV: 2, p. 120.

104 Meenakshi Mukherjee has observed that de Zoysa has become an iconic figure in Sri Lanka. M. Mukherjee, 'A Blighted Garden', *The Hindu*, Sunday April 1 2001, pp. 3–4.

105 D.C.R.A. Goonetilleke, 'Sri Lanka', *Journal of Commonwealth Literature*, 1991, XXVI: 2, p. 152. Elsewhere Goonetilleke does acknowledge the prophetic role of de Zoysa's work but precedes it with this reflection on the 1983 violence that triggered the armed conflict: 'It was no Holocaust, negligible compared to the number of Sinhalese and Muslims villagers/civilians massacred by the LTTE'. Goonetilleke, *Sri Lankan English Literature*, op. cit., p. 83.

106 Goonetilleke, *Sri Lankan English Literature*, op. cit., pp. 93 and 45–46.

107 D.C.R.A. Goonetilleke, 'Beyond Alienation: The Efflorescence of Sri Lankan Literature in English', *Journal of Commonwealth Literature*, 1986, XXI: 1, p. 30.
108 Goonetilleke, 'Sri Lanka's "Ethnic" Conflict', op. cit., p. 452.
109 J. Arasanayagam, *A Nice Burgher Girl*, cited in de Mel, op. cit., p. 174.
110 Goonetilleke, 'Poetry (Sri Lanka)' in Benson and Conolly, op. cit., p. 1281. Goonetilleke, 'Sri Lanka's "Ethnic" Conflict', op. cit., p. 452.
111 V. Walker, 'Woman, Identity and the Other in Jean Arasanayagam's Fiction', *Navasilu: Journal of the English Association of Sri Lanka*, August 2000, 17, p. 140.
112 It is worth noting that Benita Parry's positive evaluation of nativism is alert to its openness to abuse by reactionary forces. Parry, op. cit., p. 174.
113 Sasanka Perera has made a similar observation in his analysis of Sri Lankan art, claiming that representationalism is a key feature of work defined as authentic. S. Perera, 'In Search of Authenticity: Politics of Inclusion and Exclusion' in *The World According to Me: An Interpretation of the Ordinary, the Common, and the Mundane*, Colombo: International Centre for Ethnic Studies, 1999, pp. 137–38.
114 This view is clearly expressed in Rajiva Wijesinha's essay 'Spices and Sandcastles'. Here the presentation of Sri Lanka as the most colonised nation in the world – which implicitly recognises the high degree of cultural syncreticism in the country – is mediated in terms that call for a resistance to such cultural domination through the reflection that Romesh Gunesekera's novel *The Sandglass* marks the destruction of 'identity' in the Sinhalese elite. R. Wijesinha, 'Spices and Sandcastles', in Silva and Wijesinha, op. cit., p. 20.
115 Kandiah, 'Towards a Lankan Canon', op. cit., pp. 62, 55 and 64. Also see R. Wijesinha, 'English Poetry in Sri Lanka' in *Breaking Bounds*, op. cit.
116 See Kandiah, ibid., p. 68. Also see: W. Perera, 'The Perils of Expatriation and a "Heartless Paradise": Romesh Gunesekera's *The Sandglass*', *Commonwealth*, Spring 2000, 22:2, pp. 93–106 and 'Images of Sri Lanka through Expatriate Eyes: Romesh Gunesekera's *Reef*, *Journal of Commonwealth Literature*, 1995, 30:1, pp. 63–78; R. Wijesinha, 'Spices and Sandcastles' in Silva and Wijesinha, op. cit., pp. 11–20.
117 Kandiah, 'New Ceylon English', op. cit., p. 91.
118 Ibid., p. 93.
119 R. Raheem, book review 'James Goonewardene: *The Awakening of Dr Kirthi*', *Navasilu*, December 1979, 3, pp. 117–19.
120 S.H.J. Suganasiri, 'Sri Lankan Canadian Poets: The Bourgeoise that Fled the Revolution', *Canadian Literature*, Spring 1992, 132, p. 69.
121 Ibid., pp. 67 and 74.
122 M. Roberts, 'Language and National Identity: The Sinhalese and Others over the Centuries', *Nationalism and Ethnic Politics*, Summer 2003, 9:2, p. 92.
123 Kandiah, 'Towards a Lankan Canon', op. cit., p. 68.
124 R. Ranasinha, 'Romesh Gunesekera's *Reef*: Writing Expatriation', *Phoenix: Sri Lanka Journal of English in the Commonwealth*, 1997, vols 5 and 6, p. 87.
125 Often the assumption that Western interpretations of a text are representationalist are based upon synoptic book reviews, which serve to popularise and market a text. This is evident in Rajiva Wijesinha's analysis of Gunesekera's *The Sandglass*, which cites such paratextual sources in order to establish the text's exoticism, but which, paradoxically, goes on to diminish the impact of these reviews outside Sri Lanka by pointing out that the text is likely to appeal to a literary rather than a popular market. Wijesinha's main concern is with the influence of Western adulation on literary culture in Sri Lanka and the fact that expatriate texts 'will not only sell better than those by more genuine writers, they will be promoted more, by book sellers and even by academics'. R. Wijesinha, 'Spices and Sandcastles' in Silva and Wijesinha. op. cit., p. 14.
126 W. Perera, 'Images', op. cit., pp. 76–77.
127 Cleary, op. cit., p. 194.

128 See Kandiah, 'Towards a Lankan Canon', op. cit., p. 48; R. Siriwardena, 'Politics of Literary Criticism Today', speech delivered at the International Centre for Ethnic Studies, 25 October 1995, published in instalments in *The Island*, 31 October 1995, 1 November 1995 and 2 November 1995; R. Crusz, '"Politics of Literary Criticism" – a Response', *The Island*, 3 January 1996.

129 E. Shohat and R. Stam, *Unthinking Eurocentrism*, London: Routledge, 1994, p. 237.

130 E. Shohat cited in R. Bromley, *Narratives for a New Belonging: Diasporic Cultural Fictions*, Edinburgh: Edinburgh University Press, 2000, p. 8.

2 James Goonewardene: allegorical islands

1 A. Samaranayake, 'James Goonewardene and the English Language Novel', *Sunday Observer*, 25 May 1997.

2 R. Wijesinha, editorial, *Journal of Commonwealth Literature*, 1998, 3:1, p. 2.

3 N. Fernando, 'James Goonewardene (1921–97)' in J. C. Sanga (ed.), *South Asian Novelists in English*, Westport, CT: Greenwood Press, 2003, p. 91.

4 R. Wijesinha, 'The Continuing Colonial Mindset', *Daily News*, 26 February 2003. Available online: www.dailynews.lk/2003/02/26/fea02.html

5 Tissa Abeysekara observes how Goonewardene wrote through penury in 'Punyakante Wijenaike: The Underestimated Writer', *Daily News*, 16 June 2004. Available online: www.dailynews.lk/2004/06/16/artscop.03.html

6 P. Rambukwella, 'Goonewardene, James (1921–97)', *The Literary Encyclopedia*. Available online: www.litencyc.com/php/speople.php?rec=true&UID=1808

7 M. Salgado, conversation with Jean Arasanayagam and Carl Muller, Queens Hotel, Kandy, 14 December 2002.

8 G. Huggan, *The Postcolonial Exotic*, London: Routledge, 2001, p. 12.

9 Lakdasa Wikkramasinha wrote that 'To write in English is a form of cultural treason', cited in the Introduction to *The Penguin New Writing in Sri Lanka*, D.C.R.A. Goonetilleke (ed.), New Delhi: Penguin Books, 1992, p. xiv.

10 Ibid., p. xi.

11 T. Kandiah, 'New Ceylon English: *The Call of the Kirala*, A Novel by James Goonewardene', *New Ceylon Writing*, 1971, p. 93.

12 Ibid., p. 94.

13 S. Rushdie, '"Commonwealth Literature" Does Not Exist' in *Imaginary Homelands: Essays and Criticism 1981–1991*, London: Granta, 1992, p. 67.

14 D.C.R.A.Goonetilleke, *Sri Lankan English Literature and the Sri Lankan People 1917–2003*, Colombo: Vijitha Yapa, 2005, pp. 45–46.

15 Wijesinha, editorial, op. cit., p. 1.

16 Y. Gooneratne, 'Introduction', *Stories from Sri Lanka*, Hong Kong: Heinemann Educational Books, 1979, p. 11.

17 See F. Fanon, 'On National Culture' in *The Wretched of the Earth*, Harmondsworth: Penguin, 1981.

18 Fernando, op. cit., p. 89.

19 Y. Gooneratne, 'The English-Educated in Sri Lanka: An Assessment of their Cultural Role', *South Asia Bulletin*, Spring 1992, XII:1, p. 14.

20 L. de Silva cited Goonetilleke, op. cit., p. 59.

21 Samaranayake, op. cit.

22 Yasmine Gooneratne described his early novels as 'romantic village idylls that [. . .] give the decisions of their respective protagonists to quit life in Colombo an unattractive appearance of escapism'. Y. Gooneratne, book review 'The Awakening of Dr Kirthi', *New Ceylon Writing*, 1979, 4, p. 111.

23 Wijesinha, 'The Continuing Colonial Mindset', op. cit.

24 R. Raheem, book review 'The Awakening of Dr Kirthi', *Navasilu*, December 1979, 3, p. 118. Raheem's is a fine example of semantically clotted criticism that almost

stumbles over its own polysyllabic registers; Goonewardene, we are told, 'is fond of using long, compound sentences. Verbs and nouns are usually modified by adverbial or adjectival clauses. A structural description of the first paragraph [. . .] reveals the pattern Adjunct [. . .], Subject [. . .], Predicate [. . .], Complement [. . .], Complement [. . .], Subject [. . .], Predicate [. . .] Complement [. . .], Adjunct [. . .], Subject [. . .], Predicate [. . .], Complement [. . .]. . .When a writer embeds a sentence within a sentence, a clause within a clause, the main action that he is trying to describe is hedged in by verbal description that tend to enumerate either the cause or effect of the action. Prose written in such a style then becomes expository, a commentary upon action, not a vivid dramatic enactment of it'.

25 Ibid., p. 119.

26 Kandiah, op. cit., pp. 92, 91, 93. Kandiah's approach is dictated by his desire to find a literary language in Sri Lankan anglophone writing that is 'a viable expression of the rhythms of Ceylonese life', p. 91.

27 H. Bhabha, 'Of Mimicry and Man' in *The Location of Culture*, London: Routledge, 1994, p. 87.

28 *One Mad Bid For Freedom* was in fact the first novel by a resident Sri Lankan to be published by Penguin India. See Rambukwella.

29 A.R. Jan Mohamed, 'The Economy of Manichean Allegory: The Function of Racial Difference in Colonialist Literature' in H.L. Gates, Jr, *'Race', Writing and Difference*, Chicago, IL: Chicago University Press, 1986, p. 82.

30 T. Todorov, '"Race", Writing and Culture' in Gates, ibid., p. 377.

31 It is worth noting that Goonewardene could be quite specific in his anti-nationalist invective, for example attacking the university-based, anti-Western Sinhala extremism of Jathika Chintanayar in his essay 'Becoming a Writer – the agony and the ecstasy' (in *The Island*, Sunday 7 February, 1993, p. 10) and explicitly connecting linguistic nationalism with race in 'A Blueprint for a Writer's Dream' in A. Halpé (ed.), *Contemporary Sri Lankan Short Stories in English*, Colombo: The English Association of Sri Lanka, 1990, p. 155.

32 É. Meyer, *Sri Lanka: Biography of an Island: Between Local and Global*, Negombo: Viator, 2003, p. 19.

33 J. Goonewardene, 'The Man Under the Tamarind Tree' in *The Awakening of Doctor Kirthi and Other Stories*, Colombo: Lake House, 1976, p. 83. All subsequent references are to this edition.

34 Meyer, op. cit., p. 17.

35 *The Māhavamsa or The Great Chronicle of Ceylon*, translated into English by Wilhelm Geiger, Colombo: Ceylon Government Information Department, 1950; first published 1912, pp. 153–54.

36 W. Jayasuriya, *Sri Lanka's Modern English Literature: A Case Study in Literary Theory*, New Delhi: Navrang, 1994, p. 63.

37 See C. Muller, 'Population – the Bomb We Can't Defuse', *Firing at Random: Selected Essays*, Colombo: Vijitha Yapa, 2001, pp. 140–45. Muller's contention that 'pessimists have this biological turn of mind. To them each new birth is the arrival of another hungry mouth' (p. 141), could be used to evaluate Goonewardene's approach to the subject.

38 J. Goonewardene, 'Nationalism and the Writer in Sri Lanka', *Journal of Commonwealth Literature*, August 1974, IX:1, pp. 54–55.

39 Ibid., pp. 52, 53, 51.

40 J. Goonewardene, *One Mad Bid For Freedom*, New Delhi: Penguin India, 1990, p. 131. All subsequent references are to this edition. In his essay 'A Blueprint for a Writer's Dream' Goonewardene also engages with the issue of social conformity and presents this as a by-product of 'mass communication and mass ideology'. J. Goonewardene, 'A Blueprint for a Writer's Dream' in A. Halpé (ed.), *Contemporary Sri Lankan Short Stories in English*, Colombo: The English Association of Sri Lanka, 1990, p. 156.

41 Bopage, cited in Jani de Silva, 'Praxis, Language and Silences: the JVP Uprising in the 1980s' in M. Roberts (ed.), *Collective Identities Revisited*, Volume 2, Colombo: Marga Institute, 1998, p. 189.
42 Goonewardene, *One Mad Bid For Freedom*, op. cit., p. 44.
43 Meyer, op. cit., p. 65.
44 J. Goonewardene, *A Quiet Place*, Colombo: K.V.G. de Silva, 1968, pp. 121, 115, 61, 41. All subsequent references are to this edition.
45 Ibid., p. 38.
46 All the stories are in *The Awakening of Doctor Kirthi*.
47 J. Goonewardene, *Dream Time River*, Colombo: Morris and Vaughan, 1984, p. 117.
48 Goonewardene, *A Quiet Place*, op. cit., p. 19.
49 E. Fromm, *The Anatomy of Human Destructiveness*, New York: Holt, Rinehart and Winston, 1973, p. 215.
50 G. Orwell, *Nineteen Eighty-Four*, Harmondsworth: Penguin, 1990; first published 1949, p. 72.
51 Goonewardene, 'The Doughty Men of Purantota' in *The Awakening of Doctor Kirthi*, op. cit., p. 54.
52 The most dramatic example of this is to be found in 'The Dark Journey'. Goonewardene's moving presentation of the experience of Tamil refugees is dramatically undermined by his dehumanisation of them as – variously – 'hungry dogs' (p. 92), 'a swarm of rats' (p. 96) led by 'a thin hungry, little man, with prominent cheekbones and sunken eyes, [. . .a] wizened little face, [who] straightened himself up like an ape and peered suspiciously around him' (p. 91). It could, however, be argued that this story serves as a rare example of Goonewardene's effort to link dehumanisation with the social conditions that make it possible.
53 For a searching evaluation of the historical development of a clan ethos and the relationship between caste and class, see K. Jayawardena, *Nobodies to Somebodies: The Rise of the Colonial Bourgeoisie in Sri Lanka*, Colombo: SSA and Sanjiva Books, 2003. Jayawardena points out that kinship and caste loyalty have proved to be central in the development of the capitalist class in the country from the 1830s, traditional social mores going hand in hand with the rise of the colonial bourgeoisie.
54 Jan Mohamed, op. cit., p. 103.
55 Uyangoda and Samaranayake cited in Jani de Silva, op. cit., p. 164.
56 Cited in Goonetilleke, *Sri Lankan English Literature*, op. cit., p. 74.
57 As Goonetilleke has observed, *An Asian Gambit* presents the insurrection as part of an international conspiracy – something that seems to be without foundation. Ibid., p. 74.
58 Fromm, op. cit., pp. 198, 131.
59 Ibid., p. 205.
60 Ibid., pp. 203–04.
61 J. Goonewardene, 'The Awakening of Dr Kirthi' in *The Awakening of Doctor Kirthi and Other Stories*, op. cit., pp. 1–33.
62 R.B. Siegle, *Mirror to Mirror: Postmodernity in South Asian Fiction*, digital publication for The Center for Digital Discourse and Culture, Virginia Tech, 2002, Chapter 8, p. 20.
63 For a review of Goonewardene's engagement with ecology see Chapter 8 of this volume: 'Romesh Gunesekera: Past Paradise'.
64 A. Appiah, 'The Uncompleted Argument: Du Bois and the Illusion of Race' in Gates, op. cit., p. 36.
65 P. Brantlinger, 'Victorians and Africans' in Gates, op. cit., p. 203.
66 J. Goonewardene, *The Tribal Hangover*, New Delhi: Penguin India, 1995. All subsequent references are to this edition.
67 Siegle, op. cit., Chapter 8, p. 16.
68 In Gooneratne (ed.), *Stories from Sri Lanka*, op. cit., p. 79.
69 Goonewardene, *The Tribal Hangover*, op. cit., p. 164.

70 It is worth noting that Goonewardene himself was raised a Methodist but had a keen interest in Taoism and Zen Buddhism. His autobiographically inflected novel *Dream Time River* reflects a dual heritage in Christian and Buddhist traditions.

3 Punyakante Wijenaike: spectral spaces

1 Cited in A. Vidler: *The Architectural Uncanny: Essays in the Modern Unhomely*, Cambridge, MA: MIT Press, 1992, p. 69.
2 A. Niven, 'The Fiction of Punyakante Wijenaike', *Journal of Commonwealth Literature*, August, 1977, XII:1, p. 55. Niven's essay focuses on evaluating Wijenaike's first novel, *The Waiting Earth* – a text denigrated by D.C.R.A. Goonetilleke as a 'one-key romantic story with a stale Victorian villain, written as an unsophisticated third-person narrative'. D.C.R.A. Goonetilleke, *Sri Lankan English Literature and the Sri Lankan People 1917–2003*, Colombo: Vijitha Yapa, 2005, p. 259.
3 H. Naficy, 'Phobic Spaces and Liminal Panics: Independent Transnational Film Genre' in R. Wilson and W. Dissanayake (eds), *Global/Local: Cultural Production and the Transnational Imaginary*, Durham, NC: Duke University Press, 1996, p. 128.
4 Laura Mulvey cited in Naficy, ibid.
5 Vidler, op. cit., pp. 9, 6, 3–4.
6 P. Wijenaike, *The Waiting Earth*, Pitakotte and Padukka: State Printing Corporation, 1993. All references are to this edition.
7 See L. Wikkramasinha, 'Note' in *Lustre: Poems*, Kandy: privately published, 1965, p. 51, cited in Goonetilleke, *Sri Lankan English Literature*, op. cit., p. 49.
8 It could be claimed that my reading here is anachronistic – that these measures have only become controversial since the war. But even B.H. Farmer, whose study of the colonisation programme is commendatory, noted in 1957 that that the scheme caused communal tensions. B.H. Farmer, *Pioneer Peasant Colonization in Ceylon*, London: Oxford University Press, 1957, p. 300.
9 Ibid., p. 291.
10 P. Wijenaike, 'Living on the Edge', *Daily News*, 17 July 2002, p. 22.
11 Cited in Vidler, op. cit., p. 23.
12 P. Wijenaike, *A Way of Life*, Nugegoda: Deepani, 1987, p. 18.
13 A. Vidler argues that spatial fear, leading to paralysis of movement, and temporal fear, leading to historical amnesia, are symptoms of the uncanny; Vidler, op. cit., p. 6. H. Naficy, in his transnational reading of spatial fear and phobic space, has claimed that agoraphobia and claustrophobia both manifest themselves in house-bondage and the need to withdraw into safe zones; Naficy, op. cit., p. 130.
14 P. Wijenaike, *Giraya*, Nugegoda, Panaluwa and Padukka: State Printing Corporation, 1990; P. Wijenaike, *Amulet*, Wellampitiya: Godage International Publishers, 2002. All references are to these editions.
15 Cited in Vidler, op. cit., pp. 4, 11.
16 The Land Reform Act of 1972 put a ceiling of 50 acres on privately owned land, and it was amended in 1975 to also cover plantations owned by joint-stock companies.
17 Ibid., p. 23.
18 M. Salgado, conversation with Punyakante Wijenaike, Colombo, 11 December 2002.
19 Cited in Vidler, op. cit., p. 26.
20 Ibid.
21 Salgado, op. cit.
22 In her award-winning short story 'Anoma', Wijenaike explores the incestuous relationship between a daughter and a father who was a migrant labourer in the Middle East.
23 I am referring here to the practice of cross-cousin marriage that works on the one hand to conserve blood lines while on other to regulate family ties. Gananath

Obeyesekere has shown, in his fascinating anthropological analysis of Oedipal myth, how this form of marriage has been idealised in both Lankan myth and familial life, and he has further suggested that the incest taboo is weaker in relation to the sister in Sri Lanka. See G. Obeyesekere, *The Work of Culture: Symbolic Transformation in Psychoanalysis and Anthropology*, Chicago, IL: Chicago University Press, 1990, pp. 145–80, 63.

24 The point has been made well by Nicholas Royle: 'To repeat: the uncanny seems to be about a strange repetitiveness. It has to do with the return of something repressed, something no longer familiar, the return of the dead, the "constant recurrence of the same thing", "a compulsion to repeat".' N. Royle, *The Uncanny*, Manchester: Manchester University Press, 2003, p. 84.

25 E. Rochberg-Halton cited in David Sibley, *Geographies of Exclusion*, London: Routledge, 1995, p. 10.

26 G. Obeyesekere has observed that it is not given much attention in Sri Lankan folk song either, thereby suggesting that it may be an area that is generally unmarked in Sri Lankan literary and oral culture as a whole. He points out 'I have not come across one Sinhala folk song directly indicating the woman's trauma of leaving the parental home for the alien home of the husband, a genre almost universal in Hindu India, especially in the north', Obeyesekere, op. cit., p. 161.

27 Royle, op. cit., p. 192.

28 G. Bachelard, *The Poetics of Space*, trans. by M. Jolas, Boston, MA: Beacon Press, 1969; first published 1958, p. xxxii.

29 Naficy, op. cit., p. 130. Naficy's reading is specifically on phobic space rather than on the evaluation of the broader unhomely.

30 The attic is of course a characteristic locus for containing madness in the nineteenth century novel. Wijenaike herself has said that *Jane Eyre* was one of her favourite novels; Salgado, op. cit.

31 Royle, op. cit., p. 67.

32 N. Rapport and A. Dawson, 'Home and Movement: A Polemic' in N. Rapport and A. Dawson (eds), *Migrants of Identity: Perceptions of Home in a World of Movement*, Oxford: Berg, 1998, p. 27.

33 P. Wijenaike, 'An Enemy Within' in *An Enemy Within*, Ratmalana: Vishva Lekha, 1998. All references are to this edition.

34 Wijenaike's daughter was traumatised by the bomb attack. Her story – along with others that Wijenaike herself investigated – appears as one of the narratives. Salgado, op. cit.

35 This is fleetingly referred to in the text when Siromi 'did not know how to convey that she was held in a grip of anxiety and fear she could not account for. She had no more control over herself, over the enemy within'. Wijenaike, 'An Enemy Within', op. cit., p. 65.

36 M. Featherstone, 'Localism, Globalism, and Cultural Identity' in Wilson and Dissanayake, op. cit., p. 53.

37 D. Sibley, *Geographies of Exclusion: Society and Difference in the West*, London: Routledge, 1995, p. 3.

38 N. de Mel, 'Fixing Uncertainties: Producing "National" Culture in an Era of Globalization – The Terrain of Sexuality in Sri Lanka', *Asian Women*, July 1999, 8, p. 90.

39 See T. Jayatilaka, 'That Day of Horror and Humanity' (book review), *The Sunday Times*, 25 April 1999. Available online: www.lacnet.prg/suntimes/990425/plus6.html

40 E. Gordon Ericksen, *The Territorial Experience: Human Ecology as Symbolic Interaction*, Austin, TX: University of Texas Press, 1980, p. 113.

41 D. DeLillo, *Mao II*, London: Jonathan Cape, 1991, p. 157, cited in A. Brink, *Reinventing a Continent: Writing and Politics in South Africa 1982–1995*, London: Secker and Warburg, 1996, p. 157.

4 Jean Arasanayagam: fugitive selves

1 'Jean Arasanayagam' in Y. Gooneratne (ed.), *Celebrating Sri Lankan Women's Writing Volume II*, Colombo: Women's Education and Research Centre, 2002, p. 24. The entry on Arasanayagam foregrounds her interest in the fine arts.
2 C. Kanaganayakam, 'Jean Arasanayagam (1930–)' in J.C. Sanga (ed.), *South Asian Novelists in English*, Westport, CT: Greenwood, 2003, p. 17.
3 A. Nigam, 'Foreword' to *The Outsider* by J. Arasanayagam, Colombo: Voice of Women, 1995, p. 2.
4 J. Arasanayagam, 'The Minority Writer in a Plural Society', keynote address delivered to the British Council seminar on 'Minorities in a Plural Society', 14 November 1987. Manuscript provided to me in loose note form and therefore unpaginated. I would like to thank Jean Arasanayagam for granting me permission to cite it.
5 N. de Mel, *Women and the Nation's Narrative: Gender and Nationalism in Twentieth Century Sri Lanka*, Colombo: Social Scientists' Association, 2001, p. 195.
6 N. Silva, 'Situating the Hybrid "Other" in an Era of Conflict: Representations of the Burgher in Contemporary Writings in English' in N. Silva (ed.), *The Hybrid Nation: Culture Crossings and the Invention of Identity in Sri Lanka*, Colombo: Social Scientists' Association, 2002, p. 111.
7 J. Arasanayagam, 'A Seasonal Judgment' in *Kindura*, Kandy: Godamunne & Sons, Kandy, 1973, p. 43; cited in de Mel, op. cit., p. 176.
8 E. Ranaweera, 'Jean Arasanayagam – An Interview'. Originally published in *Voice of Women* in the early 1980s; manuscript supplied to me by Jean Arasanayagam, p. 1.
9 R. Radhakrishnan, *Diasporic Mediations: Between Home and Location*, Minneapolis, MN: University of Minnesota Press, 1996, p. 159.
10 M. Bakhtin, *Problems of Dostoevsky's Poetics*, ed. and trans. by C. Emerson, Minneapolis, MN: University of Minnesota Press, 1984, p. 301, note 7.
11 J.S. Duncan, *The City as Text: The Politics of Landscape Interpretation in the Kandyan Kingdom*, Cambridge: Cambridge University Press, 1990, p. 18.
12 I am most grateful to Jean Arasanayagam for giving me a copy of the manuscript of the play and permitting me to cite it.
13 J. Arasanayagam, 'Sanctuary' in *In the Garden Secretly and Other Stories*, New Delhi: Penguin India, 2000, p. 68.
14 De Mel, op. cit., p. 179.
15 J. Arasanayagam, 'April 1971', in *Kindura*, p. 50. Cited in de Mel, op. cit., p. 180.
16 J. Arasanayagam, 'The Witness' in *The Dividing Line*, New Delhi: Indialog, 2002, p. 45.
17 Ibid., p. 47.
18 Arasanayagam, 'The Minority Writer in a Plural Society', op. cit.
19 J. Arasanayagam, *Inheritance*, Colombo: S. Godage & Brothers, 2001, p. 138.
20 Ibid., p. 145.
21 J. Arasanayagam, 'Defeat' in *Apocalypse '83*, Colombo: International Centre for Ethnic Studies, 2003, p. 79; first published 1984.
22 J. Arasanayagam, 'Aftermath', ibid., p. 86.
23 R. Crawford, *Identifying Poets: Self and Territory in Twentieth-Century Poetry*, Edinburgh: Edinburgh University Press, 1993, p. 11.
24 J. Arasanayagam, 'Return' in *Out of Our Prisons We Emerge*, Kandy: Ariya Printers, 1987, p. 36.
25 J. Arasanayagam, *A Nice Burgher Girl*, manuscript, pp 3–4; cited in de Mel, op. cit., p. 174.
26 J. Arasanayagam, 'I Have No Country' in *Reddened Water Flows Clear*, introduced by N. Simms, London: Forest Books, 1991, p. 86.
27 C. Kanaganayakam, interview: 'Jean Arasanayagam' in *Configurations of Exile: South Asian Writers and Their World*, Toronto: TSAR, 1994, p. 21.

28 N. Simms, 'Introduction' to *Reddened Water Flows Clear* by J. Arasanayagam, op. cit., p. xiv.
29 De Mel, op. cit., p. 196.
30 E. Dissanayake, 'Poet of the Cataclysm: *Reddened Water Flows Clear* by Jean Arasanayagam', *The Sunday Observer*, 26 September 1993.
31 Radhakrishnan, op. cit., p. 159.
32 For a feminist reading of excess in Arasanayagam's fiction, see. V. Walker, 'Woman, Identity and the Other in Jean Arasanayagam's Fiction', *Navalisu*, August 2000, 17, p. 142.
33 J. Arasanayagam, From 'Bullets that Smash Through Screens' in *Out of Our Prisons We Emerge*, op. cit., pp. 33–34.
34 J. Arasanayagam, 'I Have No Country' in *Reddened Water Flows Clear*, op. cit., p. 86.
35 J. Arasanayagam, interview, in Kanaganayakam, op. cit., p. 25.
36 The second citation is from G.S. Morson and C. Emerson, *Mikhail Bakhtin: Creation of a Prosaics*, Stanford, CA: Stanford University Press, 1990, pp. 50–51; both citations are in Crawford, op. cit., p. 11.
37 J. Arasanayagam, 'Medusa' in *Out of Our Prisons*, op. cit., p. 29.
38 J. Arasanayagam, 'Narcissus' in *Reddened Water Flows Clear*, op. cit., p. 93.
39 J. Arasanayagam, 'Personae' in *Apocalypse '83*, Colombo: International Centre for Ethnic Studies, 2003, pp. 27–28.
40 J. Arasanayagam, 'The Death Carvers' in *Reddened Water Flows Clear*, op. cit., p. 62.
41 J. Arasanayagam, 'I have no country', ibid., p. 87.
42 D. Sibony cited in A.-B. Steen Preis, 'Seeking Place' in K.F. Olwig and K. Hastrup (eds), *Siting Culture*, London: Routledge, 1997, p. 96.
43 K.F. Olwig, 'Cultural Sites: Sustaining a Home in a Deterritorialized World', ibid., p. 35.
44 De Mel, op. cit., p. 187.
45 A. Rai, 'O Blessed Isle!: Insight into Strife-Torn Lanka', *India Today*, 15 October 1995, p. 220.
46 See J. Arasanayagam, 'Refugee Camp', 'Poems from a Refugee Camp', 'Night-Refugee Camp', 'Refugee Camp – 1983', 'Refugees – As We Move On, As We Move On', 'I Watch My Own Death', 'In Hiding', 'Refugee – Old Man – Part II' and 'Refugee' in *Apocalypse '83*, op. cit.
47 Arasanayagam, 'The Minority Writer in a Plural Society', op. cit.
48 E.G. Ericksen, *The Territorial Experience: Human Ecology as Symbolic Interaction*, Austin, TX: University of Texas Press, 1980, p. 113.
49 J. Arasanayagam, 'Fear: Meditations in a Camp' in *All is Burning*, New Delhi: Penguin India, 1995, p. 396.
50 J. Arasanayagam, 'The Dividing Line' in *The Dividing Line*, New Delhi: Indialog, 2002, p. 170.
51 J. Arasanayagam, 'Fear' in *All is Burning*, op. cit., p. 391.
52 J. Arasanayagam, *The Captain Has Come*, unpublished manuscript: 1991, pp. 46–47.
53 Arasanayagam, 'Fear: Meditations in a Camp' in *All is Burning*, op. cit., p. 417.
54 This is clear in *The Captain Has Come* when one of the characters observes of the camp: 'Being here is what places you on the other side of the fence', p. 27.
55 'Fragments from a Journey' is published in *All is Burning*, op. cit., pp. 229–63; 'The Crossing' is published in *In the Garden Secretly and Other Stories*, New Delhi: Penguin India, 2000, pp. 75–109.
56 'Exodus' is published in *The Dividing Line*, op. cit., pp. 123–40.
57 J. Arasanayagam, 'The Prediction', ibid., pp. 121–22.
58 J. Arasanayagam, *The Captain Has Come*, op. cit., p. 35. Also see J. Arasanayagam, 'Fear: Meditations in a Camp' in *All is Burning*, op. cit., and 'The Dividing Line' in the collection of stories published under the same name.
59 Arasanayagam, 'The Minority Writer in a Plural Society', op. cit.

5 Carl Muller: genealogical maps

1 M. Salgado, conversation with Jean Arasanayagam and Carl Muller, Queens Hotel, Kandy, 14 December 2002.
2 Linguistic hybridity, as Robert Young has shown in his consideration of Bakhtin, takes broadly two forms: organic hybridity and dialogic hybridity. Organic hybridity involves the fusion of disparate elements; dialogic hybridity is dialectical and contestatory, setting up one discourse against another. R. Young, *Colonial Desire: Hybridity in Theory, Culture and Race*, London: Routledge, 1995, pp. 21–22.
3 The text introduces fictional characters and narrative into an anthropologically saturated account of the capital and is therefore better described as a cultural biography of the city.
4 As David Scott has pointed out in his excellent critique of Gunawardana's text, 'It is central to the apparatus of Sinhala ideology that the idea of historical continuity of an inaugural authentic community informs and serves to guarantee the legitimacy of political claims in the present' – a logic that of course holds true for Tamil nationalism too. D. Scott, *Refashioning Futures: Criticism after Postcoloniality*, Princeton, NJ: Princeton University Press, 1999, p. 98.
5 Gunawardana, of course, contests Sinhala nationalist ideology but does so, as Scott points out, from a historicist basis. Scott, ibid., p. 103.
6 Ibid.
7 For other evaluations of the way current constructions of ethnicity are anachronistically imposed upon the past see S. Kemper, *The Presence of the Past: Chronicles, Politics, and Culture in Sinhala Life*, Ithaca, NY: Cornell University Press, 1991, pp. 96–98, 105–34; M. Angell, 'Understanding the Aryan Theory' in M. Tiruchelvam and C.S. Dattathreya (eds), *Culture and Politics of Identity in Sri Lanka*, Colombo: Institute of Cultural and Ethnic Studies, 1998, pp. 41–71; A. Guneratne, 'What's in a Name? Aryans and Dravidians in the Making of Sri Lankan Identities' in N. Silva (ed.), *The Hybrid Island: Culture Crossings and the Invention of Identity in Sri Lanka*, Colombo: Social Scientists' Association, 2002, pp. 20–40; S. Perera, 'The Presence of the Past in the Present' in *The World According to Me: An Interpretation of the Ordinary, the Common, and the Mundane*, Colombo: Institute of Cultural and Ethnic Studies, 1999, pp. 103–34.
8 Scott, op. cit., p. 95.
9 This also applies to the apocalyptic drive of his recent novel *Exodus 2300* (2003).
10 R. Radhakrishnan, *Diasporic Mediations: Between Home and Location*, Minneapolis, MN: University of Minnesota, 1996, p. 159. I consider these in more detail in Chapter 9: Conclusion.
11 C.P. Sarvan, 'Carl Muller's Trilogy and the Burghers of Sri Lanka', *World Literature Today*, Summer, 1997, 71:3, p. 529.
12 'The people who had Dutch ancestry were first class, those who claimed some Dutch blood second. If you didn't know what "Dutch" meant you were third class!' Carl Muller cited in P. Jones, 'Encapsulating the Spirit of the Burghers', *Daily Mirror*, 20 December 2003.
13 Young, op. cit., p. 21.
14 Ibid., p. 5.
15 Ibid., p. 18.
16 Ibid., p. 25.
17 C. Sarvan, 'Carl Muller (1935–)', *The Literary Encyclopedia*, 17 September 2003. Available online: www.litencyc.com/php/sepeople.php?=true&UID=4953
18 C. Muller, *The Jam Fruit Tree*, New Delhi; Penguin India, 1993. All subsequent references are to this edition.
19 C. Muller cited in Jones, op. cit.
20 N. Silva, 'Situating the Hybrid "Other" in an Era of Conflict: Representations of the Burgher in Contemporary Writings in English' in N. Silva (ed.), *The Hybrid Nation:*

Culture Crossings and the Invention of Identity in Sri Lanka, Colombo: Social Scientists' Association, 2002, p. 104.

21 See Young, op. cit., pp. 25–26.

22 'The ever-bearing tree. And never dying, too. Like the stout Burgher women of the age: fruitful, tough, always in bloom, earthy. Like the men too. Hard-working, hard-drinking, as lusty as life itself. Such a tree: always sprouting, reaching out, spreading over the leaf-strewn earth with its umbrella branches.' Muller, *The Jam Fruit Tree*, op. cit., p. 20.

23 C. Muller, *Children of the Lion*, New Delhi: Viking, Penguin India: 1997. All references are to this edition.

24 The *Mahavamsa*, or 'Great Chronicle', is a court chronicle which provides an originary myth of the nation that has gained symbolic political weight in the past decades. Written in the sixth century AD by a Buddhist monk who was brother to the Sri Lankan King Dhatusena, it closely connects the genealogy of kingship with the consecration of the island as a Buddhist land. The chronicle, along with its successor, *The Culavamsa*, provides a continuous historical record of the island over two millennia and is one of the oldest written histories in South Asia.

25 Here Muller is taking his cue from the *Mahavamsa*.

26 Written in Pali, an ancient liturgical language, the *Mahavamsa* is primarily accessible in translation. Wilhelm Geiger's translation is the best known and appears to be Muller's source text.

27 There are several examples of this: for example the Buddha's life and genealogy are mapped in relation to Vijaya's; Vijaya's arrival in the island is shown to be inscribed in Buddhist prophecy; and the Buddha's visits to the island are geographically situated in a way that marks the nation as a Buddhist land.

28 N. de Mel, personal communication; originally in a review of the novel in *Cat's Eye*.

29 The *Mahavamsa* itself relegates the early history of the island to fabular status, depicting it as a land visited by the Buddha before Vijaya's conquest and populated by magical beings and spirits. These Yakshas and Nagas (now considered the indigenous tribal groups) occupy an ambiguous status, on the boundaries of human agency. Vijaya's human status in contrast is never in doubt, despite the fact that he is the direct descendant of a bestial union.

30 Uma Chakravarti argues that the Buddha's teaching reveals 'a very deep-seated suspicion of female sexuality'. She goes on to claim that 'the woman who's privileged the most in the Buddhist texts is not [. . .] any one of the bhikshunis; it is [. . .] Vishakha Migara Matha [. . .] the model-woman, the matriarch of great fecundity, the good woman who supported the sangha from outside'. U. Chakravarti, 'Buddhism as a Discourse of Dissent?: Class and Gender', *Pravāda*, May 1992, 1:5, pp. 16–17.

31 Silva, op. cit., p. 120.

32 *The Mahāvamsa or the Great Chronicle of Ceylon*, trans. W. Geiger, Colombo: Ceylon Government Information Department, 1950; first published 1912, p. 1. All subsequent references are to this edition.

33 See Chapter 2 of the *Mahavamsa*.

34 Kemper, op. cit., p. 118.

35 The sentiment is affirmed in the novel's dedication to Sri Lanka and India so that 'the understanding between our peoples will never be lost'.

36 This term has come into popular use to characterise the primordialist strain of Sinhala ethnic chauvinism. See Kemper, op. cit., p. 105. Kemper also points out that 'the story of Dutugämunu and Elāra has been the most common figure for characterizing relations between Sinhalas and Tamils', p. 125.

37 Michael Roberts has also contended that Elara may have been neither Tamil nor Hindu – an assertion 'deliberately cast [. . .] so as to draw fire'. M. Roberts, *Burden of History: Obstacles to Power Sharing in Sri Lanka*, Colombo: Marga Institute, 2001, p. 9.

38 It could also be argued that Elara's exclusion is marked by his failure to fit the mythological register of the island. Elara's killing of his own son breaks with the model of the Oedipus myth found in the island which endorses parricide but never the killing of one's child. See G. Obeyesekere, *The Work of Culture: Symbolic Transformation in Psychoanalysis and Anthropology*, Chicago, IL: Chicago University Press, 1990, p. 183.
39 Kemper, op. cit., p. 112.
40 A. Paasi, 'The Political Geography of Boundaries at the End of the Millennium: Challenges of the De-terrotorializing World' in H. Eskelinen, I. Liikanen and J. Oksa (eds), *Curtains of Iron and Gold: Reconstructing Borders and Scales of Interaction*, Aldershot: Ashgate, 1999, p. 10.
41 K.M. De Silva, *Reaping the Whirlwind: Ethnic Conflict, Ethnic Politics in Sri Lanka*, New Delhi: Penguin India, 1998, pp. 303–4.

6 A. Sivanandan and Shyam Selvadurai: border dialogues

1 M. Heidegger, 'Building, Dwelling, Thinking' in *The Question Concerning Technology and Other Essays*, New York: Harper and Row, 1977, p. 116; cited in I. Chambers, *Migrancy Culture, Identity*, London: Routledge, 1994, p. 64.
2 H.K. Bhabha, 'DessemiNation: Time, Narrative, and the Margins of the Modern Nation' in H.K. Bhabha (ed.), *Nation and Narration*, London: Routledge, 1990, p. 320.
3 N. Papastergiadis, *Modernity as Exile: The Stranger in John Berger's Writings*, Manchester: Manchester University Press, 1993, p. 112. Also see N. Papastergiadis, 'Signs of Silence, Lines of Listening' in I. Chambers and L. Curti (eds), *The Postcolonial Question: Common Skies, Divided Horizons*, London: Routledge, 1996, p. 53.
4 In foregrounding the significance of ethnic difference in relation to their experience, I am aware of suppressing other social contradictions that may have influenced their work. For example, Sivanandan has drawn attention to the religious, class, regional and cultural conflict generated by his being born a rural Tamil, raised a Hindu, educated in the English medium in Catholic schools and having middle class aspirations while learning 'the culture of the slum'. See A. Sivanandan, 'The Heart Is Where the Battle Is: An Interview with the Author', *Communities of Resistance: Writings on Black Struggles for Socialism*, London: Verso, 1990, p. 2.
5 Rajiva Wijesinha contends that 'Tamil expatriate writers' do a 'better job' of presenting complex Sri Lankan political realities' and suggests that this is due to the fact that they have been 'less thoroughly colonised' than their Sinhalese and Burgher counterparts Romesh Gunesekera and Michael Ondaatje, preserving their 'distinct identity'. R. Wijesinha, 'Spices and Sandcastles: The Exotic Historians of Sri Lanka' in N. Silva and R. Wijesinha (eds), *Across Cultures: Issues of Identity in Contemporary British and Sri Lankan Writing*, Colombo: The British Council, 2001, p. 15. Such reasoning of course subscribes to a logic of difference and essentialisation that both Sivanandan and Selvadurai contest in their work.
6 Sivanandan, 'Interview', *Communities of Resistance*, op. cit., p. 9.
7 S. Selvadurai, 'Introducing Myself in the Diaspora' in S. Selvadurai (ed.), *Story-Wallah!: A Celebration of South Asian Fiction*, Toronto: Thomas Allen, 2004, p. 2.
8 See R. Wijesinha, 'Aberrations and Excess: Sri Lanka Substantiated by the "Funny Boy"', Features Section, *Sunday Observer* (Sri Lanka), 17 March 1996, for a consideration of these issues. In his article Wijesinha contends that 'It is generally acknowledged [. . .] that shame is a far more prominent socializing factor than guilt in Sri Lanka, in common with most South Asian countries'. Also published in *Miscelánea*, 1997, 18, pp. 347–55.
9 M. Salgado, 'Writing Sri Lanka, Reading Resistance: Shyam Selvadurai's *Funny Boy* and A. Sivanandan's *When Memory Dies*', *Journal of Commonwealth Literature*, 2004, 39:1, p. 8. Some of the points made in this chapter draw directly from this essay.

10 Bhabha, 'DessemiNation', op. cit., pp. 297–99, 306.
11 C. Searle 'Teacher and Interrupter' in C. Prescod and H. Waters (eds), *A World to Win: Essays in Honour of A. Sivanandan. Race and Class: A Journal for Black and Third World Liberation*, July–December 1999, 41:1/2, p. 110.
12 A. Sivanandan 'All that Melts into Air Is Solid: The Hokum of New Times', *Communities of Resistance*, op. cit., p. 50.
13 Ibid., p. 57.
14 Ibid., p. 48.
15 Searle, 'Teacher and Interrupter', op. cit., p. 114.
16 The critical paradigms of the performative and pedagogical are drawn from Homi Bhabha's 'DessemiNation', op. cit., pp. 297, 304.
17 Ibid., p. 303.
18 Timothy Brennan has also identified a rupture between the fictional and political in Sivanandan's work. He has observed that Sivanandan's 'rhetoric is driven [in the novel] by the force of principle to a truth-telling that would, politically, have been better to fictionalise. To describe the collapse of contemporary Sri Lanka into a berserk communalism in the novel's third section [. . .] is both to rob the reader of the earlier chapters' confident flow, and to convert the anger of analysis into the lament of fate'. T. Brennan, 'Poetry and Polemic' in Prescod and Waters, op. cit., p. 32.
19 H. Bhabha, 'Representation and the Colonial Text' in F. Gloversmith (ed.), *The Theory of Reading*, Brighton: Harvester Press, 1984, p. 98.
20 Ibid.
21 A. Sivanandan, *When Memory Dies*, New Delhi: Penguin India, 1998. All subsequent references are to this edition.
22 Raj Pal, 'An Interview with Sivanandan', September 2000. Available online: www.birminghamblackhistory.com/Sivanandan1/Sivanandan2
23 Nagesh Rao has pointed out that the novel insists on the recoverability of history. N. Rao 'Communalism, Socialism and Liberation in *When Memory Dies*' in Prescod and Waters, op. cit., p. 177.
24 S. Jayawickrama, 'Cross-Cultural Resistance in A. Sivanandan's *When Memory Dies*', *Cross-Cultural Perspectives in Sri Lankan Literature*, unpublished doctoral dissertation, Darwin College, Cambridge, 2005, p. 54.
25 S. Perera, '"We Can Be Killed but we Can Never Be Silenced": Narratives of Coexistence in Recent Sri Lankan Fiction', *CRNLE Journal: Sri Lankan and Indian Diasporic Writing*, 2000, p. 15. Perera's analysis focuses on the posthumously published novel of Chitra Fernando, a Sri Lankan writer resident in Australia, claiming that it is ideologically aligned to Sivanandan's text in its bid to articulate alternative understandings of Sri Lankan history.
26 As Ram Manikkalingam has pointed out 'The Tigers are anti-historical in that they are committed to denying that the Tamil identity also includes a history of co-existence with other communities'. R. Mannikkalingam, *Tigerism and Other Essays*, Colombo: Ethnic Studies Group, 1995, cited in S. Perera, 'Unmaking the Present, Remaking Memory: Sri Lankan Stories and a Politics of Coexistence' in Prescod and Waters, op. cit., p. 194.
27 Perera, '"We Can Be Killed But We Can Never Be Silenced"', op. cit., p. 16.
28 Ibid.
29 This approach is supported by Sivanandan's socialist reading of subject constitution: 'By himself or herself the individual is nothing [. . .] we need to confirm and be confirmed by each other.' Sivanandan, 'All that Melts into Air Is Solid', op. cit., p. 58.
30 For an exuberant and syntactically innovative representation of subaltern cultural hybridity by a resident writer read Jagath Kumarasinghe's *Kider Chetty Street*, Colombo: Sooriya, 2005.
31 N. Lazarus, 'The Prose of Insurgency' in Prescod and Waters, op. cit., p. 38.
32 Sivanandan's essay 'Sri Lanka: A Case Study' provides an invaluable insight into the

author's non-fictional scripting of this past. Another useful contextual grounding to the novel is to be found in Nagesh Rao's 'Communalism, Socialism and Liberation in *When Memory Dies*' in Prescod and Waters, op. cit.

33 Perera, 'We Can Be Killed but we Can Never Be Silenced', op. cit., p. 15.

34 Rajiva Wijesinha, in an otherwise favourable evaluation of the novel, has also contended that Sivanandan falsifies history in attributing the authoritarianism of J.R. Jayawardene's government to racial motives. R. Wijesinha, 'Spices and Sandcastles: The Exotic Historians of Sri Lanka' in Silva and Wijesinha, op. cit., p. 17.

35 R. Siriwardena, book review: 'A Sivanandan *When Memory Dies*, *Nēthrā*', July–September 1997, 1:4, p. 79.

36 H.K. Bhabha, 'Introduction', *The Location of Culture*, London: Routledge, 1994, p. 7.

37 Bhabha, 'DissemiNation', op. cit., p. 303.

38 T. Brennan, 'Poetry and Polemic', in Prescod and Waters, op. cit., p. 24.

39 Jayawickrama, 'Cross-Cultural Resistance in A. Sivanandan's *When Memory Dies*', op. cit., p. 69.

40 A. Sivanandan, 'Sri Lanka: A Case Study', *Communities of Resistance*, op. cit., pp. 199, 211–12.

41 Sivanandan, 'The Heart is Where the Battle Is', op. cit., p. 2.

42 In an interview he claimed, 'I am at home in myself. [. . .] I may be in the literal sense exiled from my country, but today, at the end of the twentieth century, when all our boundaries are breaking down, we should be looking not to roots in some place but to resources within ourselves for understanding our place in society [. . .] I do not understand the question of exile. I do not understand the question of domicile. The heart is where the battle is'. Sivanandan, ibid., p. 16.

43 Lazarus, op. cit., p. 39. Lazarus cites these as 'Shakespeare and Donne; the Romantic poets (Keats, Wordsworth, Blake and Shelley above all); the novelists from Austen to Joyce and Lawrence and beyond; Wilde; Eliot, Yeats, and the modernist poets.' He goes on to point out how Sivanandan simultaneously echoes and subverts Keatsian idiom.

44 Sivanandan, 'The Heart is Where the Battle Is', op. cit., p. 6. For an interesting corollary read Gāmini Salgādo's personal recollections of the domestication of English literature in 'Shakespeare and Myself', *The True Paradise*, Manchester: Carcanet, 1993.

45 Sivanandan, 'The Heart is Where the Battle Is', op. cit., p. 5.

46 S. Rushdie, '"Commonwealth Literature" Does Not Exist', *Imaginary Homelands: Essays and Criticism 1981–1991*, Harmondsworth: Granta, 1991, p. 67.

47 Bhabha, 'DissemiNation', op. cit., p. 306.

48 Sivanandan, 'All that Melts into Air Is Solid', op. cit., p. 48.

49 Sivanandan has analysed in detail how different classes mediated ethnic difference in divergent ways. See Sivanandan, 'Sri Lanka: A Case Study', op. cit., pp. 203–04.

50 Perera, 'We Can Be Killed but we Can Never Be Silenced', op. cit., p. 22.

51 S. Selvadurai, *Funny Boy*, New Delhi: Penguin India, 1994. All subsequent references are to this edition.

52 P. Jeganathan, 'All the Lord's Men?: Recollecting a Riot in an Urban Sri Lankan Community' in M. Roberts (ed.), *Sri Lanka. Collective Identities Revisited Volume 2*, Colombo: Marga, 1998, pp. 221–45. Jeganathan's article offers an invaluable insight into – and provides a damning indictment of – the silencing of this event in Sri Lanka.

53 J. Butler, *Gender Trouble: Feminism and the Subversion of Identity*, London: Routledge, 1990, p. 137; cited in A. Sinfield, *Gay and After*, London: Serpent's Tail, 1998, p. 33.

54 R. Raj Rao's critique, focusing on the representation of the 'male fanatical self', argues that in the final analysis the novel affiliates itself more closely with gay fiction rather than Sri Lankan or South Asian writing. R.R. Rao, 'Because Most People Marry their Own Kind: A Reading of Shyam Selvadurai's *Funny Boy*', *ARIEL*, January 1997, 28:1, pp. 117–28.

55 Sinfield, op. cit., p. 31.
56 Selvadurai, 'Introducing Myself in the Diaspora', op. cit., p. 4.
57 C. Patton and B. Sánchez-Eppler (eds), Introduction, *Queer Diasporas*, Durham, NC: Duke University Press, 2000, p. 3.
58 S. Jayawickrama, 'At Home in the Nation? Negotiating Identity in Shyam Selvadurai's *Funny Boy*', *Journal of Commonwealth Literature*, 2005, 40:2, pp. 129–30, 131, 133.
59 It is worth noting that Selvadurai has pointed out that English is the only language he can read and write, marking perhaps a strong sense of the impermeability of linguistic boundaries in his work. Selvadurai, 'Introducing Myself in the Diaspora', op. cit., p. 8.
60 Bhabha, 'DissemiNation', op. cit., p. 304.
61 S. Selvadurai, *Cinnamon Gardens*, New Delhi: Penguin India, 1998. All subsequent references are to this edition.
62 C. Wickramagamage, 'A Fish Without a Bicycle? Annalukshmi's Choice in Selvadurai's *Cinnamon Gardens*', *CRNLE Journal: Sri Lankan and Indian Diasporic Writing*, 2000, p. 134.
63 It is interesting to note that Selvadurai claims that the novel was written for a Sri Lankan readership. See J. James, 'The Toronto Circle', *The Atlantic Monthly*. Available online: www.theatlantic.com/issues/2000/04/james2.htm
64 As Jamie James has pointed out the 'flat prose [. . .] appears to be an attempt to reproduce the ironic understatement of the English novelists writing at the time in which the book is set', ibid. Wickramagamage also refers to the novel's reliance on English idiom; see Wickramagamage, op. cit., pp. 133, 136.
65 T.B. Macaulay, 'Minute on Indian Education' in W. Theodore de Bary (ed.), *Sources of Indian Tradition*, Vol. 11, New York: Columbia University Press, 1958, p. 49; cited in H.K. Bhabha, 'Of Mimicry and Man', *The Location of Culture*, London: Routledge, 1994, p. 87.
66 Bhabha, ibid., pp. 87, 86.
67 S.J. Tambiah has contended that the epoch of the Donoughmore Constitution which followed the Donoughmore Commission established forcefully the reality of Sinhalese majoritarian rule. S.J. Tambiah, *Buddhism Betrayed?: Religion, Politics and Violence in Sri Lanka*, with a foreword by L. Jayawardena, Chicago, IL: Chicago University Press, 1992, p. 10.
68 I am drawing upon R. Radhakrishnan's evaluation of metropolitan and postcolonial hybridity here. R. Radhakrishnan, *Diasporic Mediations: Between Home and Location*, London: Routledge, 1996, pp. 159–62.
69 Bhabha, 'Representation and the Colonial Text', op. cit., p. 98.
70 Wickramagamage, op. cit., pp. 131–32.
71 Ibid., pp. 130, 132.
72 This is also evident in her reading of this instability as an 'ambivalent *self*-fashioning' (my emphasis), ibid., p. 132.
73 Bhabha, 'Introduction', *The Location of Culture*, op. cit., p. 8.

7 Michael Ondaatje: place as palimpsest

1 Patricia Lawrence is citing S. Felman and D. Laub, 'Grief on the Body: The Work of Oracles in Eastern Sri Lanka' in M. Roberts (ed.), *Sri Lanka: Collective Identities Volume 2*, Colombo: Marga, 1998, p. 284.
2 M. De Certeau, *The Practice of Everyday Life*, trans. Steven Randall, Berkeley, CA: University of California Press, 1984, p. 109.
3 G. Huggan, *The Postcolonial Exotic: Marketing the Margins*, London: Routledge, 2001, p. 116.
4 W. Waring, cited ibid., p. 166.
5 Ondaatje has claimed in the 'Acknowledgements' to *Running in the Family* that the text

is a 'communal act'. The point is explored in more detail in M. Jaggi, 'In Conversation with Michael Ondaatje', *Wasafiri*, Autumn 2000, 32, p. 9.

6 R. Wijesinha, 'The Continuing Colonial Mindset', *Daily News*, 26 February 2003. Available online: www.dailynews.lk/2003/02/26/fea02.html

7 Huggan, op. cit., p. 173.

8 M. Ondaatje, *Running in the Family*, London: Picador, 1983. All subsequent references are to this edition.

9 N. Silva, *The Gendered Nation: Contemporary Writings from South Asia*, New Delhi: Sage, 2004, pp. 116, 137.

10 D. Leahy, '*Running in the Family*, *Volkswagen Blues* and *Heroine*: Three Post/Colonial Post-Modernist Quests?', *Kunapipi*, 1992, XIV:3, p. 70.

11 D. Coleman, *Masculine Migrations: Reading the Postcolonial Male in 'New Canadian' Narratives*, Toronto: University of Toronto, 1998, pp. 113, 117.

12 A.P. Mukherjee, 'The Poetry of Michael Ondaatje and Cyril Dabydeen: Two Responses to Otherness', *Journal of Commonwealth Literature*, 1985, XX:1, p. 57.

13 S.H.J. Suganasiri, '"Sri Lankan" Canadian Poets: The Bourgeoisie that Fled the Revolution', *Canadian Literature*, Spring 1992, 132, p. 64.

14 C. Kanaganayakam, 'A Trick with a Glass: Michael Ondaatje's South Asian Connection', *Canadian Literature*, Spring 1992, 132, p. 39.

15 Suganasiri, op. cit., p. 69. One Sri Lankan reader has gone so far as to catalogue the 'lies' in the text in a blatant act of cultural reclamation. G. Uswatte-Aratchi, 'Fact, "Faction" or Fiction? On Reading Michael Ondaatje's *Running in the Family*', *The Island*, 7 January 2001, p. 13.

16 E. Ty, 'The Other Questioned: Exoticism and Displacement in Michael Ondaatje's *The English Patient*', *International Fiction Review*, 2000, 27, p. 19.

17 Suganasiri, op. cit., p. 63.

18 L. Hutcheon, 'Interview with Michael Ondaatje' in L. Hutcheon and M. Richmond (eds), *Other Solitudes: Canadian Multicultural Fictions*, Toronto: Oxford University Press, 1990, p. 201.

19 G. Huggan, 'Decolonizing the Map: Post-colonialism and the Cartographic Connection' in I. Adam and H. Tiffin (eds), *Past the Last Post: Theorizing Post-Colonialism and Post-modernism*, Calgary: University of Calgary, 1990, p. 127.

20 See E. Said, *Orientalism*, Harmondsworth: Penguin, 1991 (first published 1978), p. 6.

21 Huggan, 'Decolonizing', op. cit., p. 127.

22 Coleman, op. cit., p. 118.

23 J.A.Thieme, '"Historical Relations": Modes of Discourse in Michael Ondaatje's *Running in the Family*' in C.A. Howells and L. Hunter (eds), *Narrative Strategies in Canadian Literature: Feminism and Postcolonialism*, Milton Keynes: Open University Press, 1991, p. 41.

24 J. Berger cited in N. Rapport and A. Dawson, 'The Topic and the Book' in N. Rapport and A. Dawson (eds), *Migrants of Identity: Perceptions of Home in a World of Movement*, Oxford: Berg, 1998, p. 7.

25 Silva, op. cit., p. 134.

26 Ibid., p. 133.

27 J. Berger, cited in Rapport and Dawson, op. cit., p. 27.

28 Rapport and Dawson, ibid., p. 29.

29 Said, *Orientalism*, op. cit., p. 7.

30 Silva, op. cit., p. 116.

31 Ibid., p. 118.

32 M. Ondaatje, *Anil's Ghost*, London: Picador, 2001. All subsequent references are to this edition.

33 Q. Ismail, 'A Flippant Gesture towards Sri Lanka: A Review of Michael Ondaatje's *Anil's Ghost*', *Pravāda*, 2000, 6:9, p. 26.

34 De Certeau, op. cit., p. 115.

35 Privileged people, they argue, tend to construct it as a domain of self-knowledge and individual narration while the less affluent tend to present it as a contested site in which the knowledge of self is mediated by the need to know the community and assert social rights. See Rapport and Dawson, op. cit., p. 17.
36 E. Said, *Culture and Imperialism*, London: Chatto and Windus, 1993, p. 120.
37 I would like to thank Nirmala Salgado for her detailed feedback on my reading of Buddhist thought and practice, which helped me to refine my argument in this section. Any existing oversights are, of course, my responsibility.
38 See for example S. Spearey, 'Mapping and Masking: The Migrant Experience in Michael Ondaatje's *In the Skin of a Lion*', *Journal of Commonwealth Literature*, 1994, XXIX:2, pp. 45–60; R. Cook '"Imploding Time and Geography": Narrative Compressions in Michael Ondaatje's *The English Patient*', *Journal of Commonwealth Literature*, 1998, 33:2, pp. 109–26.
39 K. Sangari, 'The Politics of the Possible' in B. Ashcroft, G. Griffiths and H. Tiffin (eds), *The Postcolonial Studies Reader*, London: Routledge, 1995, pp. 143–47.
40 M. Ondaatje, 'Pale Flags: Reflections on Writing *Anil's Ghost*', *Wasafiri*, Summer 2004, 42, p. 61.
41 A.K. Coomaraswamy, *Christian and Oriental Philosophy of Art*, New York: Dover, 1956, p. 41.
42 A.K. Coomaraswamy, *On The Traditional Doctrine of Art*, Ipswich: Golganooza Press, 1977, p. 7. Ondaatje's volume of poetry is called *Handwriting.*
43 Coomaraswamy, *Christian and Oriental Philosophy of Art*, op. cit., p. 39.
44 Ibid., p. 41.
45 Ondaatje, 'Pale Flags', op. cit., p. 62.
46 Coomaraswamy, *On The Traditional Doctrine of Art*, op. cit., p. 13.
47 A.K. Coomaraswamy, *The Transformation of Nature in Art*, New York: Dover Publications, 1934, p. 33.
48 B.C. Suzuki, *Mahayana Buddhism: A Brief Outline*, New York: Macmillan, 1969, p. 35.
49 A. Halpé, 'Ondaatje's Symphonic Ode: Michael Ondaatje's *Anil's Ghost* – a Reader's Response', *Phoenix*, 2005, VII, p. 24.
50 J. de Falbe, 'Tinker, Tailor, Soldier . . .: Anil's Ghost by Michael Ondaatje' *Spectator*, 29 April 2000. Available online: http://findarticles.com/p/articles/mi_qa3724/is_200004/ai_n8900862/print
51 G. Kamiya, 'Painting the Eyes of a God', *Salon*, 25 April 2000. Available online: http://dir.salon.com/books/feature/2000/04/25/ondaatje/index.html?pn=3; Ismail, op. cit., pp. 27, 28.
52 G. Obeyesekere, 'The Vicissitudes of the Sinhala Buddhist Identity through Time and Change' in M. Roberts (ed.), *Sri Lanka: Collective Identities Volume 2*, Colombo: Marga, 1998, p. 382.
53 Ismail, op. cit., p. 28.
54 R. Coomaraswamy, 'In Defense of Humanistic Way of Knowing: A Reply to Qadri Ismail', *Pravāda*, 2000, 6:9, p. 29.
55 Coomaraswamy, *On The Traditional Doctrine of Art*, op. cit., p. 16.
56 Theravada Buddhists traditionally cremate rather than bury their dead.
57 Suzuki, op. cit., pp. 21, 30.
58 In his historical reflection on the development of Mahayana Buddhism in India, Senerat Paranavitana has contended that for Mahayanists 'the aim of a true follower of the Buddha should be to tread the path followed by the Master Himself, i.e. to postpone one's own liberation so as to be able to aid others to end suffering, by attaining Buddhahood. A person who pursued this ideal of attaining Buddhahood, i.e. a Bodhisattva, need not necessarily be a monk'. S. Paranavitana, *Sinhalayo*, Boralesgamuwa: Visidunu Prakashakayo, sixth edition, 2004, first published 1967, p. 16. Gombrich's study of Theravada Buddhism makes clear that the penetration of the bodhisattva ideal in Sri Lanka has been 'extraordinarily slow'. R.F. Gombrich,

Theravāda Buddhism: A Social History from Ancient Benares to Modern Colombo, London: Routledge and Kegan Paul, 1988, p. 161.

59 Sukuzi, op. cit., pp. 33, 35; also see R. Gombrich and G. Obeyesekere, *Buddhism Transformed: Religious Change in Sri Lanka*, Princeton, NJ: Princeton University Press, 1988, p. 23.

60 N. Wilson Ross, *Hinduism, Buddhism, Zen: An Introduction to the Meaning and their Arts*, London: Faber, 1978, p. 124.

61 Ibid.

62 Gombrich, *Theravāda Buddhism*, op. cit., p. 28.

63 M. Salgado, 'Complexity and the Migrant Writer: Chaotics in Michael Ondaatje's Fiction', *Angles on the English-Speaking World*, 2001, 1, pp. 89–106; 'Nonlinear Dynamics and the Diasporic Imagination' in M. Fludernik (ed.), *Diaspora and Multiculturalism: Common Traditions and New Developments*, Amsterdam: Rodopi, 2003, pp. 183–98.

64 Jaggi, op. cit., p. 7.

65 Gombrich, *Theravāda Buddhism*, op. cit., p. 203.

66 J.S. Walters, 'Multireligion on the Bus: Beyond "Influence" and "Syncretism" in the Study of Religious Meetings' in P. Jeganathan and Q. Ismail (eds), *Unmaking the Nation: The Politics of Identity and History in Modern Sri Lanka*, Colombo: Social Scientists' Association, 1995, pp. 30–38.

67 K.M. De Silva, *Reaping the Whirlwind: Ethnic Conflict, Ethnic Politics in Sri Lanka*, New Delhi: Penguin India, 1998, p. 110. For a historical reflection on the embattled relationship between Mahayanists and Theravadins in ancient Sri Lanka, see Paranavitana, op. cit., pp. 16–17.

68 Gombrich endorses this view. Gombrich, *Theravāda Buddhism*, op. cit., p. 146.

69 A.K. Coomaraswamy, *Mediaeval Sinhalese Art*, New York: Pantheon, 1979, p. 71. Coomaraswamy claims that 'The ceremony would seem to be rather Hindu than Buddhist in origin; the underlying idea seems to be an endeavour to secure good "conditions" at the time of definitely consecrating the image as a medium which shall put the worshipper in touch with the unseen god whose symbol is set forth, and this is rather a Hindu than a Buddhist idea; for Southern Buddhism does not regard Buddha as a still existent personal God, and would not have been likely to originate such a ceremonial'.

70 Ross, op. cit., p. 124.

71 Coomaraswamy, *Mediaeval Sinhalese Art*, op. cit., p. 71.

72 For a consideration of the proliferation of Hindu deities to be found and actively worshipped in Buddhist temples in the country, see Walters, op. cit., pp. 37–38.

73 D. Rajasingham-Senanayake, *Identity on the Borderline: Multicultural History in a Moment of Danger*, Colombo: Marga Institute, 2001, p. 18.

74 D. Bullis, 'Painting the Buddha's Eyes', *Bodhi Leaves*, Kandy: Buddhist Publication Society, 1992, 126, p. 9.

75 A. Burton, 'Archive of Bones: *Anil's Ghost* and the Ends of History', *Journal of Commonwealth Literature*, 2003, 38:1, p. 52.

76 Marlene Goldman has described an alternative cultural role for Palipana in her reading of him as a representative of nationalist discourse. M. Goldman, 'Representations of Buddhism in *Anil's Ghost*', CLC Web: Comparative Literature and Culture: AWWWeb Journal, 6.3, September 2004. Available online: http://clcwebjournal.lib.purdue.edu/clcweb04–3/goldman04.html

77 The broad correspondence between the short story and *Anil's Ghost* was drawn to my attention by Rajiva Wijesinha, who had been alerted to it earlier by Anne Ranasinghe, the editor of *Channels* in which the story appeared. I am most grateful to them both for drawing attention to this story. The critical interpretation of the story and the basis of its links with the novel are of course mine.

78 U. Gunethilake, 'Continuity', *Channels*, November 1998, 8:1, p.57.

79 Marlene Goldman also focuses on this episode in her detailed evaluation of the text, but her emphasis is somewhat different; she claims that in it 'Ondaatje gestures toward the ideals of transcendence, wholeness, and unity' while ultimately refusing to reinscribe them. Goldman, op. cit.
80 Ibid.
81 Suganasiri, op. cit., p. 74.
82 J. Lethem, 'An Interview with Michael Ondaatje', *Book Forum*, Summer 2000, p. 33.
83 D. Finkle 'A Vow of Silence – Canadian Author Michael Ondaatje', *Saturday Night*, November 1996. Available online: http://findarticles.com/p/articles/mi_m1494/is_n9_v111/ai_19022342/print Finkle cites this in relation to Ondaatje's written reply to Ed Jewinski's request for an interview for his biography, *Michael Ondaatje: Express Yourself Beautifully*.
84 D. Weich, 'Michael Ondaatje's Cubist Civil War', Powells.com, 23 May 2000. Available online: www.powells.com/authors/ondaatje/html

8 Romesh Gunesekera: past paradise

1 G. Huggan, *The Postcolonial Exotic: Marketing the Margins*, London: Routledge, 2001, pp. 13, 14.
2 Ibid., p. 264.
3 *The Shorter Oxford English Dictionary on Historical Principles*, third edition, rev. G.W.S. Friedrichsen, London: Guild Publishing, 1983, p. 1507.
4 J. Thieme, 'Are we all Migrants?' *Literary Review*, February 1998, p. 24.
5 Ibid.
6 P. Binding, 'A Tear-Shaped Homeland: *The Sandglass* by Romesh Gunesekera', *The Independent on Sunday Review: Books*, 22 February 1998, p. 29.
7 It should be noted that Perera contends that Binding's reductive reading does in fact not do the novel justice. W. Perera, 'The Perils of Expatriation and a "Heartless Paradise"', *Commonwealth*, Spring 2000, 22:2, p. 104.
8 G. Salgādo, *The True Paradise*, Manchester: Carcanet, 1993, p. 164.
9 W. Perera, 'The Phases and Guises of the Twentieth-Century Expatriate Sri Lankan Novel', *CRNLE Journal 2000: Sri Lankan and Indian Diasporic Writing*, 2000, p. 56.
10 T. Kandiah, 'Towards a Lankan Canon in English Creative Writing: Subversions of Post-colonialism and the Resisting Representations of Chitra Fernando's Fictional Voice', *Phoenix: Sri Lanka Journal of English in the Commonwealth*, 1997, 5/6, pp. 50, 51, 53.
11 R. Ranasinha, 'Romesh Gunesekera's *Reef*: Writing Expatriation', *Phoenix: Sri Lanka Journal of English in the Commonwealth*, 1997, 5/6, p. 87.
12 G. Kundu, 'Romesh Gunesekera (1954–)' in J.C. Sanga (ed.), *South Asian Novelists in English*, Westport, CT: Greenwood Press, 2003, pp. 93, 96.
13 Kundu argues that it is 'inevitable' on the basis that, unlike Michael Ondaatje, Gunesekera has made Sri Lanka his 'centre of gravity' while simultaneously 'mining its resources for his fiction', ibid., p. 97. I am inclined to contend that it is inevitable for a different reason: that is that Gunesekera explicitly engages with the exotic in his work.
14 T. Kandiah, 'New Ceylon English: *The Call of the Kirala*, A Novel by James Goonewardene', *New Ceylon Writing*, 1971, p. 93.
15 Kandiah, 'Towards a Lankan Canon in English Creative Writing', op. cit., p. 48.
16 W. Perera, 'Images of Sri Lanka through Expatriate Eyes: Romesh Gunesekera's *Reef*', *Journal of Commonwealth Literature*, 1995, 30:1, p. 67.
17 Perera, 'The Perils of Expatriation and a "Heartless Paradise"', op. cit., p. 102.
18 Ibid.
19 Perera, 'Images of Sri Lanka through Expatriate Eyes', op. cit., p. 67.
20 Walter Perera has pointed out that Gunesekera's *Reef* and Goonewardene's *One Mad Bid For Freedom* have similarities in their common focus on marine conservation. See Perera, ibid., p. 71.

21 T. Todorov, '"Race", Writing and Culture' in H.L. Gates (ed.), *'Race', Writing and Difference*, Chicago, IL: Chicago University Press, 1986, p. 377.
22 E. Fromm, *The Anatomy of Human Destructiveness*, New York: Holt, Rinehart and Winston, 1973, p. 205.
23 E. Dodson Gray, *Green Paradise Lost*, Wellesley, MA: Roundtable Press, 1979, p. 76.
24 S. Nasta, *Home Truths: Fictions of the South Asian Diaspora in Britain*, Basingstoke: Palgrave, 2002, pp. 226, 227, 226.
25 P. Middleton and T. Woods, *Literatures of Memory: History, Time and Space in Postwar Writing*, Manchester: Manchester University Press, 2002, p. 131.
26 Ibid., p. 130.
27 Ibid., p. 39.
28 Gunesekera invites such a reading, pointing out that the names of the two families replicate the Buddhist conception of Dukkha and the Sinhala word for 'fall'. *The Sandglass*, London: Granta, 1999, p. 93. All subsequent references are to this edition.
29 Huggan, op. cit., p. 22.
30 See Goonewardene's essay 'Nationalism and the Writer in Sri Lanka' *Journal of Commonwealth Literature*, August 1974, IX:1, pp. 50–56.
31 Stanley Fish, cited in Huggan, op. cit., p. 124.
32 Perera, 'The Perils of Expatriation and a "Heartless Paradise"', op. cit., p. 94.
33 Ibid., p. 93.
34 Ibid., p. 99.
35 Ibid., p. 93.
36 Ibid., p. 101.
37 R. Wijesinha, 'Spices and Sandcastles: The Exotic Historians of Sri Lanka', in N. Silva and R. Wijesinha (eds), *Across Cultures: Issues of Identity in Contemporary British and Sri Lankan Writing*, Colombo: The British Council, 2001, pp. 19, 16.
38 Perera in fact refers to the 'completing' of identity in his essay: 'The other factor which prevents her from completing a new identity is the inexorable presence of the past'. Perera, 'The Perils of Expatriation and a "Heartless Paradise"', op. cit., p. 96. Wijesinha, 'Spices and Sandcastles', op. cit., p. 20.
39 Huggan, op. cit., p. 173.
40 R. Gunesekera, *Reef*, London: Granta, 1994. All subsequent references are to this edition.
41 S. Jayawickrama, 'Consuming Desire: Identity and Narration in Romesh Gunesekera's *Reef*', *Postgraduate English*, September 2003, 8. Available online: www.dur.ac.uk/postgraduate.english/reef.html
42 R.G. Davis, '"I Am an Explorer on a Voyage of Discovery": Myths of Childhood in Romesh Gunesekera's *Reef*', *Commonwealth*, Spring 1998, 20:2, pp. 14–25.
43 For example Walter Perera has contended that the focus on cuisine threatens the integrity of the novel. Perera, 'Images of Sri Lanka through Expatriate Eyes', op. cit., p. 72.
44 Prakrti, '"The Breach": Three Sri Lankan-Born Writers at the Crossroads', *Lanka Outlook*, Summer 1997. Available online: www.is.lk/is/spot/sp0151/clip5.html
45 Huggan, op. cit., p. 32.
46 See A. Jamison, *The Making of Green Knowledge: Environmental Politics and Cultural Transformation*, Cambridge: Cambridge University Press, 2001, pp. 109, 121. Jamison distinguishes between 'utilitarian' and 'romantic' conceptions that emerged from the American experience of conquest and domination – oppositional models that continue to inform our approach to the environment.
47 Huggan, op. cit., p. 157.
48 Gautam Kundu appears to undertake such a reading. He contends 'It is part of the questionable political ideology of the novel that the preservation of tradition and national culture and the Sri Lankan "way of life" are left in the hands of Mr Salgado, a member of the bourgeois elite, whose understanding of the actual dynamics of

political radicalism and state terror and their toll of violence and death in Sri Lanka is class-based and biased. It is ironic that the politics of the book is conservative even when the national elite's efforts at ecological and environmental protection are recognized and praised'. G. Kundu, op. cit., p. 95.

49 J. Clifford, cited in Huggan, op. cit., p. 158.

50 It is interesting to note the suggestion that the possibility for such a sanctuary is likely to be in England rather than Sri Lanka, a factor which lends itself to Perera's reading of England as 'a haven' despite its drab representation in the novel.

51 See Jayawickrama, op. cit.

52 D.D. Elgin, 'Literary Fantasy and Ecological Comedy (1985)' in D. Sandner (ed.), *Fantastic Literature: A Critical Reader*, Westport, CT: Praeger, 2004, p. 269.

53 B. Attebery, 'Fantasy as Mode, Genre, Formula (1992)', ibid., p. 294.

54 R. Jackson, *Fantasy: The Literature of Subversion*, London: Methuen, 1981, p. 70. Also see N. Cornwell, *The Literary Fantastic: From Gothic to Postmodernism*, London: Harvester Wheatsheaf, 1990, p. 27.

55 Thieme's review of *The Sandglass* identifies this as a central concern of the novelist.

56 This is qualitatively different from other novels that also focus on the illegibility of political violence. For example in Ondaatje's *Anil's Ghost* the sense of conceptual crisis generated by this context foregrounds the need for a nuanced understanding of political violence.

57 Thieme, op. cit., p. 24.

58 Sandner, op. cit., p. 9. David Sandner claims that 'the fundamental characteristic of the fantastic is displacement; the fantastic signifier does not point, even superficially, to any clear signified and so causes the reader to experience a lack, a disruption, inviting (if not provoking) an interpretation'.

59 Ibid.

60 U. Le Guin, 'From Elfland to Poughkeepsie (1973)' in Sandner, ibid., p. 146.

61 Huggan, op. cit., p. 13.

62 R. Gunesekera, *Heaven's Edge*, London: Bloomsbury, 2002. All subsequent references are to this edition.

63 Nasta, op. cit., p. 213.

64 H. White, *Metahistory: The Historical Imagination in Nineteenth Century Europe*, Baltimore, MD: Johns Hopkins University Press, 1973, p. 25.

65 See B.R. Sørenson, 'The Experience of Displacement: Reconstituting Places and Identities in Sri Lanka' in K.F. Olwig and K. Hastrup (eds), *Siting Culture: The Shifting Anthropological Subject*, London: Routledge, 1997, p. 145.

66 Perera, 'Images', op. cit., p. 76.

67 B. Curtis and C. Pajaczkowska, '"Getting There": Travel, Time and Narrative' in G. Robertson, M. Mash, L. Tickner, J. Bird, B. Curtis and T. Putnam (eds), *Travellers' Tales: Narratives of Home and Displacement*, London: Routledge, 1994, pp. 206–12.

68 I am paraphrasing Maggie Nolan here; cited in Huggan, op. cit., p. 175.

69 A. Brink, *Re-Inventing a Continent: Writing and Politics in South Africa 1982–1995*, with an introduction by Nelson Mandela, London: Secker and Warburg, 1996, p. 203.

9 Conclusion: destinations

1 That is April 2006, a month that has seen an escalation of political violence and the death of over 100 people (about 70 of them army personnel) culminating in the LTTE suicide bomb attack on the chief of the Sri Lankan Army and retaliatory air strikes by the military in eastern areas on 26 April; events that mark the first large-scale military engagement since the 2002 ceasefire agreement.

2 D. Scott, *Refashioning Futures: Criticism After Postcoloniality*, Princeton, NJ: Princeton University Press, 1999, p. 10.

3 B. Anderson, 'Long-Distance Nationalism', *The Spectre of Comparisons; Nationalism, Southeast Asia and the World*, London: Verso, 1998, pp. 58–74.
4 N. Papastergiadis, *Modernity as Exile: The Stranger in John Berger's Writings*, Manchester: Manchester University Press, 1993, p. 112.
5 P. van der Veer, 'Introduction: The Diasporic Imagination' in P. van der Veer (ed.), *Nation and Migration: The Politics of Space in the South Asian Diaspora*, Philadelphia, PA: University of Pennsylvania Press, 1995, p. 6.
6 I. Chambers, *Migrancy, Culture, Identity*, London: Routledge, 1994, p. 10.
7 H.K. Bhabha, 'Cultures in-Between' in S. Hall and P. du Gay (eds), *Questions of Cultural Identity*, London: Sage, 1996, p. 58. See V. Kalra, R. Kaur and J. Hutnyk, *Diaspora and Hybridity*, London: Sage, 2005, p. 102.
8 I. Chambers, op. cit., p. 115.
9 L. Warley, 'Locating the Subject of Post-Colonial Autobiography', *Kunapipi*, 1993, XV:1, p. 25.
10 G.C. Spivak, *Critique of Postcolonial Reason: Towards a History of the Vanishing Present*, Cambridge, MA: Harvard University Press, 1999, pp. 168–69, 319. See Kalra, Kaur and Hutnyk, op. cit., p. 102.
11 R. Radhakrishnan, *Diasporic Mediations: Between Home and Location*, Minneapolis, MN: University of Minnesota, 1996, pp. 159, 162.
12 Ibid., pp. 161, 166.
13 D.C.R.A. Goonetilleke, *Sri Lankan English Literature and the Sri Lankan People 1917–2003*, Colombo: Vijitha Yapa, 2005, p. 293.
14 E. Dissanayake, 'Poet of the Cataclysm: *Reddened Water Flows Clear* by Jean Arasanayagam', *The Sunday Observer*, 26 September 1993.
15 Radhakrishnan, op. cit., p. 159.
16 Kalra, Kaur and Hutnyk, op. cit., p. 17.
17 Ibid., pp. 84–85.
18 S. Sayyid, 'Beyond Westphalia: Nations and Diasporas – the Case of the Muslim *Umma*' in B. Hesse (ed.), *Un/Settled Multiculturalisms: Diasporas, Entanglements, Transruptions*, London: Zed Books, 2000, p. 42; cited in Kalra, Kaur and Hutnyk, op. cit., p. 34.

Select bibliography

Adam, I., and Tiffin H. (eds), *Past the Last Post: Theorizing Post-Colonialism and Post-modernism*, Calgary: University of Calgary, 1990.

Anderson, B., *The Spectre of Comparisons: Nationalism, Southeast Asia and the World*, London: Verso, 1998.

Angell, M., 'Understanding the Aryan Theory', in M. Tiruchelvam and C.S. Dattathreya (eds), *Culture and Politics of Identity in Sri Lanka*, Colombo: Institute of Cultural and Ethnic Studies, 1998, pp. 41–71.

Appiah, A., 'The Uncompleted Argument: Du Bois and the Illusion of Race', in H.L. Gates, Jr, (ed.), *'Race', Writing and Difference*, Chicago, IL: Chicago University Press, 1986, pp. 21–37.

Arasanayagam, J., *Apocalypse '83*, Colombo: International Centre for Ethnic Studies, 2003; first published 1984.

—— *Out of our Prisons we Emerge*, Kandy: Ariya Printers, 1987.

—— *Reddened Water Flows Clear*, with an introduction by Norman Simms, London: Forest Books, 1991.

—— *All Is Burning*, New Delhi: Penguin India, 1995.

—— *The Outsider*, with a foreword by Alka Nigam, Colombo: Voice of Women, 1995.

—— 'Sri Lankan Writing in English: The Bi-Cultural Experience in a Post-Colonial Context', *Wasafiri*, Spring 1995, 21, pp. 63–64.

—— *Peacocks and Dreams*, New Delhi: Navrang: 1996.

—— *In the Garden Secretly and Other Stories*, New Delhi: Penguin India, 2000.

—— *Inheritance*, Colombo: S. Godage & Brothers, 2001.

—— *The Dividing Line*, New Delhi: Indialog, 2002.

Attebery, B., 'Fantasy as Mode, Genre, Formula' (1992), in D. Sandner (ed.), *Fantastic Literature: A Critical Reader*, Westport, CT: Praeger, 2004, pp. 293–309.

Austin, D., *Democracy and Violence in India and Sri Lanka*, London: Pinter, 1994.

Bachelard, G., *The Poetics of Space*, trans. M. Jolas, Boston, MA: Beacon Press, 1969; first published 1958.

Bakhtin, M., *The Dialogic Imagination: Four Essays*, ed. M. Holquist, trans. C. Emerson and M. Holquist, Austin, TX: University of Texas Press, 1981.

—— *Problems of Dostoevsky's Poetics*, ed. and trans. by C. Emerson, Minneapolis, MN: University of Minnesota Press, 1984.

Benson, E., and Conolly, L.W. (eds), *The Encyclopedia of Postcolonial Literatures in English*, vol. 2, London: Routledge, 1994.

Bhabha, H., 'Representation and the Colonial Text: A Critical Exploration of Some Forms of Mimeticism', in F. Gloversmith (ed.), *The Theory of Reading*, Brighton: Harvester, 1984, pp. 93–121.

—— (ed.), *Nation and Narration*, London: Routledge, 1990.
—— *The Location of Culture*, London: Routledge, 1994.
—— 'Cultures in-Between', in S. Hall and P. du Gay (eds), *Questions of Cultural Identity*, London: Sage, 1996, pp. 53–60.
Brantlinger, P., 'Victorians and Africans: The Genealogy of the Myth of the Dark Continent', in H.L. Gates, Jr, (ed.), *'Race', Writing and Difference*, Chicago, IL: Chicago University Press, 1986, pp 185–222.
Brennan, T., 'The National Longing for Form', in H.K. Bhabha (ed.), *Nation and Narration*, London: Routledge: 1990, pp. 44–70.
—— 'Poetry and Polemic', in C. Prescod and H. Waters (eds), *A World to Win: Essays in Honour of A. Sivanandan, Race and Class: A Journal for Black and Third World Liberation*, July–Dec. 1999, 41:1/2, pp. 23–34.
Brink, A., *Reinventing a Continent: Writing and Politics in South Africa 1982–1995*, London: Secker and Warburg, 1996.
Bromley, R. *Narratives for a New Belonging: Diasporic Cultural Fictions*, Edinburgh: Edinburgh University Press, 2000.
Bullis, D., 'Painting the Buddha's Eyes', *Bodhi Leaves*, Kandy: Buddhist Publication Society, 1992, no. 126.
Burnett, P., 'The Captives and the Lion's Claw: Reading Romesh Gunesekera's *Monkfish Moon*', *Journal of Commonwealth Literature*, 1997, 32:2, pp. 3–15.
Burton, A., 'Archive of Bones: *Anil's Ghost* and the Ends of History', *Journal of Commonwealth Literature*, 2003, 38:1, pp. 39–56.
Butler, J., *Gender Trouble: Feminism and the Subversion of Identity*, London: Routledge, 1990.
Chakravarti, U., 'Buddhism as a Discourse of Dissent?: Class and Gender', *Pravāda*, May 1992, 1:5, pp. 12–18.
Chambers, I., *Migrancy, Culture, Identity*, London: Routledge, 1994.
Chandraprema, C.A., *Sri Lanka: The Years of Terror, The JVP Insurrection 1987–1989*, Colombo: Lake House, 1991.
Chatterjee, P., *Nationalist Thought and the Colonial World: A Derivative Discourse*, London: Zed, 1986.
Cheran, R., *The Sixth Genre: Memory, History and the Tamil Diaspora Imagination*, Colombo: Marga Institute, 2001.
Cleary, J., *Literature, Partition and the Nation State: Culture and Conflict in Ireland, Israel and Palestine*, Cambridge: Cambridge University Press, 2002.
Coleman, D., *Masculine Migrations: Reading the Postcolonial Male in 'New Canadian' Narratives*, Toronto: University of Toronto Press, 1998.
Cook, R., '"Imploding Time and Geography": Narrative Compressions in Michael Ondaatje's *The English Patient*', *Journal of Commonwealth Literature*, 1998, 33:2, pp. 109–26.
Coomaraswamy, A.K., *Christian and Oriental Philosophy of Art*, New York: Dover, 1956.
—— *The Transformation of Nature in Art*, New York: Dover, 1957; first published 1934.
—— *On the Traditional Doctrine of Art*, Ipswich: Golganooza Press, 1977.
—— *Mediaeval Sinhalese Art*, New York: Pantheon, 1979.
Coomaraswamy, R., 'In Defense of Humanistic Way of Knowing: A Reply to Qadri Ismail', *Pravaḏa*, 2000, 6:9, pp. 29–30.
Cornwell, N., *The Literary Fantastic: From Gothic to Postmodernism*, London: Harvester Wheatsheaf, 1990.
Crawford, R., *Identifying Poets: Self and Territory in Twentieth-Century Poetry*, Edinburgh: Edinburgh University Press, 1993.
Curtis, B., and Pajaczkowska, C., '"Getting There": Travel, Time and Narrative', in

G. Robertson, M. Mash, L. Tickner, J. Bird, B. Curtis and T. Putnam (eds), *Travellers' Tales: Narratives of Home and Displacement*, London: Routledge, 1994, pp. 199–215.

Davis, R.G., '"I am an Explorer on a Voyage of Discovery": Myths of Childhood in Romesh Gunesekera's *Reef*', *Commonwealth*, Spring 1998, 20:2, pp. 14–25.

De Certeau, M., *The Practice of Everyday Life*, trans. Steven Randall, Berkeley, CA: University of California Press, 1984.

De Mel, N., 'Fixing Uncertainties: Producing "National" Culture in an Era of Globalization – The Terrain of Sexuality in Sri Lanka', *Asian Women*, July 1999, 8, pp. 87–105.

—— *Women and the Nation's Narrative: Gender and Nationalism in Twentieth Century Sri Lanka*, Colombo: Social Scientists' Association, 2001.

De Silva, J. 'Praxis, Language and Silences: The JVP Uprising in the 1980s', in M. Roberts (ed.), *Collective Identities Revisited Volume 2*, Colombo: Marga Institute, 1998, pp. 163–98.

De Silva, K.M., *Reaping the Whirlwind: Ethnic Conflict, Ethnic Politics in Sri Lanka*, New Delhi: Penguin India, 1998.

Dissanayake, E., 'Poet of the Cataclysm: *Reddened Water Flows Clear* by Jean Arasanayagam', *The Sunday Observer*, 26 September 1993.

Dodson Gray, E., *Green Paradise Lost*, Wellesley, MA: Roundtable Press, 1979.

Duncan, J.S. *The City as Text: The Politics of Landscape Interpretation in the Kandyan Kingdom*, Cambridge, Cambridge University Press, 1990.

Elgin, D.D., 'Literary Fantasy and Ecological Comedy (1985)', in D. Sandner (ed.), *Fantastic Literature: A Critical Reader*, Westport, CT: Praeger, 2004, pp. 255–70.

Ericksen, E.G., *The Territorial Experience: Human Ecology as Symbolic Interaction*, Austin, TX: University of Texas, 1980.

Fanon, F., *The Wretched of the Earth*, Harmondsworth: Penguin, 1981; first published 1961.

Farmer, B.H., *Pioneer Peasant Colonization in Ceylon*, London: Oxford University Press, 1957.

Featherstone, M., 'Localism, Globalism and Cultural Identity', in R. Wilson and W. Dissanayake (eds), *Global/Local: Cultural Production and the Transnational Imaginary*, Durham, NC: Duke University Press, 1996, pp. 46–77.

Fernando, B., and Puvimanasinghe, S., *An X-ray of the Sri Lankan Policing System and Torture of the Poor*, Hong Kong: Asian Human Rights Commission, 2005.

Fernando, N., 'James Goonewardene (1921–97)', in J.C. Sanga (ed.), *South Asian Novelists in English*, Westport, CT: Greenwood Press, 2003, pp. 88–92.

Finkle, D., 'A Vow of Silence – Canadian Author Michael Ondaatje', *Saturday Night*, November 1996. Online: http://findarticles.com/p/articles/mi_m1494/is_n9_v111/ai_19022342/print.

Foucault, M., *Power/Knowledge: Selected Interviews and Other Writings 1972–1977*, edited by C. Gordon, New York: Random House, 1981.

Fromm, E., *The Anatomy of Human Destructiveness*, New York: Holt, Rinehart and Winston, 1973.

Gates, H.L., Jr, *'Race', Writing and Difference*, Chicago, IL: Chicago University Press, 1986.

Geiger, W., trans., *The Mahāvamsa or The Great Chronicle of Ceylon*, Colombo: Ceylon Government Information Department, 1950; first published 1912.

George, R.M., *The Politics of Home: Postcolonial Relocations and Twentieth Century Fiction*, Berkeley, CA: University of California Press, 1999.

Glasius, M., 'The European Union and Sri Lanka: Tsunami Response and the Long-Term Policy', Centre for the Study of Global Governance, LSE publication, 14 October 2005. Online: www.lse.ac.uk/Depts/global/2securitypub.htm

Goldman, M., 'Representations of Buddhism in *Anil's Ghost*', CLC Web: Comparative Literature and Culture: AWWWeb Journal, 6.3, September 2004. Online: http://clcwebjournal.lib.purdue.edu/clcweb04-3/goldman04.html

Gombrich, R.F., *Theravāda Buddhism: A Social History from Ancient Benares to Modern Colombo*, London: Routledge and Kegan Paul, 1988.

—— and Obeyesekere, G., *Buddhism Transformed: Religious Change in Sri Lanka*, Princeton, NJ: Princeton University Press, 1988.

Gooneratne, Y. (ed.), *Stories from Sri Lanka*, Hong Kong: Heinemann Educational Books, 1979.

—— Book Review: 'The Awakening of Dr Kirthi', *New Ceylon Writing*, 1979, 4, pp. 108–15.

—— 'The English Educated in Sri Lanka: An Assessment of Their Cultural Role', *South Asia Bulletin*, 1992, 12:1, pp. 2–33.

—— 'Making History in Sri Lanka: Comic Modes of Satire and Fiction', in E. Thumboo and T. Kandiah (eds), *The Writer as Historical Witness: Studies in Commonwealth Literature*, Singapore: Unipress, 1995, pp. 368–79.

—— (ed.), *Celebrating Sri Lankan Women's Writing Volume II*, Colombo: Women's Education and Research Centre, 2002.

Goonetilleke, D.C.R.A., 'Beyond Alienation: The Efflorescence of Sri Lankan Literature in English', *Journal of Commonwealth Literature*, 1986, XXI:1, pp. 26–38.

—— (ed. and introduced), *The Penguin New Writing in Sri Lanka*, New Delhi: Penguin, 1992.

—— 'Sri Lanka's "Ethnic" Conflict in its Literature in English', *World Literature Today*, 1992, 66:3, pp. 449–53.

—— (ed. and introduced), *Sri Lankan Literature in English 1948–1998: A 50th Independence Anniversary Anthology*, Nugegoda: Department of Cultural Affairs, 1998.

—— *Sri Lankan English Literature and the Sri Lankan People 1917–2003*, Colombo: Vijitha Yapa, 2005.

Goonewardene, J., *A Quiet Place*, Colombo: K.V.G. de Silva, 1968.

—— 'Nationalism and the Writer in Sri Lanka', *Journal of Commonwealth Literature*, August 1974, IX:1, pp. 50–56.

—— *The Awakening of Doctor Kirthi and Other Stories*, Colombo: Lake House, 1976.

—— *Dream Time River*, Colombo: Morris and Vaughan, 1984.

—— 'A Blueprint for a Writer's Dream', in A. Halpé (ed.), *Contemporary Sri Lankan Short Stories in English*, Colombo: The English Association of Sri Lanka, 1990, pp. 154–56.

—— *One Mad Bid for Freedom*, New Delhi: Penguin India, 1990.

—— 'Becoming a Writer – The Agony and the Ecstasy', *The Island*, Sunday 7 February, 1993, p. 10.

—— *The Tribal Hangover*, New Delhi: Penguin India, 1995.

Gunesekera, M., 'Language and Identity: In a Class of their Own', in N. Silva and R. Wijesinha (eds), *Across Cultures: Issues of Identity in Contemporary British and Sri Lankan Writing*, Colombo: The British Council, 2001, pp. 81–89.

—— *The Postcolonial Identity of Sri Lankan English*, Colombo: Katha Publishers, 2005.

Gunesekera, R., *Monkfish Moon*, London: Granta, 1992.

—— *Reef*, London: Granta, 1994.

—— *The Sandglass*, London: Granta, 1998.

—— *Heaven's Edge*, London: Bloomsbury, 2002.

Guneratne, A., 'What's in a Name? Aryans and Dravidians in the Making of Sri Lankan Identities', in N. Silva (ed.), *The Hybrid Island: Culture Crossings and the Invention of Identity in Sri Lanka*, Colombo: Social Scientists' Association, 2002, pp. 20–40.

Gunethilake, U., 'Continuity', *Channels*, November 1998, 8:1, pp. 57–60.

Halpé, A., 'Ondaatje's Symphonic Ode: Michael Ondaatje's *Anil's Ghost* – A Reader's Response', *Phoenix*, 2005, VII, pp. 21–24.

—— Nuhman, M.A., Obeysekere, R. (eds), *A Lankan Mosaic: Translations of Sinhala and Tamil Short Stories*, Dehiwala: Three Wheeler Press, 2002.

Heidegger, M., *The Question Concerning Technology and Other Essays*, New York: Harper and Row, 1977.

Hoole, R., *Sri Lanka: The Arrogance of Power, Myths, Decadence and Murder*, Colombo: University Teachers for Human Rights (Jaffna), 2001.

Huggan, G., 'Decolonizing the Map: Post-Colonialism, Post-Structuralism and the Cartographic Connection', in I. Adam and H.Tiffin (eds), *Past the Last Post: Theorizing Post-Colonialism and Post-modernism*, Calgary: University of Calgary, 1990, pp. 125–36.

—— *The Postcolonial Exotic: Marketing the Margins*, London: Routledge, 2001.

Hutcheon, L., and Richmond, M. (eds), *Other Solitudes: Canadian Multicultural Fictions*, Toronto: Oxford University Press, 1990.

Ismail, Q., 'A Flippant Gesture towards Sri Lanka: A Review of Michael Ondaatje's *Anil's Ghost*', *Pravāda*, 2000, 6:9, pp. 24–29.

—— *Abiding by Sri Lanka: On Peace, Place and Postcoloniality*, Minneapolis, MN: University of Minnesota Press, 2005.

Jackson, R., *Fantasy: The Literature of Subversion*, London: Methuen, 1981.

Jaggi, M., 'In Conversation with Michael Ondaatje', *Wasafiri*, Autumn 2000, 32, pp. 5–11.

James, J., 'The Toronto Circle', *The Atlantic Monthly*, April 2000. Online: www.theatlantic.com/issues/2000/04/james2.htm

Jamison, A., *The Making of Green Knowledge: Environmental Politics and Cultural Transformation*, Cambridge: Cambridge University Press, 2001.

Jan Mohamed, A.R., 'The Economy of Manichean Allegory: The Function of Racial Difference in Colonialist Literature', in H.L. Gates,Jr, (ed.), *'Race', Writing and Difference*, Chicago, IL: Chicago University Press, 1986, pp. 78–106.

Jayasuriya, W., *Sri Lanka's Modern English Literature: A Case Study in Literary Theory*, New Delhi: Navrang, 1994.

Jayatilaka, T., 'That Day of Horror and Humanity' (book review), *The Sunday Times*, 25 April 1999. Online: www.lacnet.prg/suntimes/990425/plus6.html

—— 'The English-Language Novel of Sri Lanka and the Critical Response to it: An Overview', *Navasilu: Journal of the English Association of Sri Lanka*, August 2000, 17, pp. 1–20.

Jayawardena, K., *Nobodies to Somebodies: The Rise of the Colonial Bourgeoisie in Sri Lanka*, Colombo: SSA and Sanjiva Books, 2003.

—— *Ethnic and Class Conflict in Sri Lanka: The Emergence of Sinhala-Buddhist Consciousness, 1883–1983*, Colombo: Sanjiva, 2003.

—— and De Alwis, M. (eds), *Embodied Violence: Communalising Women's Sexuality in South Asia*, London: Zed, 1996.

Jayawickrama, S., 'Consuming Desire: Identity and Narration in Romesh Gunesekera's *Reef*', *Postgraduate English*, September 2003, 8, Durham University. Online: www.dur.ac.uk/postgraduate.english/reef.html

—— 'At Home in the Nation? Negotiating Identity in Shyam Selvadurai's *Funny Boy*', *Journal of Commonwealth Literature*, 2005, 40:2, pp. 123–39.

—— *Cross-Cultural Perspectives in Sri Lankan Literature*, unpublished doctoral dissertation, Darwin College, Cambridge, 2005.

Jeganathan, P., 'All the Lord's Men? Ethnicity and Inequality in the Space of a Riot', in M. Roberts (ed.), *Sri Lanka: Collective Identities Revisited*, vol. 2, Colombo: Marga, 1998, pp. 221–45.

—— and Ismail, Q. (eds), *Unmaking the Nation: The Politics of Identity and History in Modern Sri Lanka*, Colombo: Social Scientists' Association, 1995.

Kalra, V., Kaur, R., and Hutnyk, J., *Diaspora and Hybridity*, London: Sage, 2005.

Kamiya, G., 'Painting the Eyes of a God', *Salon,* 25 April 2000. Online: http://dir.salon.com/books/feature/2000/04/25/ondaatje/index.html?pn=3

Kanaganayakam, C., 'A Trick with a Glass: Michael Ondaatje's South Asian Connection', *Canadian Literature*, Spring 1992, 132, pp. 33–41.

—— *Configurations of Exile: South Asian Writers and their World*, Toronto: TSAR, 1994.

—— 'Dancing in the Rarefied Air: Reading Contemporary Sri Lankan Literature', *ARIEL*, January 1998, 29:1, pp. 51–65.

—— 'Literature and the Politics of Ethno-Nationalism in Sri Lanka', *The Sri Lanka Journal of the Humanities*, 2000, XXVI:1/2, pp. 29–43.

—— (ed.), *Lutesong and Lament: Tamil Writing from Sri Lanka*, Toronto: TSAR, 2001.

—— ' Jean Arasanayakam (1930–)', in J.C. Sanga (ed.), *South Asian Novelists in English*, Westport, CT: Greenwood, 2003, pp. 16–20.

Kandiah, T., 'New Ceylon English: *The Call of the Kirala,* A Novel by James Goonewardene', *New Ceylon Writing*, 1971, pp. 90–94.

—— '"Kaduva": Power and the English Language Weapon in Sri Lanka', in P. Colin-Thomé and A. Halpé (eds), *Honouring E.F.C. Ludowyk: Felicitation Essays*, Dehiwela: Tissa Prakasakayo Ltd, 1984, pp. 117–53.

—— 'Towards a Lankan Canon in English Creative Writing: Subversions of Post-colonialism and the Resisting Representations of Chitra Fernando's Fictional Voice', *Phoenix: Sri Lanka Journal of English in the Commonwealth*, 1997, vols 5 and 6, pp. 47–72.

Keith, M., and Pile, S., *Place and the Politics of Identity*, London: Routledge, 1993.

Kemper, S., *The Presence of the Past: Chronicles, Politics, and Culture in Sinhala Life*, Ithaca, NY: Cornell University Press, 1991.

Krishna, S., *Postcolonial Insecurities: India, Sri Lanka and the Question of Nationhood* New Delhi: Oxford University Press, 2000.

Kundu, G., 'Romesh Gunesekera (1954–)', in J.C. Sanga (ed.), *South Asian Novelists in English*, Westport, CT: Greenwood Press, 2003, pp. 93–99.

Lawrence, P., 'Grief on the Body: The Work of Oracles in Eastern Sri Lanka', in M. Roberts (ed.), *Sri Lanka: Collective Identities Revisited*, vol. 2, Colombo: Marga, 1998, pp. 271–94.

Lazarus, N., 'The Prose of Insurgency', in C. Prescod and H. Waters (eds), *A World to Win: Essays in Honour of A. Sivanandan, Race and Class: A Journal for Black and Third World Liberation*, July–Dec. 1999, 41:1/2, pp. 35–47.

Leahy, D., '*Running in the Family*, *Volkswagen Blues* and *Heroine*: Three Post/Colonial Post-Modernist Quests?', *Kunapipi*, 1992, XIV:3, pp. 67–82.

Le Guin, U., 'From Elfland to Poughkeepsie (1973)', in D. Sandner (ed.), *Fantastic Literature: A Critical Reader*, Westport, CT: Praeger, 2004, pp. 144–55.

Lethem, J., 'An Interview with Michael Ondaatje', *Book Forum*, Summer 2000, pp. 32–33.

Manikkalingam, R., *Tigerism and Other Essays*, Colombo: Ethnic Studies Group, 1995.

Meyer, É., *Sri Lanka: Biography of an Island: Between Local and Global*, Negombo: Viator, 2003.

Middleton, P., and T. Woods, T., *Literatures of Memory: History, Time and Space in Postwar Writing*, Manchester: Manchester University Press, 2002.

Mukherjee, A., 'The Sri Lankan Poets in Canada: An Alternative View', *Toronto South Asian Review*, 1984, 3:2, pp. 32–45.

—— 'The Poetry of Michael Ondaatje and Cyril Dabydeen: Two Responses to Otherness', *Journal of Commonwealth Literature*, 1985, XX:1, pp. 48–67.

Mukherjee, M., 'A Blighted Garden', *The Hindu*, Sunday April 1, 2001, pp. 3–4. Online: www.hinduonnet.com/2001/04/01/stories/1301067j.htm

Muller, C., *The Jam Fruit Tree*, New Delhi: Penguin India, 1993.

—— *Yakada Yakā: The Continuing Saga of Sonnaboy von Bloss and the Burgher Railwaymen*, New Delhi: Penguin India, 1994.

—— *Once Upon a Tender Time: The Concluding Part of the Von Bloss Family Saga*, New Delhi: Penguin India, 1995.

—— *Colombo: A Novel*, New Delhi: Penguin India, 1995.

—— *Children of the Lion*, New Delhi: Viking, Penguin India: 1997.

—— *Firing at Random: Selected Essays*, Colombo: Vijitha Yapa, 2001.

—— *Exodus 2003*, Colombo: Vijitha Yapa, 2003.

Naficy, H., 'Phobic Spaces and Liminal Panics: Independent Transnational Film Genre', in R. Wilson and W. Dissanayake (eds), *Global/Local: Cultural Production and the Transnational Imaginary*, Durham, NC: Duke University Press, 1996, pp. 119–44.

Nasta, S., *Home Truths: Fictions of the South Asian Diaspora in Britain*, Basingstoke: Palgrave, 2002.

Niven, A., 'The Fiction of Punyakanate Wijenaike', *Journal of Commonwealth Literature*, August, 1977, XII:1, pp. 55–65.

Obeyesekere, G., *Land Tenure in Village Ceylon: A Sociological and Historical Study*, Cambridge: Cambridge University Press, 1967.

—— *The Work of Culture: Symbolic Transformation in Psychoanalysis and Anthropology*, Chicago, IL: Chicago University Press, 1990.

—— 'The Vicissitudes of the Sinhala Buddhist Identity through Time and Change', in M. Roberts (ed.), *Sri Lanka: Collective Identities Revisited*, Volume 2, Colombo: Marga, 1998, pp. 355–84.

Obeyesekere, R., *Sri Lankan Theater in a Time of Terror: Political Satire in a Permitted Space*, New Delhi: Sage, 1999.

Olwig, K. F., 'Cultural Sites: Sustaining a Home in a Deterritorialized World', in K.F. Olwig and K. Hastrup (eds), *Siting Culture: The Shifting Anthropological Subject*, London: Routledge, 1997, pp. 17–38.

Ondaatje, M., *Running in the Family*, London: Picador, 1983.

—— *The Cinnamon Peeler: Selected Poems*, London: Picador, 1989.

—— *Handwriting*, London: Bloomsbury, 1998.

—— *Anil's Ghost*, London: Picador, 2001; first published 2000.

—— 'Pale Flags: Reflections on Writing *Anil's Ghost*', *Wasafiri*, Summer 2004, 42, pp. 61–62.

Paasi, A., 'The Political Geography of Boundaries at the End of the Millennium: Challenges of the De-terrotorializing World', in H. Eskelinen, I. Liikanen and J. Oksa (eds), *Curtains of Iron and Gold: Reconstructing Borders and Scales of Interaction*, Aldershot: Ashgate, 1999, pp. 9–24.

Pal, R., An Interview with Sivanandan, September 2000. Online: www.birminghamblack history.com/Sivanandan1/Sivanandan2

Papastergiadis, N., *Modernity as Exile: The Stranger in John Berger's Writings*, Manchester: Manchester University Press, 1993.

—— 'Signs of Silence, Lines of Listening', in I. Chambers and L. Curti (eds), *The Postcolonial Question: Common Skies, Divided Horizons*, London: Routledge, 1996, pp. 47–62.

Paranavitana, S., *Sinhalayo*, Boralesgamuwa: Visidunu Prakashakayo, 2004; first published 1967.

Parry, B., 'Resistance Theory/Theorising Resistance, or Two Cheers for Nativism', in F. Barker, P. Hulme and M. Iversen (eds), *Colonial Discourse/Postcolonial Theory*, Manchester: Manchester University Press, 1994, pp. 172–96.

Patton, C., and Sánchez-Eppler, B. (eds), Introduction, *Queer Diasporas*, Durham, NC: Duke University Press, 2000.

Perera, Sasanka, *Living with Torturers*, Colombo: International Centre for Ethnic Studies, 1995.

—— *The World According to me: An Interpretation of the Ordinary, the Common, and the Mundane*, Colombo: International Centre for Ethnic Studies, 1999.

Perera, Suvendrini, 'Unmaking the Present, Remaking Memory: Sri Lankan Stories and a Politics of Coexistence', in C. Prescod and H. Waters (eds), *A World to Win: Essays in Honour of A. Sivanandan, Race and Class: A Journal for Black and Third World Liberation*, July–Dec. 1999, 41:1/2, pp. 189–96.

—— '"We Can Be Killed but we Can Never Be Silenced": Narratives of Coexistence in Recent Sri Lankan Fiction', *CRNLE Journal: Sri Lankan and Indian Diasporic Writing*, 2000, pp. 13–23.

Perera, W., 'Images of Sri Lanka through Expatriate Eyes: Romesh Gunesekera's *Reef*', *Journal of Commonwealth Literature*, 1995, 30:1, pp. 63–78.

—— 'The Perils of Expatriation and a "Heartless Paradise": Romesh Gunesekera's *The Sandglass*', *Commonwealth*, Spring 2000, 22:2, pp. 93–106.

—— 'The Phases and Guises of the Twentieth-Century Expatriate Sri Lankan Novel', *CRNLE Journal 2000: Sri Lankan and Indian Diasporic Writing*, 2000, pp. 52–60.

Perera-Rajasingham, N. (ed.), *July '83 and After, Nēthrā: Special Issue*, April–Sept., 2003, 6:1/2, Colombo: International Centre for Ethnic Studies.

Prakrti, '"The Breach": Three Sri Lankan-Born Writers at the Crossroads', *Lanka Outlook*, Summer 1997. Online: www.is.lk/is/spot/sp0151/clip5.html

Radhakrishnan, R., *Diasporic Mediations: Between Home and Location*, Minneapolis, MN: University of Minnesota Press, 1996.

Raheem, R., Book Review 'James Goonewardene: *The Awakening of Dr Kirthi*', *Navasilu*, December 1979, 3, pp. 117–19.

—— and Fernando, S., 'Women Writers of Sri Lanka', *New Ceylon Writing*, 1979, 4, pp. 88–98.

Rahula, W., *History of Buddhism in Ceylon: The Anuradhapura Period, 3rd Century BC–10th Century AD*, Dehiwala: The Buddhist Cultural Centre, 1993, first published 1956.

Rai, A., 'O Blessed Isle!: Insight into Strife-Torn Lanka', *India Today*, 15 October 1995, p. 220.

Rajasingham-Senanayake, D., *Identity on the Borderline: Multicultural History in a Moment of Danger*, Colombo: Marga Institute, 2001.

—— 'Identity on the Borderline: Modernity, New Ethnicities, and the Unmaking of Multiculturalism in Sri Lanka', in N. Silva (ed.), *The Hybrid Island*, Colombo: Social Scientists' Association, 2002, pp. 41–70.

Rambukwella, P., 'Goonewardene, James (1921–97)', *The Literary Encyclopedia*. Online: www.litencyc.com/php/speople.php?rec=true&UID=1808

Ranasinha, R., 'Romesh Gunesekera's *Reef*: Writing Expatriation', *Phoenix: Sri Lanka Journal of English in the Commonwealth*, 1997, vols 5 and 6, pp. 87–91.

Rao, N., 'Communalism, Socialism and Liberation in *When Memory Dies*', C. Prescod and H. Waters (eds), *A World to Win: Essays in Honour of A. Sivanandan, Race and Class: A Journal for Black and Third World Liberation*, July–Dec. 1999, 41:1/2, pp. 175–88.

Rao, R.R., 'Because Most People Marry their Own Kind: A Reading of Shyam Selvadurai's *Funny Boy*', *ARIEL*, January 1997, 28:1, pp. 115–28.

Rapport, N., and Dawson, A. (eds), *Migrants of Identity: Perceptions of Home in a World of Movement*, Rapport and Dawson (eds), Oxford: Berg, 1998.

Roberts, M. (ed.), *Sri Lanka. Collective Identities Revisited*, vols I and II, Colombo: Marga, 1998.
—— 'Sinhala-ness and Sinhala Nationalism', *A History of Ethnic Conflict in Sri Lanka: Recollection, Reinterpretation and Reconciliation*, Colombo: Marga Institute, 2001.
—— *Burden of History: Obstacles to Power Sharing in Sri Lanka*, Colombo: Marga Institute, 2001.
—— 'Language and National Identity: The Sinhalese and Others over the Centuries', *Nationalism and Ethnic Politics*, Summer 2003, 9:2, pp. 75–102.
—— *Firstness, History, Place and Legitimate Claim to Place-as-Homeland in Comparative Focus*, Colombo: International Centre for Ethnic Studies, 2005.
—— Raheem, I., and Colin-Thomé, P., *People Inbetween: The Burghers and the Middle Class in the Transformations within Sri Lanka, 1790s-1960s*, vol. 1, Ratmalana: Sarvodaya, 1989.
Ross, N. Wilson, *Hinduism, Buddhism, Zen: An Introduction to the Meaning and their Arts*, London: Faber, 1978.
Royle, N., *The Uncanny*, Manchester: Manchester University Press, 2003.
Rushdie, S., *Imaginary Homelands: Essays and Criticism 1981–1991*, London: Granta, 1992.
Said, E., *Orientalism*, Harmondsworth: Penguin, 1991; first published 1978.
—— *Culture and Imperialism*, London: Chatto and Windus, 1993.
Salgādo, G., *The True Paradise*, Manchester: Carcanet, 1993.
Salgado, M., 'Complexity and the Migrant Writer: Chaotics in Michael Ondaatje's Fiction', *Angles on the English-Speaking World*, 2001, 1, pp. 89–106.
—— 'Nonlinear Dynamics and the Diasporic Imagination', in M. Fludernik (ed.), *Diaspora and Multiculturalism: Common Traditions and New Developments*, Amsterdam: Rodopi, 2003, pp. 183–98.
—— 'Writing Sri Lanka, Reading Resistance: Shyam Selvadurai's *Funny Boy* and A. Sivanandan's *When Memory Dies*', *Journal of Commonwealth Literature*, 2004, 39:1, pp. 5–18.
Samarasinghe, S.G., 'Language Policy in Public Administration, 1956–94: An Implementor's Perspective', in K.N.O Dharmadasa (ed.), *National Language Policy in Sri Lanka: 1956 to 1996, Three Studies in its Implementation*, Kandy: International Centre for Ethnic Studies: 1996, pp. 79–112.
Sandner, D. (ed.), *Fantastic Literature: A Critical Reader*, Westport, CT: Praeger, 2004,
Sanga, J.C. (ed.), *South Asian Novelists in English: An A-to-Z Guide*, Westport, CT: Greenwood Press, 2003.
Sangari, K., 'The Politics of the Possible', in B. Ashcroft, G. Griffiths and H. Tiffin (eds), *The Postcolonial Studies Reader*, London: Routledge, 1995, pp. 143–47.
Sarachchandra, E.R., 'Tradition Overturned: A Modern Literature in Sri Lanka', in G. Amirthanayagam (ed.), *Asian and Western Writers in Dialogue: New Cultural Identities*, London: Macmillan, 1982, pp. 209–220.
Sarvan, C., 'Carl Muller's Trilogy and the Burghers of Sri Lanka' *World Literature Today*, Summer, 1997, 71:3, pp. 527–32.
—— 'Carl Muller (1935–)', *The Literary Encyclopedia*, 17 September 2003. Online: www.litencyc.com/php/sepeople.php?=true&UID=4953
Sayyid, S., 'Beyond Westphalia: Nations and Diasporas – the Case of the Muslim *Umma*', in B. Hesse (ed.), *Un/Settled Multiculturalisms: Diasporas, Entanglements, Transruptions*, London: Zed, 2000, pp. 33–51.
Scott, D., *Refashioning Futures: Criticism after Postcoloniality*, Princeton, NJ: Princeton University Press, 1999.
Searle, C., 'Teacher and Interrupter', in C. Prescod and H. Waters (eds), *A World to Win: Essays in Honour of A. Sivanandan, Race and Class: A Journal for Black and Third World Liberation*, July–Dec. 1999, 41:1/2, pp. 109–21.

Selvadurai, S., *Funny Boy*, New Delhi: Penguin India, 1994.

—— *Cinnamon Gardens*, New Delhi: Penguin India, 1998.

—— 'The Influence of Canada in *Funny Boy*', in N. Silva and R. Wijesinha *Across Cultures: Issues of Identity in Contemporary British and Sri Lankan Writing*, Colombo: The British Council, 2001, pp. 3–10.

—— 'Introducing Myself in the Diaspora', in S. Selvadurai (ed.), *Story-Wallah!: A Celebration of South Asian Fiction*, Toronto: Thomas Allen, 2004, pp. 1–14.

Shapiro, M.J., *Violent Cartographies: Mapping Cultures of War*, Minneapolis, MN: University of Minnesota Press, 1997.

Shohat, E., and Stam, R., *Unthinking Eurocentrism*, London: Routledge, 1994.

Sibley, D., *Geographies of Exclusion: Society and Difference in the West*, London: Routledge, 1995.

Siegle, R.B., *Mirror to Mirror: Postmodernity in South Asian Fiction*, Virginia Tech: Digital publication for The Centre for Digital Discourse and Culture, 2002.

Silva, N., 'Situating the Hybrid "Other" in an Era of Conflict: Representations of the Burgher in Contemporary Writings in English', in N. Silva (ed.), *The Hybrid Island: Culture Crossings and the Invention of Identity in Sri Lanka*, Colombo: Social Scientists' Association, 2002, pp. 104–26.

—— *The Gendered Nation: Contemporary Writings from South Asia*, New Delhi: Sage, 2004.

—— and Wijesinha R. (eds), *Across Cultures: Issues of Identity in Contemporary British and Sri Lankan Writing*, Colombo: The British Council, 2001

Sinfield, A., *Gay and After*, London: Serpent's Tail, 1998.

Siriwardena, R., book review, 'A Sivanandan *When Memory Dies*', *Nēthrā*, July–Sept. 1997, 1:4, pp. 74–82.

Sivanandan, A., *Communities of Resistance: Writings on Black Struggles for Socialism*, London: Verso, 1990.

—— *When Memory Dies*, New Delhi: Penguin India, 1998.

—— *Where the Dance Is: Stories from Two Worlds and Three*, London: Arcadia, 2000.

Sjöbohm, A., '"Someone Smashed in the Door and Gave me my Freedom": The Writings of Jean Arasanayagam', *Wasafiri*, Spring 1991, 13, pp. 14–16.

Soja, E.W., *Postmodern Geographies: The Reassertion of Space in Critical Social Theory*, London: Verso, 1989.

Sørensen, B.R., 'The Experience of Displacement: Reconstructing Places and Identities in Sri Lanka', in K.F. Olwig and K. Hastrup (eds), *Siting Culture: The Shifting Anthropological Subject*, London: Routledge, 1997, pp. 142–64.

Spearey, S., 'Mapping and Masking: The Migrant Experience in Michael Ondaatje's *In the Skin of a Lion*', *Journal of Commonwealth Literature*, 1994, XXIX:2, pp. 45–60.

Spivak, G.C., *Critique of Postcolonial Reason: Towards a History of the Vanishing Present*, Cambridge, MA: Harvard University Press, 1999.

Steen Preis, A.-B., 'Seeking Place: Capsized Identities and Contracted Belonging among Sri Lankan Tamil Refugees', in K.F. Olwig and K. Hastrup (eds), *Siting Culture: The Shifting Anthropological Subject*, London: Routledge, 1997, pp. 86–100.

Suganasiri, S.H.J., '"Sri Lankan" Canadian Poets: The Bourgeoisie that Fled the Revolution', *Canadian Literature*, Spring 1992, 132, pp. 60–79.

Suzuki, B.C., *Mahayana Buddhism: A Brief Outline*, New York: Macmillan, 1969.

Tambiah, S.J., *Buddhism Betrayed?: Religion, Politics, and Violence in Sri Lanka* Chicago, IL: University of Chicago Press, 1992.

Tennekoon, N.S., 'Rituals of Development: The Accelerated Mahavali Development Program of Sri Lanka', *American Ethnologist*, 1998, 15:2, pp. 294–310.

Thieme, J., '"Historical Relations": Modes of Discourse in Michael Ondaatje's *Running in the Family*', in C.A. Howells and L. Hunter (eds), *Narrative Strategies in Canadian Literature: Feminism and Postcolonialism*, Milton Keynes: Open University Press, 1991, pp. 40–48.

—— 'Are we all Migrants?' *Literary Review*, February 1998, p. 24.

Thumboo, E., and Kandiah, T. (eds), *The Writer as Historical Witness: Studies in Commonwealth Literature*, Singapore: Unipress, 1995.

Tiruchelvam, M., and Dattathreya, C.S. (eds), *Culture and Politics of Identity in Sri Lanka*, Colombo: International Centre for Ethnic Studies, 1998.

Todorov, T., '"Race", Writing and Culture', in H.L. Gates, Jr, (ed.), *'Race', Writing and Difference*, Chicago, IL: Chicago University Press, 1986, pp. 370–80.

Ty, E., 'The Other Questioned: Exoticism and Displacement in Michael Ondaatje's *The English Patient*', *International Fiction Review*, 2000, 27, pp. 10–19.

Uyangoda, J., 'Biographies of a Decaying Nation-State', in M. Tiruchelvam and C.S. Dattathreya (eds), *Culture and Politics of Identity in Sri Lanka*, Colombo: International Centre for Ethnic Studies, 1998, pp. 168–86.

—— *Questions of Sri Lanka's Minority Rights*, Colombo: International Centre for Ethnic Studies, 2001.

van der Veer, P., 'Introduction: The Diasporic Imagination', in P. van der Veer (ed.), *Nation and Migration: The Politics of Space in the South Asian Diaspora*, Philadelphia, PA: University of Pennsylvania Press, 1995, pp. 1–16.

Vidler, A., *The Architectural Uncanny: Essays in the Modern Unhomely*, Cambridge, MA: Massachusetts Institute of Technology, 1992.

Walker, V., 'Woman, Identity and the Other in Jean Arasanayagam's Fiction', *Navasilu: Journal of the English Association of Sri Lanka*, August 2000, 17, pp. 126–44.

Walters, J.S., 'Multireligion on the Bus: Beyond "Influence" and "Syncretism" in the Study of Religious Meetings', in P. Jeganathan and Q. Ismail (eds), *Unmaking the Nation: The Politics of Identity and History in Modern Sri Lanka*, Colombo: Social Scientists' Association, 1995, pp. 25–54.

Warley, L., 'Locating the Subject of Post-Colonial Autobiography', *Kunapipi*, 1993, XV:1, pp. 23–31.

Weich, D., 'Michael Ondaatje's Cubist Civil War', Powells.com, 23 May 2000. Online: www.powells.com/authors/ondaatje/html

White, H., *Metahistory: The Historical Imagination in Nineteenth Century Europe*, Baltimore, MD: Johns Hopkins University Press, 1973.

Wickramagamage, C., 'A Fish without a Bicycle? Annalukshmi's Choice in Selvadurai's *Cinnamon Gardens*', *CRNLE Journal: Sri Lankan and Indian Diasporic Writing*, 2000, pp. 130–40.

Wijenaike, P., *A Way of Life*, Nugegoda: Deepani, 1987.

—— *Giraya*, Nugegoda, Panaluwa and Padukka: State Printing Corporation, 1990, first published 1971.

—— *Yukthi and Other Stories*, Kelaniya: New Kelani Printers, 1991.

—— *The Waiting Earth*, Pitakotte and Padukka: State Printing Corporation, 1993; first published 1966.

—— 'Anoma', *Commonwealth Currents*, 1996, 3, pp. 4–5.

—— *An Enemy Within*, Ratmalana: Vishva Lekha, 1998.

—— *Amulet*, Wellampitiya: Godage International Publishers, first published 1994; third edition 2002.

—— 'Living on the Edge', *Daily News*, 17 July 2002, p. 22.

Wijesinha, R. (ed.), *An Anthology of Contemporary Sri Lankan Poetry in English*, Kelaniya: English Association of Sri Lanka: 1991.

—— 'Aberrations and Excess: Sri Lanka substantiated by the "Funny Boy"', Features Section, *Sunday Observer* (Sri Lanka), 17 March 1996. Also published in *Miscelánea*, 1997, 18, pp. 347–55.

—— *Breaking Bounds: Essays on Sri Lankan Writing in English*, Belihuloya: Sabaragamuwa University Press, 1998.

—— 'Spices and Sandcastles: The Exotic Historians of Sri Lanka', in N. Silva and R. Wijesinha (eds), *Across Cultures: Issues of Identity in Contemporary British and Sri Lankan Writing*, Colombo: The British Council, 2001, pp. 11–20.

—— 'The Continuing Colonial Mindset', *Daily News*, 26 February 2003. Online: www.dailynews.lk/2003/02/26/fea02.html

Wilson, R., and Dissanayake, W., *Global/Local: Cultural Production and the Transnational Imaginary*, Durham, NC: Duke University Press, 1996.

Young, R., *Colonial Desire: Hybridity in Theory, Culture and Race*, London: Routledge, 1995.

Index

For Product Safety Concerns and Information please contact our EU representative GPSR@taylorandfrancis.com
Taylor & Francis Verlag GmbH, Kaufingerstraße 24, 80331 München, Germany

www.ingramcontent.com/pod-product-compliance
Lightning Source LLC
Chambersburg PA
CBHW071356100726
47908CB00004B/1008

* 9 7 8 0 4 1 5 6 5 3 4 3 5 *